Integrated Marketing Communication

A Practical Guide to Developing Comprehensive Communication Strategies

Edited By

Robert A. Sevier
Vice President for Research and Marketing
Stamats Communications, Inc.
and
Robert E. Johnson
Vice President for Enrollment
Albion College

CASE. Books

COUNCIL FOR ADVANCEMENT
AND SUPPORT OF EDUCATION®

ISBN 0-89964-341-8

Printed in the United States of America.

Council for Advancement and Support of Education (CASE) is the international education association serving professionals in the disciplines of alumni relations, communications, and philanthropy.

CASE offers high-quality training, information resources, and a wide variety of books, videotapes, and materials for advancement professionals.

For more information, or to place an order, call (800) 554-8536 (US and Canada) or (301) 604-2068 (International). To receive our catalog, call (202) 328-2273.

Visit CASE Books online at *www.case.org/books.*

Book design: Fletcher Design
Editors: Laura Henning and Shirley Rosenberg
Researcher: Barbara Perkins

COUNCIL FOR ADVANCEMENT
AND SUPPORT OF EDUCATION®

1307 New York Avenue, NW
Suite 1000
Washington, DC 20005-4701

Table of Contents

PREFACE...v
ACKNOWLEDGMENTS..ix

Section I: The Basics

Chapter 1: Understanding Integrated Marketing Communication,
by Robert Sevier...3
Chapter 2: Some Communication Theory and a Little Bit More,
by Robert Sevier...11
Chapter 3: Developing the Integrated Marketing
Communications Plan, *by Robert Sevier*..25
Chapter 4: Using Research to Enhance Your Strategic Plan, *by Robert Sevier*.........49
Chapter 5: Creativity and Concepting, *by Pat Sellergren*..65

Section II: Strategies and Tactics

Chapter 6: Developing a Visual Identity System, *by Harry Battson*.......................79
Chapter 7: Defeating the Grapevine: Building an Effective Internal
Communication Strategy, *by Jeannie S. Morelock*.......................................99
Chapter 8: Presidential Image-Enhancement Strategies, *by Michael Norris*.........111
Chapter 9: Building a Message-Driven Media Relations Plan, *by Harry Battson*.........129
Chapter 10: Crisis Communication, *by Harry Battson*...143
Chapter 11: Special Events, Anniversaries, and Celebrations, *by Larry D. Lauer*.........153

Section III: Taking It to the Next Level

Chapter 12: Integrated Publication Strategies, *by Robert Sevier*........................169
Chapter 13: Creating an Integrated Advertising Campaign, *by A. R. (Andy) Kesling*...193
Chapter 14: More than Direct Mail: Developing a Direct
Marketing Strategy, *by Robert Johnson*..211
Chapter 15: Marketing on the Web: Blending the New
and the Newer, *by Robert Johnson*..239
Chapter 16: Getting It Together, *by Robert Johnson* 265

Section IV: Appendices

Appendix A: Designing a Research Study, *by Robert Sevier*...............................271
Appendix B: Elements of a Graphics Standards Manual, *by Robert Sevier* 285
Appendix C: Useful Web Sites...289
Appendix D: Organizations and Associations 297

ABOUT THE EDITORS AND CONTRIBUTORS 301

Preface

Welcome to *Integrated Marketing Communication: A Practical Guide to Developing Comprehensive Communication Strategies*, the second book in CASE's Integrated Marketing Series.

By any definition, this new publication is a "how-to" book. It is designed to help both the novice and the seasoned professional communicate the outcomes of strategic decisions involving product, price, and place (or, as some might prefer, consumer, cost, and convenience).

Not surprisingly, this book builds on the groundwork laid in *Integrated Marketing for Colleges, Universities, and Schools: A Step-by-Step Planning Guide,* published by CASE in 1998. There is, however, an important distinction between the two. The first book presented the need for integrated marketing and outlined in detail the integrated marketing planning process. This second book stresses the creation of specific integrated communication strategies. As a consequence, most chapters open with a brief overview of a specific communication strategy and then move to a discussion of how this strategy can be applied to your institution. Examples of good practices from public and private academic institutions are presented in each chapter; each chapter also includes numerous "how-to" and "don't forget" lists and closes with a short list of recommended readings or other sources.

The book is arranged in three sections: The Basics, Strategies and Tactics, and Taking It to the Next Level.

Section One: The Basics

Chapter 1: *Understanding Integrated Marketing Communication* makes the case for integrated marketing communication and explores how it differs from marketing and promotion. The chapter also presents the three levels of integration that are required for the creation of a truly integrated marketing strategy and then concludes with a decision tree to help you determine whether you should consider developing a more strategic integrated marketing plan or an integrated marketing communication plan.

Chapter 2: *Some Communication Theory and a Little Bit More* outlines the many challenges of communicating in our message-saturated society. It then presents what we term the "listening-first" model of communication that stresses listening to and responding to the needs of the target audience as the essential first steps in any effective communication strategy. The chapter concludes with a discussion of the characteristics of successful messages and presents a schematic for developing messages.

Chapter 3: *Developing the Integrated Marketing Communications Plan* addresses your overall communication planning process. It begins with the integration of your institutional mission, vision statement, and strategic initiatives into the planning process and moves through audience definition, clarification of communication goals, development of vivid descriptors, refining of target geographies, creation of the media mix and calendar, and budgeting.

Chapter 4: *Using Research to Enhance Your Strategic Communications Plan* introduces you to basic research terminology and outlines the steps for undertaking your research project. These steps include developing the research agenda, identifying target audiences, selecting the initial research methodology, writing the research instrument, drawing the sample, executing the study, analyzing the data, and presenting the results. The chapter also reviews basic research methods and lists sources for obtaining inexpensive research data.

Chapter 5: *Creativity and Concepting* looks at how you can become more creative, first by understanding what limits creativity and then by understanding your own attitude toward creativity. It also offers suggestions on how you can get to great concepts faster and includes an often overlooked step between concepting and execution, namely, how you can help ensure your concepts will win approval at your institution. We'll also give examples of some concepts that have served academic institutions well.

Section Two: Strategies and Tactics

Chapter 6: *Developing a Visual Identity System* identifies the importance of creating a signature look as part of your image-building communications plan. It addresses the idea of brand, the steps for establishing and managing a visual identity system, winning compliance across campus, and even integrating the athletics program. Tips on what goes into an identity standards manual and how to distribute it are also included.

Chapter 7: *Defeating the Grapevine: Building an Effective Internal Communication Strategy* focuses on the critical need to capitalize on internal marketing and strategic internal relations. It defines your institution's internal audiences and what types of information they want to know. This chapter offers numerous ideas for improving your internal communications efforts as well as tips for evaluating the effectiveness of your program.

Chapter 8: *Presidential Image-Enhancement Strategies* suggests concrete ways to increase your president's visibility, ability to persuade, and overall effectiveness. It begins with the assumption that image-enhancement initiatives will be most successful if individually tailored to reflect the personality of your president. It then presents a range of image-building activities and approaches and illustrates these with examples of strategies that have worked for leaders at both public and private institutions of various sizes.

Chapter 9: ***Building a Message-Driven Media Relations Plan*** addresses a strategic focus for media relations activities. Your institution's media relations team must target your audiences through the media gatekeepers, find the institution stories that support your marketing communications messages, and develop a plan for getting those messages out that includes capitalizing on standard university events. Your plan also should address accountability and evaluation. This chapter also includes information on media training, how to make media contacts, and media resources.

Chapter 10: ***Crisis Communication*** identifies the types of crises most likely to confront an academic institution and sets forth a four-step plan to prepare for handling such events. Using four actual examples, this chapter shows how staying true to your marketing messages actually can turn a crisis into a successful image-building opportunity. It also addresses the impact of new media.

Chapter 11: ***Special Events, Anniversaries, and Celebrations*** recognizes that special events are primary tools in integrated marketing. They provide effective opportunities for you to build strong relationships with stakeholders and opinion leaders who represent your key target market segments. Simply put, strategically designed events gather the right people in controlled settings, facilitating the communication of carefully crafted messages to them and enabling the kind of interactive communication you need to build long-term commitments. This chapter discusses special events in the context of a larger integrated marketing program and offers specific suggestions for designing them as effective marketing tools.

Section Three: Taking It to the Next Level

Chapter 12: ***Integrated Publication Strategies*** is a primer on creating publications. It presents a step-by-step process for developing publications and outlines strategies for evaluating the effectiveness of existing publications. This chapter also presents information on copywriting, design, use of photography, and options for reducing cost, and addresses the 10 biggest mistakes people make when creating publications.

Chapter 13: ***Creating an Integrated Advertising Campaign*** prepares you to make the most of advertising for your institution. "Getting the Word Out" is a phrase often mentioned by individuals who are considering using advertising. Effective advertising gets the word out, and more. This sponsored mass communication transmits a clear message stated as a benefit to the audience, urges action that will benefit the advertiser, and costs less per contact than any other communication tool in the promotional mix.

Chapter 14: ***More than Direct Mail: Developing a Direct Marketing Strategy*** introduces the basic principles of professional direct marketing as the starting point for a long-term relationship-building program for prospective students and donors. The fundamental points of creating strong prospect pools from ACT, PSAT and SAT test-takers are covered in detail, followed by a review of how to develop an effective communications package for the highest possible response rates. Also included are the most effective "power" words to get your DM letters off to a great start.

Chapter 15: *Marketing on the Web: Blending the New and the Newer* ventures into the rapidly changing world of Web marketing to point out the most essential elements you need to know to thrive in this vital new communications area. You'll learn about "collaboration marketing," an extension of direct marketing well suited to academic institutions looking for prospective students and potential donors. You'll explore the expanding world of e-mail communications and how to develop e-mail newsletters that take best advantage of what interests people. No marketing professional knows exactly where Web marketing is headed, but this chapter will give you the basic tools to keep up with whatever happens next.

Chapter 16: *Getting It Together* summarizes the information presented in the 15 preceding chapters. It points to the growing commitment of academic institutions to marketing, image-enhancement, personal communications, database management, marketing research, integrated internal communications, and Web communications. And it urges you to become a campus champion of your institution's marketing efforts.

The appendixes contain useful information above and beyond that included in the chapters. Appendix A, "Designing a Research Study" supplements the material in Chapter 4 on research. Appendix B, "Elements of a Graphics Standards Manual," will assist you in an essential component of your communication program. Appendix C contains a list of valuable and interesting Web sites and Appendix D contains a list of useful organizations.

Acknowledgments

It is impossible, in a few short paragraphs, to thank all the people who contributed to this book. There are simply too many to mention by name, and I am afraid that if I tried, someone would slip by unmentioned. So for those who offered ideas, sent examples, reviewed sections, and offered support and insight, you have my deep appreciation.

Even as I acknowledge the contributions of many, there is a small handful who deserve special mention. First, Bob Johnson, my co-editor, for his professionalism, the quality of his ideas, and his sense of humor. He helped make this task enjoyable. Second, I would like to thank Nancy Raley at CASE for her faith in and patience with me. I missed a few deadlines here and there. Her graciousness was greatly appreciated. And finally, I would like to thank Harry Battson and Mike Norris. Both of these gentlemen contributed far more than chapters to the book. They were my "go-to" guys and helped me out time after time. I am honored to know them, and I look forward to future opportunities to work together.

I would also like to thank three people who work with me on an almost daily basis: Toni LeVasseur, Annette Stahr, and Becky Morehouse. Toni's and Annette's help— especially with proofing, editing, and tracking down all those pesky permissions—was greatly appreciated. Becky's frank insights, candor, and delight in bringing me back to earth were as constant as they were valued. And Annette, I promise to learn the difference between an em dash and an en dash before my next book.

Finally, as with most endeavors, I would like to acknowledge the two people closest to me, my wife and son, Pat and Andy. They are the very best part of my life.

Like my first book, I willingly share the credit for this work with all these people, both named and unnamed, and reserve only the mistakes for me.

—*Bob Sevier*

I owe thanks to many people. First, to everyone who has shared their commitment to the positive role of marketing in higher education. Without your constant feedback to my presentations and newsletters, I would not be writing this introduction now. Next, to Tom Colaner, Tom Hayes, Charlie Hutchins, and Kate O'Connor for their friendship, help, and frank feedback over the years that help me do what I do as well as I can do it.

Bob Sevier deserves special thanks. As in any endeavor with Bob, there are special rewards that come from contact with a true professional who never stops exploring new ways to do things better than anyone else has done them. And a final word of thanks to Jeanne Umholtz, a constant source of personal and professional support.

A friend once asked me "Why do you do this?" To make you and myself better marketing people. I hope our efforts in this book move us all in that direction.

*—**Bob Johnson***

Making the case for a long-term commitment to strategic communication must be the first priority for all communications professionals.

Section I
The Basics

1

Understanding Integrated Marketing Communication

By Robert Sevier

Few would debate the importance of effective communication on campus. And even a cursory list of the benefits of an effective communication strategy would include:

- A stronger, more consistent institutional image;
- Increased coordination and stewardship of marketing dollars;
- Increased support from such funding publics as legislatures and churches;
- More satisfied alumni;
- Lower costs to recruit students and raise dollars;
- A general public that is more aware of your accomplishments, value, and needs;
- The ability to attract and retain better administrators, faculty, and staff; and
- Greater employee satisfaction including an increased sense of pride and loyalty.

Of course, it would be a mistake to imply that every good thing comes from the ability to communicate effectively, strategically, and in an integrated fashion. But at the same time, it would be a mistake to discount the importance of effective integrated communication.

Not surprisingly, this leads us to a conundrum. If the benefits of communicating effectively are so apparent, why do so few colleges and universities undertake the creation of an effective communication program?

Why don't more colleges and universities communicate strategically?

Ultimately, we believe that there are four reasons why colleges and universities have trouble communicating strategically. They are:

- Inability to prioritize audiences, messages, and media,
- Lack of internal expertise,
- Unwillingness to address turf and territory issues, and
- Failure to truly understand and appreciate the importance of strategic communication.

> **A lack of financial resources is rarely the reason for poor strategic communication.**

First, there is an inability to prioritize audiences, messages, and media consistently. There is no sense of which audiences are most important to institutional success. There has been no research on audience needs, expectations, or media habits. And the enduring—truly enduring—messages have not been developed to reach them. In other words, the strategic communication plan has not been tied closely to the strategic plan.

Second, there is a lack of internal expertise. Few colleges, in large part because of budget cutbacks or long-term staff openings, have enough seasoned communications professionals who understand relational databases, direct mail, advertising, publications, interactive media, and the whole host of other communication options. And often on the college campuses that do have them, such communications professionals are horrendously overloaded and their budgets and expertise are stretched painfully thin.

Third, there is an unwillingness on the part of many senior administrators to address turf and territory issues. Often, communication and marketing functions are spread across a number of departments and divisions. The publications office reports to one vice president, while interactive media, advertising, and special events report to others, allowing little sharing of communication goals, budgets, and talent.

And finally, there is a failure truly to understand and appreciate the importance of strategic communication. Perhaps it is this root failure that undermines an institution's ability—or even desire—to prioritize audiences, messages, and media that preclude the nurturing of internal expertise, and highlight the unwillingness on the part of senior administrators to address turf and territory issues. Making the case for a long-term commitment to strategic communication must be the first priority for all communication professionals. We hope their entreaties will be more warmly received in the future than they have been in the past on many campuses.

Notice anything missing from the above list of obstacles to more effective communication? Chances are some of you are wondering why we left out money.

In our opinion, a lack of financial resources is rarely the reason for poor strategic communication. More often, lack of money is the excuse used when an institution is unable to deal with its inability to prioritize, lack of internal expertise, and lack of commitment. We have seen great communication plans and strategies run on a shoestring. At the same time, we have seen hundreds of thousands of dollars wasted on ill-conceived and ill-executed communication strategies.

The issue is seldom solely the amount of money available. Rather it is the quality of the ideas and concepts that support the overall strategic communication plan and the commitment of the institution to strategic communication. More often than not, people and institutional will, not money, are the issues.

What is integrated marketing communication?

Before we proceed too much further, we should take a minute to define integrated marketing communication:

> In our opinion, integrated marketing communication (IMC) is... a comprehensive, coordinated, institution-wide effort to communicate mission-critical values and messages in ways that target audiences notice, understand, and respond to. IMC stresses data-driven segmentation, message integration and coordination, and evaluation.

Don Schultz, Stanley Tannenbaum, and Robert Lauterborn writing in their book *Integrated Marketing Communications: Putting it Together and Making it Work* were among the first to coin the term *integrated marketing communication,* but the concept— and the need IMC fills—clearly predates their writing on the subject.

Let's spend some time dissecting the four essential components of integrated marketing communication:

First, IMC is *comprehensive, coordinated, and institutionwide.* Because its goal is to communicate strategic messages, it must be able to draw on the full range of resources at the institution: people, budgets, and time. It cannot be driven from the bottom. Rather, it must have the ongoing and visible support of the institution's president and chief administrators. In this regard, as noted by Don Schultz and colleagues, IMC *is* fully integrated.

Second, integrated marketing communication *focuses on strategic communication, not merely promotion.* Strategic communication involves careful listening. In fact, aggressive listening must precede the crafting of messages.

Floyd Akins, director of a fund-raising campaign at Grinnell College, makes this point:

> Listening is a major part of what I do as a fund raiser so I have a better understanding of how to approach individual prospects and donors. Sometimes you do not always know the exact amount of a gift at the beginning of the relationship. But after a while, during the cultivation process, you listen carefully for key words and phrases. Often you query a donor, 'What kind of legacy would you like to leave Grinnell.' Recently, I asked that question of a donor and discovered that she was very interested in supporting scholarships. We had been talking to this woman for a number of years but this was the first real insight we had into what her interests were. As a result, our future contacts with her will be much more focused and will be much more likely to be successful both for her — and for Grinnell.

Third, *integrated marketing communication has as its goal the transmission of mission-critical values and messages.* You want to transmit not simply slogans and themes that are often as temporary as they are cliché, but enduring messages that represent core values that grow directly from the institution's mission and vision.

And finally, *IMC seeks to communicate to target audiences* in ways they *understand and to which they will respond.* Rather than trying to meet the needs of every definable target audience, IMC recognizes that some audiences are more important. Institutions must develop segment-based, often highly customized, messages that these strategic audiences understand, appreciate, and act on.

How does integrated marketing communication differ from marketing?

Table 1-1
The Four Ps and Four Cs of Integrated Marketing Communication

The 4 Ps	The 4 Cs
Product	Consumer
Price	Cost
Place	Convenience
Promotion	Communication

Integrated marketing communication is a subset of marketing. Traditional definitions of marketing have focused on the 4 Ps: product, price, place, and promotion. More recently, Schultz and others introduced us to the idea of the 4 Cs of IMC: consumer, cost, convenience, and communication. As Table 1-1 shows, the 4 Ps and 4 Cs are remarkably similar. There is a strong feeling among students of marketing that the 4 Ps are developed from the perspective of the organization—in this case an academic institution—and that the 4 Cs are developed from the perspective of the consumer.

Marketing and strategic communication

In general, marketing is involved in discussions of what you do (product and consumer), how much you charge (price and cost), and where you do it (place and convenience).

Strategic communication, on the other hand, tends to focus more on promotion and communication. In a sense, it concentrates on getting the word out on what you have decided about the other 3 Ps and 3 Cs and giving you feedback (that's the listening part) so that you can initiate changes in the strategic mix. Our concern, and the concern of this book, of course, is the final P and C—promotion and communication—in the context of a larger, strategic commitment to marketing.

Levels of integration

For integrated marketing (of which integrated marketing communication is a part) to be successful, this integration must be evidenced at three levels:
- Strategic integration
- Organizational integration
- Message integration

Strategic Integration
Strategic integration (Figure 1-1) requires the assessment of target audience needs with-

in the constraint of your institutional mission. It involves a willingness to make data-based decisions. It involves a desire to segment and mix strategic assets such as product, price, and place (or, if you prefer, consumer, cost, and convenience). And it relies on feedback to help assure that strategic decisions are on track.

Organizational integration

Organizational integration is another requirement. In fact, it is organizational integration that—from a systems perspective—allows or encourages strategic communication. At its most basic, organizational integration involves coordinating resources and sharing goals. In an ideal world, this is accomplished through the creation of organizational structures such as those outlined below.

In the next model (Figure 1-2), all marketing functions—we include student recruiting and fund raising—are arrayed under one vice president. Clearly, this is a dramatic, some might even say irrational, departure from how most current colleges and universities are organized. It does, however, reflect both the importance of and the need for coordinated marketing strategies.

More often than not, colleges and universities are unwilling or simply unable to change their organizational structure radically, even if it will increase their ability to communicate. As a compromise, they will seek to share goals and resources on an ad hoc or team basis. Although we believe structure is exceedingly important, it is possible, though probably more difficult, to achieve the effects of organizational integration when there is strong leadership and buy-in among senior administrators for an ad hoc or team-based approach to marketing.

Message integration

The last component of strategic integrated marketing communication is message integration, that is, your messages are consistent and coordinated. They have a common look, sound, and feel across various media and over time even though they may still be segmented to reflect different target audience needs and expectations.

How does integrated marketing communication relate to image building?

All communication strategies have as their end goal the purpose of informing or persuading people. Integrated marketing communication is no different. Its goal is to com-

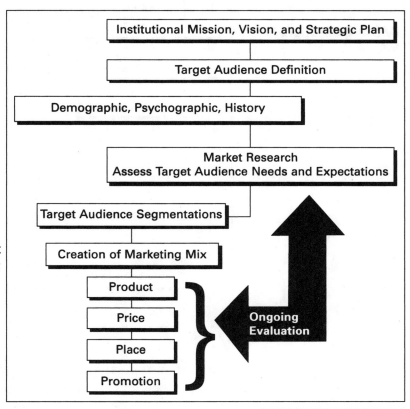

Figure 1-1
IMC Strategic Integration

Figure 1-2
IMC Organizational Integration

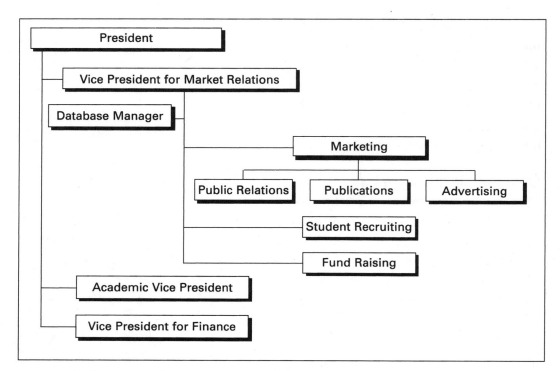

municate mission-critical values to essential target audiences with the hope of changing their awareness and, ultimately, their behavior. With this in mind, one of the most important outcomes of integrated marketing communication is the creation and maintenance of a strong institutional image.

Few would disagree that it is difficult, if not impossible, to overestimate the impact that a strong image has on student recruiting or fund raising. Even so, institutions often have difficulty managing their images—this most important asset of all assets. Although the decision about what image you wish to create is strategic, the maintenance and ongoing evaluation of this image is clearly within the purview of integrated marketing communication.

Is integrated marketing communication always coupled with integrated marketing?

In an ideal world, the answer is yes. But because we don't live in an ideal world, we need to recognize that sometimes it is necessary to proceed with integrated marketing communication without addressing strategic issues of product and consumer, price and cost, and place and convenience. In some cases, such as when there is little time or when the campus is highly politicized, it might be unwise to initiate a true integrated marketing effort. And while there are no absolute guidelines to help you decide whether your plan should embrace the 4 Ps or the 4 Cs or simply integrated marketing communication, the following decision tree (Figure 1-3) may help guide your thinking. As you examine the tree, keep in mind the difference between the decision to develop a more comprehensive integrated marketing plan (of which IMC is a part) and the decision to develop an integrated marketing communication plan.

Deciding on an integrated marketing communication plan

If times are tense or issues are pressing, in some cases it might be wise to proceed with an integrated marketing communication plan rather than with a more comprehensive integrated marketing plan. In a sense, this will allow you to show more progress on generally accepted goals, achieve some quick and necessary wins, and buy some time before addressing the larger, more strategic, and often more politically charged issues that naturally fall under the purview of an integrated marketing plan. In addition, the less political approach may allow you the opportunity to build some bridges— even a consensus— that will help you develop a more comprehensive integrated marketing plan at a later date.

We believe strongly that most institutions would benefit from the creation of an integrated marketing plan; however, practical realities indicate that the emphasis must sometimes be limited to communication. It is at these times that fully integrated marketing communication is often more important.

Recommended Readings

Beckwith, Harry. *Selling the Invisible: A Field Guide to Modern Marketing.* New York: Warner Books, 1997.

Bennis, Warren and Patricia Ward Biederman. *Organizing Genius: The Secrets of Creative Collaboration.* Reading, MA: Addison-Wesley Publishing Company, 1998.

Katzenbach, Jon R. and Douglas K. Smith. *The Wisdom of Teams.* New York: Harper & Row, 1994.

Keller, George. *Academic Strategy: The Management Review in Higher Education.* American Association for Higher Education. Baltimore: Johns Hopkins University Press, 1983.

Nanus, Burt. *Visionary Leadership: Creating a Compelling Sense of Direction for Your Organization.* San Francisco: Jossey-Bass Publishers, 1992.

Parker, Glenn M. *Cross-Function Teams: Working with Allies, Enemies, and Other Strangers.* San Francisco: Jossey-Bass Publishers, 1994.

Peppers, Don and Martha Rogers. *Enterprise One to One: Tools for Competing in the Interactive Age.* New York: Doubleday, 1997.

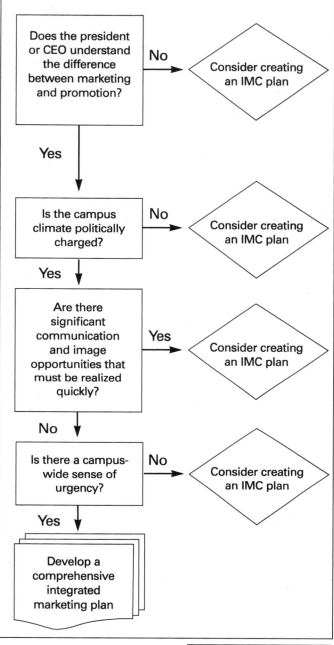

Figure 1-3
IMC Decision Tree

Schultz, Don E., Stanley Tannenbaum and Robert F. Lauterborn. *Integrated Marketing Communications: Putting It Together and Making It Work.* Lincolnwood, IL: NTC/Contemporary Publishing Group, 1992.

Schultz, Don E., Stanley Tannenbaum and Robert F. Lauterborn. *The New Marketing Paradigm: Integrated Marketing Communications.* Lincolnwood, IL: NTC/Contemporary Publishing Group, 1994.

2

> 66 **Most messages either never get noticed or are not compelling enough to cause an action.** 99

Some Communication Theory and a Little Bit More
Lessons Learned from the Field

Robert Sevier

Chapter 1 introduced us to an important conundrum: If academic institutions are filled with sincere and bright people (and we believe they are) and most people understand the importance of strategic communication (and we believe they do), why don't more institutions communicate better? During the course of that chapter, we offered the following four explanations for why many communication efforts fail or are not as effective as hoped:

■ Inability to prioritize audiences, messages, and media
■ Lack of internal expertise
■ Unwillingness to address turf and territory issues
■ Failure to truly understand and appreciate the importance of strategic communication

Let's begin with a little communication theory

These barriers to communication are certainly worth noting, but we also believe that something else is occurring, something a little more subtle and ill-defined. In this chapter, we explore some other issues related to communication theory that may help explain why institutions—and other organizations and even individuals—are poor communicators. We will also offer some insight and ideas on how the quality and effectiveness of communication might be improved.

But first we need to buy a little life insurance to protect ourselves from the communication purists who might read this book. We, therefore, state at the outset that our goal is not to explore and debate the nuances of every communication theory ever proposed. There are others far more qualified for this course of action than we are. Rather, our goal is to address communication theory in a straightforward fashion, in other words, what works, what doesn't work—and if not, why not—based on our experience as professional communicators.

One of the biggest reasons communication strategies fail is due to the "from on high" approach to communication, an approach that stresses downward communication or promotion almost exclusively—namely, what the institution wants the audience to know. For the most part, there is little consideration about what the audience actually wants to hear. The two chief characteristics of this largely promotion-based model are (1) no listening, and (2) a single, usually unsegmented message.

A cacophonous approach to communication, which has inconsistent, sometimes inappropriate, messages flying around to all audiences is another fault with many communication programs. This model also has two overarching characteristics: (1) It is usually quite reactive, and (2) it stresses a large volume of uncoordinated messages.

Both of these models have a number of fundamental flaws. In the first place, the message flow is one-way, and there is little opportunity for feedback. Second, there is no recognition of noise or barriers to communication. Third, there is little segmentation based on audience needs. And finally, there is little or no opportunity for message evaluation and modification.

Use of these downward-only and uncoordinated communication models is still very widespread. However, there is increasing evidence that institutions are looking for a model or models that more adequately meet both their needs and the needs of their target audiences. We sense that some institutions, for example, are spending more time listening to their target audiences. At the same time, we note that target audiences are increasingly willing to throw their weight around, demanding not just information, but dialogue. Also, we see a new (some might say renewed) emphasis on stewardship as institutions recognize their responsibility to become more adroit at measuring the effectiveness of their communication programs.

Barriers to communication

It is clear that the two downward-oriented communication models just discussed probably never did serve academic institutions well and will not serve it well in the future.

With this in mind, we have spent a great deal of time reviewing the literature on communication and speaking with professional communicators. But perhaps most importantly, we listened to target audiences. We wanted to know, from their perspective, why so much of the communication directed at them failed. The most important lesson we learned from these interviews and research was:

> Most messages either never get noticed or are not compelling enough to cause an action.

Before you take umbrage at this finding (either you will disagree with it entirely or you will find it painfully simplistic), we would like to take a quick trip into the minds and lives of our target audiences so that we can more completely understand the most common barriers to communication and all become better communicators.

Barrier # 1: 'I can't hear you.'

This barrier reminds us that the marketplace is loaded with messages, interference, and distractions, and that even the most important messages are sometimes just not heard. In fact, even when people actually look forward to your message, they sometimes don't notice it. Witness, for example, the promising young prospective student who is contacted by more than 500 different recruiters, or the alumnus who receives more than 20 solicitations from museums, police associations, and the local zoo each month. Sometimes—even most times—the messages we send just aren't getting noticed.

Barrier #2: 'I'm really, really busy.'

This second barrier acknowledges that our target audiences are extraordinarily busy. The demands of school, work, family, sports, religion, and many other commitments mean that each minute of each day is as precious as it is contested for time on your agenda. As a consequence, messages received and even noticed may not be acted upon because there is only so much time and your message didn't make the cut.

Barrier #3: 'What's in it for me?'

Most people find themselves on a continuum that begins with savvy and ends with cynicism, and today's target audiences, besieged by dozens and hundreds of competing messages, are becoming increasingly choosy about the messages to which they will respond. While they may not be calculating their exact return on investment, they often ask themselves, "How will I benefit by responding to his message?" If the answer isn't obvious, there is a high likelihood that the message will fail to elicit a response.

Barrier #4: 'I'm not as rational as you think.'

As professional communicators, we often assume too much rationality on the part of our target audiences. "This message is so important," we think, "that surely our target audience will read it and act today." Ahhh, if only it were so, but it isn't. In fact, there is some strong evidence that suggests the opposite may be true; today's target audiences, for a number of reasons, simply don't spend too much time thinking, at least thinking rationally, about the bulk of the messages they receive.

Dick Canterbury, direct marketing expert, is convinced of this point, especially as it applies to the search for students. "We treat high school students like young adults," he notes, "when in fact they are still kids. They think like kids. Act like kids. And react like kids." To illustrate his point, Canterbury developed what he calls "The Clouds of Late Adolescence" (Figure 2-1). Each cloud represents a major shadow or concern in the lives of today's adolescents. "We design these beautiful messages that will appeal to today's logical teenager," he says wryly. "But who out there really knows a teenager that is logical? We are asking them to make the most important decision of their lives, and they just discovered that they have a pimple in the middle of their forehead and they have a big date on Friday."

Figure 2-1
The Clouds of Late Adolescence
Courtesy of Richard M. Canterbury

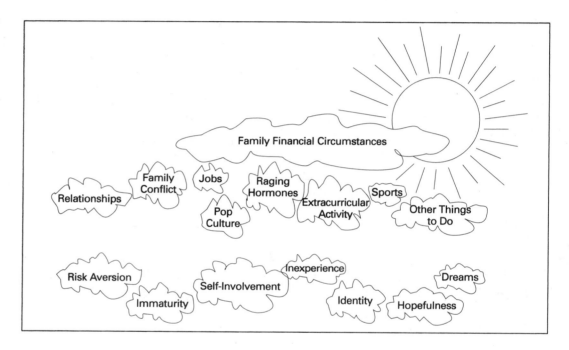

There is no reason to believe that young alumni and older donors don't also have similar clouds in their lives. Perhaps clouds of tight finances, health problems, troubles with a spouse or work, concerns about children—or even the lawn. Sometimes, possibly even most times, our target audiences just aren't thinking, or at least not thinking the way we would like them to.

One note is worth making here. Even though our target markets may be less rational then we might hope, we should still approach message design and construction in a rational fashion that begins with basic research to help clarify the behaviors of audiences.

Barrier #5: 'I really don't care as much about your message as you hope I do.'

Many messages fall, if not on deaf ears, on cold hearts: the announcement of the 25th anniversary alumni gathering, the centennial celebration for Old Siwash, the fund raiser for the new science building, or the retirement of the beloved physics professor.

Increasingly, messages that are important or even urgent to the sender are seldom as important or urgent to the recipient. Target audiences quickly learn that most of them can be safely ignored and that seemingly urgent and critical messages are, at least from their perspective, seldom really that urgent or critical.

Barrier #6: 'I meant to do that.'

Even when our target audiences desire to act on our messages, the odds are still high that they will not. Good intentions are delayed or forgotten or ignored. Each one of us could probably look at our desks and see messages we intended to respond to, ads for books we were going to buy, subscription cards for magazines to which we were going to subscribe, even concerts we were going to attend. But we didn't follow through. We meant to, but we just didn't get around to it.

The listening-first model

As we were writing this chapter, we struggled with the challenges represented by these communication barriers. We were particularly interested in how they might impact the communication model we hoped to develop. After debate and discussion, synthesis and supposing, we came up with a model that addresses these potential communication stumbling blocks. We call our model, with tongue firmly in cheek:

> The listening-first-and-then-communicating-to-a-very-busy-audience-that-is-probably-less-interested-in-what-we-want-to-say-than-we-think-they-are-and-we-aren't-the-only-ones-talking-to-them-anyway model.

Or, for the hyphen-challenged: "The listening-first" model

The listening-first model understands that successful communication:
- Is two-way, not simply downward;
- Recognizes the self-interests of both the sender and the receiver;
- Is part of an ongoing relationship;
- Occurs in a very dynamic, busy, cacophonous environment; and
- Is long-term and enduring.

Our listening-first model is designed to address a number of key communication realities.

First, most audiences weary quickly of downward communication. As noted by expert marketers Don Peppers and Martha Rogers, audiences want, and increasingly demand, to be listened to. And they expect you not only to modify and customize your message, but your product as well.

Second, today's audiences are extraordinarily busy. Not only do they overlook messages that don't interest them, they often overlook messages that would interest them if only they noticed them. Communication theorists and marketing practitioners note that the average person—adult or child—in our society is bombarded with thousands of messages every day, seven days a week, 52 weeks a year. Thousands and thousands and thousands of messages all compete for their attention and action.

Third, our target audiences are wily consumers of communication messages. They have heard all the promises and claims and exhortations. And their defenses are up. They can sense baloney a mile away.

Fourth, our target audiences suffer from what Erik Larson, writing in *The Naked Consumer*, called "pitch pollution." They receive dozens, even hundreds, of messages from other organizations competing for their attention, time, and dollars. They are numbed by the chaos of messages that flow from their mailboxes, telephones, televisions, radios, and computers. When asked if they received a message, they are increasingly likely to respond, "I don't know."

Fifth, we are not the only ones communicating with our audiences. Other like-minded, or at least like-motivated, organizations and causes are all turning to psychographics, geodemography, segmentation, and list merges and purges to reach the same target audiences. It's a communication free-for-all. Everyone in communications today has access to telephones, mailing houses, and the Internet.

Sixth, our model recognizes that our goal is not simply to send messages, but to garner responses. We want people to act after hearing, viewing, or seeing our message, and data suggest that this action will not occur as a consequence of one mailing or one telephone call. Psychologists tell us that it takes five discrete steps to motivate people to act:

1. Get their attention
2. Cause them to read or hear or view your message
3. Convince them to contemplate your offer
   - Weigh benefits against other offers
   - Weigh benefits against inactivity or no decision
4. Motivate them to act
5. Convince them to follow through on their decision to act

Will these five steps occur in a single action message? Sometimes, but sometimes not. Depending on such variables as complexity and cost of the commitment, it may take more than one message to move a respondent to the decision to buy. The likelihood is high that a series of communications based on a thorough knowledge of the needs of your target audience will reach that audience and, as result, they will be able to make complex decisions.

Characteristics of successful messages

As part of our discussion on both the theoretical and practical implications of our listening-first model, we posed the following question to ourselves:

> What are the characteristics of a successful message?

To answer this question, we looked at books and articles on communication theory. We interviewed practitioners in the media, advertising, direct marketing, and direct mail. We looked at short- and long-term communication campaigns for higher education, other nonprofits, and for-profits. We looked at business-to-business communication strategies and business-to-consumer communication strategies. In short, we looked at this question from every direction. The result we came up with is represented by a simple pie chart (Figure 2-2).

And finally, our model stresses that long-term success depends on a mutually satisfying relationship between the sender (the institution) and the receiver (the target audience) based on trust.

In our minds, successful messages have three overarching characteristics:

- ■ They are noticeable.
- ■ They are salient.
- ■ They are memorable.

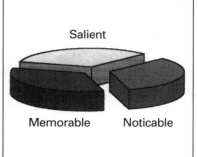

Figure 2-2
Message-Effectiveness Variables

First, against the backdrop of the thousands of messages that a person receives each day, the successful message is noticed. It arrives with flair. It is packaged uniquely. It has texture where others do not. It yells when other messages are quiet; it is contemplative when others are brash. It transcends the average. It is received with an "Ah-ha," a recognition that it is special.

Second, successful messages are salient. They strike a cord with the recipient. They meet a need, provide an answer, act on a dream, or resolve an issue. They resonate with the target audience. They fill a hole that the recipient may not even have known existed. They have meaning because they acknowledge the environment in which this person is functioning.

And third, successful messages are remembered after they are received. Either their initial impact or cumulative impact lodges in the memory of the recipient. They nag. They remind. They are an itch that can't be scratched until they are acted on.

Mixing the three message characteristics

We believe that these characteristics are common to all successful messages. And although the pie chart implies that each quality must be equally represented, we don't necessarily believe that this is always the case. For example, a series of messages may first strive to be noticed, especially when delivered amidst a great barrage of other messages or when delivered to target audiences who have no initial awareness. Over time, however, as the recipient or target audience becomes more aware, the saliency of individual messages may increase.

Creating successful messages

The crafting of successful messages is a somewhat complex undertaking that includes the following seven steps:

1. Audience definition
2. Audience research
3. Development of communication goals

4. Clarification of vivid descriptors
5. Concept creation
6. Development of the media mix
7. Message evaluation and modification

Note: This process, not surprisingly, fits neatly into the communication plan outline that will be presented in Chapter 3. Elements and examples of these seven steps are presented in greater detail in other chapters throughout the book. In particular, note the chapters on developing a communication plan, communication research, and creativity. It is important to remember, too, that a basic messaging strategy is similar, in many respects, to creating the overall communication plan; thus, there will be some necessary overlapping of content.

1. Audience definition

All successful communication and message strategies depend on a clear definition of your target audience. This may sound straightforward, but it seldom is. Often institutions find themselves trying to communicate with multiple, ill-defined target audiences. Consider, for example, the potential target audiences shown in Table 2-1.

Table 2-1
Potential Target Audiences

Stakeholders	**Customers**	**Influencers**	**Resource Providers**
Faculty	Current students	Media	Donors
Staff	Prospective students	Parents	Alumni
Administrators		Peers of the target audience	Foundations
Alumni		Church and religious leaders	Legislators
Board members		Business leaders	Business leaders
		High school guidance counselors	Grantors
		High school club advisers	
		Coaches	

Is it reasonable to think that one message strategy will meet the needs of these diverse target audiences? No, of course not. But still, institutions try it.

Target audience categories. Because the seven-step list can be daunting, it may help to think of target audiences as members of one (and in some cases more than one) of the following four categories:

1. Stakeholders
2. Customers
3. Influencers
4. Resource providers

Stakeholders are the individuals and groups involved in delivering your product. Some common stakeholders are faculty, staff, and administrators. They are critical audiences, but it is very important not to confuse stakeholders with customers. Often their needs and expectations are quite different.

Customers are the people who pay the bills. In most cases, they are students. Sometimes, however, you may have other customers, such as corporations for whom you offer classes or conduct research. Some public institutions may try to make the case that taxpayers are also customers and, in a somewhat convoluted fashion, they probably are.

The third group is the influencers. These are people who influence both customers and resource providers. Influencers, for example, may be high school guidance counselors, club advisers, coaches, parents, the media, and business leaders. Although this is the most amorphous of all the categories, it is still exceedingly important.

Finally, resource providers include donors, parents (here's one group that fits in more than one category), legislators, alumni, and voters, among others.

Customizing the message. One of the greatest communication challenges facing institutions is coming up with a coherent message flow that meets the often different and sometimes conflicting information needs and expectations of their stakeholders, customers, influencers, and resource providers.

Let's say, for example, you are interested in developing a brochure that highlights academic quality. Will one definition of academic quality meet the needs and expectations of each of these four diverse groups? No, probably not. Ask faculty (stakeholders) to define academic quality and you will hear about the quality of the curriculum, facilities, faculty credentials, and the academic ability of students. Students (customers), however, often define academic quality with strong components of convenience: Which classes are taught when? Is there a place to park? Will they take credit cards in the business office? Parents, taxpayers (resource providers), and high school club advisers (influencers) will all have their own interpretations of academic quality. Because of these varied expectations, there is little likelihood that one message strategy will work. Instead, integrated marketing communication demands a segmented message strategy that is dependent on the different expectations of different target audiences.

Defining your target audiences. Identifying your target audiences is but half the battle. Now you must define them—and their interests—in greater detail. You may wish to know their ages, where they live, their household incomes, and other demographic characteristics. At the same time, you might also want to have an understanding of such psychographic and behavioral characteristics as:

- Who and what influences them;
- How they perceive (and misperceive) you and your competitors;
- Their attitude about you; and
- Their short- and long-term motivations and desires.

Obtaining this information and other data about your target audiences may require audience research.

2. Audience research
The odds are high that you don't know as much about your target audiences as you might wish. For example, you probably don't know what motivates major donors or how prospective students compare you with competing institutions. You may not clearly understand how commuter students define academic quality or how parents feel about

campus safety. Obtaining this and other information is the critical goal of audience research, the second step in the message creation process. Without research, there is little likelihood that your messages will have the saliency they need. In fact, audience research is the step in the message process that addresses the need to listen first and, by extension, to listen often.

It is foolish on the one hand, and dangerous on the other, to base an enduring integrated communication plan on scant or faulty research. Undertaking audience or communication research will help you refine messages, clarify which media are most effective, and generally help you focus your overall communication plan.

Note: Chapter 4 explores communication research in much greater detail.

3. Development of communication goals

After your audience research is completed, it is time to outline your broad communication goals. This requires that you do two things. First, as we have already discussed, you must identify the specific target audience. And second, you must anticipate the desired outcome of your messages to them. Here are some sample communication goals:

- Develop greater institutional name recognition among prospective students.
- Persuade more alumni to contribute to the alumni fund.
- Reduce dissemination of incorrect information among part-time faculty.

It is very important to settle your broad communication goals before creating your vivid descriptors (see below) and developing your creative concept. This allows you to test initial vivid descriptors and creative concepts on subsets of the actual target audiences.

4. Clarification of vivid descriptors

After you have defined your target audiences, conducted the necessary audience research, and begun to outline your communication goals, it is time to clarify your vivid descriptors, or as some call them, points of pride—the institutional core values you most often wish to communicate. Insight into the importance of vivid descriptors can be obtained by asking and answering this question: When your target audiences hear your name, what words and phrases do you want to come to their minds? More often than not, these words and phrases—descriptors, if you will—will be the institutional core values that you most often wish to convey.

A large, private university in the Midwest, for example, wanted to communicate the following vivid descriptors:

- Academic quality
  - Innovative programs
  - Great faculty
  - Great facilities
- Solid administrative leadership
- Outstanding graduates
- Economic and cultural partnership with the community

Are the above vivid descriptors unique? No, but they are still significant and important. And more often than not, what will make them unique is the degree to which they are interpreted and communicated in ways that target audiences will understand, appreciate, and remember. This interpretation is an important part of the audience research discussed earlier.

As noted previously in this chapter, it is very important that you communicate a quality or attribute in ways that your target audiences understand and even appreciate. In our earlier discussion, it was noted that different audiences often define academic quality in different ways. Early in your message development strategy, you might ask members of each target audience to define academic quality. Listen to their words and phrases. Determine their expectations. Ask them to describe academic quality. Perhaps they can give some examples from their own experiences. It is very important that you use as much of the target audience's definition of academic quality as you can to craft your messages.

5. Concept creation

The next step in the messaging process is the creation of the driving concept. Sometimes we term this the "big idea," the catalytic engine that drives the creative effort and even helps guide decisions about the choice of one or more media to use.

It is the creation of a great driving concept that is at the core of successful messages. Without it, messages will seldom be noticeable, salient, or memorable. Solid creative driving concepts are built on the communication goals and vivid descriptors outlined above.

Note: The development of the creative driving concept is the focus of Chapter 5.

6. Development of the media mix

After you have created the driving concept, it is time to begin formulating the media mix. The media mix is the array of communication media used to execute the communication strategy. To give you some idea of the variety of media available, some options are presented in Figure 2-3.

Media relations – PSAs	Magazine advertising
Media relations – Feature stories	Outdoor/transit advertising
Media relations – Hometowners	Specialty advertising
Media relations – Wild art	Environmentals/signage
(photos with captions but no accompanying article)	Web/Internet/Intranet
Media relations – Tip sheets	Video/audio
Media news	Compact discs
Alumni relations	Publications
High school relations	Direct mail
Public relations	Special events
Radio advertising	TV/cable advertising
Newspaper advertising	Telemarketing/Word of mouth

Figure 2-3
Communications Options

Note: Additional information on creating and customizing the media mix appear in the chapters dealing with the creation of the integrated marketing communication plan and communication research.

7. Message evaluation and modification

The last step in the message process is to evaluate and modify the overall message strategy. One of the basic assumptions of the listening-first model is that all messages and message strategies can be fine-tuned.

Evaluating the effectiveness of the overall message strategy means answering simple questions: Did the campaign help you reach your communication goals? Were more people informed? Were donors motivated? Did annual fund participation increase? Was there more awareness among prospective students? In other words, did the cumulative effect of the messages achieve the goal you established at the outset?

Evaluation can also occur at another level and with another goal. Although it is extremely important to evaluate the effectiveness of the overall campaign, it is also useful to evaluate individual messages during the campaign so that subsequent messages can be refined. For example, you might ask a focus group of members of your target audience how they responded to a television spot. This would allow you to use the insights gained from this group to refine future spots.

Note: Chapter 4 outlines a number of communication research strategies that can be used to enhance individual messages.

A couple of final words

(Well, maybe more than a couple.) During the course of this chapter, we presented the components of what we termed our listening-first model of communication. Although some of our comments were intended to be humorous, the overall point we tried to convey is quite serious. To be effective, communication must be two-way and must involve aggressive listening at two levels. First, listening must be part of an initial assessment of target audience needs and expectations. This must occur very early in the message-creation process. And second, listening must occur as part of the ongoing evaluation and modification of individual messages and larger message strategies.

In our opinion, there is no excuse for failing to listen to target audiences if we are sincere in our desire to communicate, not merely promote. Institutions that elect not to listen to their constituencies imperil themselves and their missions. In an earlier age, we used the term *caveat emptor*—let the buyer beware. Recognizing the power, influence, and long memory of the buyer, we must revise our Latin to *cave emptorum*—beware of the buyer.

Recommended Readings

Bittner, John R. *Mass Communication*. New York: Allyn & Bacon, 1995.

Caywood, Clarke L. *The Handbook of Strategic Public Relations & Integrated Communications*. New York: McGraw-Hill Book Company, 1997.

Gregory, James with Jack G. Wiechmann. *Leveraging the Corporate Brand*. Lincolnwood, IL: NTC/Contemporary Publishing, 1997.

Larson, Erik. *The Naked Consumer: How Our Private Lives Become Public Commodities*. New York: Viking Penguin, 1994.

Martin, David N. *Romancing the Brand*. New York: AMACOM, 1989.

McQuail, Denis. *Mass Communication Theory: An Introduction*, 3rd ed. Thousand Oaks, CA: Sage, 1994.

Percy, Larry. *Strategies for Implementing Integrated Marketing Communications*. Lincolnwood, IL: NTC/Contemporary Publishing Group, 1997.

Ries, Al and Jack Trout. *The 22 Immutable Laws of Marketing: Violate Them at Your Own Risk!* New York: Harper & Row, 1994.

Roman, Erman. *Integrated Direct Marketing*. Lincolnwood, IL: NTC/Contemporary Publishing Group, 1995.

Schoell, William F. and Joseph Guiltinan. *Marketing: Contemporary Concepts and Practices*, 6th ed. Englewood Cliffs, NJ: Prentice-Hall, 1995.

Schultz Don E., Stanley Tannenbaum and Robert F. Lauterborn. *The New Marketing Paradigm: Integrated Marketing Communications*, Lincolnwood, IL: NTC/Contemporary Publishing Group, 1994.

Sevier, Robert A. "Shifts and Nudges: Important Lessons from Old and New Approaches to Marketing Colleges and Universities." *White Paper No. 5*, Cedar Rapids, IA: Stamats Communications, Inc., 1997. (This white paper is available on www.stamats.com.)

Vivian, John. *The Media of Mass Communication*, 5th ed. New York: Allyn & Bacon, 1998.

Weinstein, Art. Market Segmentation: *Using Demographics, Psychographics, and Niche Marketing Techniques to Predict and Model Customer Behavior*. Chicago: Probus Publishing Company, 1993.

3

> **Effective integrated marketing communication plans are built on a foundation of institutional core values.**

Developing the Integrated Marketing Communications Plan

Robert Sevier

This chapter outlines the components of the integrated marketing communication plan and walks you through the steps of the planning process. Because some of you may never have seen an integrated marketing communication plan, we begin with a basic plan outline so that you start out familiar with the ground we are going to cover.

The IMC planning process

First, a few quick notes are in order. We are aware that the outline presented here is similar to the planning outline presented in the first book, *Integrated Marketing for Colleges, Universities, and Schools,* published by CASE Books in its integrated marketing series. However, as we wrote this book, we kept reminding ourselves that many readers will not be familiar with that first book, a companion volume to this one. For this reason, it is necessary to address some of these key planning steps again.

Another reason is that despite a similarity between the two planning processes, there is at least one important distinction. The steps for creating a comprehensive, institution-wide integrated marketing plan address the following three levels of integration:

■ Strategic
■ Organizational
■ Message

But because the focus of this book is the creation of an integrated marketing communication plan, our discussion in this chapter will center on the third level of integration: message. As you can see from Figure 3-1, the plan has 10 basic components. Some plans vary in slight detail, but we believe that the following plan elements, taken in this order, will serve most institutions well.

Figure 3-1
Outline of an Integrated Marketing Communication Plan

1. Mission statement	6. Vivid descriptors
2. Vision statement	7. Clarification of target geographies
3. Strategic plan and initiatives	8. Create media mix
4. Definition of target audiences	9. Media calendar
5. Communication goals	10. Budgets

The outline presented here closely parallels the messaging strategy outlined in Chapter 2. This, too, was intentional on our part. Successful messages depend greatly on the effectiveness of the larger communication plan. Later in this chapter we move through the overall planning process. But before we can step up to that challenge, we need to spend some time introducing and explaining the individual plan elements.

Mission statement, vision statement, and strategic plan and initiatives

Effective integrated marketing communication plans are built on a foundation of institutional core values. These core values arise from the institution's historical mission, the first item on the list, and are reinterpreted through the second and third items, namely its vision and strategic plan and initiatives. We believe that communication plans that do not acknowledge these core values can never be truly strategic, fully integrated, or enduring. In addition, we believe that communication plans without this foundation will ultimately fail because they cannot resist the vagaries of whim and fashion. To stay on track and on target, the communication plan must fully embrace the core values of the sponsoring institution.

Target audiences

The next element in the integrated marketing communication plan is a detailed list of target audiences, the people whom you wish to inform or influence. Surprisingly, the list of target audiences in a successful communication plan is generally quite small, usually no more than about a half-dozen. It is important to keep in mind that because integrated marketing communication plans emanate directly from the strategic plan, it is reasonable to assume that the target audiences must also be of strategic importance. In other words, the plan must focus on meeting the information needs of the relatively small number of people who will truly, quickly, and significantly impact your institution's future.

Communication goals

Next, the plan outlines the overall communication goals. Message goals express the desired outcomes of the overall communication plan and campaign. As you think about communication goals, keep in mind that the clearer the goals, and the more they are built on solid research, the easier it will be to evaluate your plan's effectiveness.

Vivid descriptors

The sixth component listed in the outline of an integrated marketing communication plan comprises the vivid descriptors. Vivid descriptors are the institutional core values expressed as words and phrases that you want to communicate to your target audiences aggressively. Like the list of target audiences, the number of vivid descriptors is usually relatively small. And like your target audiences, your vivid descriptors must also be strategic.

Target geographies

Following the vivid descriptors is a clarification of your target geographies—the geographic areas where your target audiences live. A clear understanding of your target geographies is extremely important because of the need to coordinate media buys, purchase mailing lists, coordinate visits, and generally steward resources. Based on our experience, too many plans founder because they try to reach target audiences spread out over too large a geographic area.

Media mix

The media mix is the array of media that are incorporated into the overall communication strategy. The media mix is heavily influenced by the media habits of the target audience, the budget, the sophistication and competitiveness of the media market, and other variables.

Media calendar

The media calendar keeps track of messages, media, and deadlines. Readers with a planning bent may find similarity between a media calendar and action plans. Both feature GANTT* charts and are designed to help keep the plan on schedule and to increase accountability and control.

Budget

The final element of the integrated marketing communication plan is the budget. Although the budget may be positioned at the end of the list, successful planners know that discussions about the budget must occur very early in the planning process. In particular, you need to know the answers to the following issues:

- How much money is allocated for the plan each year?
- How long will the plan run?

---

*A GANTT chart is a chronological overview of a series of activities in which each is represented as a bar or symbol on a calendar. GANTT charts allow you to see at a glance when everything is happening.

Planning relationships

It is often useful to have a sense of how the integrated marketing communication plan relates to the institutional mission, vision, and strategic plan. Earlier, we noted that integrated marketing communication plans must flow directly from mission and vision. Figure 3-2 outlines a typical relationship between mission, vision, the strategic plan, and the integrated marketing communication plan. The purpose of the IMC plan is to help influence, inform, and persuade strategic audiences.

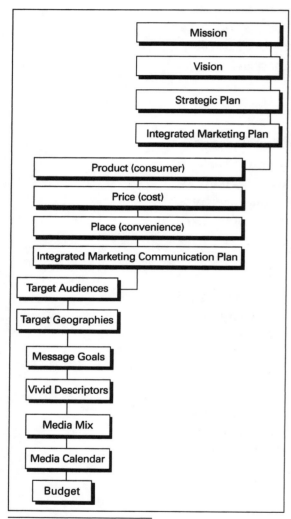

Figure 3-2
The Strategic Communication Plan: Planning Relationships

The integrated marketing communication planning process

The IMC planning process we have developed encompasses nine essential steps. We don't want to turn this book into a primer on planning—after all, our goal is to spend the majority of our time discussing individual communication strategies—but we believe it is useful to understand in some detail the overall components of an integrated marketing communication plan. In addition, we want to point out some pitfalls to avoid so that your overall planning effort will be as successful as possible.

The planning steps are as follows:
1. Achieve buy-in.
2. Choose the planning champion and assemble the planning team.
3. Define and prioritize your target audiences.
4. Establish communication goals.
5. Settle on vivid descriptors.
6. Clarify target geographies.
7. Create the media mix.
8. Develop the media calendar.
9. Implement, evaluate, and modify the plan.

Step 1: Achieve buy-in

The first step in creating an integrated marketing communication plan is similar to the first steps required for creating strategic and marketing plans—achieving buy-in. For any plan and planning process to succeed, it must have the active, visible, and demonstrated support of the president and senior administrators. In addition, it must have as much campus-wide buy-in as possible. If the president and senior administrators are not active supporters in the planning process, or the need for the planning process has not been demonstrated to the larger campus community, then there is little likelihood that it will succeed.

Buy-in of the president and senior staff. There are a number of reasons why the support of the president and senior staff is critical, but only a handful should suffice to make the case. First, if the integrated communication plan will truly promulgate institutional core values, it must have the support of senior leadership. Second, for the communication budget to be long-term and of sufficient size, there must be consensus at the senior level. Third, communication strategies, like marketing strategies, are often far-ranging and cross-departmental, and the support of senior staff will help reduce turf warfare and increase efficiencies.

The active, aggressive support of the president and senior administrators will also accomplish the following:

- Increase the likelihood of shared goals.
- Heighten the stewardship of resources.
- Maximize coordination.
- Help establish a consistent and integrated message.

Finally, and perhaps most importantly, the involvement of the president and senior administrators legitimizes integrated marketing communication to the larger campus community from the beginning of the planning process to the resulting plan. The involvement of the senior staff sends an important, clear message that this undertaking is of strategic interest to the institution.

Campuswide buy-in. Although support of the president and senior staff is important, equally important is the support of the larger campus community. For any IMC planning effort to succeed, the need for the plan, or at least its anticipated results, must be felt by faculty, staff, administrators, and even students. If the body politic does not feel the need, then the plan will never be accepted and the activities outlined in the plan will never be acted upon.

Students of organizational change note that buy-in almost never occurs without a burning platform: an event or series of events that ignites the interest of the community in taking a specific course of action. The burning platform may be an outside threat, such as the opening by a competitor of a branch campus just down the street. A burning platform may also be a concern about enrollment or a decline in annual fund contributions. Planning and coordinated action works best in a climate of demonstrated need, a need to respond to a threat or to take advantage of a significant opportunity. Without a sense of widely felt need, the planning effort will often fall on deaf ears, or at least inattentive ones. ·

Clarifying the role of the president
The president's first duty is to empower the planning process. To do this, he or she must be willing to do the following:

- Spend time, money, talent, and political capital.
- Make tough decisions.
- Reallocate institutional priorities and funds.
- Address territoriality.

If the president is unwilling to empower the process in this manner, then the planning team should seriously question his or her commitment and the decision to proceed with an integrated marketing communication plan.

Second, the president must clarify the planning mandate. This involves demonstrating how the communication plan will build on the institutional mission and vision and may also include some preliminary discussion of target audiences and broad communication goals. It is very important that the planning champion and planning team be in sync with the president's mandate because it is against this mandate that the president will evaluate the individual components of the plan and the completed plan itself.

Third, the president must establish a preliminary communication budget and give the planners a sense of whether the plan should run one, two, three, or more years. It is essential that the president acknowledge this responsibility because there is little likelihood that a planning team can develop a plan that will be approved at a later date without this initial guidance. Fourth, the president must serve as the chief decision maker. This includes selecting the planning champion, approving the team, developing the initial budget, and approving the individual components of the plan. A flowchart outlining the presidential decision points is presented in Figure 3-3.

Finally, the president selects the planning champion and approves the planning team.

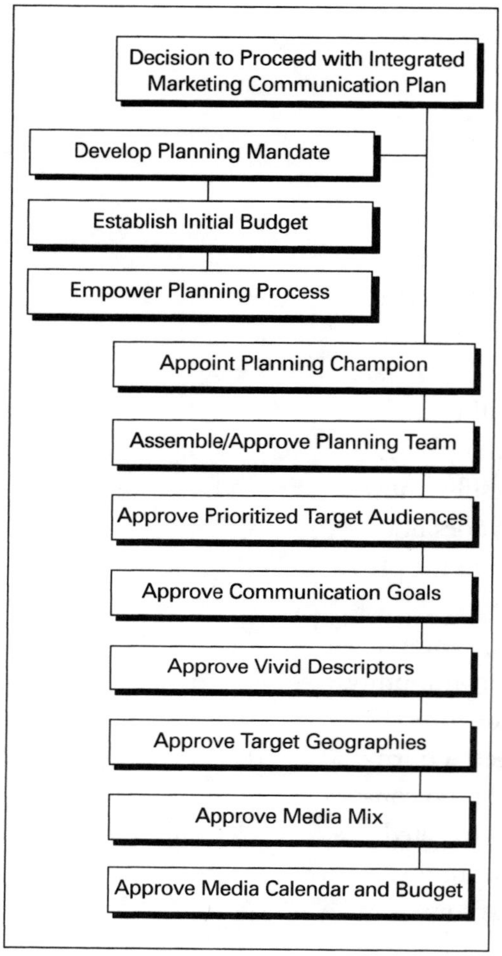
Decision to Proceed with Integrated Marketing Communication Plan
Develop Planning Mandate
Establish Initial Budget
Empower Planning Process
Appoint Planning Champion
Assemble/Approve Planning Team
Approve Prioritized Target Audiences
Approve Communication Goals
Approve Vivid Descriptors
Approve Target Geographies
Approve Media Mix
Approve Media Calendar and Budget

Figure 3-3
Key Decision Points for the President

Step 2: Choose the planning champion and assemble the planning team

One of the most important decisions the president makes is appointing the planning champion, the single person most responsible for the overall planning process. Presidents who are sincere about the planning process will select a champion who has four characteristics. First, he or she must have the respect of the campus community. Second, the person should have both a theoretical and an experiential understanding of marketing and communication. Third, the champion must have power and clout. And fourth, he or she must be able to lead and motivate people.

The role of the champion

As the head of the planning effort, the champion has a number of responsibilities, including those that follow:

- Assembling the planning team
- Representing the president's mandate to the planning team
- Interfacing with the president and other senior administrators
- Overseeing the internal and external planning liaisons
- Serving as planning leader
- Serving as planning delegator
- Keeping the president continually informed

Presidents don't like surprises. One way the champion can keep from surprising the president is to keep him or her informed at each stage in the planning process. We've learned from experience that presidential approval of each step in the planning process is best accomplished by:

- Keeping him or her involved at key junctures

- Heightening his or her confidence in the champion, the planning team, the planning process, and the final plan
- Keeping the plan focused on strategic, mandated issues

Address the budget issue now

We believe strongly that the president should commit an amount or range of dollars to both the planning and implementation of the integrated communication plan at the outset.

We make this recommendation for a number of reasons. First, if the president won't commit dollars, chances are that he or she is not committed to the overall planning process. If this is truly a strategic integrated marketing communication plan, then it must be supported with strategic assets: people, time, and dollars.

Second, if you do not know how much money you have to work with, it is likely that the plan you develop will be either too limited or too far-reaching in scope. A sense of the real dollars that are available will help you make decisions that allow you to focus the plan more correctly throughout its development.

And third, if the president says, "Go ahead and write the plan and we'll talk about budgets later," the champion and the team will be in an extremely awkward spot if, after the plan is written, the president is not able to keep his or her promise about funding.

If you look closely at the planning-team organization chart (Figure 3-4), you will notice someone who might surprise you—the chief finance officer. This inclusion is not accidental. Rather, it is a measure of the institution's commitment to fund the plan. We have discovered that when the chief financial officer is involved at the beginning of the planning process, the likelihood that sufficient resources will be available increases. By involving the chief financial officer at the plan's inception, you increase his or her ownership in the plan as well.

A final word about the plan budget. It is much more effective to budget fewer dollars over a longer period of time rather than more dollars for a shorter period of time. If, for example, you have $100,000 , it makes more sense to spend $30,000 for each of three years than $100,000 in one year. By leveraging your dollars over time, your plan is much more likely to have a lasting impact.

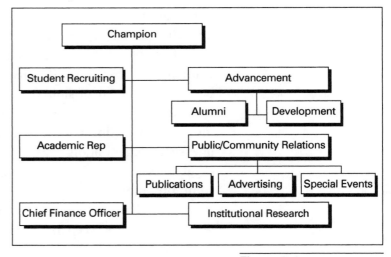

Figure 3-4
The IMC Planning Team

Responsibilities of the planning team

Like the planning champion, the planning team has several important tasks. The team must handle these tasks:

- Oversee the planning process.
- Interface with internal and external stakeholders.
- Gather data and insight from internal and external sources.
- Make preliminary planning decisions.

■ Spread ownership of the planning process.
■ Oversee implementation of the plan.
■ Monitor and evaluate the plan and plan activities at key junctures.

Assembling the planning team

One of the first responsibilities of the planning champion is to assemble the team of individuals who are responsible for first writing and then implementing the integrated marketing communication plan. Although there are no hard and fast rules, some general guidelines may provide insight and direction.

First, keep in mind that this is a team, a group of individuals working toward a common, often heart-felt, goal. At this point, it is important to state something that might not be so obvious: Everyone on the team should be committed to the president's mandate and the IMC plan's raison d'être. The team should never include someone who is not committed to marketing and communication. Resist the temptation to include someone who represents interests not consistent with those of the larger team. Sometimes people believe that such a person is a valuable counterbalance. In our experience, this person becomes a tremendous drag on the planning process and more often than not poisons the interaction of the team members and the interaction between the team and the larger campus community.

Second, the team should include at least some individuals who most likely will be charged with implementing the plan. This serves two important purposes. It increases ownership of the plan. And it keeps the plan goals more realistic since some of the people responsible for writing them know they will be involved in their implementation.

Third, because planning teams are increasingly likely to be cross-functional, great effort must be expended in developing a work climate that recognizes the need to integrate team members who often have different backgrounds, expectations, and goals— and who may have never worked with one another—into a truly effective team.

It is not possible to make a blanket recommendation about who should be on the planning team because of the great diversity not only in educational institutions, but in how institutions are organized and in the range of problems and opportunities they face. To deal with this situation, it is important to look beyond titles and offices and instead to marketing and communication principles. Rather than dotted and straight lines on an organization chart, let's concentrate on involving those with the essential capabilities and functions needed to implement and monitor the integrated marketing communication plan.

With this goal in mind, we have listed the titles of members of a sample planning team in Figure 3-4. Keep in mind, that this is only an example; it is not prescriptive. Your goal must be to develop a planning team made up of individuals who are knowledgeable, enthusiastic, and participatory, and who recognize the context, qualities, opportunities, and problems that are unique to your institution.

Before we proceed with the next step in the planning process, let's take a few minutes to examine the role and function of individual team members. Titles are flexible and approximate. What is more important are the conceptual and technical skill sets and spheres of influence and responsibility they bring to the job, and that all target audiences are represented.

The champion. The person the president selects as the champion sends an important signal to the campus community about how the president perceives the value of the plan and planning process. Often, the champion is drawn from recruiting or advancement for the simple reason that people in these offices generally have a greater understanding of and appreciation for not only marketing and communication, but also for target audiences and marketplace dynamics. In addition, the success of a communication plan will have a direct impact on the champion's ability to meet the challenges of his or her primary responsibilities.

The champion may come from the faculty. This will work if the faculty member has ample time and all four of the characteristics of a champion—the respect of the campus community, an understanding of marketing, an understanding of communication, and plenty of power and clout. Because the champion often becomes a lightning rod for campus concerns and frustrations—especially those of faculty, it is important that a planning champion who is a faculty member also have one other important quality—a sense of humor.

Like all members of the planning team, the champion is responsible for communicating with and managing internal and external constituencies who may include those listed in Table 3-1.

Planning Team Member/Office	Internal Staff	Constituencies

Planning Champion	President
	Senior administrators
		Trustees
		Key external opinion
		  leaders and
		  influentials

Advancement Office	Advancement staff Alumni staff	Donors Alumni Foundations
Public Relations Office	Public relations staff Publications staff Community relations staff Media relations staff Advertising staff Special events staff	Community relations Business leaders Opinion leaders Media
Recruiting Office	Field recruiters	Prospective students -traditional -of color -international -nontraditional -graduate

Table 3-1
Communicating with and Managing Internal and External Constituencies

Planning secretary. Because of the great volume of information that will flow to and through the planning team, it is helpful to have a secretary. He or she may be a contributing member of the team or a clerical assistant recruited or appointed to serve. Ideally, the planning secretary should report directly to the champion.

The secretary is the chief recorder and document specialist for the planning team. He or she is responsible for recording the minutes from each meeting; collecting, organizing, and distributing materials; handling correspondence; coordinating meetings and schedules; and generally keeping things under control. In most cases, the secretary is responsible for assembling and formatting the final written plan.

The planning secretary should have one other important skill—the ability to keep confidences.

Advancement representative. In all likelihood, the planning team should also include someone from the advancement office. This person is responsible for serving as a communication and information-gathering liaison with key internal and external constituencies. The advancement office's constituencies are shown in Table 3-1.

All advancement staff, via the advancement representative on the planning team, are involved in the planning process, and it is up to the advancement representative to see that the perceptions, needs, and expectations of their key external constituencies are sought.

Public/community relations representative. The planning team should also include a representative from the PR office, especially if the public relations function does not report to advancement. The public relations liaison must communicate with and gather insight and data from the constituencies listed in Table 3-1.

Student recruiting representative. Another important member of the communication planning team is the representative from recruiting. In an ideal world, this person would serve as a liaison for all recruiting functions, including undergraduate, graduate, adult, commuter, part-time, and international students. Table 3-1 lists the office's constituencies.

Institutional research representative. The planning team will also benefit by including a member from institutional research. This representative has three potential tasks: (1) to assemble all relevant current research conducted by individuals and departments at the institution, (2) to make sure the team does not initiate communication research now being undertaken by some other entity, and (3) to oversee the primary and secondary research undertaken as part of the planning process.

Finance representative. Another important member of the planning team is a senior representative of the finance office. Only someone from the finance office can determine how much money all departments are currently spending on communication-related activities. Involving a person from finance early will increase the likelihood that he or she will more completely understand the benefits of marketing and communication, their significance, and therefore more readily espouse the need for long-term funding from the institution in support of the planning team's activities. Finance people often become important allies when it comes time to develop or argue for a budget.

Academic representative. Strong academic representation on the planning team is critical. Just as the team champion is responsible for interacting with senior administrators, the faculty representative must serve as a liaison with other faculty.

Faculty from no one particular discipline make better team members than others, and, contrary to popular notion, business faculty bring no essential skill set to the plan-

> " Faculty from no one particular discipline seem to make better team members than others, and, contrary to popular notion, business faculty bring no essential skill set to the planning process. "

ning process. Rather, faculty who serve best in this role have a varied set of skills and attributes, including the following:

- They are perceived by other faculty as honorable and trustworthy.
- They are able to consider all faculty needs—not just those of their department.
- They are able to understand and appreciate all faculty ranks and categories, including part-time and adjunct.
- They are knowledgeable about the institution and its history.
- They are knowledgeable about competing and noncompeting institutions.
- They are knowledgeable about the institution's obstacles and opportunities.
- They are sensitive to students and to student needs.

After working with a number of faculty members over the years, we have noticed other skills and attributes often found in the best faculty representatives. They must:

- Be willing to examine issues critically from all sides
- Be willing to interact with faculty from other disciplines
- Be willing do the homework—read the books, papers, reports; conduct the interviews; and complete the assignments
- Be able to meet deadlines
- Be thick-skinned because they will often serve as the lightning rod for all faculty concerns and complaints

Perhaps most importantly, they must have an appreciation for the planning process and believe that creating and implementing an integrated marketing communication plan is in the best interest of all campus stakeholders, including faculty.

Who's missing?
Unless there is a compelling reason, I do not generally recommend that the communication planning team include representatives from the following constituencies:

- Current students
- Alumni
- Trustees
- Community residents
- Business leaders
- Donors
- The president

Of course, you're probably wondering why these people have been omitted from the planning process. Well, actually, they haven't been excluded. Rather, we believe that their needs and the needs of the institution are best served by team members aggressively soliciting their input. This is especially important at the situational-analysis stage.

There are two other issues to address. First, the team should include people who will actually oversee the plan's implementation. If it doesn't, they will never have the necessary ownership, and you will miss the benefit of their experience and expertise. Second, the process outlined in this chapter for creating a team can easily grow to an unmanageable size if care is not taken. Remember, you must try to keep the size of the team as small as possible. It is difficult, if not impossible, for large teams to meet often enough to get the job done in a timely fashion.

Space and resources

Now that you have a planning team, you need somewhere to meet and work. Your meeting room should have the following supplies:

- An overhead projector
- A slide projector
- A screen
- Large chalkboards or dry-marker erasable boards with chalk or dry markers
- Flip charts and easels
- A telephone
- Quick access to a photocopier
- A computer with access to the Internet
- Work tables
- Access to coffee, soft drinks, and restrooms

Computer and software resources

If they are available, certain software and computer resources will make your work more efficient and effective. A linked or network-based meeting-scheduling software package such as Microsoft Outlook will make scheduling your meetings much easier. E-mail can cut down on the need for so many meetings. You can use e-mail to query team members about a particular topic or issue, poll them about a decision, or even schedule meetings.

I strongly suggest you also use planning software such as ManagePro, On Target, or Fast Track Schedule. Planning software such as this will save you an enormous amount of time and frustration as the plan is developed, refined, implemented, and changed. We will explore the use of planning software in greater depth later in this chapter.

A computer-based projection system helps, too. A good system will allow you to project your monitor's image to a large screen. This is especially useful when compiling initial lists and ideas and for projecting initial concepts and dummies. Using a computer to record and project the team's comments and ideas makes the process much more engaging and efficient. It is also helpful to use a projection system when examining Web sites.

Step 3: Define and prioritize your target audiences

One of the most important steps in the integrated marketing communication planning process is to define and then prioritize your target audiences first. Often the single biggest mistake that people make when developing their communication plan is to focus on too many target audiences or on audiences that are ill-defined. Consider, for a minute, the four groups of target audiences outlined in Table 2-1 in Chapter 2.

Most communication plans would falter if they had to meet the information needs of even half the audiences of an average institution. However, there are a number

> " Not only must you identify your target audiences, you must define them as succinctly as possible so you can avoid any confusion or misinterpretation. "

of options for reducing the size of the list of potential target audiences.

In this era of finite resources, it is important to ask the following question as early in the planning process as possible: Who matters most?

This is a tough, political, and often contentious question. It is, however, an extremely important one because it immediately helps you make some rough decisions about which audiences are truly most important.

Obviously, the who-matters-most question has a number of permutations that can help you prioritize potential target audiences. Consider, for example, the following:

- Which audiences will have an impact on student recruiting most quickly?
- Which audiences will have an impact on major gifts most quickly?
- Which audiences have the most far-reaching strategic significance?
- Which audiences will lead to other, perhaps more important, audiences?
- Which audiences can be safely delayed—even ignored?

Second, remember the president's mandate. Often the president's mandate will provide some insight into which target audiences are important.

Remember that your plan will run three or more years. With this in mind, it is sometimes wise to focus on a small group of target audiences in the first year of the plan and then add one or two target audiences in succeeding years.

Identifying your plan's target audiences is the first order of battle. For example, suppose one of your target audiences is faculty. Are you referring only to full-time faculty? What about adjunct faculty? How about retired faculty? Or consider alumni. All alumni? Alumni who actually graduated? Alumni who completed a specific number of courses? What about alumni who have donated versus alumni who have not?

Not only must you identify your target audiences, you must define them as succinctly as possible so you can avoid any confusion or misinterpretation. Fortunately, there are a number of demographic, psychographic, and behavioral variables you can use to help clarify your target audiences.

Some basic demographic characteristics follow:

- Age
- Distance from the institution
- Household income
- Relationship to the institution (alumni, parent, faculty, donor)
- Giving history
- Year of graduation

Marketing expert Philip Kotler and others believe that audiences should also be defined psychographically, attitudinally, and, when possible, behaviorally. Kotler, for example, stresses a series of audience characteristics based on benefits sought, user status, loyalty status, readiness stage, and attitude toward the institution. As Table 3-2 indicates, these segments have great potential for student recruiting and fund raising.

Step 4: Clarify your communication goals

Now that you have defined your target audiences—the groups of people who are of

Table 3-2
Potential Target Audiences

Stakeholders	Customers	Influencers	Resource Providers
Faculty Staff Administrators Alumni Board members	Current students Prospective students	Media Parents Peers of the target audience Religious leaders Business leaders High school guidance counselors Grantors Club advisers Coaches	Donors Alumni Foundations Legislators Business leaders

strategic importance to your institution—it is time to establish your strategic communication goals.

It is sometimes helpful to think of communication goals as desired outcomes: in other words, how you wish to influence, inform, or move a specific target audience. Some communication goals might be to accomplish the following:

- Increase our ability to communicate to faculty and staff.
- Help city residents become more aware of the economic value of our institution.
- Enhance the image of our new president.
- Raise the sense of awareness of the new capital campaign.
- Enhance the perception of our institution as a friendly, caring, supporting college of liberal arts within the greater metropolitan area.

Good communication goals have a number of key characteristics. For example, they are:

- Built on research—they are not simply hopes and dreams, but based on solid data
- Important—they represent essential, core, widely shared values
- Achievable—they are realistic; something you can strive for yet still accomplish
- Differentiating—they help you stand out from your competitors
- Measurable—they have a positive impact on the two key barometers: fund raising and student recruiting
- Directed both inward and outward—they target both internal and external audiences
- Energizing—they have a galvanizing, catalytic impact on the campus community

As you think about communication goals, keep in mind a number of issues. First, the goals should reflect the emphases of the original planning mandate as often as possible. Second, they should be directed at the most important target audiences. Third, because the communication goals will be distilled as vivid descriptors, they should be as focused as possible. And finally, because of increased interest in stewardship and return on investment (ROI), the communication goals should be both achievable and measurable.

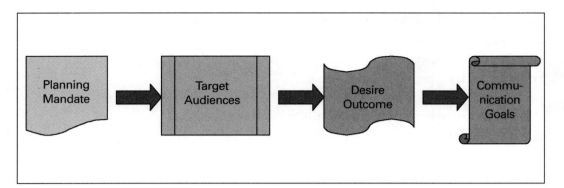

Figure 3-5
**Relationship
Between Planning
Mandate and
Communication
Goals**

Step 5: Settle on vivid descriptors

As noted earlier, vivid descriptors, sometimes called points of pride, describe your institutional core values. As such, they become the heart and soul of your messages and overall communication campaign. The best vivid descriptors emanate from the mission, vision, and strategic plan, and are both enduring and long-term. In addition to representing core values, successful vivid descriptors must also resonate solidly with your target audiences.

Consider, for example, the following vivid descriptors from a private college in the Midwest:

- A caring, supportive campus culture
- High-quality faculty, facilities, programs, and graduates
- A valuable economic, cultural, and intellectual asset to the region

A public, regional university in the West established the following vivid descriptors:

- Small classes
- Undergraduate focus
- Leadership in and partnership with the community
- Access to faculty
- Curriculum focused on real-world issues

Vivid descriptors as positioning elements

At this stage in the communication planning process, it is absolutely essential that you establish, test, and settle on a handful of vivid descriptors because these descriptors will become the central themes for your integrated marketing communication plan. They will be used in tag lines, advertising, publications, media relations, and other media. They will become, in sum, the position you hold in the minds of your target audiences.

As you think about your vivid descriptors, remember to keep their number as small as possible. There are few instances where more than half a dozen are justified. It is also important to realize that not all target audiences will be interested in all of your vivid descriptors. Furthermore, not all audiences will define all the vivid descriptors the same way. Earlier, we presented examples of how different target audiences define academic quality, and it is time to revisit those examples. Faculty may interpret academic quality to mean the quality of your faculty, facilities, curriculum, and students. Students, however, may think academic quality means access to faculty, convenience, and accelerated programs. It is very important to ask the target audience to define, from their perspective, your vivid descriptors and, where possible, use their definitions in the messages you send back to them (Figure 3-6).

Step 6: Refine your target geography

After you have created and tested your vivid descriptors, it is time to refine your target geography: the physical landscape in which your target audiences live. One of the biggest mistakes that planners make is to overestimate the size of their target geography. A useful way to get a clear sense of where your most important target audiences live in sufficiently dense numbers is to use mapping software such as Microsoft ACCESS for Windows 97 or MapLinx.

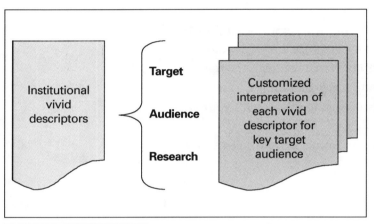

Figure 3-6
Using Vivid Descriptors to Reach Your Target Audience

Based on our experience, many communication plans fail or are not budgetarily sustainable because they try to address geographies that are too large, too distant, or too disparate. All things considered, it is more efficient and more effective to work in a smaller area than a larger one. We realize that this may not be as glamorous but we are convinced it is a better stewardship of dollars and time.

As you can see from Figure 3-7, although a college located in Michigan may attract students from 42 other different states, the majority of students come from the upper Midwest. This information would be extremely helpful to the institution as it develops an advertising campaign or seeks to establish alumni clubs where they would have the most impact on student recruiting. On a single map, plot the following seven databases:

Database 1: Current students
Database 2: Prospective students
Database 3: Alumni
Database 4: Alumni clubs
Database 5: Feeder high schools
Database 6: Feeder religious organizations
Database 7: Two- and four-year competitors (both public and private)

The depiction of these databases on a single map can offer much insight as you plot your communication strategy. If your resources are tight, for example, you might want to focus on areas and regions where these databases overlap because these target geographies offer the greatest synergy.

With your target geography in hand, it is time to create an appropriate media mix. For the most part, developing a media mix involves answering a series of questions. Two of these questions (Who are your target audiences? Where do they live?) have already been answered. The other target audience questions are:

■ What is their awareness of or attitude toward your institution?

- What are their media habits?
- What media are available within your target geography?
- What media can you afford to use?
- What are your communication goals? To create initial awareness? To persuade? To motivate?
- What is the character and complexity of your message?

As you examine the above questions , you may realize that several can be answered only with audience research. This is especially true for questions dealing with audience awareness and media habits. See Table 3-3 for a list of target audience characteristics.

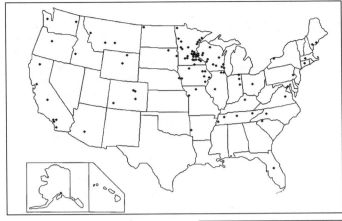

Figure 3-7
Geographic Distribution of Target Audiences

Step 7: Create the media mix

As you can see from Table 3-4, there is no shortage of media options for you to consider and use. As you review them, you will quickly discover that we encourage a very rich definition of "media." This expanded definition intentionally includes many types of media or forms of communication for two reasons: (1) many plans falter because they focus on a media array that is too narrow, and (2) it is our belief that the media plan should embrace all communication and outreach, not merely print or broadcast.

Assessing initial awareness
In developing a media mix, it is extremely important to assess initial audience awareness. For example, if you are developing a message strategy for prospective students who have never heard of you, it is relatively ineffective to focus on highly personalized telemarketing or direct mail. Rather, you should consider a mix that seeks to establish an initial awareness before you develop customized, and often more expensive, messages.

Figure 3-8 suggests you use different methods of communication depending on how familiar the target audience is with your institution. If the level of awareness is low, then your initial plan should involve most mass, attention-generating media from the bottom of the communication ladder.

As the level of awareness changes, you should move from mass media to more personal types of media. The goal with important audiences, of course, is to move as quickly away from the mass media as you can. It is always better to be personal than mediated.

Customizing messages for different media and audiences
A little later in this chapter, we discuss the overall media calendar. But

Table 3-3
Target Audience Characteristics

Benefits sought	Academic quality
	Job skills
	Social life
User status	Nonuser
	Ex-user
	Potential user
	First-time user
	Regular user
	Completed user
Loyalty status	None
	Medium
	Strong
	Absolute
	Switcher
Readiness stage	Unaware
	Aware
	Informed
	Interested
	Desirous
	Intend to apply/donate
Attitude toward institution	Enthusiastic
	Positive
	Indifferent
	Negative
	Hostile

Table 3-4
Media Mix Options

Media relations – PSAs	Outdoor/transit advertising
Media relations – Feature stories	Specialty advertising
Media relations – Hometowners	Environmentals/signage
Media relations – Wild art (photos with captions but no accompanying article)	Web/Internet/Intranet
	Video/audio
Media relations – Tip sheets	Compact discs
Media news	Publications
Alumni relations	Direct mail
High school relations	Special events
Public relations	Telemarketing
TV/cable advertising	Radio advertising
Newspaper advertising	Word of mouth
Magazine advertising	

before we can move on to that step, we need to emphasize that different media, used in conjunction with different audiences, may not require different messages, but variations on message themes.

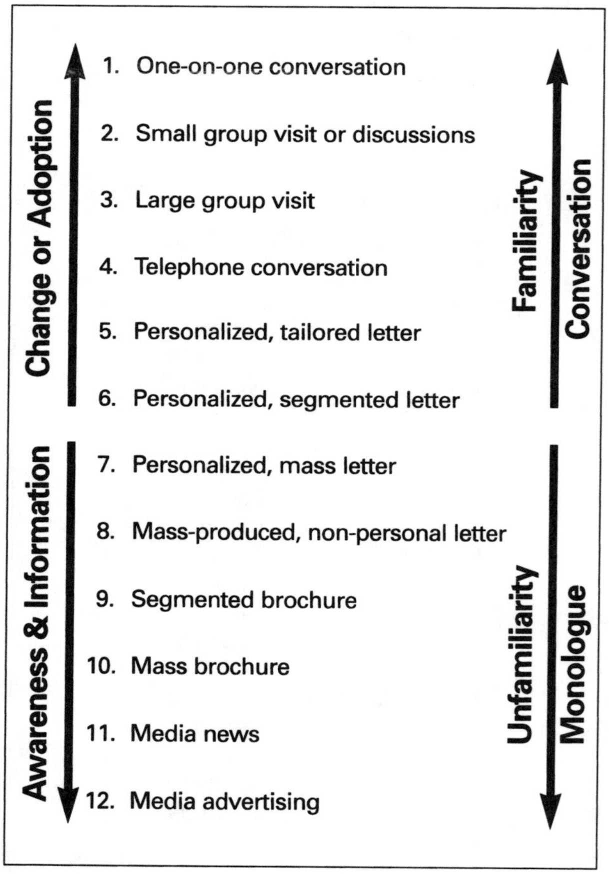

A radio spot that stresses academic quality, for example, has to be less sophisticated and less detailed than an editorial on the op-ed page of the local newspaper or even a print ad in a regional magazine. Although academic quality may be the focus of all three messages , the messages are intended for different audiences and should respond to the characteristics of each medium.

In some respects, this need to customize and modify will force you to be more creative than you might normally be, but, remember, all these variations on the same theme will help reinforce your theme in your marketplace.

Creating a communication grid

A useful tool to help you develop an effective media mix is to prepare a simple grid with three columns (Table 3-5). In the left column, list your primary target audiences. In the center column—based on the audience research you have completed—list how your particular target audience defines and interprets your vivid descriptors. In the right column, list the media habits of your individual target audience, once again based on audience research. This simple grid will help you keep track of the essential elements of your integrated marketing communication plan.

Change or Adoption / Familiarity / Conversation

1. One-on-one conversation
2. Small group visit or discussions
3. Large group visit
4. Telephone conversation
5. Personalized, tailored letter
6. Personalized, segmented letter

Awareness & Information / Unfamiliarity / Monologue

7. Personalized, mass letter
8. Mass-produced, non-personal letter
9. Segmented brochure
10. Mass brochure
11. Media news
12. Media advertising

Figure 3-8
Communication Ladder

Some rules of thumb

Without knowing context and need, it's always a bit dangerous to offer "rules of thumb." However, some basic guidelines about media mixes might be useful.

First, make sure the mix you adopt is sustainable over time. Big splashes are just that—splashes—and seldom have any long-term impact.

Second, avoid the temptation to turn to mass advertising automatically. It is seldom a good first choice unless you have substantial dollars at your disposal and you have carefully matched different media buys to the media habits of your target audiences. Keep in mind, too, that even mass advertising should be supported by other media such as direct mail, special events, etc.

Third, try to develop a media mix that serves more than one audience. It is very confusing and time consuming to develop highly segmented mixes.

Fourth, don't overlook "low-end" but incredibly powerful media such as word-of-mouth or special events. They may not be particularly sexy, but they are often highly effective.

Fifth, take the time to test your messages and media on smaller subsets of your target audience before the big roll-out. You will almost always be glad that you pretested because it gives you one last chance to catch any mistakes and to refine your concepts one more time.

Finally, and perhaps most importantly, make sure the media you choose and the messages you craft target the needs and expectations of your target audiences, not simply those of your president, faculty, or major donors.

Table 3-5
Communication Grid

Target Audience	Vivid Descriptors	Media Habits
1.		
a.	a.	
b.	b.	
c.	c.	
d.	d.	
2.		
a.		a.
b.		b.
c.		c.
d.		d.
3.		
a.		a.
b.		b.
c.		c.
d.		d.
4.		
a.		a.
b.		b.
c.		c.
d.		d.

Step 8: Develop the media calendar

The media calendar is a management tool that helps you coordinate all your communication activities. Table 3-6 is a sample calendar that directs the communication activities for four key groups for the first quarter of the year:
- Faculty, staff, and administrators
- Alumni
- High school influencers
- Community residents

Step 9: Implement, evaluate, and modify the plan

You are now at the end of the planning process. It's time to begin implementing your plan. Most often, this simply involves following the media calendar developed in Step 8. Unfortunately, no matter how well conceived the plan might be, there will always be instances when activities run behind schedule and over budget. At times like these, some mid-course corrections may be in order.

As a guide to which activities should receive additional time or money, or both, and which activities should be cut back or even eliminated, keep in mind the original planning mandate. In times of uncertainty or stress, it is almost always a good idea to stick closely to the mandate and use it to guide your actions.

In addition to implementation, we now concern ourselves with two more ongoing

Target Audience	Start Date	Cost	28	4	11	18	25	2	9	16	23	30	6	13	20	27
					Apr '99				May '99					Jun '99		
Faculty/staff/admin																
Quarterly newsletter	4/4/99	$125		◆												
Quarterly newsletter	6/2/99	$125										◆				
Quarterly newsletter	8/12/99	$125														
Quarterly newsletter	11/17/99	$125														
Summer retreat	8/25/99	$6,300														
Alumni																
Create alumni Web page	7/29/99	$18,000														
Magazine	4/21/99	$6,000				◆										
Magazine	7/22/99	$6,000														
Magazine	9/22/99	$6,000														
Magazine	11/24/99	$6,000														
Europe Tour	9/22/99	$15,000														
Homecoming	10/13/99	$20,000														
H.S. Influencers																
High school newspaper ad series	3/11/99 4/1/99 4/15/99 4/28/99 5/12/99 5/26/99 6/10/99 9/8/99 9/23/99 10/7/99 10/21/99 11/3/99 11/18/99 12/2/99	$15,500	◆		◆		◆		◆		◆		◆			
Create H.S. database	3/3/99	$3,000														
H.S. newsletter	3/24/99 5/12/99 9/22/99 11/3/99	$6,000							◆							
Spring high school tour	5/2/99										▬▬▬	▬▬▬				
Fall high school tour	9/16/99	$68,000														
Counselor open house	10/28/99	$25,000														
Community residents																
Community open house	10/28/99	$25,000														
Quarterly ad series	3/17/99 6/9/99 9/9/99 11/25/99	$20,000											◆			
Kiwanis	4/8/99			◆												
Rotary Club	5/19/99															
Chamber of Commerce	8/4/99								◆							
Progress 2000	11/11/99															
		$281,300	28	4	11	18	25	2	9	16	23	30	6	13	20	27

Table 3-6

Communication Plan Media Calendar

activities, evaluation and modification involved in Step 9.

As practitioners, we believe strongly that there isn't a plan or series of messages that can't be improved. To that end, our listening-first model reminds us of the need to constantly monitor how target audiences are receiving—and acting—on our messages. This, of course, necessitates ongoing research. Evaluation of current messages and modification of future messages are essential components of any successful communication planning process.

Some guiding principles
Before we close this chapter, we offer five guiding principles that will help your planning efforts go more smoothly and will increase the effectiveness of your overall communication plan.

1. Don't try to write the perfect communication plan. Endless analysis and debate can cost you dearly. Not only will there be lost opportunities but you might also lose the initiative. It is much better to develop a pretty good plan quickly than to take months, and even years, developing a perfect plan that is never implemented.

2. Appoint the most credible, knowledgeable, powerful planning champion you can.

3. Don't forget to address the needs of internal audiences. Too often, we have a tendency to focus our efforts on external constituencies and fail to anticipate the needs of internal audiences. The pie chart in Figure 3-9 is designed to give you a sense of how to apportion your time, resources, and strategies between these two audiences. Keep in mind that this is a general allocation. If your campus environment is more stressful or anxious or if mistrust is high, you will need to consider spending more time and attention on internal needs.

4. Emphasize accountability of all active participants at both the planning and implementation stages.

5. And, finally, don't begin something you can't sustain budgetarily . It is much better to fund a plan at $30,000 a year for five years than to allocate $150,000 for one year. Resist the temptation to go for the big, though short-lived, splash.

Why communication plans fail
We want to close with a brief list of why communication plans fail. In some cases, this list reiterates points made earlier in this chapter. However, because of their importance, we believe they are worth repeating.

- Lack of top-down buy-in and commitment.
- The plan did not have a credible champion.
- The president did not approve individual planning steps.
- Too many target audiences.
- Unfocused target geography.
- Message goals and target audiences were not adequately defined or of strategic importance.
- The plan was not founded on research.
- There was no audience differentiation, no message segmenting.
- The plan was overdesigned—too complex.
- The plan failed to anticipate the need for internal marketing.
- There was no ongoing evaluation.

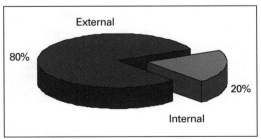

Figure 3-9
Ratio of Internal and External Resource Allocations for Communication Plans

- There was no budget, or the budget was not realistic.
- The budget was not sustained over time.

A final word

The purpose of this chapter was briefly to outline the communication planning process. It was not designed to be definitive. Rather, our goal was to present you with the various components of a communication plan so that you might better understand how they build upon and support one another, making your overall planning efforts more effective, efficient, and fruitful. We hope we have accomplished this goal.

Recommended Readings

Beckworth, Harry. *Selling the Invisible: A Field Guide to Modern Marketing.* New York: Warner Books, 1997.

Beemer, C. Britt and Robert L. Shook. *Predatory Marketing: What Everyone in Business Needs to Know to Win Today's Consumer.* New York: William Morrow and Company, 1997.

Brooks, Larry and James Hammond. "Has Higher Education Been Using the Wrong Marketing Approach?" *Journal of Marketing for Higher Education,* 4, no. 1-2 (1993): 27-48.

Bryson, John. *Strategic Planning for Public and Nonprofit Organizations: A Guide to Strengthening and Sustaining Organizational Achievement.* San Francisco: Jossey-Bass Publishers, 1995.

Dolence, Michael G., Daniel James Rowley, and Herman D. Lujan. *Working Toward Strategic Change: A Step-by-Step Guide to the Planning Process.* San Francisco: Jossey-Bass Publishers, 1997.

Hall, Cindy. "Demystifying Marketing. Campuses Use and Confuse This Concept. To Understand It, Start by Cutting Through the Fog." CURRENTS, 19, no. 2 (February 1993): 30-31.

Kotler, Philip and Karen Fox. *Strategic Marketing for Education Institutions.* Englewood Cliffs, NJ: Prentice-Hall, 1995.

Lewis, Herschell Gordon. "*Before I Forget: The Core of Any Successful Direct Marketing Strategy Has to Be the Ability to Convince the Reader, Viewer, or Listener. That Ability Stems from Astute Word-Choice.*" Direct Marketing, 58, no. 12 (April 1996):38-39.

Mintzberg, Henry. *The Rise and Fall of Strategic Planning: Reconceiving Roles for Planning, Plans, and Planners.* New York: Free Press, 1994.

Myers, James H. *Segmentation and Positioning for Strategic Marketing Decisions.* Chicago: American Marketing Association, 1996.

Percy, Larry. *Strategies for Implementing Integrated Marketing Communications.* Lincolnwood, IL: NTC/Contemporary Publishing Group, 1997.

Ries, Al and Jack Trout. *Marketing Warfare.* New York: McGraw Hill, 1986.

Ries, Al and Jack Trout. *The 22 Immutable Laws of Marketing: Violate Them at Your Own Risk!* New York: Harper & Row, 1994.

Roman, Erman. *Integrated Direct Marketing.* Chicago: NTC/Contemporary Publishing Group, 1995.

Sevier, Robert A. "Why Marketing Plans Fail: Nine Reasons Student Recruitment Efforts Break Down— And How to Avoid Them." CURRENTS, 20, no. 10 (November–December 1994): 48-53.

4

Using Research to Enhance Your Strategic Plan

This chapter has two purposes. First, it provides an overview of communication research so you can have a better understanding of research terms, methodologies, and how studies are developed. And second, it presents some ideas and insights that will help you use research to refine your larger communication strategies and individual messages. In particular, you will find ideas to help you handle these research tasks:

Robert Sevier

- Gather initial data on audience perceptions and values
- Assess audience information needs and expectations
- Gather audience media habit information
- Develop vivid descriptors and initial message strategies
- Test and refine concepts
- Ascertain the effectiveness of your overall communication strategy

When to conduct research

There are many reasons to conduct research. First, do it when you sense your market-place or target audiences are changing. You might want to undertake research if you are facing more competition for each donated dollar, struggling to recruit students, or if you are discovering that fewer and fewer members of your target audiences have a clear sense of what you are all about. I remember working with a small Catholic institution in the Midwest. They were concerned that donations from older alumni had dropped and wanted me to help them find out why. We discovered that the older alumni were reacting to the institution's decision to become a university. The older alumni no longer felt a sense of ownership. In addition, they felt that if the institution had the money to become a university, it no longer needed their donations. Using data from the research, the institution was, over time, able to restore its relationship with these older alumni. Donations are now rising.

Second, conduct research when you want to test a new idea or concept. Sometimes, a great brainstorming session can leave you with many good ideas. Research can help you determine to which idea your target audiences are most likely to respond. Spending a few thousand dollars on research at the concept stage can prevent you from making very costly and very public advertising or publication mistakes.

Third, conduct research if you are new, are working in a new area, or have lost your perspective. Research can quickly clarify and prioritize the issues and options before you. A college president once hired me to complete a study because he had lost faith in a senior administrator and wanted to conduct research to find out what was happening and why he was not being adequately informed about a specific issue.

Fourth, conduct research to identify meaningful audience segments. For example, do women donors think and act differently than men? What about older donors? Or younger? I conducted a study for a law school in the Pacific Northwest and discovered that women alumni were keenly interested in supporting initiatives related to ethics, social improvement, financial aid, and women's issues. Men alumni, however, wanted to contribute to buildings.

Fifth, conduct research to determine how to improve an alumni magazine. Use focus groups to break the publication down by its component parts. This will help you find out what parts of the magazine your alumni value most.

And last, conduct research when you cannot afford to be wrong. When dollars are tight, time is critical, or public opinion is shaky, research can keep you from making poor decisions.

A foundation of research

It is not an overstatement to say that solid integrated marketing communication plans rest on sound, ongoing research. In fact, any communication plan that does not include research at its base is almost surely flawed. Like the well-constructed building on a foundation of sand, communication plans written without research will eventually fail. They may become unfocused, take more time and money to execute, or simply have no impact on the intended audiences. Research, especially at the earliest stages of the planning process, will help make sure that your communication is firmly grounded.

As I was writing this chapter, I realized that I was using the terms market research, audience research, and communication research almost interchangeably. This is

> " As you prepare to develop a research study, it is important that you be aware of the definitions of confidentiality and anonymity, and the differences between them. "

because these three terms are synonyms when you consider the basic definition of market research: the systematic design, collection, analysis, and reporting of data and findings relevant to the specific marketing situation an institution faces. In short, research involves finding specific answers to specific questions—information that you will use to refine your messages and message strategies.

Research can help you in a variety of ways. First, you can use it to gather perceptual data. Because people act on their perceptions, learning how strategic target audiences perceive, and sometimes misperceive you, is critical. Second, you can use research to provide answers. One client was interested in fine-tuning a campaign case statement. I tested a variety of concepts and wordings on a sample of the intended target audience. The result was a case statement that was more on target.

Third, audience research helps you clarify and set priorities. In today's marketing, fund raising, and recruiting environments, the problem is generally not a lack of options; rather, it is determining which ones are most likely to succeed or provide the greatest return in the shortest time. If you have $10,000 to buy advertising aimed at nontraditional students, you can use research to pinpoint the media to which they are most likely to respond.

And finally, communication research allows you to test ideas. With research, you can evaluate publication concepts, logo ideas, even signage. You can evaluate potential new majors. You can even test audience response to moving from one football league to another. Using research in this way can often prevent you from making expensive and very public mistakes.

It is not difficult to generate research data. The odds are high that you have volumes of data sitting on a shelf somewhere in your office. But more than yielding just data, successful research must generate information you can act upon. In other words, it is not the collection of data that matters most, but its interpretation and application.

Good research, research that can be used to support an integrated marketing communication plan, must be more than simply a collection of data. It must provide answers to real questions. It must provide clear direction. And it must set out options in order of priority.

As you prepare to develop a research study, it is important that you be aware of the definitions of confidentiality and anonymity, and the differences between them. Confidentiality means you will not release the data or findings to outside parties. This sounds simple but it is usually quite difficult. One of Erick Larson's laws of data dynamics suggests that data migrate and often end up in places distantly removed from the study. In our era of e-mail and photocopiers, it is very difficult to keep studies confidential.

Anonymity means that you will not attempt to match the name of the respondent to his or her individual survey responses. Anonymity is especially important if you are going to ask respondents questions dealing with such sensitive issues as household income, giving patterns, perceptions of leaders, and similar topics.

Like confidentiality, preserving anonymity can also be a challenge. This is especially true for surveys of prospective students, donors, and alumni when there is incredible pressure to use the findings immediately to enhance the "sell." For example, I am aware of one college that wants to undertake an anonymous survey of prospective students and then use the data collected on individual surveys to customize their telemarketing efforts. This approach is unethical, potentially illegal, and just plain dangerous.

Be very careful about promising confidentiality and anonymity. If they are promised, those responsible for the survey—including the institution itself—are bound by honor to deliver.

Before discussing how to develop a research strategy or how to use research to improve your communication efforts, it is important to review some basic research methodologies and some important terms and definitions.

Designing a research study

" Like any specialized endeavor, market research has its own vocabulary. "

Thoughtful methodology is important for any research study, but it is especially important in communication research for a simple reason: If you make a mistake in communication research, you make that mistake in public. A faulty sample or a misinterpretation of a confusing question can have disastrous and very public results. For this reason, research designed to support the creation of an integrated marketing communication plan must be extremely well planned and executed.

A detailed discussion of these steps can be found in Appendix A.

Research methods

It is helpful when undertaking a research project to follow a basic methodology. This is especially important when the data to be gathered will be used to support decisions that have strategic, economic, or political consequences. A solid research methodology helps preserve the integrity of your data.

Focus groups
Focus groups are designed to target discussions around a specific topic so people's attitudes, perceptions, and language can be captured and analyzed. This is why focus groups are ideal for exploring opinions and attitudes held by students, donors, parents, and others.

Typically, focus groups involve 10 to 12 people in sessions about 60 minutes long that are directed by a moderator. Respondents are selected and screened so they make up a relatively homogeneous group, thereby minimizing both conflicts on issues not relevant to the study and wide-ranging differences in perceptions, experiences, and verbal skills.

During the discussion, the moderator follows a guide, actually a pre-established list of questions and topics to address during the session. Sessions are usually audiotaped. The tape transcriptions and the moderator's notes become the raw data that are analyzed and presented in the final report.

Mail surveys

Mail surveys are widely used research methods for examining geographically dispersed groups, such as alumni, community residents, or —if you use campus mail—students or faculty. When you write and pretest the survey instrument, draw on a representative sample of the population or audience to be investigated. In some cases, you should send a presurvey postcard to notify the people in your sample that they will be part of an important research project. The survey instrument goes out with a cover letter that explains the need for research. Depending on the audience, these surveys may include some sort of incentive to increase response.

After a short period, you may send a follow-up letter to people who have not returned the survey. This letter helps increase response. As the surveys come in, you or your researcher review them for completeness and validity.

The actual analysis involves frequency counts (percentages) of the answers to each question and cross-tabulations (comparisons of how different groups answered the same question). In some cases, you may want to apply more sophisticated statistical analyses so you can do a better job of isolating cause and effect. For example, it is possible through multiple regression to track down the impact of a single mailing on the decision of a group of alumni to give or not to give. Of course, more sophisticated analyses will generally require larger samples so that they might not be appropriate in all instances.

Telephone surveys

Telephone surveys are a combination of in-depth interviews and mail surveys. The methodology is largely similar to mail surveys, but the interview is conducted over the phone. Because the interviewer reads all the questions, telephone surveys tend to be less sophisticated and shorter than mail surveys. In addition, telephone surveys often have difficulty with handling sensitive issues.

In-depth interviews

Lasting 30 to 45 minutes, in-depth, or one-on-one, interviews are designed to elicit information and opinions from people who are unable or unwilling to be approached through other research techniques. Like other forms of research, in-depth interviews are conducted according to an interview guide, that is, a series of questions that serve to direct the discussion. Most in-depth interviews are conversational in nature.

Table 4-1 shows the strengths and weaknesses of these four types of research in greater detail.

Research terms and definitions

Like any specialized endeavor, market research has its own vocabulary. It is important to understand some key terms and phrases at the outset.

Type of Research	Strengths	Weaknesses	Best Uses
Focus groups	1. Informal 2. Often uncover ideas never anticipated by researcher 3. Great for capturing anecdotal data useful for illustration, for comparisons, or to gather insight before developing a quantitative research instrument 4. Often spontaneous	1. Require an experienced moderator 2. Group dynamics can be problematic 3. Can turn into gripe sessions 4. Heavily anecdotal and nonquantitative 5. Often difficult to arrange 6. Relatively expensive for the quality of data obtained	1. Early in the research process to provide initial direction 2. To test concepts, especially visuals 3. To test and compare messages and media from competing institutions
Mail surveys	1. Relatively inexpensive if an adequate sample can be obtained 2. Can contain more questions 3. Can ask complex or sensitive questions 4. Can use illustrations and graphics 5. No geographic limitations	1. Take longer to complete 2. Offer less control over response rate 3. Can be perceived as impersonal 4. Offer less control over timing 5. Depend heavily on quality of mailing list 6. May require an incentive for completion	1. For audiences who have a great affinity for the institution (alumni, parents) and who are more likely to respond 2. To gather comprehensive data 3. To survey audiences who are dispersed geographically
Telephone surveys	1. Offer more control over response rates 2. Can be completed quickly 3. Confer anonymity 4. Can be highly representative	1. Must be shorter and less complex 2. Difficult to establish initial rapport 3. Sometimes difficult to gather sensitive or personal data 4. Relatively expensive 5. Cannot use illustrations and graphics 6. Telephone numbers of respondents may not be available	1. Reach audiences who may not respond to a mail survey 2. Short surveys 3. Yields a great deal of data in a short time
In-depth interviews	1. Interviewer can probe and follow lead of respondent 2. Good for highly political audiences 3. Don't always strike respondent as "research" 4. Often can gather data and build bridges with audience 5. Difficult to be representative of target audience	1. Very expensive 2. Depend heavily on skill of interviewer 3. More potential for interviewer bias 4. Can take a great deal of time 5. Difficult to input; data often subject to multiple interpretations	1. For high-profile audiences not available through other means 2. When validity is not a big issue or when population is very small

Table 4-1
Comparison of Four Research Methods

Primary research and secondary research

Essentially, there are two sources of research data: primary and secondary. Primary research uses data that come out of your study. Secondary research uses existing data from a completed study that may be applicable to your research.

Suppose, for example, you want to know why alumni give to your institution. If you conduct a survey on this topic, you are engaged in primary research. On the other hand, if you use data from a study completed by a colleague at another institution, you are using secondary research.

The difference is important. First, because primary research involves designing an original study, it is more expensive and time consuming. Secondary research is usually less expensive or even free and is usually available quickly.

A second major difference involves the quality, suitability, and integrity of the data. A well-designed primary research study should offer high-quality data results. With secondary data, you are inferring conclusions from someone else's research, so you must take extra care to ascertain the relevance of the data, examine the impartiality of the study sponsor, and ensure that the correct methodology was followed.

Quantitative research and qualitative research

Just as there are two broad sources of research, there are two broad types of research: quantitative and qualitative.

Quantitative research uses a statistically valid and randomly generated sample to represent a larger population. Validity is important because you want to project data obtained from a relatively small sample to the larger population. Quantitative research requires a carefully designed methodology. For this reason, it is usually fairly expensive and may take some time. Mail surveys and telephone surveys are two forms of quantitative research.

Qualitative research, on the other hand, is not statistically valid, and the data cannot be projected to larger populations with any degree of certainty. Because qualitative research uses a much less strict methodology, it can usually be conducted more quickly and at lower cost. Focus groups and in-depth interviews are two kinds of qualitative research.

The key difference between quantitative and qualitative research is how you wish to use the data. Qualitative research is descriptive, but it is not projectionable. In other words, you cannot project the findings from a focus group of six students to predict how other students might react to your new viewbook. However, with a well-designed quantitative study, you can project the findings to a larger population with a high degree of reliability. If 73 percent of your sample responded a certain way to a question, you can be reasonably sure that roughly 73 percent of the larger population will respond in the same manner.

Populations and samples

A population is the group of people to be studied. For example, you may have a population of faculty, staff, donors, alumni, current students, prospective students, parents, and community residents.

A sample is a small subset of the population. In statistical or projectionable studies, the sample must be of a particular size, representative of the larger population, and randomly generated to be considered valid.

Sampling is important for three reasons. First, it involves smaller groups. Second, correctly drawn samples are highly representative. And third, it takes less time to survey a sample than an entire population.

Reliability

Reliability, often called confidence or validity, is usually expressed as a percentage. A study that is reliable at the 95-percent level has a range of error of 5 percent. If 68 percent of respondents say yes to a particular question, the assumption for the population as a whole could range from 63 percent (68 percent minus 5 percent) to 73 percent (68 percent plus 5 percent). The greater the percentage of reliability, the more valid the findings.

However, there is a trade-off. The more reliability you want, the greater the sample must be. Table 4-2 illustrates this point.

For example, suppose you have a population of 4,000 alumni (see arrow in table). If you want 95 percent reliability, you must survey 350 (right column). A confidence level of 95 percent is very good. Note, however, how much larger the sample would have to be if you wanted a confidence level of 98 percent. Instead of 350 alumni, you would need 1,500.

As you can see, moving from 95 percent to 98 percent means sampling four times as many alumni. Of course, this will have a tremendous impact on the cost of the research. Clients often begin projects with the hope of achieving 99 percent reliability. However, 95 percent is really a much better goal. This level is a good balance between cost and validity.

Table 4-2
Sample Size and Reliability

Size of Population	Sample Size for Reliability				
	+/-1%	+/-2%	+/-3%	+/-4%	+/-5%
1,000	**	**	**	375	278
2,000	**	**	696	462	322
3,000	**	1,334	787	500	341
4,000 ←	**	**1,500**	842	522	350 ✓
5,000	**	1,622	879	536	357
10,000	4,899	1,936	964	566	370
20,000	6,489	2,144	1,013	583	377
50,000	8,057	2,291	1,045	593	381
100,000	8,763	2,345	1,056	597	383
500,000	9,423	2,390	1,065	600	384

Develop a research cycle

Though any research project can provide important information, single projects at best are a snapshot that show how people think at a specific time. One study is certainly better than none, but it is often much more helpful to know how those data have changed over time. Suppose your research revealed that 23.5 percent of alumni do not read any portion of your quarterly magazine. Many people would find this distressing. However, you know that two years ago this number was 31.4 percent. Or, let's say that your average response to an annual fund solicitation is $37.00. Is that good or bad? Well, considering that two years ago, your average response was $43.00, you can conclude that your current solicitations are not as effective. Rather than being distressed, you are elated because you are making progress. Trend or longitudinal data provide an important research perspective: rather than a single snapshot, they are an ongoing movie.

To collect trend data, you must routinely survey the same audience using the same sampling methodology, and the same basic instrument. This is the only way that you can make truly meaningful and accurate comparisons.

One way to develop trend data is to implement a research cycle. A research cycle allows you to survey strategic audiences in a systematic and consistent fashion. Although the nature of your institution, its budgetary commitment to research, and its specific marketing challenges will affect the design of your research cycle, the cycle presented in Table 4-3 offers some initial direction and insight as to the frequency of oft-undertaken studies.

Survey Cycle	
Annually	nonmatriculants nonapplicants prospective students
Every two years	current students noninquirers high-school influencers annual fund donors donors community leaders
Every three years	parents community residents alumni former donors faculty and staff media

Table 4-3
Sample Research Cycles

Using research to enhance your strategic communication plan

Up to this point, I have discussed research in a more general fashion. And while this background is essential for complete understanding of research, it is now time to turn to using research to develop communication strategies, support the development of an integrated marketing communication plan, and to refine and evaluate the plan over time. To that end, I want to offer some guidelines on using research to:

■ Gather initial data on audience perceptions and values.
■ Assess audience information needs and expectations.
■ Gather audience media habit information.
■ Develop vivid descriptors and initial message strategies.
■ Test and refine concepts.
■ Ascertain the effectiveness of your overall communication strategy.

Gather initial data on audience perceptions and values

One of the greatest mistakes you can make when writing an integrated marketing communication plan is to overlook the need to gather initial data and insight on audience perceptions and values. If you don't know how your target audiences perceive you, if you fail to anticipate their behavioral or readiness state, or don't understand their values and motivations, there is little likelihood your messages will be credible or will resonate with them.

To guide the planning process, you must conduct research to yield a variety of data:

■ Determine how key audiences perceive you.
■ Learn the words and phrases they use to describe you.
■ Ascertain how these audiences compare you with other institutions (Learn their motivations for attending college, donating, supporting the alumni association, etc.).

At this stage it, is also a good idea to gather preliminary information on target audience media habits. It will provide significant insight into the motivations and behaviors of your target audiences. In addition, this perceptional data forms an initial baseline against which you will later evaluate the effectiveness of your communication plan and activities. For this reason, the data must be captured and analyzed in a manner that allows for easy comparisons. For example, suppose one of your perceptual studies of alumni asks how they believe the institution is being managed. Their responses are outlined below.

- 27 percent describe your institution as well managed
- 36 percent describe your institution as adequately managed
- 18 percent describe your institution as poorly managed
- 15 percent describe your institution as very poorly managed
- 4 percent "don't know"

Capturing data in this fashion will allow for easy comparisons later on.

> **"Communication research can help you develop your institution's vivid descriptors."**

Assess audience information needs and expectations

Early in the communication planning process, it is also helpful to determine clearly the information that most interest your target audiences. For example, a client recently decided to develop a publication for parents of traditional-aged prospective students. After surveying nearly 400 parents, I discovered that they were most interested in the following items and topics:

- Academic emphases
- Student access to technology
- Data on placement and outcomes
- Safety
- Who will be teaching their children
- Curricula
- Academic advising
- Student counseling services
- Financial aid
- Residence life
- Career development
- Student social activities
- Internship opportunities
- Sports schedules
- Comments from other parents

Later, we completed a series of focus groups with parents during which they helped us refine these topics. They also suggested how this information might be illustrated.

Gather information on audience media habits

Obtaining insights into the media habits of target audiences is a good use for research, especially if you plan to spend significant time and money expanding your media strategy. Depending on the characteristics of your target audiences and the scope of your plan, here are some good media habit questions :

■ To what newspaper(s) do you subscribe?
■ What sections of the newspaper do you read first?
■ What radio formats do you prefer?

■ At what time of day are you most likely to listen to the radio?
■ What TV channel do you watch most often?

■ What magazines do you subscribe to or read regularly?
■ What section of the alumni magazine do you read first?
■ About how much time do you spend reading each issue of the alumni magazine?

Questions such as these will help you reduce waste in your media buys and increase the likelihood of your messages being noticed.

Develop vivid descriptors and initial message strategies

Communication research can help you develop your institution's vivid descriptors. Early on, you might ask your target audiences of donors, prospective students, faculty, staff, alumni, and others to describe the qualities and characteristics they would value most in a college or university. They might respond with answers similar to those below:

■ Academic quality
■ Jobs
■ Quality and accessible faculty
■ Intellectual, cultural, and economic asset to the community
■ Friendly, caring, and supportive atmosphere

The next step is to make sure that these descriptors fit comfortably within your institutional mission, vision, and strategic plan and that they represent enduring, core values. After this is done, research can be used to refine the vivid descriptors. You might, for example, ask prospective students to expand on the notion of academic quality by asking them the following questions:

■ How do you define academic quality?
■ What are some words and phrases you use to describe academic quality?
■ Can you think of instances from high school where academic quality was demonstrated?
■ When you think of colleges and universities with high academic quality, what institutions come to mind?
■ What kinds of photographs illustrate academic quality?

It is important to develop a series of questions such as these for each target audience. This will allow you to develop message themes based on their definitions and insights. These themes, of course, will be used as the foundation for customized message strategies that each involve slightly different interpretations of your core values—your vivid descriptors.

Test and refine concepts

Research (especially focus groups) is an ideal way to test concepts before the big roll-out. Not only does this give you an opportunity to refine your concepts, but it can also help prevent some colossal and very public misfires.

Suppose, for example, you have developed two or three tag lines based on your vivid descriptors. You can test these tag lines in a focus group comprising members of your target audience. Input from the focus group can help you choose which tag line is most on target or, as is more often the case, the focus group will help you refine one tag line.

You can also use research to test and refine such things as:
■ Photography
■ Cover designs
■ Web layouts
■ Campaign case statements
■ Logos
■ Signage templates
■ Color palettes and paper stocks

As I write these paragraphs, I am thinking of a story that ran on the AP wire recently. Evidently a university adopted the tag "… the independent Ivy." The institution noted that the slogan resonated well with prospective students. What it failed to anticipate, however, was the backlash from such stakeholders as current students and faculty. One current student called it, "...a wannabe slogan." Other students parodied the slogan with "Hydrox, the independent Oreo," and "RC, the independent Coke." A little research among stakeholders would probably have warned the institution that its new tag line would be a problem.

As you can see, the uses of research to refine concepts are almost endless. In addition, advances in computer design mean that concepts can be developed to a much higher degree of completeness so the testing is even more accurate. Instead of asking people to interpret thumbnails or add color to a blueline, they can view designs and illustrations that look amazingly finished.

Take the time to test your concepts. You will always be glad you did.

Ascertain the effectiveness of your overall communication strategy

One of the final uses of communication research is to help you assess the overall effectiveness of your integrated marketing communication plan and the ensuing communication strategies. The best way to do this is to repeat the image and perception studies undertaken at the beginning of the planning process. Remember the discussion of trend data. The initial image and perception study created the baseline. That was a data snapshot. Repeating the study will show you direction, and the snapshot will become a movie. To truly ascertain the effectiveness of your plan, you must repeat those original studies exactly. The same instrument. The same target audience. The same way of drawing your sample.

Remember our fictitious study of alumni and their perceptions of how well the institution is managed. Let's further pretend that this research generated a strong interest on the part of the president to stress institutional management and that this became a key theme in the larger, ongoing communication plan. Now pretend that three years later, that study of alumni is repeated. As you can see in Figure 4-1, the data clearly show that alumni—in part because of the emphasis of the communication plan—have a much better feeling about how the institution is being managed.

Do the research yourself or go outside?

As you think about research, you are probably also wondering whether you want to conduct it yourself or whether you want to seek outside help.

Undertaking the research yourself may save you money. Your familiarity with your institution is a bonus, you are aware of in-house research resources upon which you can depend, and the odds are high that there are already some existing budgets for such items as postage, stationery, and clerical support that you can tap into. For these reasons, conducting your communication research internally might be a good idea.

Going outside will save you time, especially when you are conducting multiple studies or when your internal resources are tight. Also, outside companies often have more expertise across all types of research methodologies and can often correctly match research questions with your target audiences and the type of study you are undertaking. In addition, an experienced outside source likely has samples of questionnaires that you can modify and customize.

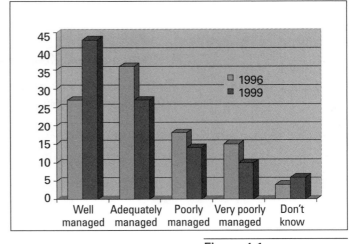

Figure 4-1
Sample Results of Repeat Research: Alumni Perceptions of Institution's Management, 1996 and 1999

An outside researcher has no stake in the findings—no hidden agenda—and is not trying to use data to prove something. This impartiality and objectivity is especially important if you are examining a sensitive or political issue. Go outside when you need perspective on the findings.

Good research is much more than simply collecting data; it uses data to provide direction in improving programs and strategies. One of the biggest reasons colleges and universities go to a company that specializes in higher education research is that they realize the importance of data interpretation and application. It is one thing to collect data, but quite another to know what to do with it.

A final word

Walter Lippman once noted that the duty of a newspaper is to provide information upon which people can act. Lippman's comments can easily be ascribed to research. As the study is conceived, designed, and executed; as the research is collected and analyzed; and as the data are presented; research should have one goal: to inform and clarify. At the conclusion of your communication research, you should be able clearly to understand how your target audiences perceive you, what motivates them, their information needs, and their media habits.

I hope this chapter will be helpful as you develop a communication research strategy. As you develop your strategy, however, keep in mind these guiding principles of research:

- Don't ask a question if you can't do anything with the answer.
- Ask important questions often and to as many different target audiences as possible.
- Balance your research methods.
- Separate what you need to know from what you are merely interested in knowing.
- Although it is important to have an idea of what you hope to learn, be prepared for some surprises.
- Remember, when all is said and done, it's not the research, it's what you do with it that counts.

Recommended Readings

Adams, James L. *The Care and Feeding of Ideas: A Guide to Encouraging Creativity.* Reading, MA: Addison-Wesley-Longman Inc., 1986.

Adams, James L. *Conceptual Blockbusting: A Guide to Better Ideas,* 3rd ed. Reading, MA: Addison-Wesley-Longman Inc., 1990.

Baldwin, Christina. *Life's Companion: Journal Writing as a Spiritual Quest.* New York: Bantam Books, 1986.

Cameron, Julia. *The Artist's Way: A Spiritual Path to Higher Creativity.* New York: Putnam Publishing Group, 1992.

Covey, Stephen R. and A. Roger Merrill. *First Things First: A Principle-Centered Approach to Time and Management.* New York: Simon & Schuster, 1994.

Crandall, Rick. *Break-out Creativity: Bringing Creativity to the Workplace.* Corte Madera, CA: Select Press, 1997.

Csikszenmihalyi, Mihaly. *Creativity: The Work and Lives of 91 Eminent People.* New York: Harper Collins Publishers, 1996.

Csikszenmihalyi, Mihaly. *Finding Flow: The Psychology of Engagement with Everyday Life.* New York: Basic Books, 1998.

Csikszenmihalyi, Mihaly. *Flow: The Psychology of Optimal Experience.* New York: Harper & Row, 1991.

De Bono, Edward. *Lateral Thinking: Creativity Step-by-Step.* New York: Perennial Library, 1970.

De Bono, Edward. *Serious Creativity: Using the Power of Lateral Thinking to Create New Ideas.* New York: Harper Collins Publishers, 1992.

De Bono, Edward. *Six Thinking Hats.* Des Moines, IA: Advanced Practical Thinking Training, 1996.

Edwards, Betty. *Drawing on the Artist Within: An Inspirational & Practical Guide to Increasing Your Creative Powers.* New York: Simon & Schuster, 1987.

Edwards, Betty. *Drawing on the Right Side of the Brain: A Course in Enhancing Creativity and Artistic Confidence.* New York: Simon & Schuster, 1986.

Garfield, Patricia L. *Creative Dreaming: Plan and Control Your Dreams to Develop Creativity, Overcome Fears, Solve Problems, and Create a Better Self.* New York: Simon & Schuster, 1995.

Goldberg, Natalie. *Writing Down the Bones: Freeing the Writer Within.* Boston: Shambhala Publications, 1998.

Kao, John. *Jamming: The Art and Discipline of Business Creativity.* New York: Harper Collins, 1996.

Kidder, Tracy. *Soul of a New Machine.* Boston: Little, Brown, and Company, 1981.

Michalko, Michael L. *Thinkertoys.* Berkeley, CA: Ten Speed Press, 1991.

Ray, Michael and Rochelle Myers. *Creativity in Business.* New York: Doubleday, 1986.

Ricchuito, Jack. *Collaborative Creativity: Unleashing the Power of Shared Thinking.* Greensboro, NC: Oakhill Press, 1996.

Von Oech, Roger. *A Kick in the Seat of the Pants.* New York: Perennial Library, 1986.

Von Oech, Roger. *A Whack on the Side of the Head.* New York: Warner Books, 1983.

Whitney, Dick and Melissa Giovagnoli. *75 Cage-rattling Questions to Change the Way You Work: Shake-Em-Up Questions to Open Meetings, Ignite Discussion, and Spark Creativity.* New York: McGraw Hill Companies, 1997.

Wycoff, Joyce. *Mindmapping: Your Personal Guide to Exploring Creativity and Problem Solving.* New York: Berkeley Publishing Group, 1991.

5

> **The good news is that it is relatively easy to become more creative.** "

Creativity and Concepting

There's bad news and good news about creativity in integrated marketing communication. The bad news is that effective communication to multiple audiences across several media requires more creativity than communicating to one audience via publications or interactive media or advertising.

The good news is that it is relatively easy to become more creative. Honest.

In this chapter, we take a look at how you can become more creative, first by understanding what limits creativity and then by understanding your own attitudes toward creativity. We offer suggestions on how you can get to great concepts faster and—an often overlooked step between concepting and execution—how you can help ensure your concepts will win approval at your institution. And we give examples of some concepts that have served colleges and universities well.

What is creativity?

Becoming more skilled in creativity takes practice. We believe it is worth the effort. Greater creativity can help you come up with concepts and themes that will funnel the disparate elements in your communication system into an integrated series of contacts whose cumulative effect is substantially more powerful than the sum of the parts. Just as a current will catch a swimmer and increase the distance each swimming stroke will

Pat Sellergren

carry him, a strong concept will enhance the movement of your audience toward fulfilling your specific organizational objectives.

Creativity is nothing more—and nothing less—than combining things in new ways. It involves opening oneself up to the widest range of possibilities—what we call "thinking outside the box." The phrase has become a cliché, but to give it meaning again all we need to do is ask what in fact it means: What is the box that we should think outside of?

Creativity depends on opening oneself to the widest range of possibilities from which to make new combinations; the box is the factor that limits the range of possibilities. The first step toward becoming more creative is understanding and removing the limitations.

The number one limitation on creativity is fear—fear of taking risks of consequences, ranging from "people will laugh at me" to "I'll go broke" to "it will mean the end of life as we know it." Fear that "people will laugh at me" will mean "the end of life as we know it" is what prevents us from acting on the impulse to stand on a busy street corner and bray like a donkey. It also prevents us from making a suggestion in a meeting we think will be met with laughter, derision, stony silence—in fact, anything short of approval.

The number two limitation is "time constraint." Good, even great ideas don't have to take longer than mediocre ones, but if you wait until the last minute to begin the concepting process, you are likely to settle for the first idea that comes to mind. Time constraints also limit your ability to come at a problem from many different directions.

The less practiced you are at creativity, the more time the process takes. The fact is, creativity is a discipline, a systematic effort, if not to climb out of the box, then push back its walls so we have more elbow room. As with any discipline, improvement comes from a deliberate process: Observe your own performance, identify weaknesses, replace those weaknesses with better methods, and then practice, practice, practice.

There are other limitations:

- Assumptions: Assumptions are things we take for granted, often without questioning their validity, for instance, assuming that a college publication should look, read, or be organized a certain way, assuming your institution's president will never stand for a particular approach in copy or design, or assuming that certain topics are taboo. You might also mistakenly assume a level of name recognition for your institution. Whenever we accept assumptions as reality, we limit our ability to come up with new ideas.
- Stereotypes push pattern recognition—an ability that allows us to get through the day without catastrophe—to the point of a vice. They prevent us from seeing what is unique or distinctive.
- Failure to pay attention accounts for most of the other limitations. Fix this and you're guaranteed more creativity. For instance, in three minutes, write as fast as you can without stopping; list, map, or web all the words you associate with creativity.

Reluctant to Share Your Ideas in a Group?

Try creating a CREATIVITY JOURNAL. Think of it as a private place for storing and ripening ideas. Any notebook will do, although it should be small enough to carry with you all the time. If you carry a planner, dedicate a section of it to a creativity journal. Record any good ideas, insights, resources, etc. that come your way. Use it to try out other concepting strategies. Every once in a while, review what you've collected to see if any ideas are ready to pick.

Did some of the words you associate with creativity show hostility, contempt, or fear? Don't be surprised—most of us are not initially aware that our attitudes toward creativity are complicated. Many of us are surprised to find that our admiration for it is directly proportional to our distance from it. If you discover that your own feelings are conflicted, paying attention to those feelings by pulling them to the surface of awareness and asking where they come from is a first step toward eliminating them—and toward greater creativity.

Ideas, good ideas, and really good ideas

The point of toning your creative muscles is to come up with better ideas. As a communication tool, creativity "captures insight," revealing connections between seemingly dissimilar things. These connections enlarge and enhance the audience's understanding and—most importantly—create the recognition and resonance necessary to get the response you want.

The creative concept expresses that connection. It's the Big Idea. A good concept communicates information more clearly. It makes the audience more receptive to the information by establishing a bond between them and your institution. This bond makes your institution "accessible."

The creative concept is the controlling idea for presenting your institution in your publications, interactive media, and other contacts you have with a given audience or audiences. It involves copy, design, photography, organizational structure, and every other element of the publication, interactive media product, and other communication vehicles. It is often expressed as a tag line or theme line, but that is actually only the bumper sticker version of the concept.

A strong creative concept has certain qualities:

- It's accurate.
- It's versatile.
- It has "legs."
- It's distinctive.
- It has freshness—or its opposite, "familiarity."
- It has a basis in research.

Let's look at each of these terms in greater detail.

Accuracy

"Accuracy" means that the creative concept fits your institution, that is, the concept represents it accurately. The image it creates has to be one that your audience will recognize as a true representation. If the audience is not yet familiar with your institution, the concept should be one that the audience can believe to be true and, in fact, will find to be true as they come to know you.

Accurate, however, does not mean "complete." No creative concept will represent your institution completely, that is, in all its "accuracies." What you want to represent is a

---

360° Creativity

Breaking through to new ideas often happens when you come at a problem from as many different directions as possible. SCAMPER is a creative exercise from Michael Michalko's book *Thinkertoys*. It's a checklist of sorts—a series of questions you ask to uncover new ideas. Here's what SCAMPER stands for:

S ubstitute
C ombine
A dapt
M odify/Magnify
P ut to other uses
E liminate
R everse/Rearrange

Here's how it works: Isolate the challenge or subject you want to think about. Go through the checklist phrasing each word as a question: What can I substitute for . . .? How can I modify . . .?

Edward de Bono's *Six Thinking Hats* is a similar checklist that will ensure you approach a subject or challenge from multiple perspectives.

---

substantive reality with which your audience will connect. If that "first impression" is acceptably accurate, your audience will have no trouble accepting the other "accuracies," even when they differ somewhat from the first impression.

Beloit College's slogan "Invent Yourself at Beloit," is a good example of an accurate concept. It portrays a college that attracts highly individualistic students with widely varied interests, offers them ample opportunity to pursue those interests or develop new ones, and encourages them to put together an eclectic educational experience. That accuracy has paid off. The concept has stood Beloit College well for several years, continuing to test favorably with students and parents. The college has been able to evolve the look of their publications, to keep them fresh, without departing from the original concept.

Versatility

How many contacts are in your funnel? A strong creative concept will have the "versatility" to adapt itself to each one.

The concept that Benedictine University in Lisle, Illinois, adopted was used not only across its undergraduate recruitment publications; it was extended to its Web site and to brochures and advertising for other student populations. Benedictine used a visual image of intersecting ripples on the undergraduate publications; it was recalled in other water imagery—ripples, waves, drops—in advertisements aimed at adults and prospective graduate students. Both the ripple image and the theme line used in the undergraduate publications, a brief quote from a faculty member, were also used on the Web site.

'Legs'

A good concept should have the "legs" to carry your marketing efforts at least several years. This is true for several reasons. The first is economic: publications and interactive media products are expensive and time-consuming to replace when they become dated. The second is related to image management—that is, making certain that when people hear your institution's name, they immediately have a clear idea of who you are and what you are about. A strong concept with good "legs" can build and sustain an image of your institution in the mind of your audience.

Distinctiveness

We can think of distinctiveness in two ways: a concept that is substantially different from concepts that competing institutions are using in their communications, and a concept that demonstrates how your institution is substantially different from the ones with which you compete. Can you have a concept that is distinct in both senses? Certainly. In fact, you should strive for it. Is one type of distinctness better than another? That depends. A concept distinct from those of competing institutions will help your publication get noticed—you're more likely to win at the mailbox. A concept that demonstrates how your institution is distinct from your competitors helps prospective students make informed decisions in the college selection process.

> " A concept, remember, is the controlling idea for your entire family of publications, interactive media products, and other communications. "

Finding points of genuine distinctness is often not easy. Almost every small liberal arts college or university says it offers prospective students small classes, personal attention from faculty, professors who prefer teaching above all else, and a better shot at leadership opportunities. All proudly sport alumni who can be called successful. An increasing number are restructuring their core curricula to incorporate a more systematic preparation for careers and emphasizing service learning and student/faculty collaboration on research projects. Large public institutions also share many surface similarities.

But regardless of whether you look a lot like the competition or are very different, a distinct concept clearly and memorably communicates the personality of your institution.

Freshness—or its opposite, 'familiarity'

Think about the jokes you laugh at. Some of them make you laugh because they are new, a fresh surprise. Some of them make you laugh because you've laughed at them a million times before—part of the pleasure is recalling all those earlier moments of laughter.

Similarly, a creative concept can take power from either its freshness or its familiarity. Which will create the right degree of recognition and resonance in your audience? Only you know, but your best creative concept will come out of that knowledge.

Grinnell College added a fresh spin to the all-too-common "small-campus-life-long-friends-close-personal-attention-from-faculty" idea by focusing on the symbiotic nature of the dialogues that happen at Grinnell—and by representing them on the cover of their viewbook with a rhinoceros and an oxpecker bird, "remarkably different animals who enjoy a mutually beneficial relationship."

Research-Based

A strong concept is based in knowledge of the institution, the audience, and the purpose for the communications. It is also based in knowledge of the competition. That knowledge comes from research of one kind or another. At the very minimum, take a good look at the publications, interactive media products, and other communications your competitors are using. Ask faculty, administrators, students, and alumni what characterizes and distinguishes your institution and how these characteristics benefit the target audience. (If you ask good follow-up questions and ask for specifics, including stories to illustrate each feature-benefit combination, you'll have the makings of a distinctive, fresh, accurate concept that will serve you well over time and over the range of your communications.)

From concept to tag line

Not every concept needs a tag line. A concept, remember, is the controlling idea for your entire family of publications, interactive media products, and other communications. A tag line is a succinct and memorable line that expresses the essence of the concept. If you use a tag line, make it as memorable as possible. A memorable tag line has one or more of the following qualities:

■ *Freshness (or surprise):* A memorable tag line will capture and express the novelty of the concept's combination of elements. The University of Minnesota Duluth's tag line, "The Lake Effect," applies a familiar meteorological phrase to the advantages UMD's proximity to Lake Superior offers students, from research to recreation. Surprise is "freshness" pushed to an extreme.

■ *Rhetorical sophistication:* This quality makes the tag line memorable by creating a pattern in the way it sounds. Kansas City Art Institute's "Balancing passion with practicality . . . intellect with imagination" uses alliteration and balance in a tag line that expresses the school's "Left Brain, Right Brain" concept. "The Way Education Should Be," a tag line Alverno College used to position its distinctive abilities-based and content-based curricula against more traditional institutions gained memorability from the rhythm of the line, as well as the question it raised in the reader's mind.

■ *Action:* A tag line that expresses or suggests motion or progress will generally be more memorable than one that is static. Southwestern College's "Come Here. Go Far." lets the verbs do most of the work in a tag line that also uses balance and opposites for its effect.

■ *Suggestion:* Because the tag line is the distillation of the concept, it should suggest the possibilities for meaning contained within the concept. When Rider University tested its "Success in Motion" tag line with prospective students, it found that when asked to explain the line, students had no trouble coming up with all the associations the creative team originally had in mind. Northern Michigan University's "Northern. Naturally" tag line was echoed in the viewbook's section heads: "Natural Curiosity" (academics), "Natural Ability" (faculty), "Natural Success" (opportunities and outcomes), "Natural Environment" (campus life), "Natural Wonder" (location), etc.

A good concept requires none of these tag-line qualities. But if, in your concepting, you come up with a strong tag line first, make certain that it expresses a concept that can carry the communications on which it will appear.

The creative process

The odds are that you not only want better ideas and stronger concepts, you want them faster. Is there a shortcut to a great concept?

If you've ever cooked Chinese food, you know it goes a good deal more smoothly if you spend time up front gathering the ingredients and chopping the vegetables. So it is with the creative process. You'll make it more efficient—as well as more productive and enjoyable—if you plan ahead.

Every creative person develops his or her own process for getting to great ideas, but what follows are some general truths :

■ *Do your homework.* Get to know your target audience or audiences. Don't stop at who they are; find out how they think. As Hood College, Director of

Admission Kerry Durgin notes in an article in the Spring 1998 issue of *College Admission,* "Students seek information to plug into mental slots that have been reserved for specific facts. Only they can determine what is distinctive, accurate, and appropriate for them." Take a look at your competitors' publications, interactive media products, or advertising. Familiarize yourself with any available research reports.

■ *Know what messages you want to send.* Have them written out to keep you on track, but don't try to communicate too many in any single communication. The messages should determine the concept, not vice versa.

■ *Set aside time for concepting.* A series of sessions a few days apart will probably be more productive than a single marathon session. The days between the sessions allow time for digesting information and ripening ideas.

■ *Know the goal of the creative session ahead of time.* Early in the creative process, you may be interested in generating as many ideas as possible. Later you may want to test the versatility or "legs" of a concept you particularly like. If you're working with a creative team, share the goal and the information you've gathered with the members. This plants a seed that can be germinating even before the first session.

■ *Have the appropriate tools.* The tools you'll need will vary with the goal of the creative session. For instance, if you're brainstorming, you'll need a way to record ideas that come fast and furious—large tablets, an easel, white boards, and markers. If you're trying to break through a creative block or open your creative team to entirely fresh ideas, you might want to try zanier tools— funny hats to break down inhibitions or blindfolds to encourage new ways of perceiving.

■ *Have the right attitude.* The creative process can be fragile. Quick judgments, for example, can shut off the free flow of ideas. To keep ideas coming, try replacing "Yes, but . . ." with "Yes, and . . .." Be aware of your own attitudes. If you're suspicious of creativity or you think creative people are all flakes, you're probably not going to enter into the creative process with an open mind.

■ *Use more than one method for generating ideas.* "Brainstorming" has become a catch-all term for any creative exercise, but it is by no means the only strategy. Try matrixes and grids, pull random words from a jar, create analogies, draw pictures, ask absurd questions: If X were an animal, article of clothing, food item, what would it be? You can use just about anything that will help you avoid limited thinking. Virtually any book on creativity will contain dozens of exercises you can use effectively.

■ *Trust the process.* Don't settle for the first idea, even if it seems like a good one. Unless you are deeply skilled in creativity, first ideas are almost always "inside the box." Don't discard the first idea either, just because it's first. Keep it in the pool of ideas you're generating, and keep the ideas coming.

■ *Pay attention to what works for you.* Remember that creativity is a discipline. Notice when, where, and how you come up with your best ideas and reproduce the conditions the next time. On the other hand, if you feel the need to give yourself a jolt, don't be afraid to change the conditions. Just expect that, for a while, your process is likely to seem inefficient and messy.

■ *Don't forget to have fun.* Creativity is a discipline, and it is also play. Enjoy the process.

Try Humor

If creativity is putting things together in new ways, humor is the essence of creativity. Humor relies on discrepancy, exaggeration, and surprise. And like a good concept, it also relies on recognition and resonance to provoke the response: laughter. The new combination has to strike the audience as right at some level. Even if you decide that a humorous concept is ultimately not appropriate for your message and the media you choose, making humor a part of the creative process will help you to break out of the box.

Myths and realities

As with any process that is relatively unexamined, many myths have grown up around the idea of creativity. Here are a few of those myths—and the realities.

Myth: Logic is schooled. Creativity is unschooled.

Reality: Creativity is not unschooled, but it is rarely taught. We are not formally taught in school to strengthen our creative muscles in the way that we are taught analytical thinking. Highly creative children are often considered to be classroom management problems. Highly creative people both understand and consciously practice the process of creativity.

Myth: Creativity is illogical.

Reality: Creativity is not illogical; it is just not narrowly logical. Instead of looking for connections between relatively closely related things or following a narrow progression of thought, creativity pushes the limits of logic to their widest extreme. Creativity sees the connection—the "logic"—in widely disparate things. It throws the door open to a much broader range of ways to approach a problem.

Myth: Great ideas strike from out of the blue.

Reality: It only seems so. Actually, when a great idea seems to appear from nowhere, the creative work has been going on below the level of awareness, behind some closed door in the mind. (In this regard, creativity is a lot like intuition, which is nothing more than experience gone underground. We distrust intuition for the same reason we distrust creativity—because we have not been consciously aware of the process.) When our defenses against creativity are down—in many cases while dreaming or thinking about something other than the problem to be solved—the creative ideas appear.

Myth: Creativity can't be learned.

Reality: Certainly some people are more creative than others—they have a genius for creativity. But everyone has the ability to be creative and, as with any other ability, can improve it with practice.

Myth: Creative people are difficult (and they dress funny).

Reality: The degree to which creative people are seen as difficult is often in direct proportion to other people's discomfort with creativity. Creative people are independent and mentally playful. They have high levels of conceptual fluency and flexibility and originality. They are also highly observant (they pay attention) and creatively motivated (they enjoy problem-solving).

Appropriate creativity

The first law of marketing communications is:

You are not talking to yourself.

When a communication fails, it is often because this law has been flung to the ground and stomped on. The "listening-first" communication model introduced in Chapter 2 has been disregarded. The effort to make messages noticeable, salient, and memorable has not taken place. And the dynamic, cacophonous message marketplace has been ignored. The result: Even if the group receiving the message has been designated—prospective students, perhaps, or parents, or "friends of the college"—little that is specific about the group, and how the institution can answer its needs, is understood.

Without this understanding, creativity is still possible, but appropriate creativity is nearly impossible.

Appropriate creativity acknowledges the context in which your communications exist. It begins with the awareness that its purpose is not just to "say something in a new way" but to "say something in a new way so as to elicit a predetermined response from a specific audience." It results in creative concepts that succeed, as mentioned earlier, because they work on the formula:

Recognition + Resonance = Response

Your concepts must establish "recognition" in the audience. Your audience must see itself in you, see how you can serve it and its interests. However, recognition alone is often not enough to overcome audience inertia or separate you from the other institutions vying for attention. Your concepts must also strike a note of resonance in the audience, establishing a comfort level that breaks down any resistance to responding.

What to do with a great creative concept

Okay, you did your research. You called together your creative team. You brainstormed and scampered and put together analogies. You challenged assumptions and took risks. And it worked: You've got a creative concept, a Big Idea. It looks promising. Now what?

Write a creative rationale. Why? Because your concept is, at this point, only potential—and because not everyone will share your enthusiasm for it.

Put the pieces together. The success of your concept lies not in the concept itself, but in the way it is executed. The process of conception and execution is something like an hourglass: Lots of thoughts and ideas are compressed into the concept itself, after which those thoughts and ideas must explode outward into copy, design, photography, and the myriad other elements that make up the viewbook, brochure, advertisement, or interactive media product.

The translation of the concept into those elements involves a series of more or less conscious decisions. (The less fluent you are in the conception-to-execution process, the more the decisions will be conscious. At some point, you will find they become almost automatic.) For instance, say your creative concept seeks to present your institution to prospective students as a place where they will be acknowledged for where they stand

Your creative rationale should present your case persuasively to your particular gatekeepers. Long or short, detailed or summarized, it should cover the following points:

- *The goals and objectives:* What the publications, interactive media product, and other forms of communication should achieve (e.g., position the institution relative to its chief competitors, raise the academic profile of students, highlight the advantages of the institution's location, etc.)
- *The strategy:* How you propose to achieve the goals and objectives
- *The concept:* A description of the concept and how its various elements (design, copy, photography, organizational structure, etc.) carry out the strategy

Planning for Persuasion

Answering a few questions will help you deal effectively with the gatekeepers at your institution:

- Who are the gatekeepers with whom I must deal?
- What obstacles does each present?
- Are those obstacles real or imagined?
- What information does each gatekeeper need to buy into my idea?
- How can that information best be presented to win each gatekeeper's support?
- Is there any particular order in which the gatekeepers should be handled?

academically and then developed from there. What does this dictate about copy? Among other things, it determines that you will use a phrase such as "teaching style" over a word like "pedagogy."

The creative rationale captures those decisions. It ensures that you give the concept enough thought to see whether it has the versatility to extend across different media, applies to all your different audiences, and has the "legs" to remain fresh for the life of the publications, interactive media products, and advertising.

Get past the gatekeepers. Too often, efforts to become more creative focus on freeing the imagination and building knowledge of the domain of effective communication. Little thought is given to getting past the gatekeepers. But it is the gatekeepers who determine whether a good idea ever sees the light of day.

A gatekeeper is anyone with the power to slow or stop the process of effectively executing your creative concept. Every institution has them. These are the individuals who approve budgets, review content, or sign off on copy, design, or photography.

In many, if not most, cases, all that these people require is a cogent argument to bring them around to your way of thinking. But creativity means taking risks. As you push the limits of your creative efforts, you are also going to have to open the minds of everyone involved in the approval process. In a very real way, these individuals constitute another audience with whom you must communicate. The creative rationale will explain your creative concept to this group—what the concept is, how it will be executed in various media, why it is appropriate for your audiences, and how it will be adapted for each use.

The creative rationale creates the context for each element in the concept. A conversational tone and style of copy, for instance, sometimes raises concerns with those reviewing copy. They protest that it is not "good writing." The creative rationale demonstrates that each of these decisions has been consciously made and is in keeping with the goals of the communication and the audience.

The last word on creativity

Just kidding. We've only begun to touch on how you can become more creative and why you should. Fortunately, there are hundreds of additional resources to help you. A few that impress us are listed below. They range from the highly theoretical to the eminently practical.

Recommended Readings

Adams, James L. *Conceptual Blockbusting: A Guide to Better Ideas,* 3rd ed. Reading, MA: Addison-Wesley-Longman Inc., 1990.

Adams, James L. *The Care and Feeding of Ideas: A Guide to Encouraging Creativity.* Reading, MA: Addison-Wesley-Longman Inc., 1986.

Baldwin, Christina. *Life's Companion: Journal Writing as a Spiritual Quest.* New York: Bantam Books, 1986.

Cameron, Julia. *The Artist's Way: A Spiritual Path to Higher Creativity.* New York: Putnam Publishing Group, 1992.

Covey, Stephen. *First Things First: A Principle-Centered Approach to Time and Management.* New York: Simon & Schuster, 1994.

Crandall, Rick. *Break-out Creativity: Bringing Creativity to the Workplace.* Corte Madera, CA: Select Press, 1997.

Csikszentmihalyi, Mihaly. Creativity: The Work and Lives of 91 Eminent People. New York: Harper Collins, 1996.

Csikszentmihalyi, Mihaly. *Finding Flow: The Psychology of Engagement with Everyday Life.* New York: Basic Books, 1998.

Csikszentmihalyi, Mihaly. *Flow: The Psychology of Optimal Experience.* New York: Harper & Row, 1991.

De Bono, Edward. Lateral *Thinking: Creativity Step by Step.* New York: Perennial Library, 1970.

De Bono, Edward. *Serious Creativity: Using the Power of Lateral Thinking to Create New Ideas.* New York: Harper Collins Publishers, 1992.

De Bono, Edward. *Six Thinking Hats.* Des Moines, IA: Advanced Practical Thinking Training, 1992.

Edwards, Betty. *Drawing on the Artist Within: An Inspirational & Practical Guide to Increasing Your Creative Powers.* New York: Simon & Schuster, 1987.

Edwards, Betty. *Drawing on the Right Side of the Brain: A Course in Enhancing Creativity and Artistic Confidence.* New York: Simon & Schuster, 1986.

Garfield, Patricia L. *Creative Dreaming: Plan and Control Your Dreams to Develop Creativity, Overcome Fears, Solve Problems, and Create a Better Self.* New York: Simon & Schuster, 1995.

Goldberg, Natalie. *Writing Down the Bones: Freeing the Writer Within.* Boston: Shambhala Publications, 1998.

Kao, John. Jamming: *The Art and Discipline of Business Creativity.* New York: Harper Collins Publishers, 1996.

Kidder, Tracy. *Soul of a New Machine.* Boston: Little, Brown, and Company, 1981.

Michalko, Michael. *Thinkertoys.* Berkeley, CA: Ten Speed Press, 1991.

Ray, Michael L. and Rochelle Myers. *Creativity in Business.* New York: Doubleday, 1986.

Ricchuito, Jack. *Collaborative Creativity: Unleashing the Power of Shared Thinking.* Greensboro, NC: Oakhill Press, 1996. Von Oech, Roger. A Kick in the Seat of the Pants.

Van Oech, Roger. *A Whack on the Side of the Head: How to Unlock Your Mind for Innovation.* New York: Warner Books, 1983.

Whitney, Dick and Melissa Giovagnoli. *75 Cage-rattling Questions to Change the Way You Work: Shake-Em-Up Questions to Open Meetings, Ignite Discussion, and Spark Creativity.* New York: McGraw Hill Companies, 1997.

Wycoff, Joyce. *Mindmapping: Your Personal Guide to Exploring Creativity and Problem Solving.* New York: Berkeley Publishing Group, 1991.

Integrated marketing is a holistic approach to mobilizing everyone in your institution to tell the institution's story.

Section II
Strategies and Tactics

6

Developing a Visual Identity System

■ Who are we?
■ What do we want to be known for?
■ What is our image?

Harry Battson

These three questions have been at the core of our discussion of strategic communication thus far. At this point, however, we want to move away from a philosophical treatment of these topics and focus on something a bit more pragmatic: the creation of a strong visual identity system.

To this end, we will discuss the pros and cons of a visual identity system, offer insights into evaluating your current identity, examine the issue of branding, and outline some strategies for maintaining a visual identity system. Finally, we will present a protocol for creating a new look.

The importance of a 'look'

In Chapter 1, we noted that integrated marketing operates at three levels:
■ Strategic
■ Organizational
■ Message

For the most part, a visual identity system or, as some call it, a graphic or family look, is concerned with the message. It has as its focus the development and maintenance of a comprehensive look. Historically, this look has been graphic in nature and impacted most directly on the way an institution's logo was to be used in publications and other printed material, such as stationery and business cards.

Today's visual identity systems are much more comprehensive and address not only use of the logo and wordmark in publications and stationery, but also in advertising, the Internet presence, signage, and even building exteriors and interiors. Today's visual identity systems are concerned with the creation and maintenance of a succinct, coordinated look.

Wally Olins, author of *Corporate Identity: Making Business Strategy Visible through Design*, says that "Everything that an organization does must be an affirmation of its identity…. The organization's communications materials, from its advertising to its instruction manuals, must have a consistent quality and character that accurately and honestly reflect the whole organization and its aims."

In 1992, *Graphic Arts* magazine related the results of a study by the Yankelovich polling firm that measured seven factors affecting how consumers rated businesses. The firm's identity system logo, letterhead, business cards, etc., ranked second only to annual sales figures in conveying prestige.

Market surveys, especially those that focus on the power of a brand name, have long shown that consumers trust the familiar. The more familiar they are with companies and institutions, the higher they tend to regard them. Presenting a consistent institutional identity mark over time builds recognition and confidence in the value of your institution.

When American University introduced a new logo in 1996, Tom Myers, the vice president for enrollment management, noted that today's consumers are more visually sophisticated than ever before, particularly the younger audiences who were raised on MTV and other visually stimulating television programming. To attract the interest and attention of those prospective students, academic institutions must copy the successful corporate techniques. "In the business world, image is everything," he notes.

In focus groups conducted by North Carolina State University in the early '90s, audiences strongly indicated that their decisions to participate in programs were linked to identification with the university, not to a particular academic or administrative unit. The findings indicated that, in a ranking of importance, audiences assign priority first to the university name, second to the title of the program, and third to the college, department, or administrative unit name.

Often, when we think of the elements of a visual identity system, we have a tendency to focus on the graphic elements. However, the creation of a succinct and successful graphic look also depends on another important component: the willingness of the president and senior administrators to deal effectively with what might be termed the *politics of identity*. Often, successful looks are more likely to be undermined from within than assailed from outside, and it is up to the senior leadership to actively support the process that creates or refines a look as well as the commitment to maintain the new look.

> " The creation of a succinct and successful graphic look also depends on another important component: the willingness of the president and senior administrators to deal effectively with what might be termed the politics of identity. "

For the most part, look-maintenance involves two issues: consistency and continuity.

Consistency is concerned with how well the look is integrated across the organization. In other words, is everyone willing to use the new look, and are the president and senior administrators committed to enforcing the look on recalcitrant departments and individuals? If not, then other, nonstandard looks will continue to be used. The commitment to a consistent look is always a political issue, an issue of will rather than design.

At one level, successful communication rests on repetition. If individual departments and programs use a separate identification wordmark or logo, they create confusion in the marketplace and limit the institutional identity's visibility. And you lose opportunities to brand this identity on the public mind.

The second issue is continuity, a willingness to commit to a new look for an extended period of time. It is our opinion that institutions seriously underestimate how long it takes to establish a new look and don't understand that the frequent every four years or so changing of the look damages their long-term image and reputation.

The continuity lesson is not lost on some colleges and universities. In its graphics standards manual, Biola University notes: "An effective logo serves two purposes: it must be easily recognizable, and it must convey a message. A logo becomes increasingly recognizable when it is used frequently and consistently."

Why build an identity system?

A strong look is not a panacea, but there are a number of reasons for establishing one. First, a comprehensive, well-managed look confers stability and professionalism. Second, a strong visual identity system is a fundamental component of an overall image strategy. Third, a consistent look will help steward dollars and time. Fourth, institutions with strong looks will be able to recruit students and raise dollars more efficiently and effectively. And finally, there is some evidence that institutions with strong looks are more likely to have a clearer sense of purpose.

Although there are a many reasons for establishing an identity system, there are also some consistent naysayers. In general, their concerns fall into two areas: loss of identity and cost.

Some individuals and departments feel that they need a separate look. Often these are graduate programs, continuing education programs, or institutions that have multiple campuses. In almost all cases, this sentiment is in error. Rather than separate looks, what is needed is an identity system that establishes individual variations of a larger institutional look.

Administrators who insist on separate looks are often dealing with the issue at an ego level and will seldom respond to the logic of a consistent look that serves the whole institution. They do not seem to care that their desire to establish their own look has two great costs. First is the cost they must incur to establish a new look. Second is the cost to the larger institution when one of its components goes off and does its own thing.

Having difficulty making the case for a stronger visual identity system? Consider conducting a brand test.

First, collect examples of your printed materials, including advertising. It is especially important to include examples of pieces that do not follow the current look. Make sure to include samples of signage (you may need to take photographs), business cards, materials from the athletic and alumni offices, student services, and continuing education. The goal is to cast a wide net and draw in as many disparate examples as possible.

Second, mount this cacophony on large pieces of foam core. The more "bad" examples the better.

Third, gather some examples of strong family looks from one or two institutions that your president and other senior administrators enjoy.

Fourth, schedule a time for a presentation. During the presentation, show the examples from your institution and from others, and ask the following questions:

- Which institution seems to be projecting a more concrete image?
- Which institution appears better managed?
- Which institution appears more professional?
- Which institution appears to be doing a better job stewarding its resources?
- Which institution is more likely to make a positive impact on donors, prospective students, business leaders, and other important audiences?

The odds are high that after this presentation, you will have a much greater opportunity to develop a family look.

Regardless of the rhetoric, arguments for a separate identity mark for an individual department, center, or program rarely have validity. As more and more programs and wordmarks and logos crop up around the college or university, the larger institutional identity fades. The individual units fail to recognize that their identities never will be as great alone as they could be by building on the institutional reputation.

The other big concern about strong identity systems is surprising. Some administrators believe that comprehensive identity systems are more expensive than less comprehensive, coordinated looks. In actuality, over time strong looks are likely to be less expensive. First, while more money may be spent on developing an enduring design, this cost will be amortized over a number of years. Second, significant money and time will be saved because there will be less likelihood of always trying to create something new. Instead, the focus will be on adaptation of the look rather than constantly creating new looks.

Granted, there is one significant cost for establishing a new look: the cost to transfer from disparate looks to a new, established look. However, if carefully timed, the cost can be greatly reduced. Introducing a new look at the end of a publication cycle or prior to printing a new batch of stationery can help reduce this cost.

The idea of 'brand'

Typically, a logo comprises the symbol, or emblem, of the institution used alone or in combination with the full or abbreviated name of the institution set in type. The typeset name is known as a wordmark. One transition we have seen over the past few years has been the move away from symbols or emblems constituting all or part of a logo to the wordmark used alone. More often than not, Latin, Greek, ivy, and even buckeye branches have been replaced by graphic presentations of the institution's name.

Consider the two graphic symbols in Figure 6-1. Which one more clearly establishes the institution's image? Only the initiated will recognize the buckeye as the symbol, or logo, for Ohio State University. As a consequence, the "buckeye" might be used only in situations in which audiences already have a high degree of familiarity of OSU. The wordmark for Stephens can be universally recognized.

It is our expectation that we will be seeing significant increases in the use of wordmarks as the central graphic in identity systems in the future.

Whether institutions that use a wordmark in place of a logo are aware of it or not, they are involved in romancing their brand. The brand, represented by a wordmark, is one of their most important strategic assets; it enhances the ability to both establish and leverage their brands, a situation of critical importance.

A brand is more than a trademark: A brand is a trustmark. David Martin, writing in *Romancing the Brand,* says that a brand is a "warranty. . . and a promise," and notes that brands must be "managed, defended, nurtured, and strengthened." Brands are a covenant between an institution and its constituents. This is not to say that the logo should be abandoned. However, we believe that logos are more correctly used in more formal situations such as on diplomas, certificates, invitations, etc.

Figure 6-1
Institutional Image: Logo versus Wordmark
Courtesy of Ohio State University and Stephens College

At a 1993 meeting of the American Business Press, Larry Light, president of the Arcature Corporation, said that "brands are an institution's most valuable asset. Yet instead of being brand builders, we are committing self-inflicted brand suicide. Our brands are being belittled, bartered, bargained, and battered."

There are many spoilers of institution brands. As noted earlier, most brand spoilage occurs because there is a lack of consistent enforcement. In particular, the following campus entities seem to undermine the notion of a single, strong brand:

- Bookstore
- Athletics department
- Alumni association
- Foundation or fund-raising office
- Graduate school or continuing education
- President's office

Any decision to develop a new identity system, or to strengthen an old one, must recognize the separate needs of these offices for identity. However, these offices must also recognize that their individual identities must be subservient to the larger institutional need for a single, comprehensive look. As one administrator said, ". . .not necessarily twins, but always part of the same family."

Deciding whether to change or update your look

At a recent CASE conference, I was asked, "What should be the life cycle of a logo or wordmark?" The questioner indicated that a new president wanted to develop a new identity mark for her college, despite the fact that it had just introduced a new logo 18 months earlier.

It is our feeling that a new logo and look should remain intact for as long as it serves the needs of your institution and your marketing communications program. If a look has been in place for a long time, it creates equity. Your institution has made a substantial investment in that mark and in gaining recognition for it. If that mark no longer reflects the nature, mission, or values of the institution, it needs to change. In the case of the college just discussed, the new identity most likely had not built up much equity in its short life. So the issue should turn on whether or not the new identity reflects the institutional message.

In some cases—perhaps most cases—a look can be updated without being totally altered. Such a transition enables you to refine the mark and the message without losing the value it has created over years of use and recognition. A new president's desire to put a stamp on the institution is not sufficient reason to create a new identity system. As the president talks to various stakeholders, she or he may find that the current identity mark is not accurately reflecting the college or enhancing the image for the university. Such was the case at Iowa State University when, two years into his tenure, the president told his marketing assistant to initiate a process for changing the identity mark. The first element of that process was stakeholder research.

" Is your current identity mark a revered icon that stimulates nostalgic memories for your big donor alumni? Does it incorporate a landmark or hero that, if replaced, would upset community leaders? Testing the idea with selected individuals could be the precursor to engaging in more verifiable research. "

Begin with research

Iowa State University conducted extensive telephone and mail surveys of prospective students as well as focus groups of community leaders, alumni, donors, corporate employers, students, faculty, and administrators to determine a new identity system. When student prospects were asked to describe Iowa State and two competitors, their image of ISU was much less distinct than the images of its competitors. They also scored ISU higher for "social life" than for "academics." The focus group determined that the distinguishing values of an organization were consistency, organization, and orderliness. These features then became the basis for the new ISU wordmark, which adopted strong block letters. The "agrarian green" color that was chosen suggested both the lush beauty of the campus and the agricultural roots of the university. Accent colors also became "natural" rather than "neon".

Iowa State is an excellent example of an institution that conducted both internal and external, quantitative and qualitative research to achieve the necessary information to create a new identity mark. The new mark is designed to reflect the desired values of the institution and to convey them to key target audiences as part of the total marketing communications program.

North Carolina State University also conducted extensive studies and focus group discussions for developing a new wordmark. Focus groups included alumni, guidance counselors, parents of college-age children, potential continuing education students, and employers. A survey of 80 academic and administrative units led to primary messages for the university. The process led to a wordmark with an all-caps, bold Universe-condensed type "NC State" followed by a light-face "University". NC State's research indicated that audiences expected the university identification to take precedence over a department or program in every communication. The boldness of the logo accomplishes this goal.

Anticipate reaction: inside and outside

Part of the research must be a political assessment anticipating the reaction of key stakeholders: alumni, donors, community and corporate officials, as well as faculty, staff, and students. Is your current identity mark a revered icon that stimulates nostalgic memories for your big donor alumni? Does it incorporate a landmark or hero that, if replaced, would upset community leaders? Testing the idea with selected individuals could be the precursor to engaging in more verifiable research.

Staff designers, while talented and familiar with identity marks, may not have the experience, perspective, and credibility to oversee the creation of your new look. But the argument for using internal personnel is persuasive; they understand the institution, its mission, and its marketing communications program, and outside firms do not. Kansas State University objected to turning to an East Coast firm that wouldn't understand the Midwestern roots of its students and community. On the other hand, the argument for hiring an outside firm is that such a firm generally commands greater respect within the campus community and brings a fresh perspective and approach. Such a firm is also outside institutional politics and unhampered by these kinds of concerns.

A logical approach is to issue an RFP (request for proposal) to local and national firms and to also include on-campus groups with the talents and abilities to create the mark and develop the system. The selection team then has the opportunity to review proposals from internal and external groups.

Regardless of the group selected, the team must make sure that the designers fully understand the task. A concise statement of the image, the mission, and the values to be conveyed, along with a list of possible institutional icons that could be incorporated, should go to the designers. Also, the team needs to determine whether the current institutional colors or other accoutrements need to remain or whether they would consider alternatives.

It is not uncommon when redesigning institution identity systems to alter the shade of the primary colors or to introduce accent colors or a palette of complementary colors.

The team should set a timeline for developing and testing the designs. In addition to the normal identity mark for print media, the team needs to receive and evaluate samples for other media, including television and video, Internet, and CD-ROM, since each media has attributes that require special consideration.

The responsibility of the team is to ensure that the right designers are selected, that the design is based on research, and that the design accurately conveys the marketing communication message.

Steps for establishing and managing a visual identity system

Increasingly, institutions are recognizing that their visual identity is a strategic asset and that, like other assets, it must be managed carefully. Part of managing an identity system is following a process for its creation and maintenance. Over the next few pages, we outline a seven-step procedure for establishing and managing a visual identity system:

1. Conducting an identity audit
2. Conducting a positioning study
3. Preparing a positioning statement

Note: The material on developing a visual identity system is adapted with permission from Barton Matheson Willse & Worthington (Author: F.E. Worthington, 1988).

4. Developing an initial look
5. Testing and refining the look
6. Adopting the final look
7. Maintaining the look

If you already have a look and merely wish to address strategies for using your look more effectively, focus on steps 6 and 7.

Step 1: Conduct an identity audit

Creating or changing your visual identity can be 95 percent politics and 5 percent design. Even in ideal conditions, you can find yourself running through mine fields. We are convinced that many ineffective graphic symbols live long lives simply because no one wants to endure the controversy that change can ignite.

An identity audit, a much larger version of the audit, can help you decide if change is indeed needed. If so, it can also help you gather the necessary support for undertaking the project. Here is a simple way to move toward an institutional decision to change visual identity:

- Gather samples of all the different visual images being used throughout the campus. They may include the official seal, various typographic treatments of the institution's name, logos, sports mascot symbols, etc.

- Collect samples of publications and other visual communications being used by directly competing institutions. These should include institutions that receive the most cross-applications from your prospective student pool, with which you compete in athletics (if, in fact, athletics are a major influence on your institution's public image), that share funding from your major contributors (individuals, foundations, corporations, and government agencies), and your competitors in your primary and secondary marketing areas.

- Assemble a committee of staff and faculty members who represent a cross-section of opinion and influence on campus. With this committee, review the samples you have assembled. Use these questions for discussing your materials.

- Imagine that you are a corporation that manufactures consumer goods. The materials you are evaluating are the containers or packages for your products. Will customers recognize each of the products as one of yours simply by the packaging? Do these materials appear to belong to the same organization? Is there a dominant theme that ties all the materials together? If so, does the theme communicate your current mission and future goals?

- Do some or all of your materials look out of date?

- Are there many different styles of type being used to portray your institution's name?

- Looking beyond the logo or wordmark, do the materials work together as a visual family in graphic, editorial, and photographic styles?

- Is there consistency in production quality? If not, do the apparent "winners" of higher production budgets reflect actual institutional priorities?

■ If you had never heard of your institution, would these materials make a favorable impression on you?

■ Bring out the samples you have gathered from other sources and compare these with yours. It may be useful to include samples from a school, college, university, or organization that "has it together."

■ Contact organizations that sponsor awards for visual-identity programs if you want a "second opinion" to validate your own impressions and gather samples of the winners. (The organizations include the Council for Advancement and Support of Education, American Society of Association Executives, University and College Design Association—See Appendix D for contact information.)

■ Reach an agreement, as a committee, as to whether the existing relationship between the institution's goals and graphic expression either is appropriate or needs improvement.

■ Present the findings of the identity audit to your president. If improvement is the goal, ask for official support to move forward with the project.

> " Creating or changing your visual identity can be 95 percent politics and 5 percent design. "

Step 2: Conduct a positioning study

The next step in creating a visual identity system is undertaking a positioning study. The goal here is to help determine the position you already hold in the minds of stakeholders and external target audiences.

Successful positioning studies use surveys, interviews, and focus groups to answer such questions as the following:

What are your institution's historic strengths?

Are there any weaknesses or vulnerabilities that concern you?

What is your vision of long-range success for your institution?

What kinds of students do you think your institution needs to attract in the future?

What does your institution need to do to attract these students?

What are your peer institutions?

What institutions are slightly above yours in "pecking order"?

When you meet someone who is unfamiliar with your institution, how do you describe it?

What are some other adjectives or descriptive phrases that describe your institution?

Do you think you communicate who you are as effectively as you can to your outside audiences? How can you improve?

If your institution has recently conducted comprehensive market research as part of a strategic-planning or marketing-planning process, most of the positioning information for developing a new visual identity has been spelled out. Your task will be one of interpreting and applying information you already have. A good market research study will alert you to external misperceptions that need to be corrected. Recommendations in the study are often your best sources for justifying an institutional commitment to the development of a new image program.

If market research has not been conducted within the past few years, and none is planned in the near future, you can gather the information a bit more informally through interviews and focus groups. Although this research is not statistically valid, and you would not rely on it for executive-level strategic planning, it can give you valuable input for visual identity design.

Key internal and external audiences to be examined as part of a visual identity audit include:

Internal
- Students—Full time, part time, nontraditional, graduate, international, of color
- Faculty
- Staff
- Administrators

External
- Prospective students
- Guidance counselors
- Parents
- Alumni
- Donors
- The community
- Government officials

To analyze the data quickly, construct a master chart that lists each audience's primary responses to each question. You will have an accurate picture of your institution's self-image and its external image. There will be many perceptions that match, and some that do not. The chart can serve as the road map for your institution's communications program.

Step 3: Prepare a positioning statement

If there is any magic in the process of developing a successful graphic reflection of your institution, it occurs during the creation of a positioning statement. In its most simple form, your positioning statement is the narrative version of your graphic image, a verbal working sketch drawn from careful observation and interpretation of the positioning research. In most cases, your positioning statement should resonate strongly with your vivid descriptors and your larger strategic communication goals.

As the process of implementing the new visual identity system expands to a wide range of communications materials, the positioning statement will serve as a guide for making appropriate design, editorial, photographic, and production decisions. It will serve as the benchmark for evaluating graphic-design appropriateness. Once you have received campus-wide endorsement of the statement, your goal is to translate the verbal language into visual imagery accurately.

Your internal interviews and focus groups gave your colleagues the opportunity to share their feelings and ideas. They now have a vested interest in the success of the identity program. If you have accurately reflected their contributions in your positioning statement, you can count on their support for the new image.

Ideally, your positioning statement should be no longer than three or four paragraphs on one side of a printed page. The positioning statement summarizes the relationship between the institution and the audience it serves. It expresses the institution's personality, major historic strengths, current direction, and significant future goals.

When you ask these same people to endorse the final design, the discussion should revolve around how well the design expresses the positioning statement rather than how well it satisfies their personal design tastes.

Step 4: Develop an initial look

With an awareness of your self-image and external perceptions and having received endorsement of your positioning statement, you are now ready to translate verbal language into visual imagery.

Developing a comprehensive identity program involves much more than designing a new logo or wordmark. The range of elements that make up an institution's identity program may include the following:

- Wordmark
- Color palette
- Typeface
- Environmental graphics and signage
- Tag line (optional)
- Layout treatments

The odds are that the final image will not emerge during the first round of exploratory design. The committee may identify one or several directions that seem interesting. The designer can rework these ideas while exploring others that come to mind during the meeting. "Back to the drawing board" is not a negative statement during the exploratory design stage. It is a necessary part of the process.

Step 5: Test and refine the look

After exploratory design has produced one or two rough images that have won the committee's enthusiasm, refine the roughs into design comprehensives, or comps.

Comps are tighter in execution; they closely resemble a printed sample and are a natural part of the screening process. Translating an image from rough to comp creates subtle changes in the design's character that may affect its viability, for better or worse, thus making it easier to arrive at a decision.

During the refinement stage, you should consider all elements of the identity program. One way to do this is by executing hypothetical designs for various projects.

Checklist for evaluating initial looks

- *Impact:* Does the image draw the observer's attention and arouse interest? Is it easily remembered?
- *Appropriateness:* Does it communicate messages contained in your positioning statement? If your statement says your institution is a friendly, informal place, does the mark look friendly and warm?
- *Originality:* Is it different from those of other academic institutions in your marketing area? Is it distinctive?
- *Aesthetics:* Does it have quality of form? Is it graceful and pleasing to the eye, along with communicating a message?
- *Adaptability:* Will it work in different sizes? Is it suitable for a wide range of applications, from printing to signs to television graphics?
- *Longevity:* Will it wear comfortably over time, or is it too "gimmicky" and transitory in its appeal?

Thorough discussion is necessary. Responses to each idea provide insight and direction for further exploration. The team members should avoid just saying they like or dislike an idea; rather, they should explain why.

Seeing your new image in specific applications will give you a chance to judge its versatility as well as its potential for unifying your overall communications program.

Remember not to limit your identity program to small applications. Test how your new image works when you increase the scale in such applications as signs or campus vehicles.

Some of the committee members will want to take the comps around campus and show off the new image. Resist the temptation to let them do this! You may feel that you solved the problem and developed the perfect identity program, but it is best to keep your tests and opinions internal at this point.

Just as you gathered input from internal and external audiences before drafting your positioning statement, so must you check with members of these same audiences for their reactions to your visual image.

These meetings are most successful when conducted one to one, following this agenda:

- Explain the process. Briefly review the visual identity audit, the positioning study, and the positioning statement.
- Ask that the meeting be kept confidential, and emphasize that the designs are proposed, not formally approved. If you feel comfortable doing so, share some of the discussion highlights from the committee's deliberations.
- Show only the final comps; do not show any of the "outtakes." As you present the comps, use the same checklist from the exploratory design review for discussion:
  - Impact
  - Appropriateness
  - Originality
  - Aesthetics
  - Adaptability
  - Longevity

The interviews will provide objective responses to your identity program. Responses will vary, but if the process of research, positioning, design, and refinement were thoroughly executed, the testing will verify the appropriateness of your visual image.

In evaluating the results, you can feel that the image is successful, if, out of every 10 persons interviewed about your identity program,

- One or two love it,
- Five like it,
- Two are not thrilled, but could live with it,
- One or two dislike it, and
- One hates it.

If this last response came from the president or chairman of the trustees, go back to "Develop an initial look" (step 4).

If the response profile matches or exceeds this profile, congratulations! You have a running start. The way in which you manage the implementation of the program will determine how well you can match these results when you introduce your new image publicly.

Step 6: Adopt the final look

How to announce the new identity mark depends on your particular system. The University of Arizona announced a new visual identity program a few years ago only to have the Arizona legislature reduce the university's budget by the reported cost of the program. In general, a planned announcement is a positive step toward explaining the program and garnering attention for its implementation. Unless you fear reprisals from funding sources, we recommend you handle the announcement in the following manner.

1. The president should make the announcement and unveil the new symbols. Her or his official sanction and imprint will carry weight both externally and on campus. The president should address the rationale for developing the new system, how the new marks were created and will be used, and the image and message that the new identity system is meant to convey.

2. Your graphics identity standards manual is the management bible for your institution's visual identity system. Without it, your identity program's integrity, effectiveness, and momentum can dissipate rather quickly. It should be distributed at the announcement. Pass out pens, cups, T-shirts, or other materials to the media and people from the institution who are attending. The media should receive complete identity-standards kits, including reproducible materials for television. If you have developed an animated version for television and the Web site, include that as well. Make sure it's possible to download the logos from the Web site, and also, if you have one, that your trademark registration is prominent. Figure 6-2 displays elements from a family of graphics standards items from Centre College. Many are appropriate for gifts at the announcement ceremony.

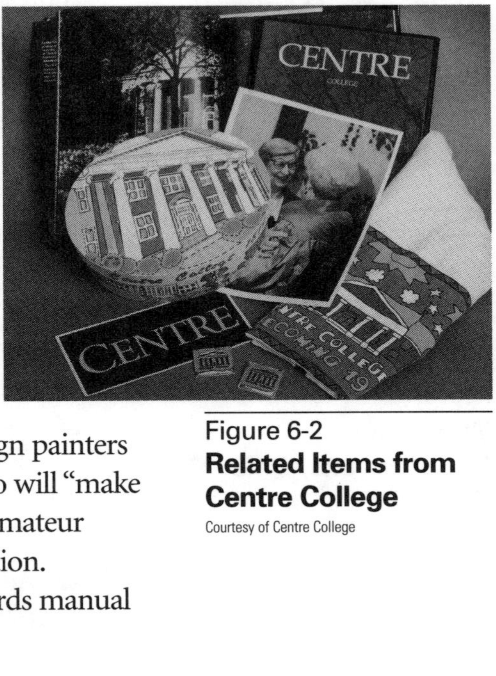

In organizations that generate communications from many departments, a comprehensive graphics standards manual is necessary. For instance, a manual for a large state institution with publications offices on each campus would include detailed specifications for letterhead design. A manual for a small institution that produces all publications from the same office need only be a basic model that includes printing specifications. Appendix B outlines many of the elements that you should consider including in a graphics standards manual designed for campus-wide use.

Institutions that do not have graphics standards manuals often find themselves at the mercy of printers who will redesign the letterhead; sign painters who fancy themselves environmental designers; advertising salespeople who will "make it look nice" as they revamp your logo to their own liking; and a crowd of amateur "designers" with Ph.Ds in scholarly fields unrelated to graphic communication.

Besides the obvious function of quality control, your graphics standards manual has other benefits:

Figure 6-2
Related Items from Centre College
Courtesy of Centre College

■ It creates confidence that your identity program is well thought out and is part of a bigger plan. Visual identity seems more important when it is an official function of the institution, complete with printed standards and operating procedures.

■ Because it is an official publication of your institution, it establishes a degree of authority and makes individuals think before creating nonconforming visual communications.

■ It serves as an "owner's manual" for your faculty and staff. An automobile owner's manual contributes to a feeling of pride and ownership of a new car; it also gives detailed instructions for maintenance and care that help preserve the car's value and performance. The same goes for your graphics identity manual.

■ It is important to take the focus off you and your staff as "design police." The style manual is an enforcement vehicle that carries the authority of official policy. This status helps to avoid conflict and bad feelings between individuals and departments.

■ It is a valuable positioning tool. It demonstrates your institution's sound management, commitment to quality, and attention to detail.

Figure 6-3 shows a page from the graphics identity manual of The Ohio State University, with directions for wordmark, color, and other specifications. The formats for graphics identity manuals vary as much as their titles. They range from modestly produced folders to elaborate, full-color books. One of the more popular formats is a loose-leaf binder that can be updated inexpensively.

Having settled on the new look, the time has come for you to implement the program.

A presidential announcement to kick off the change and to gain media attention as well as internal compliance can set the stage. Having a fully supportive president is critical to a successful program even if you elect not to make a formal announcement. Other ways to make sure your president is seen as a driving force for the identity system include:

■ Leading off your graphics standards manual with a letter from your president stating his or her support and asking all the various campus departments and units to comply;

■ Sending a memo from your president to all department heads and college deans announcing the change and indicating that he or she expects all departments to follow the program;

■ Kicking off a campus-wide workshop with remarks from your president to show all those involved in university publications, stationery, or other related projects that he or she supports their efforts to learn about the new system and to use it correctly;

■ Adopting an institution policy statement that explicitly requires all units to follow the system and authorizes various offices, including marketing communications, printing, and purchasing, to enforce it.

Figure 6-3
Wordmark
Specifications, Ohio
State

Although your president needs to support your program visibly, the integrated marketing communication planning champion needs to lead its implementation throughout the institution. Figure 6-4 is an example of a sign at Salem State University that extends the graphics look to campus markers. Through personal meetings with top officials, vice presidents and deans, directors and department chairs, the champion can explain the system and its value, show how the change will affect individual department materials, and solicit their support and compliance. Persuasion needs to be the first weapon in your arsenal.

It would be desirable to achieve compliance with your new graphic identity immediately (as corporations often do when "launching" a new identity), but it is not cost-effective for higher education institutions; they are inevitably resource-challenged. Modestly priced items with the old image that change infrequently should be replaced as soon as possible. Items like stationery should be replaced as supplies run out, assuming it's within a period of weeks or months, not years. More expensive items, such as signs, will likely take years to replace. Changes should be planned and budgeted, however, to make sure that they occur in as timely a fashion as practical.

Make sure that your plan adequately addresses the needs of individual institutions and units on your campus that require special recognition. Organizations that are based on your campus but may have other national or state affiliations may require a special treatment. For instance, a public broadcast station may need to incorporate the institution's logo along with the NPR logo.

The marketing communications planning champion should be the individual to apply to for approval of any exceptions. In general, approving different logos for individual enterprises should be discouraged. Short-term events, such as anniversaries or special celebrations, may warrant a special identity mark.

Existing marks of individual units should become part of their "look" but not interfere with the institutional identity symbol's use as "the signature."

Make sure that you distribute the graphics standards manual broadly and that you periodically send out memos or e-mail to all units to remind them to adhere to the program. In cases where programs violate or resist the standards, provide a corrected mock-up of the offending material. In many cases, the department is either unaware of the proper use of the identity mark or is uncertain how to apply the mark to its particular needs.

Step 7: Maintain the look

Support for your new image will grow quickly. After 18 months of exposure, you can expect that seven out of every 10 people on campus will like the image, two will accept it with reservation, and one will still dislike it. Considering that, in the biggest landslide in presidential election history, the losing candidate still received 45 percent of the votes, your program's 75 percent popularity will be impressive.

Maintaining the consistency of your institution's communications materials as the

---

Distributing the graphics standards manual

Consider the distribution of your graphics identity manual. Typically, copies should be given to the following:

■ Offices on campus that produce publications independently of the publications staff, from the admissions department to any institutionally related publishers

■ Vendors who produce visual and interactive communications for your institution, from printers to fund-raising consultants

Executive leaders in your institution should receive courtesy copies of all communications for reference and periodic review.

Figure 6-4
Signage at Salem State University

Photographer: Aton Grassel. Courtesy of Selbert Perkins Design and Salem State University.

Trademark Registration

Views differ on the importance of registering your visual identity mark as a trademark. If you have developed a wordmark for your image, it may not be registerable as a trademark. Protection for a wordmark is of questionable importance since your institution's name is unique.

If your primary image is a symbol, the chances of infringement are still questionable. We suggest that you provide a copy of the mark to your institution's legal representative for appropriate counsel.

For detailed guidelines and procedures for registering trademarks, contact the United States Patent and Trademark Office. It can be reached at *www.uspto.gov* or via the main switchboard at (800) 786-9199. The Patent and Trademark Office also allows you, via the Web, to download a series of documents and brochures that will help you both research and register trademarks. You can also check out *www.trademarks.com*. This fee-based site lets you search the entire federal trademark database. Be sure you ascertain how to display the trademark symbol if you choose to apply for it.

program reaches full penetration requires careful monitoring. Here are a few suggestions that will help:

- Establish "gatekeepers" to serve as an early warning system for spotting nonconforming applications of your new identity. These may include your institution's purchasing agent, in-house print shop manager, and bookstore manager. Special training sessions may be necessary with these "design deputies" to ensure that they are representing the program's objectives accurately.

- Periodically repeat Step 1: the identity audit. Occasional identity audits help you see how your comprehensive program is working as a visual family. These mini-audits will provide positive reinforcement for you and your staff and, at the same time, help identify inconsistencies.

- Make a list of design-related activities such as layout drafting, type specifications, photo editing, and pasting-up. Keep a log of staff hours spent on these functions. Measure these against schedules from your old projects. This analysis should reveal increased efficiency.

- Compare your design and prepress budgets with those of similar projects prior to your new program. Your new program should trim these budgets somewhat. This benefit will help in perpetuating the president's enthusiasm for your program.

- Refer to your positioning statement during each project. Identity programs evolve with each new special communications need. Your positioning statement will ensure that the identity program and your institution grow in the same direction.

As you implement your new program, frequent appeals for exceptions to your specifications will be a constant challenge. Although you will have made every attempt to anticipate problems when you prepared the graphics standards manual, there will still be many questions. Most can be easily addressed by explaining the guidelines in the manual in more detail. For some projects, you may want to seek further consultation from the designer. Consistency is important, but you do not want to produce "clone" projects. That is not the purpose of the identity system.

If you are the primary custodian of the identity system, be firm yet understanding with those who violate the guidelines. Maintain a service attitude. As the system evolves, new design approaches, and new layout grids can be added, and display type can be manipulated for special effects. The "spirit" of the identity program is more important than the rules and guidelines.

The key is to centralize the authorization process so that creative expansion of institution's program is not accidental but occurs in a meaningful, coordinated fashion. If you love the visual identity you have developed, you will honestly believe that everyone on campus will be best served if the system's integrity is preserved. You will not be doing anyone a favor by permitting unauthorized departures from the guidelines.

Although you will be making every effort to monitor the program's application across campus, there will be surprises. Printed publications may appear on your desk that bear little resemblance to your other materials and will stand out like a sore thumb during your next identity audit. What can you do? Invite the responsible party to your audit review.

Covering all the bases

It has been my experience that institutions seriously underestimate how many graphic items are affected by a comprehensive visual identity system. Of course, failing to anticipate the total impact of the new look and identity system also leads to miscalculations of the dollar costs involved in the changeover. Although no list of graphic items involved in a visual identity system will be totally comprehensive, the following is a good place to start:

- Stationery, from letterhead to purchase forms
- Publications, from annual reports to catalogs
- Advertising, from classified ads to exhibits
- Electronic media, from TV to the Web
- Architecture, signs, and structures
- Vehicle identification tags
- Parking permits and decals

Integrating athletics into your identity system

The ball's in your court! Wouldn't it be wonderful to see your university identity mark on national television as your Division III football team wins the national championship?

All too often, athletic logos and marks bear no resemblance or relationship to the college or university they represent. Frequently, the athletic symbols appear alone, without even a reference to the college name. A bull adorns the helmet, but no label identifies it. A cardinal graces a track warm-up jacket but, without further identification, it can be meaningless.

Granted, this is not always the case. Consider, for example, Notre Dame. The block letters that identify the university are prominent on the athletic uniforms. But this is the exception that proves the rule. One can only extrapolate that the stronger the link between the college identity and the athletic identity, the greater the recognition of both the image and the advantages that will accrue to the institution and all its programs.

The University of Wyoming—athletically, the Cowboys—is currently engaged in an evaluation and redesign of its logos, both institutionally and athletically. The objective, if possible, is to ensure that the athletic programs are integrally connected to the university.

With the visibility from the media, athletic events, and sponsorships, and even from licensed merchandise sales, it's important to make sure that your institutional

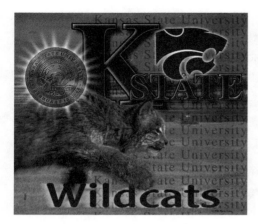

Figure 6-5
The Athletic Symbol of Kansas State
Courtesy of Kansas State University

identity and the athletic identity are linked. After its 1994 review of its athletic identity program, Illinois State University now requires its Redbird to appear with the words "Illinois State."

Many colleges and universities are updating their athletic symbols with a trend toward greater dynamics, aggressiveness, and color. The University of North Carolina replaced its 50-year-old strutting ram with a bolder version. Kansas State introduced a more aggressive wildcat (Figure 6-5). Baylor created a growling bear; secondary marks feature just the head and paw. Wright State, with the athletic team name of Raiders, changed its logo from a Viking to a wolf.

Following in the footsteps of professional sports, institutions are attempting to cash in on new merchandise sales. In 1994, Villanova University switched to a new mascot, a more aggressive-looking wildcat with new colors. Licensing royalties went from $35,000 to over $200,000 in two years. Such sales also result in tremendous additional visibility.

The process for developing a new athletic identity should mirror that of developing your new institutional identity, including the research process. Research told Iowa State University, the Cyclones, that even its fans didn't understand why it also used a cardinal as a mascot. The new athletic identity mark incorporates the cardinal with the cyclone, effectively linking two disparate elements of its image. Multiple versions also ensure the identification with Iowa State or ISU.

One difference in developing new athletic marks is the increasing importance of coordinating the change with merchandise manufacturers and your bookstore. Plan an announcement date that takes into account the time your manufacturers need to get new uniforms developed and produced. Your bookstore and other vendors also need time to promote and sell existing merchandise before bringing in a new mark that will reduce the value of their inventory.

Evaluating the program and analyzing results

After you've developed and implemented the program, you will need to evaluate and assess it on a continuing basis. Initially, you'll want to assess how the process went, including the actual announcement of the program. What was the initial reaction of alumni, faculty, staff, and students? Did it create an air of excitement or positive feelings about the college? Did comments match your research, or did new factors emerge? Was the rationale for the new mark understood? Did you get the media coverage you expected? Were the media supportive or critical of this waste of money? How did your other stakeholders, donors, legislators, corporate, and community leaders react?

Second, you'll want to do follow-up research to see how well your new identity marks are accepted. After a year of use, research if and how target audience attitudes about your institution have changed. Is your new identity helping to create the image and communicate the values that you sought? Periodically review this issue. If you don't find the movement you expected, you might want to delve into the problem. If you do find the cause, you'll want to make sure that all participants in the process, including the president, are aware of it. And you'll want to keep monitoring.

Recommended Readings

Aaker, David A. Managing Brand Equity: *Capitalizing on the Value of a Brand Name.* New York: Free Press, 1991.

Arnold, David. *The Handbook of Brand Management.* Reading, MA: Addison-Wesley-Longman Publishing, 1993.

Beckworth, Harry. *Selling the Invisible: A Field Guide to Modern Marketing.* New York: Warner Books, 1997.

Illustration Annual. Palo Alto, CA: Communication Arts (Coyne and Blanchard), 1999. [Annual]

Crispell, Diane and Kathleen Brandenburg. "What's in a Brand?" *American Demographics,* 15, no. 5 (May 1993):26-32.

Custer, Carol. "Rebuilding an Athletic Program Visual Identity: A Research-Based Approach Used at a Public University." 1997 Symposium for the Marketing of Higher Education, Eighth Annual Symposium Proceedings Series. Chicago: American Marketing Association, 1997.

—."'So, Someone Thinks You Need a New Logo for Your University?': A Research-based Approach Used at a Public University," 1996 Symposium for the Marketing of Higher Education, Seventh Annual Symposium Proceedings Series. Chicago: American Marketing Association, 1996.

Gregory, James with Jack G. Wiechmann. *Leveraging the Corporate Brand.* Lincolnwood, IL: NTC/Contemporary Publishing Group, 1997.

Gregory, James R. *Marketing Corporate Image: The Company as Your Number One Product.* Lincolnwood, IL: NTC/Contemporary Publishing Group, 1991.

Jones, John Philip. *What's in a Name? Advertising and the Concept of Brands.* Lexington, MA: Lexington Books, 1986.

Loden, D. John. Megabrands: *How to Build Them, How to Beat Them.* Homewood, IL: Business One Irwin, 1992.

Magrath, Allan J. *The Six Imperatives of Marketing: Lessons From the World's Best Companies.* New York: AMACOM, 1992.

Martin, David N. *Romancing the Brand.* New York: AMACOM, 1989.

Murphy, John M. Branding: *A Key Marketing Tool.* New York: McGraw Hill Companies, 1987.

Olins, Wally. *Corporate Identity: Making Business Strategy Visible Through Design.* Cambridge, MA: Harvard Business School Press, 1990.

Pearson, Stewart. *Building Brands Directly.* New York: New York University Press, 1996.

Reitan, Cheryl. "Get Audited: A Critical Examination of Your Print Publications Can Lead to Cost Savings and a More Cohesive Institutional Identity." CURRENTS, 24, no. 10 (November-December), 1998:34-39.

Ries, Al and Jack Trout. *Assessing the Cost of Student Recruitment at Smaller Independent Colleges and Universities.* Washington National Association of College and University Business Officers, 1989.

Ries, Al and Jack Trout. *Marketing Warfare.* New York: McGraw Hill Companies, 1997.

Ries, Al and Jack Trout. *Positioning: The Battle for Your Mind.* New York: Warner Books, 1981.

Ries, Al and Jack Trout. *The 22 Immutable Laws of Marketing: Violate Them at Your Own Risk!* New York: Harper & Row, 1994.

Interbrand and Nicholas Kochan. *World's Greatest Brands: An International Review by Interbrand.* New York: John Wiley & Sons, 1996.

Topor and Associates. "Athletics and Marketing: An Appeal to Change Perceptions about the Value of Athletics in Marketing Higher Education." *Marketing Higher Education,* (March 1995).

Worthington, F.E. *Visual Identity for Marketing Results.* Baltimore, MD: Barton Matheson Willse & Worthington, 1998. (Call (410) 298-0390 for copies.)

7

> **Most people would agree that internal communication is extraordinarily important.**

Defeating the Grapevine
Building an Effective Internal Communication Strategy

Jeannie S. Morelock

Some problems are so difficult they can't be solved in a million years— unless someone thinks about them for five minutes. – H.L. Mencken

Most people would agree that internal communication is extraordinarily important. Unfortunately, most would also agree that few institutions have truly effective internal communication programs. To help you develop a more comprehensive internal communications plan, this chapter explores the following key issues:

- The importance of effective internal communication
- Recognizing the information needs of four key constituencies
- Determining the information of most interest to internal audiences
- Components of an internal communication plan
- Evaluating the effectiveness of your internal communications effort

In earlier chapters, we emphasized that we are in the communication—not merely the promotion—business. This tenet holds true here. Our goal is not the creation of more effective promotion, or even downward communication strategies within the institution. Rather, our goal is true internal communication. Not surprisingly, this brings us back to the listening-first model of communication introduced in Chapter 1.

The four key internal constituencies

Before we proceed much further, it might be helpful to clarify who are the customers of our internal communication plans. Internal communication programs are designed to meet the information and communication needs of four key constituencies: students, faculty, staff, and administrators.

Students

Among the most important internal audiences are the students. The flow of information to and from students is critical to their sense of belonging and overall satisfaction with the institution. Students who feel that they are aware of the "goings on" around the campus will be more likely to be involved in campus activities and to persist.

Faculty

The second major internal audience is faculty. Perhaps more than any other internal audience, faculty have a keen desire to be made aware of key decisions and information at the earliest stages. If they feel excluded or overlooked, they will quickly make their dissatisfaction known. Faculty are particularly sensitive to the ebb and flow of information between them and the administration. George Keller, writing in *Academic Strategy*, notes:

> At one campus . . . the president was visited by a disgruntled group of engineering professors who informed him that while enrollments in engineering had gone up by one-fifth in the last three years, the number of faculty positions had not. They were surprised that he was not aware of this situation. A week or so later, I mentioned this to a leading historian at the same university. He quickly put his forefinger to his lips, urging quiet. "The history department," he said, "has lost one-third of its students since the early 1970s and we still have the same number of faculty."

Clearly, a vacuum existed between administration and faculty. Sound familiar?

Staff

The third significant internal audience is staff. Sometimes overlooked in the educational pecking order, a knowledgeable and in-the-know staff play a pivotal role in college life, and staff members who are included and made aware of what is going on are more likely do a better job. In addition, staff who feel informed will likely have higher morale and less turnover.

Steven Lincoln, communications coordinator at Hastings College, states,

> When employees know more about the institution and are happy about their work, they will be more positive about the college when they are out in the community. If we are successful in our internal communication efforts, we believe that gives us an edge with our external communications.

A professional communicator at Harvard University, Ann Hall, notes,

I think internal communication is particularly important with regard to morale. If you get a lot of information from your employer, whether it is information to help you do your job better, or . . . it is about your benefits, you feel the organization hasn't forgotten you.

President and senior administrators

The fourth key internal audience is made up of the president and senior administrators. In theory, this group should be aware of all major and most minor events and issues. In the world of institutional administration, however, we know this isn't always the case. And we know, too, that this problem isn't endemic at only large institutions. Sometimes smaller institutions, where communication would appear to be more intuitive and easier, suffer the same maladies as their larger cousins.

Communication is listening, too

As we think about internal communications, we need to remind ourselves that effective communication involves listening. Successful internal communication efforts include "listening" as well as "promotion" components.

Now that we have the basis for whom we need to address and include in our internal communications program, it is time to explore why it pays to keep people informed.

> " As we think about internal communications, we need to remind ourselves that effective communication involves listening. "

Some common listening options

If you are interested in developing the "hearing" component of an internal communications plan, you might consider the following options for listening to campus constituencies. The choices are divided into two groups: passive and active. Passive listening involves monitoring existing communications to keep track of emerging issues and concerns. Active listening solicits direct input from internal audiences.

- ■ Passive listening
  - Reading campus bulletin boards and kiosks
  - Reading student newspapers
  - Reading on-line forums and listservs
  - Reading faculty and staff newsletters
  - Listening to campus radio and television
  - Reading minutes from open meetings
- ■ Listening actively
  - Holding open houses
  - Holding receptions
  - Conducting an open-door policy
  - Conducting "brown bag" meetings with the president (or other senior administrators)
  - Leading by walking around

- Spending time in the cafeteria or faculty lounge
- Attending athletic and cultural events

Why we need to keep our customers informed

The importance of timely, interactive communications simply cannot be overemphasized. A. Westley Rowland, writing in the *Handbook of Institutional Advancement*, says,

> . . . if people in and around a college or university are uninformed or misinformed, if they have little opportunity to respond to messages received, if they are not persuaded to identify with institutional objectives, then the institution is in deep trouble.

Like nature, rumor loves a vacuum. In the absence of clear and accessible information, the truth can become distorted. Or, it can be mangled by gossip, hearsay, and scuttlebutt. A campus, teeming with constant talk among its internal constituencies, can provide a potent breeding ground for misinformation. And when communication suffers, the institution suffers.

Minor miscommunications can become major image headaches for an institution when the miscommunications wind their way through the front gate and into the general community. Donors, parents, prospective students, the media—any or all may become disenchanted with your institution after hearing "the bad news."

Goals of an internal communication plan

With this commitment to listening, we believe that an internal communication plan should :

- ■ Set up appropriate channels of communication.
- ■ Disseminate accurate information in a timely fashion.
- ■ Anticipate information needs among key constituencies.
- ■ Serve as an early warning system of internal concerns and issues.

Appropriate channels of communication

The first goal of an effective internal communication strategy is the creation of appropriate and timely channels of communication. Our four audiences—students, faculty, staff, and administrators—have different information needs and prefer different channels of communication.

Because our goal is to communicate, not to simply add more clutter to the communication channels, it is very important to research the optimal methods for both listening to and communicating with different audiences.

Consider Table 7-1. It shows how different internal audiences voice their concerns and how they expect you to communicate to them. Note that although most people use a variety of options to communicate their concerns, they almost always wish to be responded to in a personal, even one-to-one, fashion.

Accurate, timely information

The second goal of an effective internal communication strategy is to communicate accurately and to communicate in a timely fashion. The title of this chapter was not unintentional. If the campus grapevine is to be truly defeated, then the channels of communication must be filled with accurate, timely information.

Earlier we noted that rumor loves a vacuum. As one administrator reminded us, "If you don't tell people what is going on, they, "will likely make stuff up."

Information needs

Legendary football coach, Vince Lombardi, among others, noted that the best defense is a good offense. He was talking about football, but his comment has currency in the field of communication as well. An effective internal communication plan doesn't wait until people demand information before kicking into gear. Rather, it supplies information in an ongoing fashion. And in doing so, it suppresses rumor and misinformation. A college in Oregon communicated to faculty and staff that the number of student applicants and paid deposits was down and that enrollment would likely be down as well. As a result, the campus was not surprised by the smaller number of students who enrolled that fall.

Internal Audience	I want to be heard or will voice my concerns to you via:	I expect you to respond to me via :
Students	1. Face-to-face • Formal • Informal – open door 2. Letters to the editor of student newspaper 3. Campus ombudsman 4. Classroom discussion 5. Telephone call 6. Protest/rally 7. Notices on bulletin board 8. Reception, open house	1. Face-to-face 2. Letter or memo
Faculty	1. Face-to-face • Formal • Informal – open door 2. Letter/memo to faculty chairs/deans 3. Department meeting 4. Letter/memo to president 5. Telephone call 6. Reception, open house	1. Face-to-face 2. Letter or memo
Staff	1. Face-to-face • Formal • Informal – open door 2. Letter/memo to department heads 3. Communication to union 4. Letter/memo to president 5. Reception, open house	1. Face-to-face 2. Letter or memo
Senior administrators	1. Face-to-face • Formal • Informal – open door 2. Letter/memo 3. Cabinet meeting	1. Face-to-face 2. Letter or memo 3. Cabinet meeting

Table 7-1
Communicating With Internal Audiences

Early warning system

Because an effective internal communications strategy is two-way, it can serve as an early warning system. It puts you in a unique position to hear about campus concerns and frustrations before they become major issues. In this way, you can gather information about issues at the grassroots level and bring them to the attention of senior administrators so issues can be dealt with in a timely way and their outcome, where and when appropriate, communicated to internal audiences.

Consider, for example, the director of public relations who carefully reads the letters to the editor in the student newspaper. She notes that in a period of three weeks, five students have complained about shortened library hours. She communicates this information to the academic dean (who oversees the library). The dean holds a meeting with student leaders and discovers that they, too, have been receiving complaints about the library hours. The dean makes the decision to keep the library open later three nights each week. This information is communicated informally to the student leaders at the same time a short article is prepared for the student newspaper and the campus Web site.

What is important to whom, and why?

Our internal customers want and need information. They want to be heard. They want to have a strong sense of being in tune and involved. But deciding what to communicate is sometimes difficult.

The Communications Task Force Report from Colorado University-Boulder recommended the creation of "a Communications Council . . . established by the Chancellor to develop and coordinate communications policy and to nurture cooperation and collaboration among campus communications professionals." This task force empowered three subcommittees: external communications, outreach, and internal communications. The internal communications subcommittee addressed four questions:

- Who are the constituent groups affected by internal communications?
- What are their needs?
- What recommendations can be made to better meet these needs?
- How are other institutions approaching internal communications?

The key is to involve the stakeholders in the process of deciding the content and direction of the information to be communicated (Table 7-2).

Communication options

Now that we have a clearer sense of what kinds of information people want, we can turn our attention to the exciting part: creating the best methods for disseminating that information to fit your institution. Traditional methods can be combined with more modern communication media to keep your audience "in the know." Consider the following communication channels:

- Newsletters
- Intranet and e-mail
- Campus television and radio
- Receptions and meetings
- Telephones and faxes
- Campus mailings

Newsletters

The internal newsletter is probably the most common communication device . It can be elaborate in design, scope, and frequency, or it may be a simple one-page update reproduced on an office copier machine, like the monthly "In a Nutshell" produced at Meredith College (Figure 7-1.)

Evaluate your audience! A change in employee benefits does not directly affect Samantha the student, but Dick the dietician will have a vested interest in this information. Conversely, the fact that the East Student Parking Lot will be closed for a day for repaving may not interest Dick. But Samantha, who commutes, will appreciate knowing the location of her alternate parking site.

Depending on the size of your institution, your newsletter can take many directions. It is important to embrace what is important to your audience. Steven Lincoln notes that Hastings College's employee newsletter:

> . . . takes a familial tone, using first names of all employees we write about. It is easy to do at a smaller institution, and it helps our readers feel like they are in the know and closer to each other. For example, they really enjoy knowing when their co-workers have birthdays, wedding anniversaries, or employment anniversaries, so we provide that in our newsletter. We consider our campus the Hastings College family.

Customer	Information Types

Students	• Program and course information
	• Financial information
	• Campus events
	• Community events
	• Maps
	• Campus news
	• Class notes, assignments, etc.
	• Club information
	• Resource information
	  1. Counseling center
	  2. Gymnasium
	  3. Library
	  4. Bookstore
	  5. Cafeteria
	• Special meetings/assemblies
	• Student government issues
	• People news
	• Internships and jobs

Faculty and staff	• Employee benefits, services • College policies, data • Special announcements • College news • New hires and job listings • Faculty or staff meeting minutes • Schedules, calendars, deadlines
President/administration	• Feedback • Updates from constituents • Potential problems or issues

Table 7-2
The Kinds of Information Internal Constituents Want

On a larger scale, Vivian Fogel, director of publications and printing services at the University of North Carolina at Charlotte, produces an in-house weekly newsletter that has been in existence for at least 27 years. Each faculty and staff member receives a copy. Says Fogel:

> *Campus News* is extremely popular. . . . If it's late, the publications office starts getting calls the next morning. . . . So much information is submitted for Campus News that it's difficult to cram it into eight standard pages . . . If the publication were a joy to behold, its popularity might be easier to understand, but it is definitely not pretty. Printed in black ink on an inexpensive mint-green bond, Campus News has no photos and often no art at all. . . . I think the secret of Campus News's success is its interactive quality . . .

There you have it. Not necessarily fancy, but informative,and popular. Fogel adds that the staff complained when the publications office switched to white paper. They were used to looking for "green," and some could not easily find the white sheet among all the other communications that they received. They looked forward to finding the internal news!

Figure 7-1.
Faculty-Staff
Newsletter.
Courtesy of Meredith College, Raleigh, NC

Newsletters are often a method of communicating with students. Similar in nature to those directed to the staff, the student newsletter can take on a "student newspaper" flavor and feature coming events, campus news, and club and other organization happenings. Again, consider your audience and what they are interested in knowing. Student newsletters have the potential for being an interactive communication tool: written, edited, and published by students, with editing supervision provided by administration. Consider involving as many curricula as possible. The journalism, art, and computer departments can gain hands-on experience while providing a quality missive for their fellow students.

Intranet and e-mail

Twenty-five years ago, we asked ourselves how we ever did our jobs without electric typewriters and copiers. Now we ask how we ever did our jobs without the computer and e-mail! Electronic mail has fast become the preferred means of communication for personal and professional use. Millions of people have logged on to commercial carriers at home. Institutions without e-mail have become as rare as manual typewriters. We "e" to our colleagues throughout the day. It is a marvel that saves time, energy, and may eventually sound a welcome death knoll for the more traditional mode of communication: the time-usurping meeting.

Chowan College in North Carolina is a completely wired campus. Bill Harlow, Web site developer at Chowan, believes that the most effective form of communication on the campus is e-mail. Says Harlow,

> Every classroom, office, dorm room, library, conference room, and . . . auditorium is connected to our campus ethernet. . . . With our network, [we have] eased the paper trail on campus. . . . We are able to e-mail everyone on campus at once. This works out great for announcing special programs.

Many other colleges make extensive use of the *Intranet.* According to Patricia Facciponti, author of a 1995 article in CURRENTS magazine, "Electronic communication is a fast, easy, inexpensive way to keep in touch with other important groups—faculty, staff, and students." She notes that the University of Pennsylvania uses its campus-wide network "to disseminate everything from course rosters to job listings to urgent safety information."

Facciponti points out that Western Illinois University's president uses e-mail to send a weekly message to update internal groups on university goals and policies, student and employee accomplishments, and activities around the campus.

Meredith College, an all-women's college in Raleigh, NC, has recently made its on-campus Intranet accessible to off-campus visitors. Meredith's Internet and Intranet are merged at *www.meredith.edu.* Says Ruth Ann Balla, director of technology services, "We found this to be a great service to the community. This benefits commuters, faculty and staff, and parents, and it gives prospective students a taste of campus life."

Campus television and radio

It's the age of MTV, sensational television courtroom dramas, and outlandish TV talk shows. For all of the cutting-edge computer technology available for consumption today, we Americans still love the old standby—television.

Rowland makes an interesting observation: "Although face-to-face communication is preferred by employees, even audiovisual presentations, such as videotapes, films, and multimedia slide shows, are considered more personal and more credible than the printed word."

In the past decade, many campuses have installed their own closed-circuit television channels. They use these channels to run custom programming, including student video productions and calendar event screens. Much like those in larger hotels, campus CCTV can provide instant visual access to maps, directions, meetings, notices, and announcements. The information can be quickly updated, and is available, 24 hours a day, 7 days a week, in monitor-equipped classrooms, meeting facilities, dining halls, lobbies, and dormitory rooms.

In addition to television, don't forget radio. More colleges and universities have radio stations than TV stations. While TV may afford more splash, radio is often more pervasive and offers a number of segmenting options.

Receptions and meetings

Why, in the age of high tech, should we have a meeting? The answer is simple: for high touch.

In face-to-face meetings, the credibility quotient is higher than in a memo or newsletter. Gathering your constituencies together for an assembly is the age-old tried-and-true means of effective internal communications, but *only* if your meetings, forums, or assemblies are substantive in content. Meetings are valuable for major institutional announcements. Hearing it straight from the "horse's mouth" can squelch the rumor mill before it has time to grind into action. Rowland notes that we all know, but don't always listen to the advice: "To be effective and productive, meetings require purpose, careful planning and arranging, and skillful direction. Exchanging views openly can benefit everyone if comments are kept on track."

Telephones and faxes

By today's standards, phones and faxes are old technologies. But they're both very useful for internal communications. They have evolved beyond their original limitations and now casually offer users broadcast-distribution capabilities.

Voice-mail messages can be tailored to spread the word to incoming callers. Campus phone systems enable users to send messages to all voice mailboxes on the system. Hotlines are frequently used to dispel rumors, list job openings, present information on events, dates, tickets, etc., and to provide immediate information in crisis situations.

Faxes, like phones, present an inexpensive and user-friendly mode of one-stop, push-button information dissemination. You put in your campus office fax numbers list once, and then simply hit the broadcast function to send your announcement to every office on the list. It's immediate, it's easy, and it works.

Campus mailings

Let us not forget the snail-mail pony express: campus mail. Regular mailings to campus offices provide information that can't be faxed, phoned, or e-mailed. Many institutions insert notices in the paycheck envelopes mailed to their employees.

Once a month, Meredith College sends a mailing to all faculty and staff department heads. The mailing is an accumulation of new Meredith publications, copies of the college's recent advertisements, and copies of recent news clippings. To save costs and trees, the recipients are asked to circulate the packet of information to their staffs.

Some reasonable outcomes

It is unreasonable to ascribe every good thing to an effective internal communication plan, but we suspect that an effective plan should contribute to some or all of the following results:

- Reduced absenteeism
- Reduced turnover
- Higher morale
- Greater sense of community
- Greater tolerance for uncertainty
- More trust and openness

Interestingly, Keller notes that "more administrators each year believe that openness about new directions the institution is taking is more conducive to rallying faculty, student, and alumni support behind initiatives as well as productive of better academic plans because of criticisms and improvements from others."

Back to the future

We've discussed who our internal stakeholders are and what they expect. We've covered many of the most effective modes of conveying information to them, some simple and inexpensive and others that are more intense from time-commitment and financial standpoints.

The final step in the communication cycle is to keep listening to your audience. Almost as fatal as not using an effective internal communications program is the failure to encourage feedback. This is an ongoing challenge. Your program should never become static. Periodic surveys can help you enhance your program continually. Ask the questions that will elicit productive feedback. Let your constituencies tell you when their interests veer off the beaten path.

Build it and they will come

People enjoy and appreciate being heard and communicated with in a timely fashion. If you decide to implement a comprehensive internal communications strategy, you must be committed for the long haul. You just can't stop when it is no longer convenient —or easy. Always remember that the people inside your campus gates are as important to the health and well-being of your institution as the potential customers and benefactors in the community at large.

Human beings react positively to being treated as individuals. When they feel "warm and fuzzy" as a name instead of "cold and forgotten" as a number, good word-of-mouth will ripple out into the community. Unfortunately, the opposite is true, when the news may not be good. Ignoring this market and taking it for granted can result in the "fatal error."

We've heard the maxims: "No man is an island." "It takes a village to raise a child." You cannot shoulder the challenge of creating an effective internal communications program alone. You now have the tools to pull the "village" together and serve the child.

The world is on the cusp of a new millennium. Technology has snowballed to the point that "new" today is "old" tomorrow. It's hard to keep up, and the most obvious source of inexpensive mass marketing (end-user word-of-mouth) can easily be over-looked.

As higher education marketing professionals, we've been drilled on selling our product. With the explosion of the Information Age, we cannot ignore—we must involve!—the market that has bought into our business. If we do, the "sold" will "sell."

Recommended Readng

Abramson, Paul. "How Schools Compute." *American School and University,* 67, no. 4 (December 1994):2A-3A.

Arden, Kelvin J. and William J. Whalen. *Your Guide to Effective Publications: A Handbook for Campus Professionals.* Washington: Council for Advancement and Support of Education, 1991.

Brown, Tom. "Leverage PR for Internal Communications: Two Pros Say It's Something Leaders Should Tune In To." *Industry Week,* 244, no. 3 (February 6, 1995):24.

Facciponti, Patricia. "Network News: E-mail, Gophers, Bulletin Boards, and More: How Communications Can Make the Most of the Internet." CURRENTS 21, no. 1 (January 1995): 22.

Footlick, Jerrold K. *Truth and Consequences: How American Colleges and Universities Respond Publicly to Public Crises.* Phoenix, AZ: ACE/Oryx Press, 1997.

Geddie, Tom B. "Internal Communication: A Model for the Future." *Communication World,* 12, no. 1 (January-February 1995):32-35.

Golden, Sandra. "A Plan for All Seasons: Putting Your Priorities and Goals in Writing Will Help Your PR Program Succeed Year Round." CURRENTS 19, no. 9 (October 1993):8-12.

Heeman, P. Warren. *Criteria for Evaluating Advancement Programs,* 2nd ed. Washington: Council for Advancement and Support of Education, 1989.

Keller, George. *Academic Strategy—The Management Revolution in American Higher Education.* Baltimore: The Johns Hopkins University Press, 1983.

Kelly, Kathleen S. *Fund Raising and Public Relations: A Critical Analysis.* Hillsdale, NJ: Lawrence Erlbaum Associates, 1991.

Larkin, T.J. and Sandar M. Larkin. "Internal Communications: Have We Missed the Mark?" *Communication World,* 12, no. 3 (March 1995):12-16.

Larson, Mark. *Making Conversation: Collaborating with Colleagues for Change.* Portsmouth, NH: Heinemann, 1997.

LaSalle, Patricia Ann. *College and University Magazines: Building Credibility to Advance Your Institution.* Washington: Council for Advancement and Support of Education, 1991.

Powers, Vicki. "Internal Communications as a Strategic Function." *Strategy and Leadership,* 25, no. 2 (March-April 1997):44.

Raley, Nancy and Laura Carter. *The New Guide to Effective Media Relations.* Washington, DC: Council for Advancement and Support of Education, 1988.

Richards, Michael D. and Gerald R. Sherratt. *Institutional Advancement Strategies in Hard Times.* Higher Education Report No. 2. Washington, DC: AAHE-ERIC, 1981.

Rowland, A. Westley. *Handbook of Institutional Advancement,* 2nd ed. San Francisco: Jossey-Bass Publishers, 1986. [Published in cooperation with the Council for Advancement and Support of Education]. *This book is now out of print, but the third edition will be available in Winter 2000.*

Warner, Carolyn. *Promoting Your School: Going Beyond PR.* Thousand Oaks, CA: Corwin Press, 1994.

Willmer, Wesley K. *Winning Strategies in Challenging Times for Advancing Small Colleges.* Washington: Council for Advancement and Support of Education, 1993. *This book is now out of print, but the second edition will be available in Winter 2000.*

8

Presidential Image-Enhancement Strategies

> **66** The one sure way to increase your chance of failure is to construct an abstract model of the perfect president and seek to impose it. **99**

Michael Norris

If you don't have regular access to the president of your institution or if you have a president or school head who's not open to image-enhancement suggestions, perhaps this chapter isn't for you. If this is the case, your time might be better spent in some of the other activities described in this book such as research, planning, and institutional image development.

But if you have ready access to a president who understands that image enhancement will enable him or her to be more successful in helping the institution achieve its goals, you'll probably find this chapter useful. It suggests concrete ways to increase your president's visibility, ability to persuade, and overall effectiveness. If you, the reader, are the president of an institution, this chapter will present straightforward ideas that you can implement directly or bring to the attention of others. It also includes detailed examples of image-enhancement strategies that have worked for leaders at public and private institutions of varying sizes.

The president as a person

In any effort to build the president's image, the one sure way to increase your chance of failure is to construct an abstract model of the perfect president and seek to impose it. (This approach can also increase your chances of being invited to seek new employment opportunities.)

No two people are exactly alike. Image-enhancement strategies will be more successful if they're tailored to reflect the real person you're promoting and flow from this person's abilities, inclinations, and interests. The bad news is that you can't pick or remake your president's personality and innate abilities. The good news is that every temperament is interesting in its own way, and any person who achieves the presidency of an institution has above-average abilities. Like a novelist, filmmaker, or biographer, you need to be very much attuned to the power of his or her personality to attract, charm, and motivate people. Your chief executive's image will make a greater impact for your institution if it is genuine, engaging, inspiring, and, to some extent, unexpected.

Why "unexpected"? It creates interest and proclaims a multifaceted, distinctive, "real" person. We remember people, like institutions, more for their differences than their similarities. A story that focuses on a president's interest in fund raising and student recruitment (essential as these are) will be a much harder sell to most media than a feature focusing on a president's experience as an expert mountain climber or a published poet.

> **The good news is that every temperament is interesting in its own way, and any person who achieves the presidency of an institution has above-average abilities.**

Winning spinning

When Rick Nahm became president of Knox College (where he served 1993-98), he made it a priority to connect with students and with members of the local community. He made considerable progress with both groups by assuming the unlikely role of disk jockey.

A lifelong lover of rhythm and blues and an avid record collector, Nahm convinced the student managers of the campus radio station to give him a weekly Friday slot from 4 to 6 p.m. The resulting music program, "Rick's Picks," won a loyal listenership among both students and townspeople and was one of the trademarks of his successful tenure at Knox. In addition to making his image "more human and well-rounded," the program was taped in advance and allowed him to "be on campus" every Friday afternoon, even when he was hundreds of miles away making fund-raising calls or attending alumni meetings.

The vivid detail

On the morning of January 30, 1998, the Centre College board of trustees announced their selection of John Roush as the institution's 20th president. That afternoon, the Centre community came to a campus-wide assembly for a first look at the president-elect.

Anticipation was high as students, faculty, and staff filed into the auditorium. After being introduced by a trustee, Roush took the stage and in just 10 minutes conveyed his excitement about joining the college and told listeners what they might expect of him: "I am relatively informal in my approach to people at work," he said, "one who believes that all honest work is honorable; a great admirer of those who show courage; a man devoted to my family; a person of faith, committed to making a difference for good; a guy who loves children and Payday candy bars."

The speech and subsequent informal question-and-answer session were extremely well received. Many things were right about this first visit with the college community—the content of the speech (conveying substantial knowledge of Centre and a commitment to shared governance), the delivery (focused, energetic), and the manner (open, engaging).

The most important thing about the visit was the overall impression the president made through innumerable communications, verbal and nonverbal. But of the things he said, the comment that clearly stood out as being the most often recounted and that lodged itself most firmly in the minds of those attending the assembly was, of course, the remark about Payday candy bars.

Meaningless? Trivial? Hardly. The detail conveyed a sense of humor and fun—and showed that although the new president took his responsibilities seriously, he didn't take himself too seriously. It helped communicate the image of a real person rather than that of a script or set of abstract policies. It even produced concrete results. On his first official day on the job, the ever-vigilant president's office staff presented Roush with a jar of bite-sized Paydays.

The first 100 days really are important

Yes, you can make a first impression only once. And students, faculty, staff, and community members—anxious about impending change—are often hypervigilant when a new president is announced. For these reasons, the process of introducing the new president to key constituencies requires careful planning.

First, to whom do you introduce the new president? Although no list of groups can be guaranteed to be comprehensive for all institutions, six groups should be on all lists.

- *Trustees:* Although some trustees should have met the new president during the search process, additional time spent in getting to know board members will provide valuable resources for good times and bad. To enhance the relationship-building process, the new president should visit with trustees on "their turf" and not just on campus.

- *Students:* Early communications will relieve the anxiety of uncertainty and, as with trustees, pay future dividends. An interview with the editor of the student newspaper for an article as early as possible is usually a good idea. (Tip: For a more relaxed atmosphere, meet the editor in student or neutral territory—library, dining hall, student center—not in the president's office).

- *Faculty:* Faculty representatives will in most cases have been involved in the search and selection process. Timely follow-ups with both the entire faculty and smaller groupings are critical to making this key constituency feel valued and positive about the new president. "Meal meetings"—breakfasts, lunches, dinners—provide a particularly good format in which to create a relaxed atmosphere and establish valuable connections.

- *Alumni:* A letter, usually from the board chair, begins the process of communicating with the alumni, which is then continued through news accounts, articles in institutional publications (such as the alumni magazine and newsletters), and other media such as the institution's Web site. Still, there's no substitute for face-to-face meetings. The new president should make attending area alumni gatherings an early priority and also play a highly visible role on occasions, such as homecoming, that bring alumni to campus.
- *Leaders of the state, region, nation (and world, if your Rolodex is that big):* Obviously, the new president should be introduced to all influential leaders with whom the institution has ties. Relationships with these individuals can have a favorable impact on everything from fund raising to student recruitment to media recognition to the ability to attract high-visibility commencement speakers.
- *Leaders and other members of the local community:* This is a group that's sometimes overlooked, but is nonetheless extremely important.

The introduction process to one key constituency

When John Roush assumed the presidency of Centre College, the institution made a concerted effort to give a wide range of community leaders an opportunity to get to know him. The primary vehicle was a series of lunches held at the president's home each Tuesday and Thursday for several months.

Lunches were intentionally kept small (usually no more than one 12-person table), informal (after a brief welcome and introductions, Roush invited questions and comments on any topics his guests chose), and lasted about 90 minutes. Representatives from over 20 groups participated (for example, chamber of commerce, convention and visitors bureau, United Way chapter, industrial commission, city and county school systems, ministerial association, regional medical center) and the reaction was overwhelmingly positive.

Participants said the process made them feel the president was accessible and committed to making a positive impact on the community. One comment focused on the intimate setting of the lunches: "I've lived here all my life and never been in Craik House [the official residence of the president] before. It feels like I have a more personal connection to the college now."

Some other ways to introduce a new president:

- *Get a jump on the game.* Of course, a president's official starting date is merely that: an official date. The real date is as soon as he or she can begin to communicate with your institution's key constituencies. In some ways, before-the-official-start-date meetings can be even more powerful than later ones because people often feel flattered to have been "singled out" for a special sneak preview.
- *Pick formats in which the president is comfortable.* Since the object is to present your new leader in a favorable light, play to the person's strengths. If formal

speeches are his or her forte, set up the lectern; if informal socializing is the preferred medium, bring on the hors d'oeuvres.

■ *Prep the president:* Consider it homework for the exam, which is, in a sense, exactly what it is. Your new president should know the key issues ahead of time as well as the danger zones and the need-to-get-to-know people. Since personal recognition is one of the things humans crave most, a few study sessions—even if your president is a whiz at names and faces—with an intelligently assembled collection of photos and biographical information will be time well spent.

■ *Scrutinize the guest list.* Sometimes it's more productive for your new president to meet with the institution's adversaries than with its friends, but a public get-acquainted event is rarely the best occasion for this. A more private setting may be better for initial meetings with individuals with long-standing differences that need to be talked out.

■ *Ask those you invite, whom to invite.* As you make initial calls to set up meetings, often the "obvious people" will be able to suggest others who, though less obvious, will prove to be valuable friends for your new president and the institution.

Slowing down the eager-beaver impulse

Being president of an academic institution is different from being president of, say, the United States. U.S. presidents-elect have often spent decades preparing to govern the country and want to use the excitement and momentum of the political victory to enact long-planned policy changes and secure quick passage of major legislative initiatives; they place enormous importance on their "first 100 days." (If the past quarter century is a guide, they should perhaps be more worried about the second term.)

The urge to make a big splash quickly is understandable and probably advisable for U.S. presidents. The new president of your institution, however, should moderate this inclination. The three key jobs of most new presidents are to reassure (without promising maintenance of the status quo), to listen, and to learn the institution. Learning the institution is, of course, a critical mandate that will be ongoing not just for 100 days, but for one or two—or more—years.

Producing quick, popular results is great

The key word here is "popular." Since fund raising and student recruitment are constant institutional priorities, these are ideal areas in which your new president should strive for early successes. Likewise, when economically feasible, improved compensation for faculty and staff will rarely spark protest riots. Finally, changes that have been thoroughly researched and have achieved institutional consensus through the strategic planning process before the arrival of your new president may be good choices for early action.

Red flags

Although these examples may seem obvious, in my experience the following principle has proved sound: Anything important enough to "go without saying" should probably be said.

Generally, A new president should avoid changes that generate significant controversy among students, faculty, staff, alumni, or members of the campus community such as:

- Firings, especially of individuals with long tenure,
- Policy changes that limit faculty tenure or make tenure more difficult to achieve,
- Dramatic hikes in tuition or other fees, or major changes to the campus, especially tearing down a building or buildings with sentimental appeal or proposing to close a street open to public traffic.

In a given situation, any of these examples might be the correct thing for a new president to do, but, in general, time will be better spent learning the institution, working to achieve widely agreed-upon goals, and making deposits in the goodwill bank account for later use.

The president on campus

In pursuing presidential image-enhancement strategies, we often focus on external constituencies and neglect internal constituencies. This is a mistake. If your president is unpopular or perceived as being inaccessible by students, faculty, or staff, these attitudes will invariably be communicated to external audiences. Little things mean a lot. Here are some examples of what the president can do:

- Show up in unexpected places such as a senior's thesis presentation, a student coffee house, a faculty member's departmental lecture, a staff member's birthday cake and coffee, a low-profile but worthwhile volunteer activity.
- Eat with the students (at least sometimes) instead of off-campus or at the faculty club. (Besides, if the cafeteria food's really that bad, your new president should know about it.)
- Remember to show respect and always use tact when possible (which is most of the time). All presidents have to tell people things they don't want to hear. But oftentimes, a person will take offense—and harbor resentment—not from the content of your president's message, but from how it's delivered. If your new president builds goodwill among students, faculty, and staff by interacting with them in a straightforward, respectful way, this feeling will be communicated over and over again to external constituencies—subtly, not so subtly, and powerfully.
- Pay attention to the details of campus appearance. If the campus looks good, people will assume that the institution is well managed. Although in this case, b doesn't necessarily follow a, the perception itself will be widespread, and perception is the "reality" that people act on.

Steve Trachtenberg, president of George Washington University, made this comment about internal perceptions of educational leaders in a telephone interview in

October 1998: "In general, college presidents are pretty hardworking and largely invisible. Most of the time, faculty and students have no idea of what they're doing." Trachtenberg gives explicit strategies for communicating the content of his job to members of the GWU community and establishing his presence around the campus. Some of his tips follow:

- Invite the editor of the student newspaper to the president's office. During these meetings, Trachtenberg goes over his weekly calendar and gives the editor an overview of his major activities and their time requirements. In general, he explains "what the president does." These visits provide a context and knowledge base for future editorial decisions, and sometimes result in "day-in-the-life-of-the-president" articles in the student newspaper.

- Spend the night in a dorm. Explains Trachtenberg, "One night a year I bring about 100 pizzas with me to one of the freshmen residence halls. We eat, meet, and I go for a tour. Then I retire to my bunk. Three weeks later, we invite everyone to my house for breakfast. I learn a lot during these visits and make friendships with students that last through their four years here and beyond."

- Advertise open office hours when any student can make an appointment and meet with the president.

- Have regular lunches with faculty members. According to Trachtenberg, "Every three weeks, we take a party of six faculty to lunch. I pick up good information—and the tab—and sometimes get a chance to nip rumors in the bud. Then I send a follow-up letter the next week with additional information on issues that were raised."

Making the president pervasive

Even if your new president is a type A+, workaholic, turbo-motivated master of the seven habits, there are more worthwhile things to be done than he or she will have time for. And though priorities—which vary widely among institutions and should ideally emerge from the strategic planning process—are critical, sheer volume counts, too.

How can a president spend the necessary time on the road to promote development, student recruitment, alumni relations, and, in general, raise the visibility of the institution, and still be an accessible, influential presence around campus?

First, even under the most ideal circumstances, a successful president will obviously have to put in long hours. It will help if he or she enjoys the social and public events that are part of the life of an educational institution. But beyond this, there are ways to increase the impact of your president around campus in the face of ever-escalating demands off campus. Some suggestions:

- E-mail can be a big time-saver that greatly extends your president's capacity to communicate and influence. It can, for example, often be an effective substitute for time-consuming in-person meetings. The "copy" function of e-mail can keep discussion flowing between large numbers of people without the hour-eating demands of scheduling, travel, warm-up chit-chat, and unproductive digressions inherent in in-person meetings.

- E-mail can also be a big time-waster. Be wary about signing up for listservs and other mailing groups, which can bury critical messages in a daily flood of largely irrelevant information. If the president wants to monitor one or more listservs, have another person on campus sign up and forward only the most pertinent messages to the president.
- A president with an Internet-capable laptop can use down time on the road to read and respond to e-mail as easily as in the office.

If you can get double or triple duty out of projects that need to be done anyway, the impact of your president's time will obviously be increased. Some examples: your president's message for the alumni magazine could be the basis for an op-ed newspaper piece or vice versa; speeches can often be recycled effectively from one audience to another with only minor changes, especially if the institution's identity and mission are well defined; and a presidential evening devoted to a phonathon can influence students, alumni, friends, and development staff members simultaneously.

Time invested in one medium can be recycled to another. Patsi Trollinger recounts a successful example from her tenure as director of public relations at Emory and Henry College. She was so impressed with the speech then-president Charles Sydnor made at the dedication of a Jewish community center on the importance of the Holocaust to all ethnic groups that she worked with Sydnor to use his remarks as the basis of a magazine article. The result? A full back-page article in the *Chronicle of Higher Education* (September 16, 1987).

Some more suggestions for the president on recycling time:

- *Make travel time serve double duty.* When the president makes development trips, look for opportunities to schedule meetings with media representatives.
- *Stay fluid:* Avoiding ruts in daily activities can bring the president in contact with new people, provide fresh insights on your institution, and make him or her a real physical presence to more members of your community. Former Knox College President Rick Nahm, for example, had a policy of never parking in the same place two days in a row. The benefits he cites include meeting students, faculty, and staff with whom he wouldn't normally cross paths; seeing the campus from new angles; and not having people assume he was off campus just because his parking space was empty. Other opportunities for making atypical choices include meetings, sports events, parties and other social events, and different routes and destinations for campus "walking around" time.
- *Live the campus life:* There will, of course, be rest and recuperation times when the president needs to be anywhere except on campus, but a good rule of thumb is "use what the campus has to offer." Examples include the exercise and sports facilities, entertainment offerings, the bookstore, the dining facilities, and the library. This general practice will not only make the president seem more pervasive, but will also give him or her a consumer's-eye-view of things that work well on campus and things that don't.

Speeding up response time

Volume of activity counts, but it's only part of the equation. Another critical component of your president's job is speed. Quick response in all types of communications (for example, letters, e-mail, and phone calls) enhances your president's image in the following ways:

- Suggests that the president is an efficient manager;
- Says to the recipient, "You're important";
- Minimizes "can't-do-anything-till-we-hear-from-the-president" downtime;
- Sets a good example.

Ensuring office support

Some things in the president's office that can help enhance the new president's image:

- *Adequate staffing.* The president represents the institution more than any other individual; the office must have sufficient personnel to keep the wheels of leadership rolling.
- A *staff of efficient self-starters.* Even one staff member who has problems meeting deadlines and keeping the information flowing can detract significantly from the president's image as an energetic, effective administrator.
- *Good equipment.* This isn't the place to squeeze a couple of more years out of cast-off computers or old, unreliable laser printers. Although the hardware in your president's office shouldn't be lavish to the point that it engenders feelings of resentment around campus, up-to-date and adequately powered computing equipment and time-saving devices (such as signature machines) are wise investments.
- *Collaborative work relationships that allow other offices to support your president's office.* For example, the development office has a vested interest in timely gift acknowledgements by the president, and the admission office has a keen interest in correspondence related to student recruitment going out expeditiously over the president's signature.
- *Good screening procedures* that divert low-priority communications such as promotional mail and routine phone calls from your president to others, so that his or her time can be spent more productively.
- A *clear understanding on the part of everyone working with your new president* that timeliness is critical and that problems of slow response should be spotlighted, so they can be solved, rather than buried.

The president in print

The phrase "Put it in writing" is shorthand for "Make an official commitment to what you're saying." When you publish what you've written, you take things one step further and make even more of a commitment, especially when the material you publish is by or about your institution's leader. Before your president appears in print, great care should be taken to ensure that his or her words and images reflect well on the person who represents your institution. Look for the following elements in all material sent out by your president:

■ *Writing style reflects the personality of the president.* Those who draft messages or articles should not only say what the president wants to say, but say it the way the president would have said it. Developing this ability requires an in-depth study of materials written by the president to acquire a feel for characteristic tone and use of rhetorical devices. It also requires coaching from your president. The result will be written communications that have an authentic feel and convey a consistent sense of personality.

■ *The article, column, or message of your president stands on its own.* It's fatal to assume anyone will read it just because your president's name is on it. In fact, research suggests that the opposite is often true. In alumni magazine surveys, for example, the president's message is often rated among the least interesting features and the one most likely to be skimmed or skipped. If the piece isn't engaging and informative, the space would probably be better used for something else.

■ *Photographs are well chosen.* No one piece of photo advice fits all people. Presidents are very formal, very informal, and everything in between. Official, widely used portraits should reflect the personality of the individual. But one piece of advice applies equally to social situations and photo editing: When in doubt, do the friendliest thing. More people will react positively to a smile than any other expression. And candid photos of your president taking part in a campus activity are often more effective than his or her formal portrait.

The president in cyberspace

Many presidents are naturally wired, but they should also be connected to the Internet. Even if you measure time in nanoseconds, there are still just 168 hours in a week—use the Internet to do more, quicker. Some advantages follow:

■ *Efficiency:* E-mail can serve as a meeting replacement and also as a faster, less expensive means of mass communication. In the right context, e-mails from the president can be more effective than tree-killing, budget-busting, blind-embossed, foil-stamped, engraved announcements —lovely as they are.

■ *Research resource:* The Internet is already the place to start when you need quick information about almost anything and its resources are growing exponentially. Your president and one or more assistants should know their way around the Internet.

■ *Keeping current:* Presidents who are proficient, regular users of the Internet will be in touch with and savvy about one of the most far-reaching technological advances of the century. And they'll be able to speak the lingo and relate to increasingly wired constituencies—from prospective students to retired alumni. Conversely, presidents who aren't up to speed on the Internet will reveal this in their interactions and lose some credibility.

■ *Web site:* Your president should have a presence here—ideally both an official page with a portrait and welcome message, and a personal page that conveys a sense of your president as an individual. The personal page should have a relaxed and even whimsical feel (if this reflects your president's personality] and focus on interesting and unexpected special interests, hobbies, and other distinctive characteristics of the president.

The president as expert

One of the first things you should do in attempting to enhance your president's image is conduct an in-depth interview to determine areas in which he or she is an expert. If you have difficulty getting a block of time with your president large enough for the interview, offer to drive him or her to an upcoming out-of-town appointment and talk in the car with a tape recorder running.

You can then market the president as an expert commentator for op-ed pieces, articles, and radio or TV and other public appearances. Don Perkins, director of public relations at Wittenburg University (1970-97), counts as one of his greatest successes a presidential op-ed program that was built around his president's expertise in admissions marketing, demographics, and budgeting.

Michael Adams, president of the University of Georgia, is also an expert in several fields, including politics (early in his career he served as an aid to Senator Howard Baker and then to Tennessee Governor Lamar Alexandar), intercollegiate athletics (a lifelong interest), and the relationship between public and private higher education.

While president of Centre College (1989-97), Adams regularly appeared as a commentator on statewide public television election-night programs and published op-ed pieces on education-related political issues. He served on several NCAA committees (including gender equity and Division III policies) and successfully placed numerous articles and op-ed pieces on intercollegiate sports. In addition, he served as president of the National Association of Independent Colleges and Universities, which further added to his national reputation and made him a sought-after writer on higher education in general.

John Silber, president of Boston University (1970-96) and now its chancellor, is one of the most dramatic examples of an educational leader who used his expertise and willingness to take a stand on controversial issues to increase the visibility of his institution. A specialist in educational reform and a passionate proponent of higher standards, Silber attracted and continues to attract national attention. During his tenure as BU president, he appeared on major television news programs such as *60 Minutes, Nightline, Today,* and *Good Morning America;* wrote op-ed pieces; and was featured in articles in publications such as the *Wall Street Journal* and *New York Times.*

Nan Keohane, president of Duke University, also illustrates the benefits of speaking out on topical issues and being receptive to opportunities that arise. As the first woman president of a major research university in the South, she received significant media attention upon assuming her duties in 1993. Keohane further increased her visibility by actively opposing proposed federal budget cuts to financial aid and research funding. In 1995, as a result of her high profile, she was invited to speak at the national convention of the American Society of Newspaper Editors. She quickly accepted, only to discover she had to share the spotlight with three other featured speakers. It wasn't so bad though: They were the president of the United States, the president of Mexico, and the prime minister of Canada.

The president as performer

Most presidents will admit they have to "perform" from time to time, but some have special entertainment-oriented abilities—singing, acting, or playing a musical instrument—that are naturals for gaining media attention. There's a special fascination about seeing a person in a highly visible leadership role operating with assurance and skill in a completely different sphere.

Jerry Farley, president of Washburn University, Topeka, has a Ph.D. in higher education administration and is an acknowledged expert in education finance. He's also an accomplished character actor. Farley recently gave a presentation at a professional meeting of college and university business officers in the character of a well-known national evangelist. His message was titled "Accounting Revival." In a previous meeting of this group, Farley appeared dressed as a rapper and delivered an update on accounting principles rap-music style. *The Chronicle of Higher Education* (July 17, 1998) featured Farley in the "Money & Management " section as "one of the country's top two or three people in education finance." The first third of the article and, indeed, its main focus were on Farley's memorable in-character presentations and his success in "defying the stereotype" of the accounting expert as a dull bean-counter.

Then there is Doug Orr, president of Warren Wilson College, who performs traditional Appalachian and Scottish/Irish music. As a member of a band, he recorded a nationally recognized CD.

Leo Botstein was a symphony conductor before he was president of Bard College. Now, in addition to his presidential duties, he conducts, and attracts significant media attention when he does.

Admittedly, these individuals are the exception rather than the rule, but participating in worthy endeavors such as singing or playing in a campus ensemble, acting in a student play, or competing on a faculty-staff intramural team will help the community get to know your president on a much more human level. In addition to contributing to a good cause, the president will also help build the image of a leader who is accessible and directly engaged in the life of the institution.

Giving the president the power of research

If you regularly provide your president with sound, institution-related research findings, you will enable him or her both to appear to be and in fact be more powerful. Accurate current research enables the president:

■ To show that he or she is on top of things and acting on more than just hunches,

> " "Free gift" didn't become one of the 20th century's most printed phrases for nothing. "

■ To tell audiences important things they didn't know (and often didn't expect), and,

■ To get a firmer grasp on the reality of the institution and thereby make more informed decisions.

Valuable types of research material you can provide include the following:

■ Color-coded maps showing where students come from—and ones that show where more students should be coming from but aren't.

■ Color-coded maps showing major concentrations of alumni and other potential donors.

■ Summaries of giving trends among different geodemographic categories of alumni and friends (e.g., class year, location, major, profession).

■ Summaries of the perceptions of key constituencies (e.g., prospective students, prospective parents, alumni) of the institution.

■ Comparative information (for example, fund raising, student recruitment, endowment per student) on peer institutions, as well as on schools that you'd like to have as your peers ("aspirant institutions").

Give your president things to give to people

"Free gift" didn't become one of the 20th century's most printed phrases for nothing. Generally speaking, people like it when you give them things. This may seem overly simple, even crass. But gift giving has been a major component of human relations in most cultures throughout history, and unless your president is unusually uncomfortable with this activity, it can be very effective in areas such as fund raising, student recruitment, and simply creating goodwill and "mind share" (the foundation of market share) for your institution.

The gift you choose, of course, depends on the recipient. It may be appropriate to give a prospective major contributor a coffee-table book on your institution, while a bumper sticker or poster may be just the thing for a prospective student. A gift can also provide an occasion for a visit or something to focus on and create a comfortable atmosphere during the initial "warming-up" stage of a meeting.

One item is especially effective: Photos of the person or friends or both at an institutional party or function. This gift has the advantages of being personal, related to your school, and inexpensive. In addition, given the human tendency toward nostalgia, its value usually increases with age. And if displayed in the recipient's home or office, as is oftentimes the case, it is a more-or-less constant reminder of your institution and its thoughtfulness.

Other things the president and staff members can give away include lapel pins (again, highly visible—think of them as apparel billboards); reproductions of campus-related paintings or historical photographs; refrigerator magnets (appliance billboards); window decals; and, in fact, anything on which the school logo or nameplate can be printed, silk-screened, or sewn—again, always keeping the status and temperament of the recipient in mind.

The effect of size and type on promotional strategies

Does one set of image-enhancement guidelines apply to all—from the private liberal arts college of several hundred students to the mega public university of 40,000 or more? Or, are fundamentally different approaches required for different kinds of institutions?

Generally speaking, the principles outlined here—promote the real person, use the power of personality, derive maximum results from time invested, and employ research findings—will be helpful in enhancing the image of the president of virtually any institution. That said, there are some differences of kind and scale that should be taken into account in image-building activities.

Public vs. private

Although state government officials are important to private institutions, they are absolutely critical to public institutions since these individuals have ongoing direct involvement in funding and other crucial policy areas. And while public institutions are becoming more and more involved in fund raising to supplement their government appropriations, constituencies that provide fund-raising support obviously are most crucial for private institutions.

Issues of scale

Even if the student body and other constituencies directly connected to your institution are the size of a city rather than a village, your institution will still have just one president and he or she must make accommodations, such as the following:

- *Bigger events.* For the president of the mega-university to have the same proportional impact as the president of a smaller institution, he or she will invariably have to come in contact with more people. The president will often need to sacrifice intimacy for exposure, and he or she must learn to function effectively and comfortably in a larger arena.
- *Symbolic events.* When there are more things to do, the frequency of some events will have to be sacrificed, and they will serve a more symbolic purpose. During his tenure at Centre College, Michael Adams met with students several times a term for question-and-answer sessions. Now, as University of Georgia president, he hosts an "Open-Mic with Mike" session with students once a term. Though the demands of his schedule preclude more frequent meetings, this opportunity for students to meet him in person signals that their input is important to the administration.
- *Greater use of your president's image.* Still photos and especially video releases and TV appearances will enable your president to become known to greater numbers of people
- *Greater use of surrogates.* At the mega-university, the percentage of invitations that the president must decline because of time limitations will be greater than a small college. In these cases, it's imperative that you say "no" nicely—

that the reason for the refusal be explained, that a surrogate be offered, that appreciation for the invitation be expressed, and, if future participation is a possibility, that it be mentioned. Vice presidents, deans, and directors can fill in for your president to accommodate the large number of invitations that come to your president's office.

When the president decides to leave

Transitions are tricky. Saying goodbye to the old president requires special care. It's really the first step in introducing the new president. If handled poorly, it can make the new person's job considerably more difficult.

Here are some general principles:

- Communicate *directly* with your institution's constituents as quickly as possible. The off-campus communication is typically in the form of a letter from the board chair. As e-mail becomes pervasive, it may become an effective medium for reaching some groups faster, to be followed by the hard-copy communication.
- On-campus groups should ideally receive the communication the day before the news appears in the local newspaper. Again, e-mail may be a good supplemental medium.
- Look for ways to send and reinforce the message that a well-organized transition process is in place and that things are running smoothly.
- In your initial letter to your constituents and in subsequent communications (such as newsletters and the alumni magazine), emphasize your institution's strong senior-staff leaders.
- Evoke the history of your institution in ways that reinforce the naturalness of change and the ability of your institution to handle it successfully.

The easy situation

While no transition of leadership should be regarded as a slam dunk, some transitions present fewer pitfalls than others. For example, the successful president retiring after 20 years is easy. Here, a key challenge will be to pay appropriate tribute to the president's accomplishments without giving the impression that he or she is irreplaceable. An emphasis on the strong position in which your institution now finds itself will both acknowledge your retiring president's contributions and inspire confidence that opportunities for even greater progress lie ahead.

The tough situation

The president who is leaving after three years, in the midst of intense disputes with faculty and staff will, of course, present great challenges. In this case, you will need to:

- Strive for even greater speed of communication with key constituencies and look for every possible way to emphasize your strong senior-staff leadership and your well-defined organization of the transition process.

■ Use diplomatic language, but be candid. In discussing the rocky tenure, place it in the context of your institution's history and long-term record of successfully dealing with challenging situations. Misrepresentations will be quickly spotted by internal constituencies and conveyed to external constituencies, making a bad situation worse.

■ Boost morale with emphasis on your institution's legitimate successes and progress.

■ Stress continuity and familiar faces at your institution. This is a good time for features on popular long-time faculty members and well-known alumni leaders in the magazine and your other institutional media.

The president is key to the plan

If well-conceived, well-integrated, and well-implemented, your institution's marketing plan will give power to and enhance the image of your president, and your president will give power to the plan. It works in these three ways:

Nine Tips for Successful Speeches

Public-speaking ability is one of the key competencies large numbers of people (many of whom will never interact with your president one to one) will use to judge his or her effectiveness as a leader. As in other areas, the strengths, weaknesses, and comfort zones of the individual must always be taken into account, but the following advice applies in most situations:

1. Avoid "read" speeches. Children love to have bedtime stories read to them, but they usually respond by going to sleep. If your speech has to be read, know it so well it sounds spoken. Fred Lowy, rector of Concordia University, surprised his communications staff the first time they handed him a written speech. "You can give me a draft," he said, "but I'm not going to read it." Instead, he scans the text, makes notes, and then stands in front of his audience and talks. His presentations are so well received that the staff now has the pleasant challenge of dealing with an ever-increasing volume of speaking invitations.

2. Use humor—unless you don't have the knack (and some people don't). Anecdotes are good; personal anecdotes are better. Audiences enjoy illustrative stories in general; if the story is from the personal experience of your president, it adds an additional layer of interest. The best models of the techniques of humor are the pros—stand-up comedians. Folks who earn their living making others laugh on demand are masters of tools such as timing, economy of language, and inflection.

3. Keep your speech short; leave them wanting more instead of looking toward the door.

4. Be mobile on stage. Unless the occasion is extremely formal, don't hide behind a lectern. Movement is an effective way to maintain interest, add drama, and emphasize key points. For larger audiences, this, of course, requires a hand-held or pin-on portable microphone.

5. Know your audience. A sentimental speech about the triumphs of your institution's past may evoke tears in a 50th reunion class and yawns in a group of prospective students.

6. Use vocal variety. Monotone, monopitch, and monovolume are deadly. Vary your delivery to complement the content. A whisper, a shout, and everything in between can be effective in the correct context. One of the most memorable commencement addresses ever given at Centre College featured at one point a spirited a cappella singing of *La Marseillaise*.

7. Master public address equipment basics. Problems such as feedback, too much volume, too little volume, and distortion can wreck an otherwise great speech. Take a lesson or two from your institution's audiovisual equipment expert to learn how to avoid or correct the most common problems.

8. Don't shuffle cards. It distracts the audience and causes you to break eye contact more often. If you need notes, put everything on one piece of paper that doesn't have to be moved.

9. The beginning and the end of your speech are most important. The middle isn't unimportant, but, if time doesn't permit complete preparation, make sure you have a good "in" and a good "out."

1. An integrated marketing plan that supports the goals of a well-executed strategic planning process gives your president a sense of focus that will enable him or her to interact more effectively with all major constituencies. If the planning process has had widespread participation and met the key goal of achieving broad consensus, it also minimizes disagreements and conflicts about resources.

2. The president, like no other person, can validate the plan, promote it, and empower the individuals implementing it. If your president's image is strong—that is, he or she is highly visible, esteemed, and perceived as a can-do leader with vision—the success of the marketing plan, and more broadly the strategic plan, will be much more likely.

3. When an able, highly regarded president converges with a well-conceived marketing plan and the broad consensus that emerges from a successful, ongoing strategic planning process, a feeling envelopes your institution that's palpable. It's a shared sense of clarity, united purpose, and excitement as your institution moves forward.

In my 20 years in higher education, I've been privileged to experience several such periods of focused synergy, but one in particular comes to mind. In the latter half of Richard Morrill's Centre College presidency (1982-88), after an intense period of strategic planning, a consultant came on campus to evaluate the general functioning of the college. His report was brief and summed up in one sentence: "At this point in the college's history, everyone seems to be in the same boat, rowing in the same direction." This conclusion came as no surprise to anyone, though we all enjoyed the third-party validation.

These are the times when institutions can make rapid and remarkable progress. The key to getting everyone on board and rowing together is a leader who both is and is perceived to be strong, energetic, and respected. This is the ultimate reason for enhancing the president's image: Not to advance an individual, but to advance your institution.

What a president can do that affects his or her image

When you look at things that can possibly affect a president's image in basic terms, the list is surprisingly short. But the additional opportunities under each heading are infinite. A consideration of this set of elemental activities is a good place to start when you're thinking strategically about ways to enhance your president's image.

To affect his or her image, your president can:

- Speak to individuals or groups in person.
- Communicate interactively with individuals or groups via electronic media such as the phone, e-mail, chat rooms, or video conferencing.
- Appear in print.
- Appear on TV.
- Appear in videos or films.
- Be heard on radio.
- Be represented on the Web.
- Be described or referred to by third parties (word-of-mouth). This is not, of course, something your president "does" directly, but you should expect that almost everything your president says or does will be recommunicated to some extent by third parties.

Recommended Readings

1994 Symposium for the Marketing of Higher Education. Chicago: American Marketing Association, 1994.

Fisher, James L. "Great Expectations: What the President Expects of the PR Director and What You Should Expect in Return." CURRENTS, 6, no. 9 (October 1980): 15-17.

Fisher, James L. *The Power of the Presidency.* Phoenix, AZ: ACE/Macmillan Publishing Co., 1984.

Keller, George. "Helping Your President Understand PR." CURRENTS, 6, no. 9 (October 1980):20.

Melchiori, Gerlinda S. "Managing Institutional Image." *Journal for Higher Education Management,* 6, no. 1, (Summer–Fall) 1990:45-58.

Pappas, Richard J. *Strategic Marketing for Presidents.* Washington DC: American Association of Community Colleges (Community College Press), 1994.

Perkins, Donald R. "Marketing Your Own Iacocca: How You Can Get Media Mileage For Your President." CURRENTS, 9, no. 8 (September 1983):22-24.

Sevier, Robert A. "Image Is Everything: Strategies for Measuring, Changing, and Maintaining Your Institution's Image." *College and University,* 69, no. 2 (Winter 1994):60-75.

Sevier, Robert A. *Integrated Marketing for Colleges, Universities, and Schools: A Step-by-Step Planning Guide.* Washington DC: Council for Advancement and Support of Education, 1998.

Topor, Robert S. *Institutional Image: How to Define, Improve, Market It.* Washington DC: Council for Advancement and Support of Education, 1986.

9

Building a Message-Driven Media Relations Plan

Harry Battson

How does your news bureau or media relations office fit into an integrated marketing communications program for your institution? How can you get outside news media, which so often seem to respond to the whims of the world, to help you deliver the messages that form the core of your institution's marketing efforts? The answer, of course, is that the processes used in developing an effective media relations program often mirror the processes used in developing your larger integrated marketing communications strategy—listening to your audiences, building relationships, and consistently communicating your messages to targeted, segmented audiences.

Historically, news bureaus or media relations offices in academic institutions have drawn the majority of staff members from the ranks of practicing journalists. Why? Because these former journalists have an innate understanding of what stories, what events, what pitches would most excite newspaper, magazine, and television reporters and editors and thus result in news coverage. From an integrated marketing communications vantage point, this ability remains vital. Any successful media program must understand the needs of the news media in its multiple formats and deliver material to each medium according to its needs. The ability to do that consistently over time leads reporters and editors to see that they can count on your institution's news bureau to provide the goods—real news—opening ever-expanding media opportunities for you.

The ability to understand the needs of the news media and to provide information, or a faculty expert, to meet those needs leads to a partnership that ultimately serves both your institution and the media. Today's media relations professional understands that building and maintaining such partnerships are the keys to obtaining good media coverage of a series of university programs, events, or activities, rather than a single episode. The media relations professional also understands that your institution will benefit from such relationships in times of trouble as well, because the news media will trust the institution to provide accurate and timely information. The news bureau has helped to create an image of the institution that should, at the least, establish the initial framework for covering any news story on your campus.

Marketing as communication

Many news bureau/public information officers object to any connection with "marketing communications." They perceive their task as one of obtaining legitimate news coverage about the institution's programs and people. They promote the institution, but they also perceive this promotion as being based on obtaining news coverage of substance and significance, not on "marketing fluff."

Their ability to provide the media with "hard" news, supported by data and enhanced by experts, gives them the aura of credibility needed to pitch future stories successfully to their media contacts. If the word "marketing" enters this relationship, it could damage their credibility—they could be perceived as part of a sales team rather than as information officers. For that reason, many media relations personnel may resist joining an "integrated marketing communication" effort. Convincing the news bureau staff to become partners on the team could be an early challenge to your initiative.

The traditional model

The traditional approach to this issue would be to show the news bureau officers how their becoming part of the integrated marketing communications team will increase their effectiveness, provide them with valuable resources (research data, information leads on priority programs, etc.) and ultimately lead to increased recognition and improved reputation. This approach leaves your organization intact but begins to tap the expertise of the news bureau staff in the development stages, rather than as an afterthought.

For instance, if your institution decides to begin a weekend MBA program at a downtown location to serve the business community, the media relations staff will join the marketing and publications staff in meeting with the MBA faculty and administrators while the program is still in development. Each member of the team will examine the issue from his or her perspective. The media relations team member will look for the news value of this program and begin to hone the messages and consider which media will be receptive. He or she may have suggestions about the program, or may volunteer to draft the copy for the brochure or advertising. If the MBA site is being remodeled, the media relations member may ask for a production schedule and try to interest a news photographer. He or she may then propose that the key administrator appear on a local talk show, and follow up with the arrangements or draft an op-ed piece on the changing nature of MBA programs. All of these suggestions and activities would be integrated into the total team plan developed with the publications and marketing staff members and then implemented with the MBA faculty and administrators.

A new model

An alternative approach to integrating the news bureau staff is based on structural reorganization. This idea was detailed in the January 1998 CURRENTS article, "The Day We Closed the News Bureau: How Indiana University Survived the Switch from Promotions-Oriented PR to Integrated Marketing." Christopher Simpson, IU's vice president for public affairs and government relations, discussed a reorganization that brought the news bureau into a new Office of Communications and Marketing. The news bureau staff members found that their specific jobs remained about 75 percent the same, but that they spent 25 percent of their time learning new ways to reach key audiences and then executing those "marketing communications" abilities. This approach is more drastic in the sense that it forces the staff members to give up identification as "news bureau" members or public information officers in favor of an identity as a member of the "communications and marketing" team. By establishing a new and different organization, this approach hopes to establish a new mindset and way of acting more quickly. Either approach can work, as long as the staff members understand the goals and dedicate themselves to implementing a marketing communications team approach.

Table 9-1 outlines some differences between a traditional media relations program and a program that is committed to integrated marketing communication.

A media relations plan for your integrated marketing communications program

Your media relations plan should follow the same format and guidelines as those of your overall integrated marketing communications program. You already have identified your key audiences and examined audience research. You have established your communication goals and clarified vivid descriptors. You have developed the big idea to drive your creative efforts. Just as your overall plan outlines a media mix, your media relations plan needs to define

Before IMC	After IMC
Institution releases segmented stories piecemeal with little relationship to college or university messages or priorities.	Staff seeks opportunities to promote planned messages linked to larger marketing efforts.
Institution views news as insular, shared with media or others by chance.	News staff participates in team development of total communications package for identified priority.
Institution highlights unconnected individual faculty or stories, hoping for cumulative impact without consistent theme.	Institution highlights its strengths consistently with common language designed to improve institution's image.
Institution pitches hundreds of unrelated stories.	Institution develops concerted plan for targeted stories supporting a specific communication theme.
Institution measures success by counting clips or newsprint inches.	Institution measures success by ability to reach targeted audiences, and achieve image and positioning results based on periodic research measures.

Table 9-1
Before and After Integrated Marketing Communication

more specifically the media opportunities that match your goals and audiences. And you need a mechanism to evaluate your media successes and a method for modifying future media efforts to achieve even greater successes. With these points in mind, we suggest the following steps for developing an integrated marketing-based media plan:

- Recast your audiences according to media.
- Research the gatekeepers.
- Research your institution.
- Build a media event planning calendar.
- Extend the media event calendar into a theme-based calendar.
- Assign specific duties to each of your media team members.
- Evaluate your successes and inform all parties involved.

1. Recast your audiences according to media.

News media reporters and editors are the gatekeepers. You must get them to open their gates to reach additional audiences—their subscribers/viewers/listeners. If your overall program identifies specific target audiences (and it should), the media relations plan should identify specific media to reach those populations. For example, if African American parents of high school-aged children in the Chicago area are a primary target audience for your integrated marketing communications program, your media relations plan needs to identify what publications, news programs, and public affairs shows are most capable of getting the key messages to that audience. Audiences need to be defined according to the media that will reach them, which in turn, identifies the media gate-keepers you must target.

At this point, you should assign an individual or team to the audiences identified in your overall marketing communications plan and research the psychographic data that link these audiences to specific media. A chart developed for each audience would look like Table 9-2.

Reaching the Audiences: African American Parents of High School Students

Media	Penetration	Priority
Chicago Tribune	47.4 percent	1
WGN 6:00 p.m. News	31.3 percent	2
Chicago Sun-Times	28.2 percent	3
The Black Defender	24.7 percent	4
WCHI 11:00 p.m. News	22.1 percent	5
Chicago Today TV Show	19.6 percent	6
WILL-FM Drive News	17.3 percent	7
Ebony Magazine	16.2 percent	8
WCHI-AM Sports Talk	15.5 percent	9
Newsweek	14.9 percent	10

Note: Not actual data.

Table 9-2
Linking Audiences to Specific Media

Such a chart provides a listing of key media for reaching this target audience. A compilation of such charts for all key audiences could provide a ranking of targeted media that would be most likely to reach the largest number of those people you wish to influence. The media team's objective is to place stories with the top priority media consistently—e.g., *Chicago Tribune*, WGN 6:00 p.m. News, and *Chicago Sun-Times*.

2. Research the gatekeepers.

In introducing this chapter, we noted that many university news bureau practitioners are chosen from the ranks of journalists because they understand what makes news. However, every news medium sets its own priorities and approach to the news. To assume that a well-developed news sense enables us to anticipate what will flow through the gatekeepers to the target audience can be a grievous error. At this stage, it is critical that we cast aside assumptions and research the gatekeepers.

The most effective media research is a one-on-one discussion, possibly over lunch or in a relaxed setting. Have a prepared list of questions. Television news is driven by local audience assessments where topics like education, the environment, and health care are regularly monitored and ranked. If you learn that WGN's top priority for the year is education, particularly issues surrounding minority student success, you have the fulcrum you need to move the market from a news perspective. If personal one-on-one discussions are not feasible for all your potential media targets, use the telephone or e-mail to do a quick check on specific media priorities and interests. Then compile a list of those media whose priorities best match your university's message priorities. This list of media should be prime targets for your message materials.

3. Research your institution.

In Step 4 of your integrated marketing communication plan, you created a list of vivid descriptors that you want your target audiences to know about your institution. For your media plan, you need to compile a list of programs and activities that support those descriptors. The University of South Florida, for instance, defines itself as a catalyst for economic development in the Tampa Bay region. Its programmatic examples include the following:

- ■ A College of Engineering initiative to attract and support microchip companies;
- ■ A grant from the Department of Defense to convert an abandoned military base into an entrepreneurial center;
- ■ The launch of a biotech initiative with the Tampa Chamber of Commerce to bring new health-related industries to Tampa locations near the College of Medicine;
- ■ A partnership with the Tampa Port Authority to open an international business center at a new downtown facility;
- ■ The creation of an entrepreneurial center to teach business and engineering students how to take new ideas and build them into new businesses;
- ■ A ranking in the top 50 for U.S. public universities attracting research dollars.

A list of concrete programs and examples that support vivid descriptors can become the basis for stories and ideas to pitch to targeted media. Each vivid descriptor should have at least 20 to 30 specific examples to support it.

Typically, media relations staff members attempt to respond to every request for news coverage assistance. Frequently, that means spending valuable staff time on marginal efforts of little consequence to the institution's overall health or well-being. Researching your institution also means making sure that the areas you promote fit your overall marketing communications strategy.

It is important to mention that your media relations team should seek out opportunities to publicize your institution's strengths in accord with your communications strategy, not just answer requests or just issue a lot of news releases. After converting from a news bureau to a communications and marketing office, the number of news releases at Indiana University dropped from 554 to 321 a year, or to about 60 percent of the previous volume. Presumably, this means that, rather than churning out releases that were insignificant or less vital to building the desired image of the institution, more time was focused on promoting the programs and activities that fit the overall strategies and messages.

4. Build a media event planning calendar.

Every institution has annual events that provide opportunities for getting messages out to targeted audiences. Build an academic year calendar that highlights those events and dates, and then develop a list of possible ways to use that list for furthering the marketing communications plan. For example, Gettysburg College has positioned itself as a leader in government policy analysis and has held international conferences on global political issues. Anticipating the scheduling of these conferences enables the media relations staff to develop materials in advance that support the college's marketing communications program.

> **Without specific assignments, your plan will falter.**

Other activities may offer lesser opportunities, but developing and maintaining a calendar enables the news staff to use all the resources available: the first day of class, an annual presidential address or convocation, homecoming, commencements, major lecturers and conferences, anniversaries, and ethnic celebrations like Hispanic Heritage Week.

5. Extend your media event calendar into a theme-based calendar.

In addition to developing ways to send your vivid descriptor messages through already scheduled activities, designate weeks for getting out news stories and pitches on specific themes related to vivid descriptors alone.

For example, using the University of South Florida economic development theme mentioned above, you could plan to release a series of materials that support economic development over a set time period. If the president's annual "state of the institution" address is scheduled for September 15, use that as a kickoff since he or she will speak at length about some of these initiatives. Then schedule the release of a university news tip or business story about another economic development initiative each Monday through Thanksgiving. The trick is to intersperse these tips and stories with news conferences or photo opportunities or other mechanisms that spark the interest of the media. Your goal is to create a succession of media stories with a common theme.

Although the media covers each lead as an independent news story, the overall message getting to the target audience in this case is that USF is a partner in fostering the community's economic development. The media themselves (with a gentle nudge from you) should start to see the string of stories as the basis for an editorial opinion or as television lead-ins to the latest developments. Altogether, you have orchestrated a drumbeat of messages that have pushed this vivid descriptor into the path of your target audience consistently week after week.

A variation is to ally yourself with a top media outlet and convince it to do a series of articles or television pieces, perhaps on three successive Sundays. USF encouraged the

Tampa Tribune to examine the efforts of peer universities with research and economic development initiatives similar to theirs, resulting in a series of articles showing the institution's initiatives and the potential positive impact on the community. When preparing a special television program on preventing teen violence, USF partnered with a local television affiliate for a "Town Hall" forum to follow the broadcast. Such partnerships provide the media with an opportunity to show in-depth involvement in an issue important to the community while also helping to convey the desired message.

6. Assign specific duties to each team member.
You've identified the target publications and broadcast programs to reach specific target audiences. You know which media representatives are most receptive to your message-driven stories. You've developed the list of programs that support your vivid descriptors and the event and theme calendars to schedule your media activities. Now it's paramount that you assign specific activities to each news bureau or media relations member of your team. Without specific assignments, no accountability is possible.

Whether your news group is organized by "beats" or by media, each event on the calendar needs to be assigned. The staff member needs to know the vivid descriptor being highlighted, the target audience to be reached, and which publications and broadcasts are most likely to reach those audiences. He or she needs a plan for each event, ranging from distributing public service announcements (PSAs) and tip sheets to developing feature stories or op-ed pieces, from staging a news conference to taking a principal player at your institution to lunch with the right reporter or editor.

Without specific assignments, your plan will falter. By making sure that each team member knows his or her responsibilities and timelines, you turn the program into an action agenda guaranteed to produce positive results.

7. Evaluate your successes and inform all parties.
Media relations is an ongoing activity. The plans, particularly the calendars, need perpetual updating. As news issues rise and fall, the gatekeepers at the various media must be monitored to make sure that opportunities are not being missed and that your institution is still driving messages that match media priorities. The primary measurement should be whether media staff were successful in obtaining coverage in the top targeted publications or on the top broadcast programs for each targeted audience. A secondary measure would determine what impact that media coverage delivered. A quarterly, or at least annual, report of the success of the media plan should go to the president and other university leadership. It is vital to your continuing efforts that the president and his or her top advisers know the plan and recognize its success.

With this seven-step format in place, your media relations team can play an integral and vital role in your marketing communications program. Additional components of a successful media relations strategy—a media training program, a media mailing system, use of a national agency, and tips for gaining media interest—are addressed below.

A media training program

Preparing your top administrators and faculty to deal effectively with the news media requires advance preparation and training. With help from your own mass communications or journalism faculty members, you should be able to set up an annual training program that is both low-cost and effective. Agree in advance with your faculty on how the program will be conducted. It is very important that the faculty understand your goals. If you don't wish to use your own faculty, an outside consultant can provide the expertise and credibility you need.

A typical format would have eight to 10 trainees each receiving at least one personal media experience that covers the gamut—a television interview, talk show, live remote radio on-air interview, news conference, or print-style interview. You may even want to include "ambush"-type interviews, particularly in aggressive media markets. By exposing the group to various forms of media interviews, you can emphasize conditions that enable trainees to get their messages across most effectively. Trainees learn, for example, that on a live television broadcast you don't even have to answer the reporter's question directly but, with a quick slide transition, can move directly to the message that you want to get across. Trainee interviews should be videotaped and immediately played back for comments, not only from the faculty, but also from the other participants. Participants should receive coaching in advance, particularly in forming messages that fit your marketing communications program. The major purpose of this exercise is to familiarize top administrators and faculty with your institution's marketing communications messages and with the news media as well.

Here's what you'll need to do to start a media training program:

■ Identify an initial group for a pilot program. At one institution, the student affairs directors—admissions, residence life, financial aid, student activities, and similar department heads—provided the pilot program. As frequent interview subjects, they were an ideal group. At another institution, the vice presidents and top administrators formed the pilot group.

■ Arrange a favorable location for recording and playing back the interviews. Line up the technical staffing through mass communications or your television studio. A recording studio is usually the ideal location.

■ Prepare a handout that summarizes quick media tips and outlines the marketing communications messages. Kansas State University's "When the Media Call" has separate sections on print, radio, and television, and gives short, basic tips to faculty. Send the handout with the letter confirming each participant's attendance. A wallet-sized laminated card provides a handy reference.

■ Write an individualized scenario for each participant. The scenario could be an actual situation that occurred at your institution, or a likely scenario based on something that has happened elsewhere. The more realistic the situation, the better the scenario usually plays out. It's important that all the players—the participant and the interviewer—have a good understanding of the scenario.

■ Involve enough faculty and staff to handle the training program. If you or

> " Trainee interviews should be videotaped and immediately played back for comments, not only from the faculty, but also from the other participants. "

your staff prepared the scenarios, you may want to be the coaches who prepare the participants to answer media questions and formulate their key messages. You will likely play the role of coach anyway in the event of a major news interview.

It's always a good idea to provide coffee and rolls in the morning training sessions and soft drinks and cookies in the afternoon. Include a luncheon with one or more local media representatives as speakers or panelists. Media representatives often reinforce information from your sessions, and participants enjoy the chance to ask questions, such as "Why is the evening newscast only broadcasting bad news?" This interchange frequently is perceived as a highlight of the event.

After the training program is completed, follow up with a survey of participants (or just sound them out individually) about the value of the experience and whether they would recommend it for others. The ideal situation is to follow up annually with a refresher that is less intense.

The objective is to make your top administrators and faculty more confident and more comfortable in answering media requests and interviews and more capable of weaving the marketing communications messages into their media responses. Criticism should focus on the positives and better ways for getting the defined messages across to the reporter and ultimately to your audience. Another advantage of the training program is its ability to help you identify individuals you don't want to put in front of the media—a poor public speaker, for example, or someone who is unfocused or too eager to provide information, even to the point of providing speculation. You need to be confident that the person you're using to brief the media will represent your institution positively and convey the appropriate image as well as the proper message.

The reporter can answer many of these questions, but News Services may also be able to help get answers as well as provide you with information about unfamiliar reporters, magazines, television shows or radio programs. We are also here to help you prepare for the interview if needed. News Services does NOT, however, grant "permission" to speak to the media—that decision that is entirely up to the individual contacted by the media.

A special case—your president

Ideally, the first person to go through your media training program will be the president of your institution. For the president, I recommend a half-day commitment with an outside media consultant. Your president is your most important spokesperson. It is vital that he or she deal effectively with the media, make a positive impression on television as well as in print, and communicate the institution's marketing communications messages. The president, however, is likely to believe that he or she already knows how to handle the media or cannot afford the time for media training, and he or she certainly does not want to be placed in a position of "performing" for vice presidents, other faculty, staff, or administrators, including you. So selling your president on a media training program may be a challenge.

When A Reporter Calls, What Do I Do?

First, decide whether you will grant the interview. To help you decide, here are some questions to ask:

- What is the subject of the interview?
- Are you the appropriate person to answer questions about the topic?
- Who is the reporter and where does he/she work?
- What will be the format of the interview? Live? Taped? Telephone? Is it a feature story, or a news story?
- Where will the interview be conducted and how long will the interview be?
- What is the reporter's deadline?

Preparing for the interview

1. **Outline your main points:** Make a list of three to five main points you would like to make during the interview. These points should each be a brief as possible — you should be able to say each of them in 20 seconds or less. Reporters are looking for quotable quotes, punchy lines that can be lifted for a "quote box" in print, or a "sound bite" of air time. Make sure you get across your main points even if you have to repeat them several times.

2. **Background:** Because it is impossible to convey all the information you would like to convey in 20-second bites, handouts and background sheets are very helpful. Reporters appreciate having ample background material, and if your topic is complex, it is crucial to have handouts for reporters. This can be in the form of a prepared press release, a brochure, historical background, a fact sheet, or statistics. Reporters love facts and figures that will lend credibility to their stories, but don't exaggerate figures or use superlatives

to make something sound more impressive than it really is.

3. **Anticipate hard questions:** Make a list of questions you'd rather NOT answer, and then think about how you might best answer them. Also think about how you might transition from answering the tough questions into making one of your key points. News Services staff members can help you anticipate and prepare for tough questions.

The Interview, Some Dos and Don'ts

1. **You are the boss.** Take the initiative, don't wait for the reporter to ask the questions. Remember your three to five key points, and begin making them right off the bat, even if it means going beyond the question you've been asked.

2. **This is NOT a conversation!** This is an interview and an exchange of information. You should not feel obligated to keep a conversation going, and resist the urge to go beyond the scope of your subject. Beware of the reporter who remains silent and waits for you to ramble or divulge more information than you intend. Also, don't let an interviewer put words in your mouth. Your answer will appear in print or on the air, the reporter's question probably won't. Be quick to correct misstatements made by the interviewer — diplomatically, but firmly.

3. **Don't go off the record.** Even though a reporter may agree that your comments won't be attributed to you personally, that information may eventually end up in print if it is confirmed by other sources. If you don't want to read it in the paper, don't say it.

Courtesy of North Carolina State University.

The president of one institution, who embraced the program for his vice presidents, deans, and others, refused to participate himself. He finally agreed when I indicated that his leadership was important for ensuring that other top administrators would participate. Noting that even presidents of the United States often spend hours preparing and rehearsing for media appearances also can illustrate how important this function is. I have had presidents who did not want even me to see them put through their paces, but I also have had presidents who wanted me to be an active participant in offering suggestions for improvement.

Note: More information on presidential image-enhancement strategies appears in Chapter 8.

Collecting information to publicize

Faculty, staff, and students don't always automatically think first about contacting the media relations or news bureau staff to publicize their most recent event, activity, or

4. **Be brief and to the point.** Remember your three to five main points and make an effort to convey those points in 20 seconds or so. If there is one key message, say it in different ways, more than once. For television, about 45 seconds of response time is the maximum you will be given to make your point.

5. **Tell the truth.** Sometimes the truth hurts, but lies hurt worse and for a longer time. Your credibility and that of your institution could be at stake.

6. **If you don't know, don't speculate.** Simply refer the person to the appropriate office or to News Services if you are unsure. Sometimes reporters will not distinguish between a personal opinion and the university's position, so it will be up to you to set the record straight. If you are the spokesman for an official committee, campus organization or group, identify yourself as speaking for that group. Faculty and staff are free to give their personal opinions to reporters, but if you don't know the university's position on a particular issue, find out or refer the reporter to the appropriate source — don't speculate.

7. **Be friendly; after all it's an interview, not an interrogation.** Try to establish rapport with the reporter and be positive and courteous at all times. Never argue with a reporter, and avoid defensive answers. A combative answer or hostile body language makes great TV, but could be embarrassing to you professionally and to the university.

8. **It's alright to make a mistake.** If you have made a mistake on camera or in an interview, or if you find that you've strayed seriously from the question asked, simply stop and correct the mistake, or ask if you can give another response. Most TV reporters will prefer your new, briefer quote.

9. **In TV or radio interviews, be aware that the electronics may be rolling at all times.** Assume that if you're in the studio, everything you say is being recorded.

10. **Anecdotes and humor have their place.** Use them, when appropriate, to liven up a story, to add a human angle.

After the interview

1. **Ask the reporter what he/she sees as the "real" story.** This can give you a second chance to correct misimpressions or restate your key messages.

2. **Don't ask to "approve" the reporter's story in advance.** Reporters rarely agree to let you see their story, but many will allow you to review details or quotes for accuracy.

3. **It's okay to ask when the story will run, but don't expect to always get the answer.** Most reporters simply don't know when the story will run because the decision is made by their editors. News Services can often find out for you, if the story has been scheduled for a later time. We can also obtain videos or clippings on request.

4. **Mistakes.** Newspapers routinely run corrections, but they try to avoid it. If the mistake is very minor, it's probably best to let it go rather than risk bringing more attention to the error. Serious mistakes, misconceptions, and unbalanced stories should be brought to the reporter's attention. If the reporter is not responsive, the problem should be taken up with the reporter's editor. News Services can help in dealing with these problems, and in deciding whether to ask for a formal correction or whether a follow up story, letter to the editor, or other response is appropriate.

achievement. Here are some suggested ways to keep that information flowing to your office:

- ■ Call or visit primary campus newsmakers regularly. Just chatting, and working in phrases like "what are you up to these days," can lead to exciting revelations.

- ■ Get department heads and deans to forward photocopies of information reports to you. Faculty have to keep their academic leaders informed of their teaching, research, and service productivity, and those reports can lead you to the kinds of targeted stories you want.

- ■ Run a faculty-staff recognition column in your internal newsletter. Faculty will send information about their latest publication or professional presentation, which could be just what you're looking for.

- ■ Create forms that departments can use to send in the latest information about student awards, faculty awards, and other honors and achievements. This information is particularly useful for news releases to hometown media.

■ Publish a guide on dealing with the news media and distribute it broadly on campus. The guide's first instruction : If you think you have a newsworthy story, contact the Media Relations Office. The second instruction : When contacted by a member of the news media, immediately inform the Media Relations Office.

Media contacts—a changing science

In times gone by, a mailing list of key media contacts was fairly simple to maintain and administer. Every news release was tagged for key higher education reporters, and releases on special topics—business, performing arts, health—were distributed to the editors or reporters who specifically covered those areas. Today, the means of getting information into the hands of the right reporter or editor is often more complicated. However, here are a few ideas to help you reach your media contacts:

■ Call to pitch important stories, then fax or e-mail pertinent information. Keep your phone calls short—reporters are busy.

■ Fax releases instead of mailing them. Generally, it's cheaper and faster and just as likely to get picked up.

Recommended Readings

Balik, Susan. "Media Training: Boot Camp for Communicators." *Communication World,* 12, no. 7 (June-July, 1995): 22-25.

"Best Practices Study Pinpoints Effective Communications Approaches." *PR Reporter,* 40, no. 13 (March 31, 1997):1.

Budd, John F. Jr. *How to Get Along with the Press...and Why: A Street Savvy Guide for Legislators.* Lakeville, CT: Turtle Publishing Company, 1995.

Building Support for Your Communications Programs: A CASE Issues Paper for Advancement Professionals, No. 21. Washington DC: Council for Advancement and Support of Education, 1995.

"Developing a PR Plan," *CASE Answer File.* Washington, DC: Council for Advancement and Support of Education, 1988.

"How to Conduct A Communications Audit." *CASE Answer File.* Washington DC: Council for Advancement and Support of Education, 1986.

Caywood, Clarke L. *The Handbook of Strategic Public Relations & Integrated Communications.* New York: McGraw-Hill Publishers, 1997.

Dilenschneider, Robert L. *Dartnell's Public Relations Handbook,* 4th ed. Chicago: Dartnell Corporation, 1997.

"Experts: In Devising a Media Strategy, Making Sense of New and Old Media Still Impossible." *PR Reporter,* 40, no. 42 (October 27, 1997): 1-2.

Harrison, Walter. "Getting Past the Gatekeepers: How to Stop Being a Pest and Start Getting Your News into Print." CURRENTS, 17, no. 1 (January 1991): 34-40.

Honnert, Gary T. "Video News Releases: Slick, Newsy Videos are Flooding TV Newsrooms. Will Yours Stand Out?" CURRENTS, 15, no. 3 (March 1989): 30-34, 36-37.

Hunt, Todd. *Public Relations Techniques,* 2nd ed. Fort Worth, TX: Harcourt Brace College Publishers, 1999.

"Items to Consider in Creating a 'Surgical' Media Strategy." PR Reporter, 41, no. 17 (May 4, 1998): 1-2.

Kotler, Philip and Karen Fox. *Strategic Marketing for Educational Institutions.* Englewood Cliffs, NJ: Prentice Hall Publishers, 1995.

Ketchum Public Relations. *A Guide to Public Relations Research.* New York: Ketchum Public Relations Worldwide, 1998.

Lesly, Philip. *Lesly's Handbook of Public Relations and Communications.* New York: AMACOM, 1991.

Malaspina, Rick. "High Tech PR: Five Case Studies in Computerized Communication." CURRENTS, 19, no. 4, (April 1993): 14-23.

Netherton, Robin. "Face to Face: An Expert Argues That One-on-One Communication is the Single Defining Factor in Public Relations Success." CURRENTS, 21, no. 5 (May 1995): 8-11.

Osborn, Bill. "Agency for Hire: Secrets of Successful Relationships Between Campus PR Pros and Media Relations Consultants," *CURRENTS,* 17, no. 5 (May 1991): 14-19.

Public Management Institute. *Successful Public Relations Techniques.* San Francisco: Public Management Institute, 1980.

Simpson, Christopher. "The Day We Closed the News Bureau: How Indiana University Survived the Switch From Promotions-oriented PR to Integrated Marketing." CURRENTS, 24, no. 1 (January 1998):26-32.

Simpson, Kristen. "Get Set for Media Training: Preparing Your Professors to Master Interviews" CURRENTS, 23, no. 4 (April 1997):43-45.

Williams, Roger L. "How'm I Doing?: A Survey of Editors Can Help You Fine-tune Your Public Relations Program." CURRENTS, 12, no. 4 (April 1986):28-31.

10

Crisis Communication

Harry Battson

" Possibly more has been written about crisis communications than any other single aspect of media relations. "

It happened:

- An earthquake hit a state university, destroying or damaging large numbers of buildings and almost totally knocking out communications.
- An animal rights activist infiltrated a research facility and took records, photographs, and videotapes of unsightly experiments on dogs and rabbits.
- A fraternity student died from excessive drinking related to a Greek organization induction ceremony.
- A campus received both a bomb and murder threat in the wake of a revelation that a former adjunct faculty member had emerged as the leader of an Islamic jihad terrorist organization.

All these instances spawned a crisis reaction on the part of the leaders of the affected academic institutions. Each situation was very different, requiring an individualized response. Each situation was a serious threat to the continuing mission of the respective institution. And each situation had the potential to affect the image of the institution for years, even decades.

Possibly more has been written about crisis communications than any other single aspect of media relations. This is due as much to its sudden, unexpected—often catastrophic—nature as from its potential consequences—the closing of a college or university, the loss of legislative and public support, even the filing of criminal charges against individuals connected to the institution. As noted in *Tips & Tactics*, the how-to bulletin of public relations methods and procedures (a supplement of *PR Reporter*), "Crisis managers who have endured the crucible of coping with a crisis have seen the soul of their organizations, and . . . their own, exposed for better and for worse."

Yet crisis communications at its core is no different from other forms of media relations activity. It requires prompt, clear communications messages. It requires handling communications activities in ways that reflect the mission and values of your institution and the public relations profession. It requires integrating your crisis communications posture with your long-term marketing communications goals.

Planning ahead

Communications experts debate the merits of developing a comprehensive crisis communication plan. Still you must do some advance planning to meet the challenges that occur during a crisis most effectively. The amount of effort involved, along with the distinctiveness of each crisis situation, argue against attempting to define every possible contingency. On the other hand, not having any crisis procedures established leaves you vulnerable not only to media questioning but also to an inability to be part of the crisis solution process. A middle ground ensures crisis preparedness but does not require the significant effort you could invest in a fully detailed crisis response plan that—if you're fortunate!—may never be needed.

The following four steps, identified and worked out in advance, will provide the basics for crisis preparedness:

■ Clarify who is the chief spokesperson.
■ Establish communication ground rules.
■ Create a back-up communication system.
■ Coordinate communication among staff.

Clarify who is the chief spokesperson

From the outset, you must clarify with your president and vice presidents that you, as the chief public relations person, are the primary spokesperson in any type of crisis, from natural disasters to high crimes, from student demonstrations to the arrest of a star athlete. As the chief spokesperson, you need to be at the center of any crisis management team and you need to be fed information by the principals as soon as facts become available. It is your job, not theirs, to determine what needs to be released to the media and the public. The classic way to establish this information link is through a telephone tree system where you are alerted to the situation at the same time as the president or immediately thereafter.

Establish communication ground rules

The next step is to establish ground rules for releasing information consistent with the policies and regulations of your institution as well as those of appropriate federal and

> **" Crisis managers who have endured the crucible of coping with a crisis have seen the soul of their organizations, and . . . their own, exposed for better and for worse. "**

state agencies. Know your applicable regulations. Have that information at hand and be able to recite chapter and verse on the release of information about students, faculty, and staff or other affected individuals. Again, you will need to take the lead at any crisis management team meeting in determining what information to release and on what grounds.

Create a back-up communication system

A natural disaster such as an earthquake could destroy your normal communication systems and make your office inaccessible. Have an alternative communication system identified and ready to use. That system could be set up through your institution's police force, the central switchboard, or a mobile network of communications based on cellular phones.

Coordinate communication among staff during a crisis

You must make sure your staff has a system devised for emergency communication with you and with each other. Each member should have a wallet-sized card that provides the telephone numbers (personal office, home, and cell or pager) for your institution president, you, and every other staff member.

During a crisis, staff members generally will continue to assume responsibilies similar to their daily tasks. But if you expect any of them to assume special responsibilities in a crisis, define those in advance. For instance, the person who puts news releases on the Web page may need to construct an emergency Web site him or herself rather than wait on help from the computer staff. One alternative is to send information to faculty and staff through e-mail. If you don't already have such a system for other types of messages, developing an e-mail or fax alert system to key college or university supporters and audiences should be done in advance also. The person charged with sending those messages should have the same responsibility during a crisis.

Determining that there is a crisis

When a crisis first emerges, no matter its nature, there is a sense of astonishment, disbelief, and uncertainty. The first task of anyone involved in media relations aspects of crisis communication is to identify that a crisis indeed is occurring or has occurred and swing into action to discover the facts. Without facts, a communication plan cannot be devised, the extent of the crisis cannot be determined, and a method for integrating the crisis messages into the institution's overall communications plan cannot be developed. In short, you need the facts to develop your messages for your target audiences.

The call for information

The first reaction to a perceived crisis is always a call for information—what has happened, to whom, where, what actions are you taking, how will it affect me, why? It is not inconceivable you may first learn of a crisis through the news media, along with their questions for your immediate response. The key is to tell them you will get the information and get back to them as soon as possible.

Often you may be tempted to speculate, or to assume this situation is similar to a previous one and make a parallel reference. Don't! Decline to comment until you have a chance to learn the particulars of the case. Also, make sure your answers adhere to your institution's policies and state and federal regulations. Provide the facts. If you can, provide a context for the facts that will align the situation with your institution's marketing communications themes.

If one of your themes is that you provide a "caring environment" for students and the reported crisis is that a female student was violently assaulted in an outlying, dimly lit parking lot, you will need to express immediate concern for the victim and her family and support for their situation. Your initial message needs to ensure that the "caring" message comes through and avoid getting sidetracked into extraneous issues. But you also will need to prepare a consistent response to questions about why students have to park in unsafe areas if the college or university truly provides a caring environment. At that point, you will have to convey your institution's additional measures of caring such as your community policing initiative, safe escort service, or plans to install additional lighting and security in the assault area.

> **Failure to address a controversy in your institution's own publications strains its credibility even with friendly audiences and leaves them in the awkward position of being unable to explain your institution's position to their colleagues and peers.**

Keep the messages flowing

During a crisis, it is almost impossible to communicate too often. If your institution is not seen as coming forth with information at regular intervals, the media and the public will begin to wonder whether you are withholding additional damning information. Fears, rumors, and often baseless suspicions fuel the fires of concern that already are ablaze during a crisis. Issuing statements with regularity is a requirement of any lingering crisis. Statements need to focus on your consistent caring message, keeping with your overall communications themes and positioning. Find the silver linings in the clouds of crises, but never obscure the facts or the truth. If, for example, you attempt to hide the fact the student assaulted in your parking lot is seriously injured and may die, your credibility will evaporate. And if you try to transfer blame to the student for not using the safe escort service, your positioning as a "caring" institution will never recover. In any situation, continuous clear communication will position your institution as responding favorably to the crisis and acting responsibly toward its publics.

A single spokesperson

As noted above, we recommend that during a crisis, your chief public relations officer should serve as the primary spokesperson. But a severe crisis may require multiple spokespersons, so it's imperative that your spokespersons all be familiar with the specific message points about the crisis as well as your institution's overall marketing communications program. Philosophies differ about using your president as crisis spokesperson. He or she is often the human icon for your institution. As such, you do not wish to tarnish the president's image in any way.

Many presidents feel strongly that they need to be seen as personally attending to the crisis situation, and a president who is a skillful communicator may turn a potentially difficult situation into a positive image message. Each situation needs to be evaluated, so you may choose to have your president initially set the stage for the institution's over-all response. But in general, the chief public relations person, supported by specialists in the specific crisis area, should take the lead in responding to crisis situations.

Peter Hollister, former vice president of advancement for Northern Kentucky University, suggests that the president's best role comes when the crisis has been resolved and the time has arrived to lay the issue to rest.

Don't forget internal audiences

Your institution's harshest critics during times of emergency may be those who normal-ly are the closest to it and its greatest supporters—your own faculty, staff, and students. Such criticisms usually result from a perceived lack of communication by your president or the administration. With today's tools for reaching our internal audience—e-mail, Web sites, voice messages, fax—you should err on the side of overcommunication rather than allow the perception that your institution is unwilling or unable to discuss the situation.

Colleges and universities have multiple layers of internal audiences just as they do external audiences. In addition to faculty, staff, and students, you should send state-ments to the legislative delegation, boards of trustees, foundation boards, alumni boards, or other community advisory boards. During times of controversy, it is impor-tant that these groups become familiar with your side of the situation, not just the fil-tered version that may appear in the media.

Presidents and other administrators frequently want internal communications, including the faculty-staff newspaper and the institution's student or alumni magazine, to ignore a crisis situation. What they fail to see or acknowledge is that these publica-tions may offer the best opportunity to state their case to a naturally receptive audience who could help sway the opinions of others.

Failure to address a controversy in your institution's own publications strains its credibility even with friendly audiences and leaves them in the awkward position of being unable to explain your institution's position to their colleagues and peers. The opportunity to extend your communication message themes and to enlist friends as ambassadors and defenders is lost.

An issues scanning team

One way to avoid or mitigate a public policy crisis is to build an issues scanning team. The team should represent a divergent spectrum of people across the campus and meet periodically—perhaps just by e-mail. The sole purpose of the issues scanning team should be to evaluate what is changing in your institution's social and political environ-ment that could lead to a problem, or even a crisis, for your institution.

Team discussions should reflect multiple scenarios and consider institutional responses. Periodically, your chief public relations person should develop a topic in a briefing paper for your president and key staff. The paper should note alternatives both for crisis situations and the anticipated consequences. Again, such activity requires an investment in time but could serve your institution well in handling and even avoiding future crises.

Legal realities

Frequently, public relations spokespersons find themselves across the crisis management table from legal counsel. The dynamic tension between planning to win the battle in the courtroom and planning to win the battle of public opinion can result in heated arguments about the appropriateness of communication during a perceived crisis. Fortunately, attorneys are beginning to understand that "no comment" seldom silences the media or the public, but only lays open your institution to assertions that go unanswered and accusations that go undefended. To win the battle of public opinion, you must state your position publicly with enough background and context to withstand media and public scrutiny but without necessarily going into vivid details.

A sense of closure

Depending on the situation, your crisis communications plan also must account for a wrap-up or follow-up. At the same time that this provides you with crisis closure, it also offers you a final opportunity to link your crisis messages to your marketing communications program. Such an opportunity would occur in the event that the assaulted student in the crisis listed above recovers and returns to classes. When you announce her release from the hospital, you may be able to note the actions the institution has taken to provide medical and psychological assistance, promote the programs and safeguards in place for students to protect themselves, and introduce any new institutional changes in policies, programs, or facilities that reduce the likelihood of another occurrence.

If, on the other hand, the student were to die, at a suitable time you might be able to announce a scholarship in her honor and, in addition to noting the great sorrow throughout the institution, announce additional safeguards to make sure that no one else suffers the same fate. It's important to bring closure to an issue and make a final statement that aligns with and supports your marketing communications messages.

Crisis categories

In general, crises can be divided into four broad categories:
- Natural or technological disaster, or the imminent likelihood of such a disaster;
- Policy or value conflict with elements of your institution or the external community, resulting in high visibility protracted exchanges and antagonistic relationships;
- Deception, scandal, or misconduct by your president or other top management officials, or by faculty, staff, and students that results in serious harm to your institution or its image;
- Criminal attack on or confrontation with the institution or one or more of its components or individuals.

Let's look at actual instances of each type of crisis.

Natural and technological disaster

When an earthquake devastated California State University-Northridge, in 1994, it was one of the greatest natural disasters ever to affect an American college or university. According to Bruce Erickson, CSUN director of public relations, every building on campus was damaged and he had no crisis communication plan. Yet without the initial use of a single building and with formidable communication problems, Erickson adopted a philosophy of always saying "yes," never saying "no," and particularly never saying "no comment." "It's a matter of the human spirit," he explained. "You really have to believe in the ethic to communicate, then have the will to communicate. . . . Ideally," he added, "you'll have a president who sees the value and importance of being open and honest and responsible enough to step up to the mike and take charge." CSUN's president did.

Media demands at CSUN were so great that all the vice presidents became spokespersons. The vice presidents and Erickson met frequently to ensure they were "on the same sheet of music." The environmental health and safety staff played a key role in discussing such issues as hazardous materials, and responding to media queries honestly, frankly, and capably. The support that his office received from such experts prevented rumors from getting out of control.

Policy or value conflict

The activist who infiltrated the animal research facility of a major academic institution was a member of a national animal rights organization. She obtained a job inside the housing facility where dogs were being infected with mites. The mites, cultivated from rabbits that also had unsightly scabs, caused itching and scabs on the dogs that would generate pity by almost anyone who saw them. The research involved various treatments to see whether ointments could be developed that might alleviate similar conditions affecting humans, especially elderly residents of nursing homes who were particularly susceptible.

The institution learned of the activist and that another staff member had enabled her to enter restricted areas to obtain records, photographs, and videotapes. When a team was convened to plan a strategy, public relations was at the table. The team decided the activist should be arrested on trespassing charges and, at the same time, that the institution should provide full disclosure and complete laboratory access to the news media.

The arrest was announced at a news conference where the lead research scientist showed photographs of afflicted nursing home residents, as well as the animals. Media were given a tour and allowed to use cameras, including taking photographs of the afflicted animals. While the animal rights organization eventually arrived to make charges and show photographs, the media coverage was balanced and noted the intended benefits of the research and positive medical advances made possible by the use of animals.

> **The dynamic tension between planning to win the battle in the courtroom and planning to win the battle of public opinion can result in heated arguments about the appropriateness of communication during a perceived crisis.**

Impacts of Technology

The ease of e-mail as a communication tool, and the proliferation of Web sites as opportunities for individuals to exercise free speech, both have serious implications for the management of information during a crisis.

The emergence of "chat-rooms" can be a tool in the public relations arsenal for scanning the environment and particularly for learning of rumors, controversies, and potential problems. Assign one individual to monitor the "chat" among employees. If you detect a rumor or a series of questionable interpretations to a new policy or program at your institution, check the facts and develop a response. The staff member can enter the "chat" with an accurate representation of your institution's position, or a campus-wide e-mail message can be distributed. At the very least, such monitoring provides a "first alert" capability.

The advent of Web sites has made more important than ever the need to correct any errors that appear in print, whether errors of fact or interpretation. Newspapers archive most of their articles on computer. An article that contains an error, if referred to in subsequent follow-up articles, may repeat the error time and time again. Other newspapers or broadcast media may repeat the same error, too.

If the newspaper will run a correction, that also enters the archive and any search for previous articles should turn up the correction as well as the initial report. Although at one time the philosophy of not responding to a minor (or even major) error in print so as not to resurrect a painful subject in front of the public may have held some validity, today the danger that the error will manifest itself a thousand times over requires that you immediately and adamantly demand a correction or clarification.

Institutions with multiple campuses also have the opportunity to conduct video conferencing for announcements about crisis situations. Your president or chief spokesperson can make a presentation from the main campus that is carried to audiences at regional sites. The presentation can also be carried live on the Web site for those who may wish to access it via that medium. Evolving technologies will continue to provide new opportunities for effectively communicating with your institution's key publics.

An unexpected consequence was that a survey in the wake of the incident showed that the public considered the institution to be strong in research, even stronger than an institution in the same community that actually attracted more federal research dollars.

Deception, scandal, or misconduct

A fraternity-related drinking death occurred at Louisiana State University in 1997. Bill Ross, the university relations director, used a team of spokespersons, including the president, whose first message was to express condolences to the family. In a national conference after the event, the president felt that by going public with the story immediately "we captured the high ground and maintained it."

Ross also emphasized getting positive, related information into the media's hands, such as the institution's alcohol policy and related national materials. The institution's police issued daily briefings on the investigation, culminating in the arrest of 10 students by the end of the second week. Ross made sure that every media telephone call was answered. Although the media and public relations strategy worked, the issue was still not totally resolved and legal issues continue to be addressed.

An unexpected result of the national publicity was that out-of-state admissions interest was higher than normal, which LSU officials attributed to the beautiful campus and the positive way that students handled the national television interviews.

Criminal attack or confrontation

A criminal attack occurred at the University of South Florida only a month after it was announced that a former adjunct faculty member at the university had emerged as the new leader of the Islamic jihad. The student newspaper received a threat from an alleged terrorist organization that gave a date in late April for the bombing of an administration building and the murder of a female faculty member.

At the same time that it turned the information over to the police, the student newspaper published an article about the letter. This spread word of the threats and caused a panic among faculty, staff, students, and parents before the threats could be analyzed. Hundreds of phone calls flooded the campus. The public affairs office responded with a statement that the letter was under investigation and that the university would consider what actions to take, but that the safety of its students, faculty, and staff was its first concern.

That statement initiated a plan that resulted in moving exams up one week so as to have students and faculty off campus on the date of the threatened bombing and murder. Staff were given options, including working at alternative sites. When the FBI failed to make any arrests the weekend before the Monday, April 29, date, campus and local police began a systematic sweep of administration buildings.

Public affairs staff provided media briefings all weekend. At 6 a.m. Monday, public affairs personnel were live on television, noting the safety precautions and expressing optimism. At noon, President Betty Castor held a news conference with the same message. By evening, a statement advising that the campus was safe and that operations would return to normal the next day, was issued.

In a public opinion survey conducted a few months later, the majority of Tampa Bay residents seemed unfamiliar with the situation. Although 15 percent gave a negative reaction to the USF Middle Eastern studies program—the highest negative among the university programs in the survey—54 percent indicated they had never heard of the program.

Although each case history provides a very different situation, the respective universities took quick control of their situation and used communications effectively to convey the values and messages of their institutions. That is the heart and soul of responding to a crisis situation and successfully integrating it into your total marketing communications program.

13 Principles of Crisis

1. Guard against paranoia.
2. Provide concise information.
3. Guide reporters—don't be impatient with lack of understanding or repetitious questions.
4. Be forthright—say what you know; admit mistakes, and apologize.
5. Tell the truth.
6. Announce bad news.
7. Remember your real audience are the targets of your media communication plan.
8. Show you care by responding to people's feelings.
9. Stick to your crisis communication plan.
10. Prepare to give a crisis a lot of time.
11. Be fair to all and avoid favorable treatment of one media outlet.
12. Stay calm.
13. Win the crisis by positioning yourself at the end.

Adapted from Joann Ellison Rodgers and William C. Adams, *Media Guide for Academics.* Los Angeles: Foundation for American Communications, 1994.

Recommended Readings

CASE Issues Papers Digest I. "Racial Incidents on Campus," "Animal Rights Break-ins and Demonstrations," "Crime Incidents on Campus," and "Communicating Campus Cutbacks," Washington: Council for Advancement and Support of Education, 1990.

CASE Issues Papers Digest II. "Closing Academic Units," "Student Alcohol and Drug Abuse," "Questionable Spending Practices by Senior Administrators," and "Sexual Harassment Incidents," Washington: Council for Advancement and Support of Education, 1991.

CASE Issues Papers Digest III. "The Abrupt Departure of a Chief Executive Officer," "HIV/AIDS on Campus," and "Acquaintance Rape on Campus," Washington: Council for Advancement and Support of Education, 1992.

CASE Issues Papers Digest IV. "Coping with Controversial Speakers," Washington: Council for Advancement and Support of Education, 1993.

CASE Issues Papers Digest V. "Natural Disasters Communications Planning," Washington: Council for Advancement and Support of Education, 1993.

CASE Issues Papers Digest V. "Communicating about Controversial Research," Washington: Council for Advancement and Support of Education, 1995.

Profolio: Crisis Planning and Management, Professional Practice Center Portfolio. New York: Public Relations Society of America, 1998.

Effective Crisis Communications Management: A Guide to Identifying Potential Crises and Developing Detailed Communications Plans to Deal with Them. New York: Public Relations Society of America, 1997.

Erickson, Bruce. "It's Not Over Yet: The Aftermath of a Crisis Can Be the Most Important Time of All for the PR Office. Here's How to Meet Your Campus' Long-term Needs." CURRENTS, 21, no. 8 (September 1995): 20-24.

Fearn-Banks, Kathleen. *Crisis Communications: A Casebook Approach.* Hillsdale, NJ: Lawrence Erlbaum Associates, 1995.

Footlick, Jerry. *Truth and Consequences: How American Colleges and Universities Respond Publicly to Crises.* Phoenix, AZ: ACE/Oryx Press, 1997.

Jackson, Patrick. "The Unforgiving Era: Why Higher Education Will Be the Next Target in an Age of Increasing Public Outrage–and What PR Pros Can Do About It." CURRENTS, (October 1998): 12-15.

Larson, Wendy Ann, ed. *When Crisis Strikes on Campus.* Washington, DC: CASE, 1994.

Lerbinger, Otto, ed. "Theorists Discuss Management Crisis Successes and Failures. *Purview,* supplement to *PR Reporter,* no. 436 (March 9, 1998): 1-2.

"Lessons Learned from Crises," *Tips & Tactics,* supplement to *PR Reporter,* 35, no. 17 (December 22, 1997):1-2.

"Most School Crises Are Unrelated to Teaching or Curriculum." *PR Reporter,* no. 29 (July 28, 1997): 4.

Rodgers, Joann Ellison and William C. Adams, *Media Guide for Academics.* Los Angeles: Foundation for American Communications, 1994.

Sabo, Sandra R. "When the Unthinkable Happens, From a Professor on a Rampage to a President Accused of Racism, a Crisis Can Shake a Campus. Here, the Best Advice for Coping When Bad News Abounds." CURRENTS, 21, no. 8 (September 1995):14-19.

Siegel, Dorothy. *Campuses Respond to Violent Tragedy.* Phoenix, AZ: ACE/Oryx Press, 1994.

Teller, Harlan. "Communicating During a Crisis Includes Research: 10 Rules of the Road." *Tips & Tactics,* supplement to *PR Reporter,* 35, no. 12 (September 8, 1997): 1-2.

Tortorella, Albert J. "Crisis Communication: If It Had a Precedent, It Wouldn't Be A Crisis." *Communication World,* 6, no. 6 (June 1989):42-47.

Videotaped Conference: "Case Study of a Response to an Alcohol-Related Death on Campus," Baton Rouge, LA: Louisiana State University, 1997.

11

Special Events, Anniversaries, and Celebrations

" The analytical process related to integrated marketing is likely to bring about fundamental changes in what your public relations and communications staff does with its time. **"**

Larry D. Lauer

Integrated marketing is a way of thinking. It is a holistic approach to mobilizing everyone in your institution to tell the institution's story. It requires that priority institutional goals be set and that all public relations, advertising, and marketing activities be combined and coordinated to focus on those goals and advance them. And it soon leads you to the realization that building loyal relationships with strategic market segments is the most effective route to achieving a lasting competitive advantage for your institution.

Indeed, the analytical process related to integrated marketing is likely to bring about fundamental changes in what your public relations and communications staff does with its time. Media relations people in this situation, as we have seen in Chapter 9, tend to work fewer stories more aggressively, reducing the total number of releases they send out. These "reputation-defining" stories are then retold repetitively, especially in the institutional magazine and newsletters, both internal and external. And so sending those releases, news clips, and stories directly to stakeholders and opinion leaders becomes an effective additional initiative, making sure that the people who affect the institution's health and future are impressed by its influence and stature. Advertising is purchased only when it is a part of a larger integrated communications mix and when the ultimate goal becomes relationship-building with key people. At this point, the staff soon begins looking for even more effective ways to interact with this constituency.

Using events for strategic communication

Strategically planned special events provide an especially appealing opportunity to help control the total communications experience and are an extremely important part of a total integrated program. Gone are the days where a reception or party was seen merely as a social activity or opportunity for key people to keep in touch with each other. Now, from the message on the invitation to the impact of the evaluation —these events become extremely critical interactive communications opportunities, planned to make certain that the right messages are communicated, meaningful feedback occurs, and the total environment and atmosphere produces a satisfying emotional reinforcement of an institution's culture and values.

What makes communications strategic? Many practitioners are today asserting that the age of mass communications is dead. It is no longer effective to think in terms of getting good placements in mass media outlets as often as possible and to send messages everywhere all the time. The age of television has produced an intensely saturated communications environment, which means that much of what we send out can end up only contributing to "message clutter" and confusion. In short, the realities of the media marketplace have forced us to cut through the clutter and establish meaningful contact with audiences by becoming more focused and strategic in setting our communications goals and expectations .

Communications becomes strategic in the process of:

- Selecting target market segments or audiences
- Understanding each market or audience in terms of its characteristics and needs
- Selecting the most effective interactive channels or media
- Dealing with the distractions in those channels or situations
- Shaping the message to be concise and connecting
- Providing for effective feedback and response

When audiences are properly identified (e.g., prospective students and parents, high school counselors, donors, alumni, legislators, city leaders, and, other groups related to the institution), a situation analysis will quickly identify the benefits of getting the critical people from each group in a place where you can control the entire communications process. It is the extremely powerful potential of orchestrated special events that can motivate you to find new and more creative ways of bringing your most important people together.

The strategic elements of an event

Special events of a strategic nature often share important characteristics, including:

- Focus on market segments
- Channel and location selection
- Distraction control
- Media selection
- Message simplification and intensity
- Feedback and response

Focus on market segments

The process of planning special events is often driven by being asked to do one. Each opportunity seems to present itself out of nowhere, connected strategically to nothing else you are doing. And the staff, in turn, ends up having to make an isolated decision about a one-time activity. Worse yet, this one-time activity can become a not-very-strategic annual obligation that is not a good use of staff time.

Integrated marketing puts the selection of the priority target market up front. You may decide that legislators are key in the spring, or that city leaders are a priority during a centennial celebration, or that a certain collection of private schools are important when their headmasters are already meeting, and so on. In other words, you select the target segment before you design the event. As a result, you inform those bringing "events opportunities" to you that you "do" them only when you have included them as a part of an overall analysis of current market segment priorities (similarly to the way you inform the advertising sales people when they call).

Of course, not every important audience segment can be addressed at the same time. Thus, what is and is not a current priority will change over time. The point is, cosponsoring a parade with the Boy Scouts may not fit your plan priorities at the moment, and it is your priorities that must drive a strategic decision unless the idea happens to be incredible.

This point is very important. When you know what your strategic market segment priorities are, you can be very confident about turning down ideas that are just "nice things to do." Analysis will also prepare you to recognize the rare idea that comes out of nowhere with such powerful communication and visibility potential that you need to change your priorities to accommodate it. Powerful events often offer vital partnership opportunities and provide many levels and kinds of communications. Timing is everything, so you must think about it from several directions at the same time.

" Strategically planned special events provide an especially appealing opportunity to help control the total communications experience and are an extremely important part of a total integrated program. "

'Channel' and location selection

The medium is a critical part of the message. For an event, the location, environment, and the place are critical. They can either reinforce and enhance your central message or they can introduce noise and distractions that undermine the whole impact. Place is critical, and there is a difference between the physical and the "experienced" place. Both are important.

The physical place is what people actually see upon first arrival. But their interactions with people will quickly define how they come to "see" it. A lot of thought and energy has to go into shaping how they are greeted, who is doing the greeting, and the overall tone and message of the greeting. This becomes part of the perception of the communication medium itself and will largely influence the impact of later messages.

Distraction control

Captured audiences can be truly captured, especially when you control the environment completely. In most every other communication situation, the "noise" is out of the communicator's control. When seeing a print ad, hearing a radio PSA, or watching television, the audience can be distracted by almost anything. But an event gives you the opportunity to control the situation, and you should not miss it. Often something as simple as a poor sound system can render the whole experience ineffective. On the other hand, a sound system that surrounds the audience can hold them and focus them on the experience you want for them. You get the point. Integrated marketing makes you appreciate and, consequently, insist on managing details.

Media selection

With events, the most powerful medium is face to face. But there are many other opportunities, all of which must be coordinated and reinforce the same central message. For example, you may be having a major dinner for legislators. The dinner speaker will be developing and delivering your central message because you have selected and worked with this person from the beginning. You have communicated the central message in the dinner invitation, so even those who have declined are exposed to it. You reinforced the message in a photographic display during the cocktail reception before the dinner. You asked the entertainers to select their material to reinforce the message theme, and you reinforced the message in the printed dinner program and other "take-home" materials or gifts you provided. In this way, you have integrated communications working for you as a part of your integrated marketing program.

Message simplification and intensity

Effective communication in a cluttered world requires simple messages repeated frequently. It's as simple as that. To be sure, this is a frustrating situation when the issue is sophisticated and complex. But the reality is that if you try too much, the message will not get through at all. So your strategy must be layered. First, get your audience's attention. Then, convince them of the urgency of the message. Then give them the five or six key points they need to know. Finally, repeat and reinforce those points in a variety of media. If they come away from the event with this much, the event has been a stunning success.

Solving problems or examining complex issues is possible only with smaller, highly interested groups. But if you achieve your event goal of communicating urgency and maybe five simple points, you are now in a better position to identify those specific groups at your event who are most likely to help you with action initiatives.

You can now invite these people to join a smaller, problem-solving task force that will meet in a business, roll-up-the-sleeves-and-go-to-work type of setting. Now you are truly implementing integrated strategic communication thinking and planning.

Feedback and response

Relationships are formed only during the response part of the communication process. There is no relationship without interaction. Every event must have a feedback mechanism, even if it is mostly in tone and style.

Your objective, of course, should be providing opportunities for feedback. Your staff, for example, might be given specific message and listening objectives to work on while talking and walking through informal receptions. Certainly, they can provide and collect evaluation or issues "talk-back" forms and invite everyone to "call us later." Where these techniques are not feasible, and even where they are, the tone of the spoken and written word should always be conversational and in the context of assuming an ongoing relationship.

Events are truly integrated strategic communications opportunities:

- They can focus on the opinion leaders within specific priority market segments.
- The invitations can introduce and communicate your central message (even to those who decline to come).
- You can transmit simple information.
- The settings are fundamentally interactive.
- The conditions are natural for relationship building.
- You can control the total environment and setting.
- They offer strong possibilities for multisensory messages.
- The impact can be strongly emotional.
- It is possible for you to evaluate the event results meaningfully.

Selecting a partner

Selecting an events partner is as important as selecting a marriage partner. You can either improve or destroy your image and reputation. You can either supplement your weaknesses or make them worse. You can either achieve a sense of mutual progress or you can come to think the other one is holding you back.

It is clear, however, that by selecting the right events partner you can, just by achieving the alliance, enhance the perception of your institution's importance and visibility in the community. You will also find that by combining resources, both human and financial, you can achieve big results for less than half the cost of going it alone. In addition, the right partner affords many communication (and news media) opportunities—before, during, and after the event itself.

Here are some characteristics to look for in a good event partner:

- Enjoys high visibility and respect in the community
- Works with a staff naturally compatible with yours
- Clearly understands who will do and pay for what
- Holds that team achievement is more important than control
- Clearly understands the benefit to the partner
- Is more compatible than competitive

A partner shares the whole event. Cosponsors give you money to help support the event in return for some name recognition. You can think about having both, because cosponsors enable even bigger results for little or none of your own money. And the more important your partner, the easier it will be to attract cosponsors. Cosponsors give you money to help support the event in return for some name recognition. And with a cosponsor, you can earn both name recognition and money for your institution, because cosponsors enable you to get even bigger results for little or none of your own money. The nice thing about cosponsors is that they, too, want the community goodwill and are always looking for good projects. When you have happy cosponsors, you can go back to them often. This is not a donation on their part; it is an advertising expense.

The chamber of commerce, local museums, public schools, private schools, the local public broadcasting organization, fine arts organizations, and even the city itself provide still more key, strategic, events-partnering opportunities. Business-issues breakfasts, arts openings, science programs, planning for college conferences, and teaching-media-literacy projects are only a few examples of projects that garner high visibility and can also be partnered effectively with organizations found in most communities.

This brings up the idea of the media as cosponsor. Often newspapers, radio stations, and television stations like to cosponsor events, and, when they do, they virtually take care of giving you the visibility you seek. To cultivate this kind of partnership, you will want your media relations people to call on the news editorial department and someone else to call on the advertising and publicity departments. You may actually find the latter more productive for you than the former.

> **The key is to figure out how to drive the right kind of positive "talk on the street."**

Using events to leverage visibility

Most academic institutions are tired of being labeled by their alumni and donors as the "best-kept secret" in town, especially when the communicators know how much communication takes place and how often the institution actually does appear in the news media. And yet there is clearly a selective-perception phenomena at work here that causes people close to an institution to "perceive" that the other guy is getting more visibility. The complaints come from trustees, donors, alumni, and even faculty and staff. Even when it isn't true, the perception of something is a professional fact of life for most of us. The questions is: Visibility with whom at what cost? And the answer has to be strategic.

The truth is that the kind of visibility the critics want to see is not affordable for most institutions. Some strive for spread name-recognition through athletics, and others gain visible presence over hundreds of years of existence. But when it comes to the kind of visibility that constituents want, it just isn't in the budget cards for most of us. The solution, therefore, can only be a strategic one.

From a strategic point of view, if the people who control the future of your institution believe the institution is visible, then for all practical purposes it is. The challenge then is to communicate so effectively with your stakeholders and priority market-segment opinion leaders that they come to believe you are visible, and in so doing see you as nationally and internationally significant.

Still thinking strategically, it is also useful to distinguish between stakeholders and opinion leaders. You will need to communicate with both groups, but not with both at the same time every time. Stakeholders are people who have an active involvement with your institution and feel influenced directly by its success or failure. These people are everyone inside your institution, plus trustees, alumni leaders, vendors, etc. Opinion leaders are nonstakeholders in priority market segments who have the capacity to influence others. It is critical in integrated relationship marketing that your record systems allow you to communicate directly with these people whenever you see the need.

Using events to improve image and build reputation

When someone observes that an institution has a good image, what do they really mean? Do they mean that the pictures on the brochures are impressive? Do they mean that the advertising they see in the newspaper is attracting attention? Or do they mean that all of these factors are important, but what is really impressing them is the perception that the institution is really on the move? If so, what has given them that impression?

When this question is probed in focus groups and interviews, participants will often say things like, "We hear exciting things are really happening out there," or "You people seem to really know what you're doing out there," or "We are really impressed with that new president." In other words, the impression is that the leadership is moving the organization ahead, and it is reported in terms of an "image." A good image, then, is the result of leadership generating the "talk" that a lot of new activity is underway. On the other hand, one might hear "I hear bad things are happening out there," or "The word is that the place is in trouble." This kind of negative image is usually driven by the collective impression that there is a decline in enrollment, a budget problem, personnel layoffs, or an athletics crisis.

If the latter is the case, what is the most effective way to orchestrate a positive image?

The key is to figure out how to drive the right kind of positive "talk on the street." And what gets word-of-mouth to work is hearing the right people say the right things at the right time to the right people. The right audiences are the stakeholders and opinion leaders in priority market segments. And the right people to do the talking are the executive leadership of the institution. The right place, of course, can be orchestrated as a highly visible special event, partnered with the right organization.

Image is often reinforced by the design and overall atmosphere of the event and how well details were handled. There is little doubt that sloppy events communicate an image of an amateurish organization overall, and that attention to detail and "class" communicate the image of an organization that knows what it's doing in other areas as well. Image is the result of collective impressions: Materials, design, and photographs are a part of the support package. The fact that the organization is perceived to be doing a lot of exciting things is best conveyed by the leadership "walking the talk" in controlled communication environments.

Selecting the right event is critical because the wrong events burn up a lot of time and waste a lot of money. In other words, getting trapped into the wrong event is one of the worst things you can do. But having the opportunity to do the right one may turn out to be the most important thing you do all year.

Anniversaries

An anniversary is a "peg," or a generally accepted good reason, to celebrate the institution. Some cannot be overlooked; a centennial, for example. Others, such as the 125th anniversary, might have marginal visibility potential. Anniversaries are a time to bring to consciousness your institution's mission and vision, two very important strategic communication concerns.

Mission is the reason an institution came into being, and vision represents what it wants to become. Both concepts are the foundation of all other goal setting and strategic planning. An anniversary year gives you the opportunity to have mission and vision understood by all your critical leaders if you focus on "staying on the message."

Inaugurations

Sometimes inaugurations are regal exercises in academic elitism and ego gratification. Other times, they can be seen as real opportunities to "position" the institution in the world of higher education. The first approach is an extravagant waste of time and money. The second approach is a fundamental requirement for integrated marketing.

Speakers at inaugurations can fulfill three key purposes. First, they can scan the higher education scene with respect to the big issues or, to put it in management terms, with respect to threats and opportunities. Second, it is critical that they observe the market niche your institution has in the larger picture. And third, it is possible for them to spark an ongoing conversation about the potential of your institution to move to the next level of distinction. These first two types of speakers should have a high reputation in higher education. The last type of speaker should be your new president. All three types of speakers can be featured in a series of events to include dinners, ceremonies, luncheons, and forums.

Fund-raising kick-off

A fund-raising event is obviously a chance to rally the troops to the cause. It should have all of the elements of an effective dinner event described previously. And don't miss the chance to play to emotions.

Speeches should be short and inspiring. They should not just restate funding needs. Rather, they should be testimonials about "why I support . . . " The video you use should also not restate the case, but rather be an emotional and fast-moving account of those who came to the rescue and made a difference at critical moments in the institution's history. The setting should be dramatic and classy. And the printed case statement, which outlines the program and dollar needs, should be present at this event, mostly as a strong visual symbol of the process that the campaign leaders participated in prior to this evening's celebration. The details of "how much we are raising to do what" can be better dealt with in small group meetings that will follow. State the big dollar goal, of course, but on this night, attach it more to a vision of possibilities than to a list of needs.

A new year

The start of a new year is an opportunity to clarify short-term goals, reward high performance, and address any anticipated crises head on. It is a state-of-the-university opportunity with a real role in an integrated marketing scheme.

Design the commemorative occasion to be a straightforward, information-giving event with the opportunity for feedback. But follow it with a lunch, dinner, reception, or even a party. After the good and bad news of a candid convocation, people find it reassuring and motivating to be provided with the place and time for informal discussion in the midst of food and drink. It works; try it.

Celebrations of service and achievement

Celebrations need to be held for faculty, staff, and volunteers, too. And yes, years of service are important. One communications staff member told the story of how he thought that years of service did not warrant much of a celebration, and that only achievement mattered. He was so sure others would agree. Wrong. Others did not agree; people throughout the organization spoke up to let him know just how important the recognition of loyal service can be. If you combine service recognition with achievement recognition, you will end up with an effective and motivating experience that also has an important place in internal integrated marketing. Such events can reinforce central messages, serve as a reminder of key values, and reward the kind of behavior that advances priority goals.

Groundbreakings and dedications

These are times to celebrate progress on specific program goals and to honor donors and others who have made the results possible. Some see these as news opportunities, but they really rarely are. A new building is not mass public news, and if you add a gimmick to try to produce it as one, you can easily detract from the impact potential that the event really has.

Groundbreakings and dedications are really institutional family occasions. They represent major milestones for insiders: the donors who stretch to help and the faculty and staff who are making the programmatic difference. These events should be taken very seriously and done very, very well. And they should focus directly on the results they can best achieve—recognizing achievement and motivating others to do the same. Handled this way, they are key to effective integrated marketing.

Commencements

In many ways commencements celebrate what academic institutions are all about. They should be family days, and they should be designed to celebrate the whole family's achievement. Long speeches are not necessary, nor are celebrities, even though some feel celebrities add significance to the moment. The key is to make each graduate feel special in whatever ceremonies and rituals take place. Your ultimate purpose should be continued relationship-building with students about to become alumni, and so the event is critical to an overall integrated relationship marketing program.

Educational events

Speakers programs, issues forums, and topical conferences offer the same opportunities to fulfill marketing goals. They feature captive and targeted audiences, and they are excellent opportunities to reinforce the institutional central message and market position while they also deal with topics of local, national, and international consequence. These events are often missed marketing opportunities.

Achieving uncommon integrated marketing impact: three cases

There are many different kinds of events that can bring positive visibility. The key is to design ones that have many promotional opportunities. Here are three examples.

INPUT: *The International Public Television Screening Conference*

Approximately 1,000 television producers from 50 or more countries hold their International Public Television Screening Conference (INPUT) in a different city in the world each year to screen and discuss the 80 or so best productions in the world. This conference became a partnership possibility for Texas Christian University in Fort Worth because of contacts the institution had with members of the INPUT board.

The university has been conducting summer studies in international communications in England for 10 years. Through the natural process of setting up field trips for students, relationships were established with producers at the British Broadcasting Corporation who were also involved with INPUT. When the organization was looking for a city in the United States to hold the conference, conversations led eventually to Fort Worth and the development of a real "win-win" situation.

The city wants to see itself more as an international center, and so hosting 1,000 international television producers was extremely appealing. The regional public television organization in northern Texas, in addition to finding an international network of potential coproducers attractive, was interested in establishing a firmer presence in Fort Worth. TCU wanted to be perceived as facilitating a major conference important to the city and, in doing so, gain better recognition for being involved in the area's development. Of course, the university also wanted to develop its international contact base in support of its growing international communications and media studies programs.

The city of Fort Worth, KERA/KDTN public television, and TCU formed a partnership to host INPUT 1999, and corporate and foundation sponsors were solicited for funding. The project was too big for any one of them to do alone. But by dividing the work, they found they not only could host this major event, but they could also meet their separate but compatible local and international visibility and reputation-building goals.

International visibility begins with announcements around the world two years before the event. A press conference is held in the host city in conjunction with a board meeting one year before the event. The public can be invited to special public screenings and you can invite special guests from the partnering hosts to various associated events during the conference. There is also the task of getting press coverage of the event itself locally, nationally, and in the 50 or so countries represented.

What's interesting about this project is that almost any academic institution in a city with international interests and a major public television organization could duplicate it. This conference has only been in the United States several times in 20 years, but INPUT is always looking for future host cities and institutions.

'Firing Line' debates

Several academic institutions around the country have hosted "Firing Line" debates, national public television events that are natural opportunities for institutions to be seen as important both locally and nationally. The hosting institution is asked to contribute some of the funding, but that can be sought in corporate sponsorships.

The appeal of the project is that it provides multiple opportunities for reputation building and visibility. For example, one can expect:

- Notices in the news media when the event is announced
- Stories in the news media prior to the event about the topic to be debated
- The opportunity to invite your stakeholders and opinion leaders to be in the television audience for the debate and to attend associated receptions, luncheons, and dinners
- Nationally known political, media, and academic figures on your campus
- Local and national news coverage of the debate itself
- National broadcast of the debate in prime time, repeat broadcasts, and associated promotion

In addition, "Firing Line" usually tapes two half-hour weekly programs at the same time so visibility is extended to these two broadcasts, too. It is a lot of work for all involved, but the multiple exposures and the perceived national stature more than compensate. Even though regular panelist William F. Buckley, Jr. is politically conservative, special care is taken to make certain the debate is balanced and fair.

The first dance at Baylor

Baylor University was chartered in 1845 by the Republic of Texas. Official dances were not allowed on the campus until the president decided in 1996 that it was time for a change. The marketing and communications professionals saw it as an opportunity to have fun, to eliminate a misunderstanding about social life at Baylor, and to get a lot of national visibility at the same time. They were right.

Their press release read:

> WACO, Texas—The Berlin Wall has fallen, Big Macs have invaded Russia and there are lights at Wrigley Field. Mankind's last great resistance is about to be history: There will be dancing at Baylor University. It's true, Boogie Fever has hit Waco. The 'D' word is no longer taboo at the world's largest Baptist university. Baylor President Robert B. Sloan, Jr., a Baylor graduate and an ordained Baptist minister who has preached throughout the world, and his wife Sue, also a Baylor grad, will perform the first dance. The heavens will not shake, but this will be an historic time for Baylor and Baptists everywhere.

The first dance was a grand success. It made a serious point in a fun way. And it certainly captured the attention of the news media. The story was carried on many national television news programs at night and in the morning. It received heavy press coverage regionally and was reported in newspapers all over the world. The story was visual, dramatic, and clearly told the world that the Baylor campus was not the stuffy place many might have thought!

Increasing the impact of special events

Here are a number of ideas to help make certain your events fulfill integrated marketing requirements and make a strong impact:

A compelling theme or topic

The topic should tie into your overall marketing message but be worded so as to grab attention. For example, "Come see our new Ferrari" might invite alumni to meet Texas Christian University's new chancellor, Dr. Michael Ferrari.

Partners and cosponsors who enhance your reputation and visibility

For example, find both a corporate and media partner for a speakers program. The corporate sponsor pays the honorarium and travel expenses of the speaker, the media organization provides the promotion, and the university provides the venue and program management. Because the corporate and media sponsors are well known, overall visibility is automatically higher.

A strategically important audience (market segment)

City and business leaders often feel people in academic institutions live in ivory towers. Events that involve them in planning at the institution and are targeted to their interests can change that view. Idea: Offer to hold a monthly business breakfast on your campus with a corporate sponsor and a speaker on an urgent business or city topic.

A physical setting that produces response

The event to introduce Chancellor Michael Ferrari might, for example, be held at a local race track. An event to announce a new Latin American music festival might be held in the courtyard of a local Mexican restaurant. This is not rocket science. But be as creative as you can in selecting a setting. This includes the use of on-campus locations: You can serve a lunch in your television studio and send attendees a videotape afterwards. Or serve a dinner on the stage of your auditorium in the middle of a theatrical set.

A focused message objective

A convocation address by your president might have the objective of communicating a 10-point plan for your institution. Organize everything around staying focused on having the audience leave knowing your president's message. Apply the journalism advice of telling them what you are going to tell them, tell them, then tell them what you told them.

A multisensory on-site communication plan
You can have your central message on a poster displayed in your reception area, above the podium in your banquet hall, in your printed program, in the remarks of your speaker, in a slide presentation, even in the music you select to play, and so forth.

An attention-getting and information-giving invitation
Select a folded invitation and use one of the sides to convey the central message of your event, keeping in mind what you want to say to those who don't attend.

Many opportunities for promotion—before and after the event
Put your central message up front in any articles you do in institutional periodicals and in any advertising you place prior to an event. Find ways to use your event to stimulate newspaper and magazine stories. Then, send the news clips to both those who attended and to those who declined. Or send them the news release itself. Don't just promote your event; communicate the message at the same time.

A feedback mechanism for evaluation and information gathering
Hand out a card asking for comments. Or conduct a follow-up telephone survey asking for comments and then reinforce the central message of your event.

Check List: Making Events Part of an Integrated Marketing Program

- ◾ Identify current priority market segments or audiences and select one.
- ◾ List opinion leaders within the segment.
- ◾ Write the key message and themes you want your targets to receive, and the behavioral response you desire.
- ◾ Pick the venue that will best support and enhance your message.
- ◾ Design your setting to reinforce your message.
- ◾ Plan your program to articulate your message in easy-to-recall points.
- ◾ Develop printed invitations that preview your message and take this opportunity to communicate with those who won't attend.
- ◾ Include a feedback or interactive feature to your event—formal question and answer session, informal discussion, evaluation forms, etc.
- ◾ Select a partner organization that can enhance your visibility, increase your prestige, and share your costs.
- ◾ Consult a standard events checklist such as the ones in April Harris' book, *Special Events: Planning for Success,* Second Edition (CASE 1998).

A final word

In sum, from an integrated marketing perspective, special events have the most impact when they are carefully shaped to advance a priority institutional goal and are a strategic part of your larger integrated marketing communications campaign or program. Thus, they should include news stories, advertisements, executive speeches, merchandise, and a full range of other communications initiatives, all reinforcing the institution's central message and themes.

In the final analysis, getting the people who will make the most difference—faculty, staff, students, stakeholders, and opinion leaders—on the same message page, and motivating them to tell your institution's story, is one of your most important marketing objectives. To this end, carefully crafted special events can become one of your most powerful integrated marketing communications tools. And what makes them even more attractive is that they are also effective in building loyal, active, long-term relationships.

Recommended Readings

Barbalich, Andrea. "Need Advice on Planning a Letter-perfect Celebration? Read on for Your Guide to Special Events from A to Z." CURRENTS, 21, no. 2, (February 1995):40-45.

Barbalich, Andrea, Donna Shoemaker and April Harris. "Great Show: Experts Share 30 Spicy Ideas for Top-performing Special Events." CURRENTS, 18, no. 7, (July-August 1992):44-53.

Catherwood, Dwight W. and Richard L. Van Kirk. *The Complete Guide to Special Events Management.* New York: John Wiley and Sons, Inc., 1992.

Freedman, Harry A. Black Tie Optional: *The Ultimate Guide to Planning and Producing Successful Special Events.* Detroit: Fund Raising Institute, 1991.

Freedman, Harry and Karen Feldman. *The Business of Special Events.* Sarasota, FL: Pineapple Press, October 1997.

Harris, April. *Etiquette and Protocol: A Guide for Campus Events.* Washington, DC: Council for Advancement and Support of Education, March 1999.

Harris, April L. "In with the New: How to Make the Inauguration of Your New Campus CEO an Event to Remember." CURRENTS, 22, no. 9, (October 1996):34-39.

Harris, April L. "New Tools for the Trade: Still Using Outdated Tactics to Plan Special Events? Five High-Tech Strategies Can Help with Everything from Room Arrangements to Guest Lists." CURRENTS, 24, no. 2, (February 1998):39-43.

Harris, April L. *Special Events: Planning for Success, Second Edition.* Washington, DC: Council for Advancement and Support of Education, July 1998.

Harris, April L. "Strike Up the Plan: Eight Steps to Organizing Special Events That Accomplish Specific Campus Goals." CURRENTS, 18, no. 7, (July–August 1992):32-36.

Lauer, Larry D. *Communication Power: Energizing Your Nonprofit Organization.* Gaithersburg, MD: Aspen Publishers, July 1997.

Levy, Barbara R. and Barbara H. Marion. *Successful Special Events: Planning, Hosting, and Evaluating.* Gaithersburg, MD: Aspen Publishers, June 1997.

McCaffree, Mary Jane and Pauline Innis. *Protocol: The Complete Handbook of Diplomatic, Official and Social Usage.* Washington: Devon Publishing Company, Inc., 1996.

Ryder, Kathleen L. "How to Sleep at Night: Check It Out. CURRENTS, 6, no. 6 (June 1980):41-46.

Soares, Eric J. *Promotional Feats: The Role of Planned Events in the Marketing Communications Mix.* New York: Greenwood Publishing Group, 1991.

Viola, Joy Winkie. *Presidential Inaugurations: Planning for More than Pomp and Circumstance.* Washington, DC: Council for the Advancement and Support of Education, 1993.

Plan to become a campus champion of your marketing efforts.
Develop new areas of marketing expertise.
Use them to help solve campus problems.

Section III
Taking It to the Next Level

12

Integrated Publication Strategies

" Printed materials have never been more effective as a communication medium, and there is every likelihood that publications will remain a mainstay no matter what technological breakthroughs may occur. "

It may be surprising to some people, but we are still in the age of publications. With the arrival of the Internet and other message technologies such as telemarketing, some trendy communicators are already working on eulogies for print publications, and we still hear predictions about the soon-to-be paperless society. The fact is, however, that printed materials have never been more effective as a communication medium, and there is every likelihood that publications will remain a mainstay no matter what technological breakthroughs may occur.

Robert Sevier

The characteristics of a successful publication

I make the above statement for a number of reasons. First, a publication is tactile. You can touch it and hold it in your hands, and careful production decisions about the trim size, paper stock, and even ink can send strong, yet subtle, messages of tradition, quality, and even exclusivity.

Second, a publication waits for the reader. It is not transient. Unlike radio or television, publications do not zoom along at the speed of light. They are ready to be read when the reader is ready to read. And they need no special equipment for viewing — save for a good lamp. Readers can read them all at once or in sections. Readers can set them aside for an hour, a day, or a month. It doesn't matter. The message will not be lost.

Third, a publication offers absolute control over the technical quality of the message. Design, typography, photography, copy, illustration, paper stock, and the type of printing all combine to give publications a special look, tone, and feel that is unparalleled.

Fourth, a publication can evoke highly personal reactions. Copy, design, and illustration—the elements of a publication—work in concert to capture an imagination, move a reader to tears, or heighten a sense of outrage.

Fifth, you can segment publications. Publications for an older alum, or a prospective student, or a wealthy donor can be highly customized, using demographic and psychographic data to meet and reflect their exact needs and expectations.

And finally, even allowing for the idiosyncrasies of the U.S. Postal Service, you have much control over timing and delivery. This helps you avoid calendar conflicts—those times when an audience may not be receptive to a particular message.

Publications have not been supplanted by technology. Rather, we are taking advantage of technology to make publications more effective than ever.

In the earlier discussion of communication theory, we noted that successful messages have three qualities. They are noticeable, they are salient, and they are memorable. Publications are not unlike messages.

Successful publications are noticeable. They have covers that attract the reader and propel him or her inside. They have writing and design that work in concert to communicate the message. They are well printed and bound. They are, as a whole, captivating.

Second, successful publications are salient. Target audiences find them meaningful because they fulfill an expectation. They might provide information. Or insight. Or humor. They assure and confirm. They inspire and challenge. In short, they find a need in the reader's life, and they fill it.

Third, successful publications are memorable. They stand out from the crowd, in part because they are noticeable and salient in ways that matter to the reader. Readers read them, reread them, remember them, and even look forward to future communication.

Some big questions to ask yourself

Before you can write and design your publication, you must address a number of important questions, including:

- Why are you doing the publication?
- Who is your target audience?
- How do you know a publication is the best answer?
- How will it fit into your larger communication flow?
- Have you anticipated the environment in which your publication must compete—and win?
- What is your budget?
- What is the shelf life of your publication?

Why are you doing the publication?

Why you are doing this is one of your first concerns before you begin to develop your publication. If your answer isn't clear and compelling, consider postponing or even not undertaking the project. Because so many publications are cyclical, it is very easy to lose sight of their original purposes. In addition, the rationales for publications often change and evolve. Military planners call this "mission creep." Before you undertake the production of a publication, make sure the need is obvious. And don't redo a publication this year just because you produced it last year.

Who is your target audience?

Any discussion about the publication's rationale will involve a discussion of intended target audiences. Throughout this book, we have repeated that the need to define your target audience clearly is a precursor to developing integrated marketing communication plans and individual message strategies. We make the same admonition again: You must have a clear idea of your publication's target audience from the outset. As you will see from the publication paradigm on the following pages, you must have not only a sense of your target audience, but also an assessment of their needs and expectations. This information is extraordinarily helpful as you begin to think about your publication's driving concept.

> **" As you consider the creation of a new publication, it is important to anticipate how it will fit into the larger flow of messages you direct at your target audience. "**

One reminder about target audiences: The more narrowly defined the target audience, the better. This will allow you to develop a highly customized message. When you try to meet the needs of too many different target audiences in the same piece, there is every likelihood that none of the readers will be particularly satisfied.

How do you know a publication is the best answer?

Often, when given a new communication challenge, we automatically respond with the familiar, "Let's do a publication." Publications will likely remain a communication mainstay for years to come, but they are seldom the only effective option. With a multitude of communication media at our disposal, it is very important to use audience research to see if other media might be more effective. Keep in mind, too, that communication strategies that embrace a variety of media are much more likely to be effective in the long run.

How will it fit into your larger communication flow?

As you consider the creation of a new publication, it is important to anticipate how it will fit into the larger flow of messages you direct at your target audience. Successful publications are seldom developed in situ and experienced practitioners know that publications and messages often build on one another. We know that the impact of an annual fund mailing will be heightened if the alumni magazine that precedes it reminds readers of the importance of their contribution to the fund. And a financial aid brochure to prospective students will be enhanced if the viewbook that precedes it helps pave the way for the brochure itself. The ability to segue from message to message in a larger communication flow can create great synergy.

Have you anticipated the environment in which your publication must compete—and win?

Don't forget to anticipate the marketing and communication environment your publication must compete in—and win. We know, for example, that middle-income people are asked more than 300 times a year by telephone or direct mail to give to a college, museum, hospital, or some other worthy cause. We also know that a prospective student of even moderate talent and means will be contacted by 400 or 500 different campuses.

In today's society, all of us are bombarded by thousands of unwanted, unappreciated, and largely unnoticed messages each day. As this cacophony increases, how can you be sure that the publication you are so carefully nurturing along will even be noticed? Satisfying this question should provide a significant impetus for concepting and concept testing.

Note: Chapter 4 outlined some of the more serious, but often overlooked barriers to communication. Your review of this information might be helpful at this early stage in the publication production process.

What is your budget?

One important issue that needs to be settled early in any discussion about publications is money. Specifically, how much money is available for the publication in your budget, and is that amount adequate for the publication you plan? Our experience tells us that many publications are severely underfunded from the beginning, and that budget realities often bring high-flying expectations back to the ground. Athough small budgets are typically blamed for many publication failures, we know that more often it is not the budget that was too small, but the concept.

In an ideal world, your publication budget should be established after the need for it was assessed and its message goals developed. In the world of academic institutions—and the rest of the world, too, for that matter—it seldom works that way. Our best recommendations are:

- ■ If you can't afford quality—a quality concept, a quality design, and quality writing—don't do anything. You simply can't afford poor publications no matter how little money you have.
- ■ If the budget is tight, turn your project over to a seasoned publications professional. The odds are high that over the years he or she has learned tricks and tactics that can reduce your cost without impairing effectiveness.

What is the shelf life of your publication?

Anticipating how long your publication will be used is often overlooked in publication development. However, determining whether a publication will be used for one, two, or three years has important implications for concepting, writing and design, and budgeting. If a viewbook, for example, is to be used for only one year, then the design and photography can be more contemporary because you expect the piece to be revised for the next cycle. Copy, too, can be more specific and include detailed information on your institution—costs, deadlines and schedules, faculty, majors, and other information that often changes quickly.

However, if for budgetary or other reasons, the piece has a two- or three-year life, then the design must be more enduring, and copy should avoid specific details that could be relegated to a less expensive accompanying piece or even a cover letter. Pieces with a longer shelf life also offer three other advantages. First, because of the longer press run, the unit cost of the publication should be less. Second, the cost for exceptional design, writing, or photography can be amortized over the longer life of the publication. And finally, publications with a longer shelf life offer significant time-savings because there is little real difference in the amount of time it takes to produce a publication with a short shelf life or a three-year shelf life.

One thing is clear as you think about the shelf-life of your publication: It is best to understand how long it will be used before you develop it, rather than afterward.

The publication process

Creating a publication is a surprisingly linear undertaking involving six basic steps. Careful readers will note that the six steps outlined in the paradigm presented in Figure 12-1 are similar to those for creating any basic message strategy. This shouldn't be surprising since publications, like other media, are message carriers. In fact, one of the most important goals of any publication is to support, rather than supplant, the message or messages it is designed to carry.

The first step in the publication process, like the first step in the creation of a larger message strategy, is to define your target audience. Before you can proceed, you must have a clear sense of who will be receiving, reading, and acting on your publication.

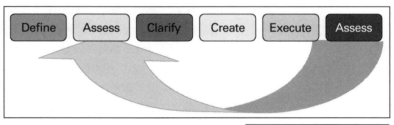

Figure 12-1
Six Steps to Creating Your Publication

Second, you must assess your target audience. What do you know about their perceptions of your institution? What are their motivations and behaviors? How do they wish you to communicate to them? Before you can proceed with the creation of your publication, you must conduct research to answer these and other questions.

Take extra care at this point to make sure that you are focusing on your target audience and not the stakeholders involved in the approval processes. We have seen many search pieces and annual fund solicitations that seem more directed at 50-year-old college administrators than at college-bound high school students and young alumni.

Third, you must clarify what you hope to accomplish with your publication. Do you want to raise money via the annual fund? Are you trying to recruit students or raise the quality of prospects? Are you trying to explain the economic impact of your institution on the community? Or are you trying to communicate information about changes in your institution's retirement benefits?

Without a clear understanding of the purpose of your publication, you are setting yourself up for two failures. First, it is unlikely that you will be able to develop a truly great concept. And second, there is little likelihood that, at a later date, you will be able to determine whether or not your publication was effective.

Ultimately, it is readers who decide whether or not a publication is successful, not the writer, designer, or chief publications officer. Not the president of your institution. And readers tell us that they are much more likely to be engaged by a publication with a single, simple, obvious purpose rather than a publication that is designed to meet the needs of multiple audiences.

If readers don't understand why they are receiving a publication, the odds are high that it will not engage them and that they will not act upon your messages. As you think about the purpose of your publication, remember this important rule: The more you try to accomplish with a single publication, the less likely that readers will respond.

Fourth, after you have defined your target audience, assessed their information needs and media habits, and clarified your rationale for the publication, it is time to begin thinking about your creative concept.

It is not an overstatement to say that a great creative concept is the lifeblood of a publication (or, for that matter, any message). A great creative concept is the wonderful sit-up-and-take-notice idea that drives almost every facet of your publication from initial design and copy through art, color, and typography selection. It is a great concept that helps diminish the impact of budget limitations. It is a great concept that helps keep your publication current, thereby extending its shelf life. And it is a great concept that assures that your publication is noticeable, salient, and memorable. (See Chapter 5 for a review of developing a creative concept.)

Great concepts depend on a number of variables, including clear audience definition, an accurate assessment of audience needs and expectations, and a clear, focused rationale for your publication. But great concepts also depend on a willingness to set aside your first good idea in favor of continuing the search for a great idea. In our experience, it is not a lack of creativity that hinders the development of great concepts. Rather, it is a willingness to settle too quickly and an unwillingness to keep pushing.

There are two research-related strategies that will help you develop your most effective concept possible. First, you should be constantly gathering data on the media to which your target audiences most often turn for information and entertainment. With this in mind, it is important to know:

- What magazines they read most often
- What radio stations they listen to
- What television programs they watch
- What kinds of books they read

Getting inside the media heads of your target audience is extremely important as you develop and refine your initial creative concepts. It is for this reason that college communications staff spend so much money on subscriptions to *Glamour, Seventeen, Rolling Stone, GQ, Sports Illustrated, Wired,* and *Campus Life.* These are the magazines that the designers and writers on staff read so that they can better understand college-bound high school students.

As part of this initial research, you also want to conduct a series of focus groups involving your target audiences. During the sessions, ask them to evaluate your past publications and those of your competitors. The insights you can gain are often invaluable.

Research also plays another important role: It helps your target audiences evaluate and refine concepts that you are currently developing. (In Chapter 4, we presented a number of ways in which research is used to learn audience media habits and refine concepts. This information and insight is especially important at this stage of your publication process. In Chapter 5, we also spent some time exploring how great concepts are created.)

Fifth, after you have created, tested, and refined your concept, it's time to translate your concept and turn it into the verbal and visual elements that become your finished publication. You must work out the marriage between design and copy. You must select the typefaces and make decisions about photography and photographic style. You must develop and even segment your mailing list. If required, you must write and test your cover letter. Then there are the details about your envelope—what message do you want it to send? And don't forget about postal regulations. In other words, you must address all the nagging little details that will turn your concept into a successful publication.

Sixth, in many respects, the last step in your publication process is the first step in the next: assessing the effectiveness of your publication after it has been received by the target audience. At this stage, you must ask yourself: Did it work? Did it achieve the goals established at the outset? Asking and answering these questions is especially important because so many of our publications are cyclical, and lessons learned can often be used to improve the effectiveness of upcoming publications. Assessment is the link between the conclusion of one publication cycle and the beginning of another.

Sometimes it is helpful to visualize the creation of your publication as a series of important and often interrelated processes. These processes are represented by the flow chart in Figure 12-2.

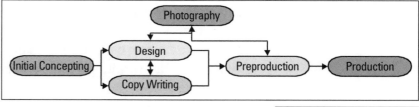

Figure 12-2
Flow chart of the publication process

Creating your publication

The process of creating your publication begins with the initial concept—the big idea that drives your design, copywriting, and photography. After you've developed, tested, and refined the concept, the process moves on to the design and copywriting stage. In most instances, these steps occur simultaneously and are highly symbiotic. It is likely that a great design idea will impact how the copy is written and, at the same time, copy often moves design.

As you develop the design and copy elements, you consider initial ideas on photography. These ideas will crystallize into a photo schedule that guides the often multiple-day photo shoot. It is a good idea at this point to have your designer direct the photo shoot. This helps heighten the relationship between design and photography.

After you've written, designed, and illustrated your publication, you move to the preproduction stage. Preproduction is a sometimes fuzzy area between the creative elements of design and copy and the actual printing and binding of your publication. It is an area fraught with technical terms such as prelim, pre-film proof, and blueline. Some of these terms reflect new technology. Some reflect technology that is little used today. But behind these terms are some important steps in the production process, and it is on these steps, and perhaps less on the terms themselves, that we focus our attention.

At its most basic, preproduction is involved with assembling the final publication. At this stage, you finalize layouts, choose and place art, position die-cuts, complete pagination and attend to a myriad of details. The goal of preproduction is simply to create a proof that comes close to simulating a printed piece that you can review and scrutinize carefully before additional, often heavy costs are incurred.

The first preproduction assemblage is the prelim. The prelim, often with low resolution or FPO (for position only) art is the first instance in which your complete publication is assembled. And while not finely tuned in some respects, the prelim does give you powerful insights into how the publication will look and feel. There may be several iterations of the prelim as it is tightened and refined.

After you finalize , you send it to the client, or the person initiating the publication, for a sign-off. The prelim must be carefully reviewed by the people who are sponsoring your publication because this is the last real check before it moves onto production where changes become much more costly and time consuming. The likelihood is very high that any errors that make it past the prelim stage will go unnoticed until the publication is printed. In addition, any errors that are caught after this stage will be costly to correct, both in terms of dollars and time.

Some words of warning here: Clients often do not scrutinze the prelim carefully and end up making type or other changes at the film stage because this stage is truly the last chance before printing. However, changes at the film stage are very expensive, and the costs and the delays that accompany them could be reduced if more attention is given to the prelim.

Once the prelim has been approved, a series of steps to move your publication to the press-ready stage are undertaken. In the old days (read that as "before computers"), keylines and mechanicals would be produced. Now, computer files are used to generate prefilm color proofs and, ultimately, the film from which final proofs and printing plates are made. Producing plates directly from computer (disk to plate) is becoming more common—thereby skipping the film stage completely—and increasing your need to check your proof earlier in the process.

After the bluelines, sometimes called dylux proofs, have been scrutinized, your publication is printed. Often your designer will undertake a series of press checks while the publication is being printed to assure that colors are running true and in register. After your publication is printed, it is bound and delivered to the client.

Terms and customs

Because design and printing technology is changing so quickly, we strongly suggest that you become—or hire someone who is—familiar with the terms used most often by your printers. The printing industry with its long and colorful history has some customs that can catch even the most savvy print buyer by surprise if he or she is not ready. For example, printers routinely charge people for overages of up to 10 percent. If you were expecting to pay for 50,000 annual fund pieces, printers often print an extra 10 percent (an additional 5,000) and fully expect to charge you for the additional pieces.

These and other printing customs are typically included with your contract or will be supplied by the printer if requested. Take the time to read the customs included in your contract carefully.

FBO

As you develop your concept, write copy, and develop your design, keep in mind the powerful differences between features, benefits, and outcomes and the need to project them effectively. A feature is a quality or characteristic. For example, you might have a library with 4.3 million volumes or an Olympic-sized swimming pool; these are features of a piece of property. Taken no further, a list of features seldom attracts or keeps the attention of a reader. Instead, readers want benefits. They want to understand clearly, from their perspective, the benefits of a large library or swimming pool. Although target audiences certainly value benefits more than features, what they are even more interested in is outcomes. They want to know how the large library will help them get better grades, land a better job, or get into a better graduate school.

When developing publications, we settle too quickly for lists of features; this many of this and that many of that. It is very important to translate those features, based on your audience research, into benefits and outcomes. Your readers are attracted by benefits, but they will invest their time and money in outcomes.

In developing your publications, you might want to consider creating a simple three-column table like Table 12-1. As you create your list of features, work hard on translating them into benefits and outcomes. It is especially important to work backward from the outcomes desired by your target audiences. For example, if nontraditional students are keenly interested in jobs, make sure your communications to them stress all the features and benefits on your campus that lead to getting jobs.

One other suggestion about features, benefits, and outcomes: Make sure you don't treat this information solely in blocks of copy. Features and benefits can often be projected visually. I remember one client who created a spread that included the business cards of recent graduates. The logos on the cards made a very compelling case about the success of its graduates. Another client arranged a photograph of a group of alumni who were working in Washington, DC. The photograph featured the alumni standing on the steps of the U.S. Capitol.

Table 12-1
Features, Benefits, and Outcomes

Features	Benefits	Outcomes
1.	1.	1.
2.	2.	2.
3.	3.	3.
4.	4.	4.
5.	5.	5.

Using testimonials

One of the questions we often receive is whether or not to use testimonials. Although there are certainly instances where testimonials don't make any sense, we believe that in most circumstances they can be an effective way to enhance a publication.

A number of years ago, I wrote a viewbook for a client in North Carolina. As part of this project we asked a young woman to sit down and write an essay on why she chose to attend this particular institution. Every so often, while she was in the throes of writing, we took her photograph. We used several of the photographs to illustrate the two-page spread that contained her essay. As a counterpoint, we mortised a smaller essay from her parents into the two-page spread. The daughter's essay was entitled, "Why I chose (the particular institution)..." The essay written by her parents was titled, "And why we're glad she did." These two testimonials, written and displayed in tandem, were extremely compelling.

I have learned over the years that the most effective testimonials are also the ones that are most believable. I remember testing a competitor's publication for a client. On one page there was a testimonial from a young woman who said, in effect, that this particular institution was the best college in the known universe. Rather than finding that testimonial compelling, the focus group of students found it amusing.

Later in the session, however, these same students highlighted another testimonial. In this one, another young woman said, "I didn't know where I wanted to go to school and someone said take a look at XYZ. I did, and I liked what I found." The young woman then went on to say that although this institution might not be right for everyone, it was right for her. The students in the focus group all said this testimonial was much more believable.

Tips for copywriting

There is perhaps nothing more important to the success of a publication than strong copy. However, even as I make this statement, I am aware that any truly effective treatment of copywriting should be of manuscript, not paragraph length. Fortunately, there are a number of excellent books on copywriting that are available, especially the books by Lewis, Blake, Ogilvy, Bly, and Yudkin listed in the recommended reading list at the end of this chapter.

Although we must leave a longer and more comprehensive commentary on the essentials of good copy to the professional writers, we offer the following more general suggestions that will help you write better copy:

- Keep focused on your creative concept. Use it like a thesis statement to keep your writing on track.
- Work from an outline.
- Hook your reader early.
- Keep your copy conversational in tone. Imagine that you are speaking to someone sitting across from you.
- Avoid polysyllabics (like this one).
- Rewrite. Rewrite. Rewrite.
- Don't bludgeon your reader with verbiage. Remember, less is more.
- Integrate copy with headlines and captions.

Design to communicate

One of the more interesting discussions related to the creation of publications is the relationship between design and communication. There are some designers who appear to care little about the need to communicate and seem more interested in serving their own needs to express themselves. Their designs seem to crowd out the message as they seek to develop pieces that have tremendous visual or emotional impact. In their use of type, treatment of photography, letter and line spacing, and white space and color, these designers do not appear to be heeding the needs of their target audience or their client.

I soundly reject this notion of design. And at the risk of offending designers everywhere, I suggest that the publications that serve colleges and universities best—the publications that raise dollars, recruit students, and build relationships should have one overarching goal: communication.

Colin Wheildon, writing in *Type and Layout,* makes the case more eloquently than I can. Although he is addressing both design and typography as elements of design, his overall message is clear. He writes:

> Design is not, nor should not be, mere decoration and abstraction, but part of the business of communication. The concern should not be for the beholder's—or creator's—eye for beauty. It should be for those who, it is hoped, will read a publication and gain sufficiently from it. . . . But how frequently are opinions on the invalidity of a typographic design cast aside, displaced by a view that legibility isn't important if the product looks exciting? This is absurd. A design that looks exciting but is incomprehensible is nothing more than a beautifully painted square wheel.

He goes on to state that publications and advertisements:

> . . . should be vehicles for transmitting ideas, and their design should be an integral part of that process, and forever under scrutiny.

> Good design is a blend of function and form, and the greater of these is function. This is as true of typography as it is of an opera house or a space shuttle.

> Typography (or design) fails if it allows the reader's interest to decline. It fails absolutely if it contributes to the destruction of the reader's interest. It is easy to accept Morison's dictum that any design which comes between the author and the reader is wrong.

Of course, good design is extraordinarily important, and I would never stand in the way of creativity. But sometimes the greatest creative challenge arises from returning to the same basic messages—enroll, donate, support—time and time again and coming up with new and unique ways to communicate these messages rather than adopting the notion that these messages are no longer important and that design should stand in its place.

As the paper carries the print, design must help carry the message.

Typography and design errors to avoid

Building somewhat on Wheildon's remarks, the following is a list of typographical and design taboos first developed by Ed Elliot. They include:

- Avoid text without sufficient contrast to the background.
- Avoid text reversed out of a dark color.
- Avoid flush-right or centered paragraphs.
- Avoid text that is too condensed.
- Avoid character spacing that is too tight.

Turning scanners into readers

One of the greatest challenges facing anyone who is interested in developing a publication is turning scanners into readers. In their book *2,239 Tested Secrets for Direct Marketing Success,* direct marketers Denny Hatch and Don Jackson, cite Ed Elliott's list of graphic devices that will help turn a publication scanner into an interested reader. Although some are obvious, others are much less so. The devices mentioned by Elliott include:

- Table of contents
- Headlines and subheads
- Photography, especially of people and action
- Tables, charts, and graphics
- Illustrations clarifying or reinforcing text
- Captions under every visual
- A word or subhead that is bigger, bolder, blacker, or in a different color from other elements on the page
- Enlarged numbers, possibly followed by an enlarged or bold lead
- Anything that interrupts a page-by-page pattern of columns
- Pull quotes
- A paragraph set off in bold or with a double indent
- Bulleted text, especially with bullets that are larger than or different from other bulleted text

Getting great photographs

Great photographs are an essential part of many great publications. To help you develop the best photographs possible, Steve Jordan, of G. Steve Jordan Photography, offers the following suggestions.

First use the 12 steps to planning a great photo shoot. Whether you run a two-person shop or are VP for communications, whether you're hiring a photographer for a day or a design firm on retainer, consider these guidelines to getting the best images possible:

1. Know what you are trying to say. Tell your photographer the tone you envision. Is there a theme to promote or a style or feeling you are trying to capture? Do you want photos that are action-packed, contemplative, or gregarious? Is there a preferred layout favoring horizontal or vertical images, close-

ups, or long shots? Don't forget ethnic and gender balance and, above all, remember who your audience is.

2. Know how the photos will be used. Will the photos be used primarily in a viewbook and related publications? These images can be more thematic, more visually daring. Conversely, more generic photos have a broader appeal and can be plugged into a variety of formats. If you need both, plan accordingly.

3. Anticipate future needs. Know your future needs, especially for seasonal shots. Your publication schedule is usually out-of-sync with what's happening outside your window, so plan to shoot your seasonal images for use months later. Even when publication plans are indefinite, there is always a place for good seasonal stock shots of your campus.

4. Don't just hope for the best, plan for it. The odds that a classroom, lab, or lounge will look the way you want on a given shooting day are slim to none—really! Although your photographer and designer may be experts at making these areas look their best on short notice, most photos can be further improved by planning for them. Scouting and prepping a location with an eye toward the visual always helps. Is that new piece of high-tech equipment just a black box? Are the areas in good shape? How about some colorful props for a blank wall? Plan ahead to assure you have well-dressed, attractive, and dynamic faculty models and a demographically diverse group of students who are fashionably, but not faddishly, dressed. It is much easier to juggle people and props to create the photo you need than it is to try and create it on the spot. (But see secret # 9.)

5. Make the most of each set-up. As long as you've gone through all the trouble, expand the potential uses of an image by having the photographer shoot horizontals and verticals, close and long, and with a mix of available students and props.

6. Alter your perspective. Have you ever been to the top of the student union building? There may be a great view of your campus from there. How about a bird's-eye view of a class circled outside around a professor? Early morning and late afternoon shadows can give a fresh graphic look to campus shots, especially from above. Inclement weather, though not usually welcome, can yield unique and exciting images. And don't forget the neighborhood around campus, especially urban campuses. Brainstorm with your photographer!

7. Plan for props. Sweatshirts and books are great but how about colorful umbrellas; musical instruments; tools from a unique course, for example, archeology, or civil engineering: or equipment used for extracurricular activities by the outing, equestrian, or drama clubs?

8. Use visual symbols. Shift your focus from a literal point of view. Books on a desk in an empty classroom may speak of potential. How about coming in close, for example, on a dancer's shoes or the hands of an artist or an athlete? These images may say more to the viewer because of their symbolic nature.

9. Be resourceful. As time permits, exploit visually stimulating situations that

present themselves. Most faculty and students are flattered by the attention you give them and will make time to participate. Be sure you're candid about how much time you'll need, especially if lighting is involved.

10. Prioritize. If you run into snags during the shoot, know which shots are "must have" and which can be put off. Try to keep in mind which scenes will be tough to reschedule or can be shot later. Does the unplanned shot of a spontaneous situation look better than the next picture on your agenda? Have a sense of how much leeway you've allowed.

11. Be realistic. So many departments, so little time. And, realistically, the best images do take time. Trying to shoot for the sesquicentennial viewbook, the six satellite brochures, and the alumni newsletter in black and white and color during commencement is like trying to cook a seven-course meal on a hot plate. And speaking of meals, do your best to allow time for lunch and a few breaks or risk burnout.

12. Communicate. Good communications by the admissions staff with your photographer, designer, and the campus community can make or break a shoot—especially where there is a specific idea to illustrate. Consider showing your photographer other viewbooks or advertising campaigns that express the feeling you'd like in your publications.

> 66 **As you refine your concept and work to translate it into publications, take the time to test different iterations.** 99

Steve Jordan also provided what he calls his secrets checklist—insider ideas to help you get the best possible photographs. They include:

- ■ Establish a theme if applicable, and talk it over with your photographer.
- ■ Delegate a key person to facilitate all aspects of your photo shoot.
- ■ Pinpoint your specific needs where applicable (e.g., vertical cover shot).
- ■ Set up a shoot list allowing one hour per set-up and indicate priority of shot, desired message, and any backup plans. Also note what to avoid (e.g., baseball caps).
- ■ Use student tour guides or ambassadors, or members of fraternities and sororities, theater groups, etc., as sources for models. Consider a payback to students to assure participation (e.g., a pizza party). Plan on a minimum of six students per hour in your photo shoot, and don't forget ethnic and gender balance.
- ■ Arrange for props, both recreational (sports equipment, Frisbees, bicycles, sweatshirts) and academic (laptop computer, calculator, maps, class-specific tools).
- ■ Make logistical arrangements, including access to classrooms, dorm rooms, and rooftops. Consider access to golf cart, ladder, and cherry picker truck.
- ■ Consider off-campus lifestyle shots and plan accordingly.
- ■ Arrange for sports set-ups or consider using in-house stock.
- ■ Don't be too literal in your planning—remember the strongest images are often symbolic.
- ■ Be sure participating faculty and students are aware of the time required for and disruption caused by your photography. Consider letting your photogra-

pher be the "bad cop" if you need to ask them to stay longer than planned.

Don't forget the envelope—unless you mean to

One of the biggest decisions you must make as you develop your publication is how it will be mailed. During my career, we have seen the pendulum swing back and forth from envelope always to envelope never. Right now, we are somewhere in the middle.

Of course, there are arguments for and against envelopes. We know, for example, that envelopes can protect the publication from damage during transit, entice the reader with cover lines, and even attract attention with the daring use of color and other design elements. We also know that the cost of the envelope can increase the expense of the mailing, that envelopes can complicate postage, and that envelopes can even impede communication.

There are no hard and fast rules on envelope use, but we concur with such savvy communicators as Ray Jutkins and Pat Friesen who hold that you should never underestimate the contribution that an envelope makes in the overall success of a mailing. To that end, Jutkins and Friesen, quoted by Denny Hatch and Don Jackson, offer the following insights on envelopes.

Jutkins explains the five basic truths about how people view the envelopes they receive in the mail:

- People look at their names. If the names on the envelope are spelled correctly and if the initials and title are right, then it becomes an invitation to be opened.
- People look at the teaser copy. They especially look at copy that is close to their name and then at copy that is elsewhere on the envelope.
- People look at who sent the piece of mail.
- People check the postage and how it is applied. Stamps get the most attention and metered mail the least.
- People turn the envelope over. They look at the back before they open it.

Freisen reminds us that as we design envelopes, we should pay attention to the following six envelope "hot spots"— opportunities to increase an envelope's ability to communicate and enhance the message. They are:

- The return address
- Addressing—window, label, computer, handwritten
- Postage
- Teaser copy
- Back envelope flap
- Back teaser copy

Remember to test

One of the themes that we have developed in earlier chapters and throughout this one is the need to test everything. As you refine your concept and work to translate it into publications, take the time to test different iterations. Test different cover designs. Test copy. Test photography. And test cover letters. An ongoing commitment to testing will dramatically increase the effectiveness of your publications and in all likelihood will reduce their production costs. And although testing may be the last thing you want to do at times, it is almost always the best thing to do. Take the time to test.

The Top 10 publication mistakes

There is no better teacher than hard-won experience. With this in mind, and borrowing a format from David Letterman, we offer the following list of Top 10 publication mistakes. (Some of the items are reiterations of key themes in this chapter and others in the book.) They are as follows:

- Not knowing enough about the publication's target audience. Too many publications are created blind. Before creating a publication, you need to know the perceptions, misperceptions, motivations, and the values, attitudes, and lifestyles (VALs) of your target audiences.
- Not meeting the information needs of your publication's target audience. Many times, publications are developed, written, and designed from the perspective of the institution rather than the intended target audience. To be successful, your messages must be meaningful to target audiences, not stakeholders such as presidents and faculty members. Ask and answer this question: What do these people want to know about you?
- Not knowing enough about your competition. You do compete—for students, for donated dollars, and for attention. Not anticipating the level of competition you face can seriously undermine your ability to communicate effectively.
- Not anticipating how this publication will fit into the overall communication flow. Seldom are publications created and executed in a vacuum. They almost always exist in the context of a larger communication flow, and the materials and information that precede your publication can dramatically enhance—or reduce—its effectiveness.
- Loss of focus—trying to accomplish too much with a single publication or aiming one publication at too many different audiences. Segmenting messages and target audiences is essential, and more narrowly focused publications directed at specific audiences will always be more successful than a more general, scattered approach.
- Letting design overshadow your message. It is tempting to focus on how good a publication looks rather than how well it works. Successful publications use design to enhance, not undermine communication. Don't spend so much time trying to be visually unique or trendy that you fail to communicate and motivate the reader to act.
- Forgetting that a publication must look good before it will ever be picked up and read. Students, donors, and all manner of people are more likely to read a publication that looks good than one that does not. And while styles may vary

among target audiences, the almost universal need for a striking cover, great art, and wonderful design and typography cannot be overestimated.

- Failure to develop a comprehensive family look. There is nothing worse—and nothing less integrated—than a cacophony of styles and looks in a communication flow. A weak family look makes publications appear disjointed, unprofessional, and reflects poorly on your institution. Settle on a basic family look that is enduring and stick to that look. Resist the temptation to change it without a strong rationale.

- Not understanding why a publication failed. A publication's success is dependent on a variety of factors including the carrier or envelope, the timing of the mailing, the quality and segmentation of the mailing list, the communication strategies that preceded the publication, and your general institutional image. Too often, however, when the response is poor, we focus our attention solely on the publication. The odds are high that other factors should also be considered.

- Forgetting the first rule of publication: Perception is the ultimate reality. If it looks good, people will assume you are good. And if it looks bad, well, people will assume some other things. When your readers view your publication, there is no one there to defend it or to talk about all the problems you had during production. No one to explain about your inadequate budget. Your target audience will judge the piece solely on its own merits, so if you can't do something great, don't do anything, because there is, after all, nothing more expensive than cheap.

Strategies for reducing publication costs

With an increased emphasis on stewardship, it is always important to seek opportunities to reduce publication costs, especially if these strategies will not negatively impact quality. Diane Fisher Johnson, college editor at Centre College, offers these suggestions:

- Don't change the blueline. Make sure those who need to sign off on a publication see it before it goes to the printer. At blueline stage, you should correct only egregious errors. Hint: Wrong phone numbers or misspelled words are egregious errors. Missing commas are not.

- Design with type. Consider snappy typography instead of photos or other expensive art. But remember: It's pointless if the message can't be read.

- Recycle. That fabulous color viewbook photo might make a great donor report cover. Since the audiences don't overlap, who's to know?

- Keep it simple. Not every project requires a press. A good laser printer and a color photocopier may be all your job requires. Keep in mind, however, that copy for copy, laser printing is more expensive than commercial printing.

- Keep it standard. You can have an odd-sized publication, but it will usually cost you. You will pay money for custom envelopes, postage, and you may even have to assemble the mailing by hand.

- Waste not, want not. You pay for the paper whether you use the whole sheet or not. If you must design a nonstandard size, use the trim for another publication. You might add a pocket schedule to an artist-series brochure, for example.
- Use color creatively. Overlapping two colors to provide a third can make a simple two-color piece seem more exciting. Screens add another color dimension. Build PMS colors out of process color.
- Design with paper. Interesting paper with flecks or texture can make one- or two-color publications look elegant for less.
- Plan ahead. Print a two-year supply of major publications such as viewbooks and catalogs, but only bind half. The following year, you can update cost and deadline information. Good printers will store the unbound pages for you at no charge.
- Make a deal. Printers, especially if they do a lot of work for you, may be willing to donate some or all of a special project as a gift in kind.

Evaluating publications

Often before undertaking the next iteration of a publication, we are asked to evaluate its predecessor. Unfortunately, there is no one tried-and-true method of determining whether a publication is good or bad—effective or ineffective. But whether the publication is designed to increase donations or recruit students, data and insights gained from these sources will help assure its success.

Essentially, you should evaluate a publication at three stages in its life cycle: (1) while it is being planned, (2) while it is being produced, and (3) after it is finished and in service.

"The key to passing client evaluation is to wed your client to the concept from the beginning."

Prepublication evaluation

A very poor reason to do a publication this year is because you did one last year. Instead, I suggest you adapt a "zero-based" approach to your first evaluation. Justify why your publication should be produced by asking yourself:

- What is the role or goal of your publication?
- What audience or audiences is it designed to serve?
- What audience needs will it meet?
- How and when and by whom were these audience needs determined?
- How will your publication fit into the marketing mix of messages that this audience is already receiving?
- Where should your publication fit into your message cycle?
- Is your publication really the best solution? Why?

After you have asked these questions, scrutinize the answers. You should be able to succinctly state the purpose and goal of your publication now. Like the thesis sentence from your high school essays, this goal definition will help you develop your publication.

These preliminary evaluations should also include the environment or context in which your planned publication will exist. Determine how it will compete with other messages in the marketplace. Analyze what is known about your target audience's disposition toward your institution and your message. Evaluate the timing of your publication and consider if it would be better to delay or advance production. Determine if your publication fits the theme and graphic style of other messages from your institution—is it part of a family?

Remember, if the goals, expectations, and environment of your planned publication are not adequately defined, then you have no benchmark against which to determine its ultimate success or failure. In addition, inadequate or uncertain definitions in the planning process may mean that the expense and time spent on it cannot be justified, and your publication should be aborted.

Evaluating during production

It is extremely important both individually and collectively to evaluate the components that form a successful publication. Simple evaluations of the copy, illustrations, graphics, and overall design can greatly reduce your chance of error.

As you begin your evaluations, remember your publication actually has two audiences: (1) the target audience for whom your publication was designed, and (2) the client—the person or group who is initiating your publication. If your target audience is not satisfied, then your publication will be unsuccessful no matter how well it is received by other end users.

The key to passing client evaluation is to wed your client to the concept from the beginning. Actively involve him or her in the early brainstorming sessions that defined the expectations of your planned publication. Ask him or her to help you answer the questions outlined above. By involving your clients in the early concept development, they will be less likely to challenge the working concepts and themes and will make all subsequent evaluations easier to obtain and interpret.

Assuming that your prepublication evaluation question-and-answer session produced a viable concept, begin your evaluating process by looking at your copy. Consider conducting a readability measure to determine the copy's reading difficulty. A readability measure assigns a numerical score to the copy. The score corresponds to the number of years of education the person reading the copy should have to read the text comfortably. Ideally, college publications should have a readability measure of about 10 to 12. This means that people with an average high school education may read them easily. Unfortunately, college publications often have scores of 20, 21, or higher. By way of comparison, news magazines aim for a score of around 8 to 10. .

Another evaluation is to pretest your copy on actual members of your publication's end-user audience. Either in a focus group or through a survey, ask the following questions:

- ■ Did the readers find the copy interesting?
- ■ What parts bored them?
- ■ Were all logical questions answered?
- ■ Was too much information presented?

■ Was the style or tone of the copy appropriate?

■ Could some of the information be presented or reinforced in graphics?

You might also ask the readers to edit the text by having them write directly on the copy. Ask respondents to indicate which sections they liked best, which sections could be left out, what parts were confusing, or what information should be added.

When you have tested and honed your copy, turn your attention to the visuals—illustrations and photographs—that you want to use. Begin by asking yourself if they are technically adequate. Then ask yourself:

■ Are the photographs current and visually interesting?

■ Are they well focused and well exposed?

■ Are they cropped adequately?

■ Are the graphics—illustrations, tables, and graphs—of production quality?

■ Do they have too much detail?

■ Do they support the story line or do they confuse the reader?

After the visuals have passed the first hurdle, evaluate them both alone and in conjunction with the text in a focus-group or open-discussion setting. Ask viewers to evaluate the visuals you are considering and to suggest ideas for additional or replacement visuals. Pay particular attention to the visuals to be used on the cover of the publication and the graphics to be used to explain important or difficult parts of the text.

Evaluating the final design before production is crucial. But if you have tested each of the discrete elements during development, this final evaluation shouldn't be a problem. Marshall McLuhan reminds us that the medium is the message. This is particularly true when evaluating full-scale mock-ups. The mock-ups must be as accurate and representative as possible for your evaluation to be legitimate.

At this stage, you are concerned with how all the elements—copy, art, and design—work together. You want to find out if your readers feel your design supports your message. You want to know if readers like the size, position, and color of photographs. Do they think the graphics are well-designed and placed? In short, do they like the publication? If they do, that's great. If they don't, find out why.

Postproduction evaluation

The final evaluations are concerned with how well the publication fulfilled the expectations outlined during the concept-development stage. Postproduction evaluations must include input from both your client and your publication's actual end users. Often, clients are asked to fill out a postmortem on the publication. A typical postmortem is a laundry list of questions covering all elements of the publication, including cover, copy, design, and production. It usually includes a section of suggestions for improvement and concludes by asking each respondent to evaluate the publication on a scale ranging from one (poor) to five (excellent).

In some cases, this postproduction evaluation may include the methods used to distribute the publication. For example, should your publication have been mailed first class instead of bulk? Would an August mailing have been more appropriate than a November mailing? Should your envelope have included cover lines to entice the reader?

> " Although it would be foolish to say a publication is the only dynamic involved in either annual fund donations or a student's willingness to attend a college night, publications often play pivotal roles in the information/ persuasion process. "

When completed, data from your postmortem form are analyzed by your project leaders and your client. Following this review, the data are added to the publication's job file so if you decide to revise your publication, your postmortem evaluation will be available.

There are numerous ways to involve the end-user audience in determining your publication's overall effectiveness. Again, you can conduct focus group evaluations. Ask your readers to list five adjectives that describe your publication. If you include it in your publication, a reader response mechanism would provide valuable information on its effectiveness. Another option is to evaluate your publication against a predetermined baseline of effectiveness. If, for example, it was an annual fund publication, did donations to the fund increase? If it was an invitation to a college night, did a significant number of students respond?

Although it would be foolish to say a publication is the only dynamic involved in either annual fund donations or a student's willingness to attend a college night, publications often play pivotal roles in the information/persuasion process. If the annual fund drive or college group discussions, postmortems or other evaluation mechanisms are successful, however, then your publication can be safely labeled as contributing to it.

Selling yourself

In May 1986, CURRENTS published an extraordinarily useful—and still fresh—article entitled, "Marketing Begins at Home" written by Ann Bennett. Within the article was a sidebar outlining a series of strategies for increasing your personal and professional effectiveness. Recognizing that some of the people who offer these insights have moved onto other positions and even other institutions, we present the text in the sidebar on page 190.

The idea box

Nearly 20 years ago, when I first began in this business, I learned how important it was to have an idea box. Mine is a beat-up, old cardboard file box held together with duct tape. This box is full of treasures. There's an old Earlham viewbook and a fund-raising piece from Clarkson University. I have an original copy of the "Ski Terra Haute" poster and the Harvey Mudd Junk Mail Kit.

There's a great poster from Ohio State with Gordon Gee and another from Marist College showing some students rowing in front of a stretch of trees in their fall colors. The tag line, "October on the Hudson," is absolutely captivating.

Some of the pieces in the idea box have nothing to do with colleges and universities. I have a great brochure that introduces a new car company—Saturn—and another that introduces a new line of furniture from Herman Miller. I even have a copy of the first issue of USA Today and the last copy of GEO. And then there are print ads: some from Nike, Xerox, and Volvo; others from Adelphi, Meredith, Houston Baptist, and NYU. The box contains an old "blue book" (not all the ideas in the box are good ones) and a copy of the Villanova CD. I have a copy of the Knox Box and the old Drake video.

Tips on Selling Yourself

Workshops, handbooks, manuals, fliers, and awards all send your campus constituents a message: We publications professionals want to help you with writing, editing, design, photography, and marketing.

But your effectiveness really boils down to how well you present the concept, copy, and layout to your clients. Here are some techniques that seasoned professionals Ann Bennett surveyed use in marketing their products on campus.

"Present tight comprehensive layouts in a formal manner. And remember, listen to the client; the designer is not always right."

Greg Dymkowski,
Director of Publications,
University of California, Irvine

"Don't create in isolation. Your results will reflect this. Involve clients in the creative process from conceptual development through approving copy and checking paste-ups to signing off on bluelines."

Linda Steele,
Director of College Relations,
Hollins College

"Try to deal only with the chief decision maker. Listen carefully. Have respect for the client's expertise. Explain your services and competencies. This reduces conflict to a negotiable and responsible level. But, protect your creative staff from the boring and the bashing."

Emily Smith,
Director of Communications,
University of New Hampshire

"Be patient. Everyone benefits from a job well done. The grief, the controversy, the time wasting, and so on are forgotten once the printed piece is delivered and put into use. Develop a realistic attitude. Not everyone will be in your corner; some people will always try to hold on to their ownership of a project. Live with it, but keep trying."

Ann Satterthwaite,
Director of Publications,
Haverford College

"Getting one's way with publications has to be based on consensus building. A good track record certainly doesn't hurt, and being consistent on 'internal market testing' is a real plus also. But you have to build a consensus so that when an important series or controversial idea seems right, you have a chance to try your idea."

Cynthia Moran,
Director of University Relations,
Drew University

"Learn to compromise. While we won't accept ideas that we don't believe are suitable, we do give clients the right to reject a concept or design. In most cases, our clients welcome any help we can give them."

Sharon Poff,
Director of Public Relations/
Publications,
Bucknell University

"Negotiate from a position of strength. You're the publications pro; he or she is the departmental pro."

Carl Magel,
Director of Publications and
Graphic Services,
University of Notre Dame

"Don't get too attached to ideas until you try them out on other people. Usually more workable or successful ones come out of such an exchange."

Joan Lentczner,
Director of News and
Publications,
Radford University

"Enlist the support of top administrators—deans, directors, and the president. My membership on the president's advisory committee allows me to present problems and proposals and receive immediate feedback."

Henry Hamlin,
Director of Publications,
Principia College

"Try a controversial idea in a scaled-down form, i.e., a flier that precedes a brochure or poster. If it flies, it's easier to convince the client to take the risk."

Judith Phair,
Director of Public Relations,
Goucher College

"Measure the value of your ideas by their potential for advancing the institution. Good ideas require adequate time and resources to develop into good products. We try to measure proposals for new projects in terms of the time and resources they will require and their potential for benefit. The same logic should also hold for perennial projects."

Jim Leach,
Director of Communications,
Colgate University

"Depending on the client, negotiate, discuss, educate, and even pray in order to get your concept accepted. But if it's a 'low-grade' client, I'll give up. Sometimes it just isn't worth the effort."

Tom Vitale,
Director of Publications, Georgia
Institute of Technology

"Plow straight ahead. Long ago I reached an agreement with the university president: Fire me if I'm way off line, but don't saddle my creativity with committees."

Douglas Geddie,
Director of the Office of External
Relations,
Brock University

"Respect the client's instincts. Butter and baloney are for politicians, not for us. Good ideas sell themselves, or maybe they're not so good. Respect for the client by itself is effective in winning support for an imaginative project."

Conrad Lulawas,
Director of Graphic Services,
Brown University

"The more I consult, the worse the product, so I avoid it at all costs. This policy requires us to take on a lot of responsibility. I tell my colleagues that they can jump on me when I fall on my face. In the meantime, they'll get a better product if they let us alone."

Bill Freeland,
Director of Communications and
Marketing,
LaGuardia Community College

"Project an authoritative image—always based on your true expertise. Tell doubting clients that if they insist on a particular idea, they may be sacrificing the effectiveness of the piece."

Marie Avona,
Director of Public Affairs,
Pratt Institute

Taken from CURRENTS article "Marketing Begins at Home." (May 1996)

This is my idea box. It is a collection of really great stuff (except for the blue book). And sometimes when I'm stuck for an idea, I pull out the box and start wading. More often than not, something in the box starts the creative juices flowing.

If you don't have an idea box, get one. And fill it with the stuff that captures your imagination.

Some final reminders

We close with three simple reminders.

First, William of Ockham reminds us that the better answers are usually the simple answers. In an era of increasing complexity and sophistication, sometimes the simple is what gets noticed.

Second, remember that all the four-color and foil stamps in the world won't save a flawed concept. Spend quality time at the concept stage and don't rush to production without an idea that sings.

Third, there is nothing more expensive than cheap. Readers don't care about your budget or your unreasonable deadlines or all the obstacles you encountered in production. All they think about is whether your publication works. This is the only litmus test that matters, and it is a litmus test against which readers will measure your publication and your institution. Don't cheap out. If you can't do quality, don't do anything.

In addition to the recommended readings and the Web resources in Appendix C, we recommend the following periodicals:

Communication Arts	(800) 258-9111
Print	(212) 463-0600
Step-by-Step	(309) 688-2300

We also suggest exploring UCDA, the University and College Designer's Association. Its contact information can be found in Appendix D.

Finally, get on the mailing list of Watson-Guptill in New York. It publishes a breathtaking array of books on design, illustration, typography, and the whole range of the printing arts. Its telephone number is (212) 764-7300.

Recommended Readings

Meggs, Philip B. *6 Chapters in Design.* San Francisco: Chronicle Books, 1997.

Bierut, Michael, William Drenttel, Steven Heller, and D.K. Holland. *Looking Closer: Critical Writings on Graphic Design,* 2nd ed. New York: Allworth Press, 1997.

Blake, Gary and Robert W. Bly. *The Elements of Copywriting: The Essential Guide to Creating Copy That Gets the Results You Want.* New York: Macmillan Publishing Company, 1998.

Bly, Robert W. *The Copywriter's Handbook: A Step-by-Step Guide to Writing Copy that Sells.* New York: Henry Holt and Company, 1990.

Hatch, Denny and Don Jackson. *2,239 Tested Secrets for Direct Marketing Success: The Pros Tell You Their Time-Proven Secrets.* Lincolnwood, IL: NTC/Contemporary Publishing Group, 1997.

Heller, Steven and Karen Pomeroy. *Design Literacy: Understanding Graphic Design.* New York: Allworth Press, 1997.

Higgins, Denis. *The Art of Writing Advertising: Conversations with William Bernback, Leo Burnett, George Gribbin, David Ogilvy, Rosser Reeves.* Lincolnwood, IL: NTC/Contemporary Publishing Group, 1994.

Lewis, Herschell Gordon. *Power Copywriting: Dynamic New Communications Techniques to Help You Sell More Products and Services.* Chicago: Dartnell Corporation, 1994.

Lupton, Ellen. *Mixing Messages: Graphic Design in Contemporary Culture.* New York: Princeton Architectural Press, 1996.

Ogilvy, David. *Ogilvy On Advertising.* New York: Crown Publishing, 1983.

Swann, Alan. *How to Understand and Use Design and Layout.* Cincinnati: F & W Publications, Inc., 1991.

Wheildon, Colin. *Type and Layout: How Typography & Design Can Get Your Message Across—Or Get in the Way.* Berkeley, CA: Strathmore Press, 1995.

Yudkin, Marcia. *Persuading on Paper: The Complete Guide to Writing Copy that Pulls in Business.* New York: NAL Dutton, 1996.

Zollo, Peter. *Wise Up to Teens: Insights into Marketing and Advertising to Teenagers.* Ithaca, NY: New Strategist Publications, 1995.

13

Creating an Integrated Advertising Campaign

A. R. (Andy) Kesling

It is Thursday morning and your phone rings. The caller is the marketing director for one of your university's continuing education programs.

"I've just bought space for a newspaper ad from a rep who offered me a great deal," the marketing director tells you. "Can you put one together for me? I already have a mock-up of what I want. I'll fax it to you in the next couple of hours. Oh, by the way, the publication says it needs camera-ready art by noon tomorrow. That's not a problem, is it?"

Does this situation sound familiar? With the information you learn in this chapter, you may not be able to cure your campus clients of the "last-minute" disease, but you will be better prepared to make the most of advertising for your institution.

The job of advertising

The American Marketing Association defines advertising as "any paid form of nonpersonal communication about an organization, product, service, or idea by an identified sponsor."

Solomon Dutka, in his book *Defining Advertising Goals for Measured Advertising*

Results, offers a more pragmatic definition. "Advertising's job purely and simply is to communicate, to a defined audience, information and a frame-of-mind that stimulates action." Dutka continues, "Advertising succeeds or fails depending on how well it communicates the desired information and attitudes to the right people at the right time and at the right cost." Later in this chapter, we will explore how to target the right people at the right cost.

"Getting the word out" is a phrase often mentioned by a person who is considering advertising. Effective advertising gets the word out and more. This sponsored mass communication is directed to a specific market segment potentially interested in the service you have to offer. It includes a clear message stated as a benefit, urges action that will be beneficial to the advertiser, and costs less per contact than any other communication tool in the promotional mix.

Advertising may be an audience's first contact with a product or service, and it can serve to reassure consumers that their decision to purchase was appropriate. Have you noticed how an automobile manufacturer's ads attract your attention after you have made the purchase?

Advertising's relation to the larger media mix

Throughout this book, we have explored the idea of a marketing mix. We have discussed the 4 Ps and 4 Cs. One of these Ps—promotion— is itself a mix comprised of the communication tools of publicity and public relations, direct marketing, sales promotion, events, personal sales, and advertising. Although tomes have been written about these tools, let's review the strengths and weakeness of some of these promotional media:

- Publicity
- Direct marketing
- Sales promotion
- Special events
- Personal sales

Publicity

One of publicity's greatest strengths is the capacity to increase the credibility of the message. An endorsement from an unbiased party leads the audience to believe that claims made are true, not just hype. Publicity is also relatively inexpensive compared with other communication options.

The downside is that you have virtually no control over the message content, and you cannot schedule the message to appear at a time you select. Both content and timing are the choice of the media gatekeeper. And measurement of effectiveness is difficult to achieve regardless of whether you succeed or fall short of your communication goal.

Direct marketing

Publicity's shortcoming on measurability is actually a direct marketing strength. With publicity, you can segment audiences with precision and personalize messages for almost every recipient if sufficient internal or external data systems are available to identify audiences.

The cost of such precision is the high expense paid per impression. And, if executed unskillfully, direct marketing can diminish favorable impressions that audiences may hold for your organization. In short, perceived junk mail can junk your brand equity.

Sales promotion

Potential students (or their parents) may not clip dollars-off coupons for tuition discounts, but many expect scholarship funds, which are a form of sales promotion. Sizable tuition discounts from the use of scholarships can prompt a student to choose one institution over another. The weakness of sales promotion is that its ability to condition the consumer to shop on the basis of price can reduce the perceived value of the service and reduce sales margins.

Special events

A special event, as we have seen in Chapter 11, offers an opportunity for rich interaction with a special audience that has chosen to attend the event. It may be a campus visit for prospective students and their parents or a periodic visit by industry representatives to a school's facilities. Typically, the audience has chosen to be a part of the activity. Handled with care and executed professionally, an event can help position an institution in people's minds. Most events, however, usually reach only a small number of the desired audience, and the cost per contact is relatively high.

Personal sales

The most effective communication tool to convert interest to commitment is the personal sale. Personal communication frees an audience to question issues not explained when other communication tools are used and provides an opportunity to get an immediate response. It gives the presenter the chance to answer any objections raised by the audience. The cost of personal sales, however, ranks as the most expensive among the communication tools.

> 66 **Advertising may be an audience's first contact with a product or service, and it can serve to reassure consumers that their decision to purchase was appropriate.** 99

Expectations from advertising

What can we expect advertising to do for our institutions? Consider:
- Awareness
- Control
- Branding

Awareness

One of the key advantages of advertising is its ability to generate awareness. By virtue of the reach factor, thousands, tens of thousands, or hundreds of thousands of readers, listeners, or viewers will be exposed to an ad or commercial. And, with a simple message and engaging delivery, an advertisement can lead to a shared, cultural experience that results in a large audience discussing the product or service highlighted in the paid announcement. A memorable Wendy's Hamburgers' commercial featured no-nonsense Claire Peller barking, "Where's the beef?" The popular query was repeated by thousands of Americans, and a presidential candidate later adopted the phrase during a series of debates. Advertising is one of the best tools available if your campus client's agenda includes "building awareness."

Control

By choosing advertising to communicate with an audience, you choose to control the messages conveyed and images portrayed. Unlike a news release, no editor will alter your message to fit it into a story. To some extent, you can direct the message to the audience you want to receive it, but you also pay for the privilege. The expense prevents many institutions from using this communication tool. Nevertheless, it is the most cost-effective way to reach a large group of people.

Branding

Another element that you can control in advertising is the image portrayed of your institution. This kind of control can create or sustain "brand equity." David Aaker, a national authority on branding, defines brand equity as "the set of brand assets and liabilities linked to the brand, its name, and symbol that add or subtract value to a product or service for a firm and/or its customers."

Houston Baptist University in Houston addressed its brand's assets and liabilities with a round of print and outdoor advertising in advance of a capital campaign (Figure 13-1). The communication objective was to raise visibility for the university's academic programs, as well as to address misperceptions regarding the ethnic composition of the student body and the university's denominational affiliation.

"We felt that we had a window of opportunity prior to launching the campaign to make some inroads into the Houston community," says Sharon Saunders, associate vice president for public relations. "The bottom line was that those who knew us loved us, but we were virtually unknown in the fourth-largest city in the United States."

Figure 13-1
Ad for Houston Baptist University
Courtesy of Houston Baptist University

Where advertising falls short

Although advertising offers many advantages, it also has some important weaknesses, including:

- Credibility
- Sale closure
- Measurement
- Clutter

Credibility

One British university recently faced censure by a national oversight group for claims made in advertisements for a school program. The Advertising Standards Authority, established to ensure that nonbroadcast advertisements are honest and truthful, took issue with the ad claim that one of its programs was "the best in Britain." The ASA said the claims were made with little or no evidence to verify them.

Negative attention such as that resulting from this incident has the potential to set back, not advance, marketing efforts. Unfortunately, the public has become accustomed to exaggeration in advertising. If you want to use hyperbole in any claim about your institution, consider the consequences. If you have evidence to support ad claims, the public will have less reason to doubt your credibility.

Closing the sale

Generally, advertising does not lead a consumer immediately to a purchase decision. Exceptions may be the Home Shopping Network or the television advertisements that offer special music collections and urge you to call a phone number where "operators are standing by." But it is unlikely that a potential student would view or hear an advertisement for your institution and call immediately to enroll.

Measurement

It is possible to measure the results of advertising by the number of inquiries or by research quantifying the change in attitude or behavior taking place between pre- and post-advertising periods. But don't be deceived into believing that advertising can be measured precisely. Variables such as the residual effect of an ad seen prior to the buyer recognizing the need for a service may influence the buyer's behavior after a campaign has concluded. And it is difficult to measure the results of advertising appearing in more than one medium. You can have a general understanding of the potential reach of an advertising campaign, but it is difficult to count with precision the total impressions generated by an ad series.

Clutter

Competition for an audience's attention is keen in the media environment. Advertising expenditures in 1996 totaled $175.2 billion, according to a McCann-Erickson Worldwide report. During the same year, the expense for advertising in the United States alone was $13.9 billion, more than the value of Switzerland's entire economy! Another example of the growing clutter of advertising is the portion of airtime allocated to sponsored messages. One-fourth to one-third of the network television day in 1996 was devoted to commercials and promotions, according to a 1997 report sponsored by the American Association of Advertising Agencies and the Association of National Advertisers.

Competition for Audience

The total of all printed knowledge doubles every eight years, according to Richard Wurman, author of *Information Anxiety.* To put this statistic into perspective, know that in late 1998, the volume of printed information had grown one hundredfold since 1990. By 2005, printed information will have doubled yet again.

More new information has been produced in the last 30 years than in the previous 5,000 years. Today's weekday edition of *The New York Times* contains more information than the average person was likely to come across in a lifetime in 17th-century England.

Planning an advertising campaign

Frequently, the discussion of advertising turns to its most visible element—the creative process—long before the essential groundwork of planning has taken place. "I want full color," demands a client. Or, "We have 32 facts that the ad must include." Or, "We need a tag line, and here's what it should be."

Without a clear and realistic understanding of what you want an ad to do, it is impossible to evaluate its effectiveness. And when a client wants an ad to accomplish a multitude of objectives, it makes it difficult to determine if the ad has achieved what it needed to accomplish. Making the phone ring may be one criterion. Generating a specific impression in a prospect's mind may be another form of a clearly defined ad goal. In every case, put the goals in writing. This step is vital for both the client and the creative team. It enables them to understand the advertising goal clearly before development of creative advertising and media planning.

Development

The following questions will help you shape a strategic advertising plan. They are as applicable to an institution-wide image campaign as they are to a narrow effort to build enrollment inquiries for a new noncredit class. Answering the following questions will help you define the information essential for either scope of effort:

- What budget is available to execute your plan?
- Who is involved in the planning process, and who will make the final decision about what goes in print or on the air?
- Are your advertising goals based on research?
- What do you know about your target audience or audiences?
- What do your audiences now think about the subject of your ad?
- What do you want your audience to think as a result of your ad?
- What message will move your audience from what it thinks now to what you would like the audience to think?
- How can your message be delivered most effectively ?
- How will results be measured?
- Once the campaign has begun, how is it working?

Budget

At a minimum, funds will be required for at least two advertising services—creative and purchase of media. A third service that may require funds is media planning to determine the most effective advertising media mix. The expense for these services will vary by media market and population of the region where your institution is located. Because media in larger cities usually have larger audiences, costs will be higher. Outside creative and media planning services, if they are used, are typically more expensive in large metropolitan areas than in smaller cities.

Some program directors and campus administrators using advertising for the first time may see only the expense of buying space in a newspaper or airtime on a broadcast station. Remember that you are responsible for what the ad says and how it is portrayed in sight and sound. If you ignore the creative process or abdicate it to a production department at a paper or at a station, you might as well save the money you were planning to spend on advertising.

Process participants

The planning process should directly involve individuals most closely affiliated with the program or event to be advertised, which may include a program director, department chair, or dean, depending on the scope of the project. Fail to clearly define with these key individuals what needs to be said, and you can be sure that the creative process will be painful and contentious. Clients who become heavy-handed in ordering repeated rounds of creative work may be clients who did not define the "what" thoroughly.

Research

Carefully review the most complete and relevant marketing information available. Review secondary research sources, such as syndicate research, industry trade reports, or data from government bureaus, or all of these. And consider any quantitative and qualitative primary research your institution conducted earlier in its integrated marketing planning process. Best guesses need to be left to picking lottery tickets.

Target audience

Knowing your target audience is crucial before beginning the media planning process. Without an audience definition, it is impossible to determine which outlets will be most useful in achieving the goals established in the previous step.

Audience perceptions

Do they think your institution is "pricey" or a solid value? What do they know about the category of services you are offering? An MBA is well established as a vital link in building a business career. But what, for example, is the value of a new master's degree that combines the disciplines of psychology and economics? You may have to educate prospective students on the benefits of a particular program, and that means your marketing communication could be considerably more expensive.

Goals

Do you want your audience to perceive your service as a low-cost alternative or the most prestigious education option available? Your creative strategy will differ accordingly.

Strategy

Frequently, I see advertisements for educational institutions that focus on the institution, not the benefit that the institution offers the potential student. The perception among some universities is, "We've been here for decades. Everyone knows we're a great educational institution. If we make the name or logo of our university large, it will lead to more calls." Unfortunately, such thinking is faulty. Consider our highly mobile and information-overloaded society. If your institution is located in a large metropolitan area, chances are thousands of residents may have no impression at all of your institution. And simply plastering a big copy of your logo at the top of an ad will do little to motivate them to learn more about it. Some element of the advertisement or commercial must appeal to a need of the prospective student.

Effectiveness

If your communication goals include building awareness and image, advertising will be among your most effective building tools. Your next consideration will be selecting the appropriate media mix for reaching your desired audiences and determining the budget to allocate for media placements. These topics are covered later in the chapter.

Measure of results

Unless you decide how your results will be measured, you will have no basis for determining if your communication goals have been met. Measurement requires identification of two points: where you are now and where you want to be. You must have some benchmark data today to compare tomorrow's results against. It may be that no benchmark data exist and must be gathered. Pre- and postcampaign research of target audiences may be necessary to evaluate advertising effectiveness. You must determine what data elements—which may include the number of potential students calling for additional information or Web site responses for a particular program offering—are essential for comparison. Be careful to limit your expectations to what advertising can reasonably deliver, not what you expect from using the combined tools of marketing communication. In every instance of advertising, make measurement part of your written plan.

Monitoring

Periodically compare the results that your advertising is generating with what you expected. Evaluate whether the media outlets you chose offer the most effective way to reach your audiences and whether your ad message is compelling enough to produce the response sought. If not, make revisions. (Chapter 4 outlines a number of research strategies you might consider before undertaking any communication strategy, including advertising.)

Here are some key ad strategy questions to ask yourself:

- Is the task your ad is to accomplish clearly and realistically defined?
- Do you understand your target audience or audiences?
- What does your audience now think about the subject of your ad?
- What do you want your audience to think as a result of your ad?
- What message will move your audience from what it thinks now to what you want the audience to think?
- How can your message be delivered most effectively?
- How will your results be measured?

Evaluating Impact

Considering the increasing emphasis on stewardship and effectiveness today, it is highly likely you will be asked to evaluate the effectiveness of your advertising campaign. If you do not take the time to gather baseline perceptual data prior to launching the campaign, there is little real expectation that you can obtain a true—or defensible—measure of effectiveness.

The creative work plan

One benefit of working with freelance creative professionals is learning better methods to accomplish what you have done less efficiently in the past. Such is the case with the creative work plan, a tool useful for identifying WHAT needs to be said before work begins on HOW to say it. A Dallas design firm developing a magazine ad for a campus client introduced me to this tool. Using the creative work plan resulted in a significantly reduced development period, and I have used the tool frequently since.

The creative work plan enables you to capsulize your advertising goals, service benefits, and the description of your target audience. A well-considered, and thus well-written plan can reduce the time required to write an advertisement. Often, key phrases from a creative work plan will appear in the ad copy or commercial script like the ones below:

- *Key fact.* Describe the essence of what you're advertising.
- *Problem your ad must solve.* Frequently the problem is defined as "awareness" of your institution, and this represents an appropriate use of mass-media advertising.
- *Ad objective.* Express what action your audience needs to take to respond to the advertisement. It may be to call, attend, visit a Web site, or consider a new idea.
- *Prospect definition.* Define the characteristics of your audience in four dimensions: (1) personal (age, lifestyle, economic status, etc.); (2) psychological (attitudes, beliefs, motivation); (3) social (family, role, status); and (4) cultural (basic perceptions, values, and desires).
- *Principal competition.* Identify other organizations offering the same or similar services you've outlined for your institution in the "Key fact." Occasionally, "competition" also may be defined as another activity that the audience could choose to do instead of what is proposed in your advertisement. If your ad focuses on going to a sporting event, competition would be not only other sporting events, but also other uses of personal time, including attending a musical performance.
- *Key consumer benefit.* Explain what potential students will gain from the service described in your advertisement. Although it is appropriate to list attributes, such as "internship program," you will also need to convey the usefulness of the attribute, such as "you will gain practical experience." Refer to the list of "vivid descriptors" (discussed in Chapters 2 and 3) to help you communicate benefits.
- *Reason why.* Briefly describe the evidence that makes your ad message claims credible.
- *Mandatories.* Your institution may require use of a specific logo or a nondiscrimination statement.

Creative Work Plan Sample, Engineering School

One of the best ways to illustrate a concept is to review a sample plan. The following plan was prepared to develop an undergraduate recruitment print advertisement for the School of Engineering and Applied Science at Southern Methodist University.

Key fact: SMU Engineering offers undergraduate students more than 20 engineering majors that can be tailored to their individual academic and career needs.

Problem the advertising must solve: Create awareness that SMU Engineering offers a high-quality engineering degree that will prepare the student for direct professional employment or as a precursor to employment in medicine, law, or business.

Advertising objective: Direct the prospective student to read the profile of SMU Engineering in the publication, complete the reader response card in the back of the book, view the SMU Engineering Web site, or call SMU for additional information.

Prospect definition: The prospect is any high school graduate with sufficient mathematics background, grade point average, and skills test scores interested in pursuing an engineering degree.

Principal competition: Regionally, SMU Engineering's key competition is made up of state-funded universities offering tuition considerably less expensive than SMU and a few private universities with reputable engineering schools.

Key consumer benefit: SMU Engineering enables the student to earn a customized undergraduate engineering degree in a personalized environment with direct access to a major U.S. city in one of the country's largest high-tech business environments.

Reasons why: SMU Engineering is located in Dallas, home to the nation's second-largest telecommunications manufacturing workforce and the nation's third-largest research and development community.

Mandatories: SMU nondiscrimination statement, SMU Engineering logo.

Media buying

John Wanamaker, a legendary Philadelphia clothing retailer in the late 19th and early 20th centuries, was one of the first U.S. merchants to engage in large-scale advertising campaigns. He once commented, "I know that 50 percent of my advertising dollars are wasted. The trouble is, I don't know which 50 percent." While precise measurement of advertising still remains elusive, today's advertisers have a host of research data and tools to use in evaluating media-buying decisions.

An effective media plan combines an optimal frequency of messages directed to your target audience or audiences. In general, you determine this by identifying the number of prospects in your media audience and evaluating the cost of ad placement divided by the number of matching prospects. What may appear to be an attractive publication based on the low cost of the placement may be relatively expensive in light of careful analysis. At the same time, a media outlet may look out of reach but become attractive following a review of the numbers. Generally, the more narrow the audience is, the more expensive is the placement.

Reach and frequency

Frequency and reach provide two critical metrics for determining the efficiency of advertising. Reach is the quantity of different households or individuals (expressed in a number or percentage) exposed at least once to an ad during a specific campaign. Frequency describes the number of times that the audience is exposed to a message during a given period of time.

Numerous studies have sought to determine the optimal number of times an ad must be received before it can be considered effective. A landmark British study done in 1966 reviewed the relationship between the opportunities to see ads for a laundry detergent and sales of the product. The study showed the optimal frequency to be three impressions. Additional research has shown that effective frequency can require as many as 10 to 15 impressions, depending on the variables of message complexity, familiarity with the service category, and the medium chosen to deliver the message.

Basic media math

Cost per thousand (CPM) compares two variables—audience and cost. Everything being equal, the lowest CPM is the most efficient. CPM calculations are useful for comparing print and broadcast advertising. CPM is determined by dividing the size of the audience into the media expense and multiplying the result by 1000. (The formula is: CPM = [Cost x 1000] / Audience.)

A thorough discussion of media buying is beyond the scope of this chapter, but the background is worthwhile if you regularly will be buying media for your institution. Consider adding a media-planning handbook, such as Jim Surmanek's *Media Planning: A Practical Guide,* to your personal library.

In addition, you will want to consider acquiring periodic statistical surveys of media rates and data. International Demographics, Inc. publishes *The Media Audit,* which has media consumption surveys for more than 100 markets throughout the United States. SRDS, a company in Des Plaines, Illinois, offers a similar service.

Other media-buying considerations

Although quantitative data are essential to determine the effectiveness of a media outlet, you should also evaluate its qualitative editorial and advertising environments as well.

Editorial environment

Take a look at the nonpaid content of your potential media outlets to see if it fits your message and your desired audience. During a recent business trip to Florida, I viewed a few minutes of one of the local television channels during a weekday afternoon. The station was airing the Jerry Springer Show, known for its raucous programming. During a commercial break, a spot for a local university made claims for the institution's high-quality programs and education tradition. While the midday commercial may have been financially inexpensive, the editorial environment carried a large cost. The message about quality was incongruent with programming content.

Advertising environment

Does your institution's ad fit with the other advertisers who are appearing in the space or time you have purchased? Daytime television on an independent station may offer affordable commercial time, but consider that your institution will be juxtaposed with advertising for personal injury lawyers and rent-to-own companies. What impression of your institution does this create among the individuals you seek?

Creative Work Plan Sample, School of Theology

Key fact: Some potential students perceive that the Perkins School of Theology at Southern Methodist University does not provide practical training for individuals who are pursuing a life as practicing ministers.

Problem the advertising must solve: Insufficient awareness of the Perkins school internship program and its benefits.

Advertising objectives: Primary objective, to change the perception of Perkins, raise the consciousness of its intern program, and clarify the fact that the program offers comprehensive preparation for the ministry. Secondary objective, to motivate prospective students to choose Perkins as the school to best help them be prepared for Christian leadership.

Prospect definition: Perkins prospects are anyone interested in preparing for ministry in and leadership of the church, friends who might recommend someone to the school, and ministers who might provide guidance to those wishing to enter the ministry.

Principal competition: Although the intern program does not have any specific competition, other schools offering similar religious training are considered competition for prospective theology students.

Key consumer benefit: The Perkins intern program offers the student an opportunity to gain in-depth academic knowledge, build spiritual awareness, and receive hands-on experience working in the church.

Reason why: The intern program places the student in parish churches, or other specialized ministries where he or she is able to work in-depth with ministers and the congregation to learn the ministerial craft.

Mandatories: SMU Perkins logo, nondiscrimination statement.

Media mix

Where should you place advertising for your institution? Should it be in print or broadcast, or perhaps some combination? The objective is to purchase media that enables you to reach your desired target audience with a frequency sufficient for the greatest number of qualified buyers to learn what you have to offer and choose to respond favorably to your call to action. As you consider the most effective way to achieve this goal, evaluate the key strengths and weaknesses of the traditional advertising media.

Newspapers. The local daily newspaper continues to be the best medium to reach a wide, regional audience in all demographic groups. A 1996 survey by Southern Opinion Research showed that more than seven out of 10 respondents said they lived in households that subscribed to a newspaper. Surprisingly, 83 percent of young adults surveyed reported being regular readers. The medium offers flexibility in the numerous sections of the paper and the greatest geographic selectivity, except for direct mail, of any medium. The nature of newspapers requires reader involvement, and readership of advertising has been reported as high as 70 percent. The strength of reaching a wide audience in newspapers is also a weakness. The extreme reach of newspapers makes it difficult to target a narrow demographic group. Another disadvantage is its short life span, often less than 24 hours. And color reproduction often is inconsistent, varying widely even within the same edition of a paper. An example of an ad that would be appropriate for a newspaper is Figure 13-2 from Southern Methodist University.

Magazines. Audiences may be more narrowly targeted with advertising in magazines, given the niches these publications serve. As with newspapers, readers often will seek out advertising that appears in magazines because of the reader involvement required by the medium. Unlike newspapers, artwork can be reproduced with top quality, more creative design and production options are available, and magazines often are retained after an initial reading. The advertising disadvantages of magazines include expense, limited reach and frequency, and long lead times. Figure 13-3 from Southern Methodist University is a good example of an appropriate ad for a magazine.

Television. TV reaches a vast audience and offers a rich media experience that includes both sight and sound, but the expense for television can be vast. In 1998, the open rate for a 30-second commercial during the nightly newscast on a station in a top-eight U.S. market was $11,000. Add to that the $10,000 to $30,000 average cost and the weeks of time it takes to produce a television commercial—all for seconds of exposure in the clutter of numerous other commercials.

Radio. Radio is to broadcast advertising what newspaper is to print advertising. This medium offers a low-cost, high-frequency option to appeal to a local audience with specific demographics given the multiple radio formats available. The creative part of radio advertising can be as few as two elements—effective copywriting and an announcer to voice the spot—and it can be executed quickly. Radio's weaknesses include recall, reach, and clutter. Phone numbers announced in a call to action are difficult to remember while driving. Your radio ad buy may require several stations to reach your particular demographic group adequately. Radio frequently is a background medium passively engaged by an audience. When your ad is one among six or more during a typical com-

Figure 13-2
Ad for Southern Methodist University
Courtesy of Southern Methodist University

Figure 13-3
Ad for Southern Methodist University
Courtesy of Southern Methodist University

mercial break, it is easy to ignore.

Outdoor advertising. Key benefits of billboard advertising include frequency and reach. Since billboards usually are scheduled on a monthly basis, the medium offers high frequency. Billboards can blanket a geographic area. The simplicity required in the medium means that a message can have a high level of impact and lead to a high level of awareness. Outdoor strengths, however, also can be weaknesses. Limited space is available to convey a message. Coverage can be greatly wasted, and audiences can grow tired of a billboard they see repeatedly during a daily commute. Billboard advertising results also are difficult to measure.

Transit advertising. Exposure time to a transit message is extended, given that the average U.S. transit time is approximately 30 minutes. Frequency is relatively high considering that most commuters ride daily, and specific coverage areas can be targeted based on transit routes. As with billboards, audience coverage can be wasted because it is difficult to target specific demographic segments, and the medium also does not afford the luxury of a lot of details. Finally, transit ads in proximity to yours may tout products and services that are inconsistent with what you offer.

So many media choices, so little to spend

Budget sources for advertising and other marketing expenses vary from institution to institution. Budgets may be derived directly from a central pool of funds, be allocated to individual program directors, or be some combination of the two models. One Midwestern university establishes an annual, institution-level budget to purchase media placements and creative services. The budget is allocated on a first-come, first-served basis to deans who request support for their schools' programs. At other institutions, program directors pay for advertising from their own budgets.

Once a budget source is identified, the next question to address is how much to spend. One popular approach to advertising budgeting is to allocate a percentage of revenues. Allocations, whether based on existing or projected revenues, range from as little as 0.5 percent to as much as 8 percent of revenues. Average allocations are 2 to 3 percent. If annual revenues from a continuing education program generate $1 mil-

---

Essential Print Ad Elements

Benefit-focused headline. Benefits are what your service means to your potential customer, not simply an attribute. For example, an attribute of a business school MBA program may be that it is nationally ranked, but how does that benefit the consumer?

Supporting body copy. Your copy should focus on presenting key selling points in logical sequence and in enough detail to convince as many as possible of your targeted audience to take the next step in the buying process. Your copy should also be believable and interesting to read.

Graphic elements. If you use any photography, illustrations, or type treatments, the graphic elements should support the copy concept outlined in the headline and body copy.

Call to action. What do you want the audience to do as a result of seeing or hearing your ad? It may be to call, access a Web site, attend an event, or honk a car horn. With an ad focused on image, not selling a particular program or event, the call to action may simply be to take notice, to build awareness.

Logo. A logo usually belongs at the bottom of an ad, not the top. Unless top placement of the logo is part of an overall branding strategy, it can be a symptom of inside-out thinking. An institution may have a great reputation, but the audience will not readily recognize the institution's logo as a mark of a quality. It is vital that the ad contain a message that will meet the need of a reader. A better practice is to anchor the ad with the logo.

Print Advertising— What Do You Need To Ask?

Deadlines, space, and art. Frequently, the deadline for reserving space in a publication is earlier than for providing camera-ready art. The range of time between space and art deadlines will be more narrow for a newspaper than it will be for a magazine, which has a longer production cycle.

Mechanical specifications. This information provides essential information to ensure your publication-ready advertisement can be reproduced. Expect to see information about line screen requirements, the preferred emulsion and the right reading regarding film negatives, and computer program requirements if the art is submitted electronically by disk or online.

---

lion, you might consider an advertising budget of $20,000 to $30,000. If projected income is expected to be $1.5 million, the advertising budget might increase to $60,000 under a 4 percent allocation.

Another approach encountered more frequently in higher education is the "all-you-can-afford" method. Often budgets are minimal under this approach and require creative use of media placement. Occasionally, all that your campus client may be able to afford will be too little to mount an effective advertising campaign.

Other factors that can have an impact on your advertising budget may be the life cycle of your program or event and the advertising done by competing institutions. New programs will require significantly more advertising than established programs that can draw on a word-of-mouth reference network. And strong competition may require more frequent and prominent advertising.

With the plethora of advertising media to choose from, consider overall advertising objectives before selecting your outlets. The more media outlets you select, the more complex and expensive your campaign will be. Your objectives may be attainable with just one or two media choices.

When Houston Baptist University launched an institutional advertising campaign, the university chose to limit its principal media mix to two media—the local daily newspaper and outdoor billboards (Figure 13-4).

The plan was executed on a tight budget, explains Sharon Saunders, associate vice president for public relations. The university worked with a Houston-area advertising agency to develop a creative series that would work both in print and on billboards. "We looked at a smart design that used word play, functioned well in one color, and could transition easily between newspapers and billboards," she says.

HBU avoided broadcast because of the expense, but it capitalized on a creative concept from the ad campaign and used it in program playbills for Houston-area arts and music performances. Ad placement in the playbills was chosen to reach an influential audience with an interest in fine arts that potentially would be interested in a university campaign to raise capital to help fund a performance facility on campus.

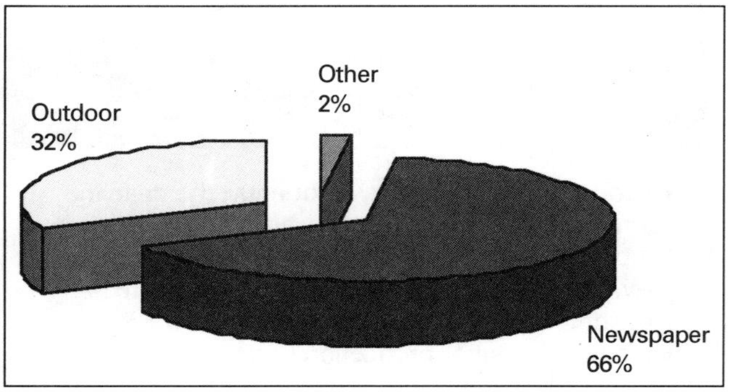

Figure 13-4
Media Budget Allocation, Houston Baptist University
Courtesy of Houston Baptist University

Use of advertising in higher education

An informal survey of universities throughout the United States in early 1998 showed that many of the respondents were seeking more coordinated advertising of their institutions, programs, and events. Southern Methodist University interviewed communication staff representatives at a dozen universities. Most of those contacted said that advertising at their universities is a growing concern and that human and financial resources have been or were in the process of being redirected to address the need. Each university representative expressed a need for institution-wide coordination of advertising.

Maximizing Advertising Efforts

How can you maximize individual advertising campaigns and budgets? Donald Jugenheimer, Professor and Director of the School of Journalism at Southern Illinois University, offers the following suggestions, excerpted from a recent American Marketing Association presentation:

Combine advertising with other promotions. Make your advertising more efficient by using the same theme in posters, mailers, public relations efforts, on-campus signs, and other promotions as you do in mass media advertising.

Use complementary media outlets and messages. If different messages are used in each advertisement, the messages need to be complementary so that they do not destroy the cumulative effect of the single theme. Similarly, your specific media outlets should complement one another: radio can support newspapers, outdoor billboards can support print and broadcast media advertising. All of this contributes to advertising "continuity," one of the best ways to maximize the efficiency of your advertising.

Stay with a single theme. The same theme should appear throughout your advertising to build recall and recognition no matter how seldom you advertise. Individual advertisements can have different specific goals and messages, but the overriding theme should not vary. This way, your message impact will build on your previous insertions instead of starting over from "ground zero" with each new advertising placement.

Use only one strong message in each ad. You might like to accomplish several things in a single advertisement: introduce a new program, remind about existing programs, tout off-campus locations, list the breadth of course offerings, make alumni feel good about the place, even reassure parents that the campus is secure. But you cannot do it. Only one strong message is feasible in a single advertisement. There can be supporting information plus the recurring campaign theme, but no more than one central purpose and one strong message per announcement. Trying to do more is confusing and counterproductive.

Courtesy of Donald Jugenheimer

Continuity leads to comprehension and recall. Advertising continuity helps your audience understand your message because it is repeated and builds on what was understood earlier. Continuity also leads to recall—not merely remembering your ad, but even to "top-of-the-head" recall that makes your institution among those that first come to mind when the public thinks of quality higher education.

Large or long advertisements are remembered better. How large an advertisement should you run? As large as you can afford, considering the overall budget. Larger print advertisements attract more attention and are remembered better and longer. A half-page newspaper placement is only about 60 percent as effective as a full-page placement, and it is usually priced at about the same ratio. Similarly, a 30-second radio placement carries more impact than a 15-second spot.

Keep promoting: less drop-off, quicker recovery. You need to keep up your advertising effort, even when the market looks poor and you do not see immediate outcomes possible. Experience shows that reducing or eliminating advertising reduces your audience's knowledge, recognition, and recall. Rebuilding these measures to previous levels is more expensive in terms of time and money than simply maintaining your ongoing advertising presence. You may want to advertise in waves, but keep your message before your target audiences.

Consult advertising professionals. Even the largest advertisers, with lots of advertising experts on staff, have advertising message development and media selection performed by outside entities, either consultants or agencies. Yet universities often call on academic deans, admissions staff, and news writers to make these expert media decisions. Use an advertising agency (an ad agency may be compensated by commissions from the media), a consultant, or advertising and marketing faculty, and even if there are expenses, the resulting efficiencies should more than offset them. Get expert assistance, react to their recommendations, and approve them if they appear sound.

The motivation to coordinate advertising is fed by a realization that advertising individual programs influences public opinion about your overall institution. The expressed desire is to leverage ad budgets to influence public perception of your institution, and, therefore, your programs. Several institutions reported working with advertising agencies for media planning and placement and for creative services. Institutions with a low volume of advertising reported fulfilling advertising needs with in-house staff. At least one institution committed two additional full-time employees to its advertising function. No institution reported having an integrated, institution-wide advertising program.

Evaluating a Full-Service Advertising Agency

Determine whether an agency personality fits your institution. An agency that tends to produce high-concept advertising and is unwilling to compromise may not be a right fit for an institution whose program directors have been producing their own ads and have experienced acceptable sales results with them. Also, is the agency willing to work in a university environment, where communication efforts can be laid to waste by conflicts between various campus power bases?

In a smaller agency, the agency principal may serve as your account representative. With a larger agency, the seniority of your representative will depend on the relative size of your account for the agency. Review agency capabilities and credentials. Ask the agency to outline a communication problem one of its clients experienced and the solution the agency proposed. How does the agency handle the essential services of account management, media planning and placement, and creative production?

Discuss with the agency how it would service your account. What will be the working relationship between the agency and your campus clients? Which agency representatives will be assigned to your institution, what are their individual responsibilities, and what relevant experience do the representatives have? How will the agency allocate time between account services, creative, and media?

The methods to pay for agency services are as variable as clients, but they usually fall into one of four categories: (1) percentage of cost of media purchase (typically 15 percent), (2) flat retainer or fixed-fee, (3) on a project-by-project basis, or (4) some combination of each of these methods.

Figuring 15 Percent The Agency Way

If you are new to how agencies bill for media, you may be convinced that the representative passed his or her art design classes but skipped out on math. The question to ask is, "What exactly is the charge 15 percent of?" The answer you will hear is that it is 15 percent of the total expense, including the commission.

Let's assume a $100-per-column-inch ad rate. The net media cost for the 10-inch ad is $1,000. At first glance, you might say that a 15 percent fee would add $150 to the media buy. In reality, such a calculation leaves the agency less than 15 percent commission. To "gross up" the media cost to include a true 15 percent fee, the agency multiplies the net media cost by 1.1765 to derive a gross media cost of $1,176.50. Calculate 15 percent of this gross figure, and the ad agency fee will come to $176.45.

The legendary image- and identity-management firm, Lippincott & Margulies, is widely credited with having invented the phrase "corporate identity." L&M has worked with more than 2,500 companies on corporate identity programs and developed hundreds of corporate and product names for The Gillette Company, Infiniti, Harcourt General, Betty Crocker, Chrysler, and others.

The late Gordon Lippincott, L&M co-founder, said, "Unless a company manages its image as professionally and systematically as it manages any other valuable business asset—with standards of accountability across all business lines, in all areas of operations, throughout the organizational ranks—the value of that asset will depreciate, along with the company's ability to achieve its business objectives." Lippincott's statement also holds true for academic institutions.

Although the higher education community is becoming aware of the need for institution-wide advertising coordination, few institutions have attempted this monumental task, let alone achieved it. Some institutions have launched image campaigns to sell their overall universities. At other institutions, integration has been achieved within specific parts of the institution, such as continuing studies or a business school.

Institution-wide advertising coordination offers the opportunity to coordinate messages and that can improve and solidify your institution's overall image. No one can expect that program–produced advertising will consistently portray your institution in its best light without institution-wide coordination.

Some closing thoughts

Any effective marketing communication requires a written, measurable strategy based upon research. Your advertising messages need to address the needs of your audience, not just what your institution has to sell. Prospects are only interested in your institution as it relates to them. Advertising, or any other marketing communication medium that makes it easy for your prospects to see clearly and quickly how your benefits relate directly to them, will serve your institution well.

Recommended Readings

Aaker, David A. *Managing Brand Equity: Capitalizing on the Value of a Brand Name.* New York: Free Press, 1991.

Bly, Robert W. *Advertising Manager's Handbook, 2nd ed.* Paramus, NJ: Prentice Hall, 1992.

Bly, Robert W. *The Copywriter's Handbook: A Step-by-Step Guide to Writing Copy that Sells.* New York: Henry Holt and Company, 1990.

Caples, John and Fred E. Hahn. *Tested Advertising Methods.* Englewood Cliffs, NJ: Prentice Hall, 1997.

Duncan, Thomas R. *Driving Brand Value: Using Integrated Marketing to Manage Profitable Stakeholder Relationships.* New York: McGraw Hill Professional Book Group, 1997.

Colley Russell. *DAGMAR: Defining Advertising Goals for Measured Advertising Results, 2nd ed.* Lincolnwood, IL: NTC/ Contemporary Publishing Group, 1995.

Hart, Susannah and John M. Murphy. *Brands: The New Wealth Creators.* New York: New York University Press, 1998.

Jones, John Philip. *What's in a Name? Advertising and the Concept of Brands.* Lanham, MD: Lexington Books, 1986.

Katz, Helen. *The Media Handbook: A Complete Guide to Advertising, Media Selection, Planning, Research, and Buying.* Lincolnwood, IL: NTC/Contemporary Publishing Group, 1995.

Ogilvy, David. *Ogilvy on Advertising.* New York: Random House, 1985.

Surmanek, Jim. *Media Planning: A Practical Guide, 3rd ed.* Lincolnwood, IL: NTC/Contemporary Publishing Group, 1995.

Resources

The Arbitron Company, 142 West 57th Street, New York, NY 10019, (212) 887-1332

The Media Audit, 3355 West Alabama, Suite 500, Houston, TX 77908-1718, (800) 324-9921

Mediamark Research, Inc., 708 Third Avenue, 8th Floor, New York, NY 10017, (800) 310-3305

Simmons Market Research Bureau, Inc., 309 West 49th Street, New York, NY 10019 (212) 373-8900

SRDS, 1700 Higgins Road, Des Plaines, IL 60018-5605, (800) 851-7737, (847) 375-5000

(See also Appendix D for other useful organizations.)

14

More than Direct Mail: Developing a Direct Marketing Strategy

Robert Johnson

- Do you want to enroll more students and raise more money?
- Do you want to begin a personal relationship with your prospective students and donors?
- Do you know the "hot buttons" that will bring responses from your target audiences?
- Do you want to deliver a detailed message?
- Do you want to track the responses of different audiences to different messages?

If you are interested in the answers to these questions, you are interested in direct marketing.

What is direct marketing—and how is it different from direct mail?

In this chapter, we explore the basics of direct marketing (DM) and one of its most popular formats—direct mail. You will learn the principles of direct marketing and how to apply them in a variety of situations. You will adapt to the opportunity presented by new technology and move on to new success.

Before we can proceed, we need to stop just long enough to explain the difference between two different, but often confused terms. Direct marketing is any marketing technique that takes place directly between the marketer and the person to whom something is being marketed. Since the objective of a direct marketing activity is always to generate a response from the person receiving the message, it is sometimes referred to as "direct response marketing".

Bob Stone, writing in *Successful Direct Marketing Methods,* reminds us that, "Direct marketing is an interactive system of marketing which uses one or more advertising media to effect a measurable response and/or transaction at any location."

Based on this understanding, we quickly realize that different media, including direct mail, can be used for a direct marketing campaign: television, telephone, mail, print advertising, and more. However, since mail has for so long been the dominant vehicle for direct marketing, especially in higher education, the term "direct mail" is often used instead of the generic "direct marketing" designation.

You can recognize a direct marketing print ad, for instance, not merely because it includes a phone number, reply coupon, or e-mail address but because it tries to motivate the reader to respond. And if you look closely, you can often note how the marketer intends to track response to the ad. Direct marketers track and evaluate everything they do. If they don't, they are not really direct marketers.

Here's another example. Listen to college radio ads. If a phone number is used, is it repeated at least once? Or more? If the phone number is given only once, a direct marketer did not do the ad. A phone number given only once is not likely to be remembered. Response will be low. And if the purpose of the ad was to build enrollment inquiries and not just awareness, low response means the ad failed.

How widespread and effective is direct marketing in higher education?

In 1995, 99 percent of colleges and universities were using direct mail as one of their student recruitment activities, but only 33 percent said it was "very effective" in enrolling students, a decrease from 37 percent in 1989.

Although I have seen no similar survey for annual fund campaigns, the personal solicitations received in my household from four private and public institutions of varying size suggest that professional techniques are largely absent from much of what is done on the fund-raising side.

Whether you are interested in the larger direct marketing field or in the more narrowly focused direct mail, the general principles presented here are applicable to any form of direct marketing.

> "Direct marketing is about creating response, a response you can use to begin a relationship with a person who has a resource—time, money, or attention—that you need."

The foundation stones of direct marketing

Direct marketing rests on three foundation stones that must be recognized at the outset:

- ■ Know your audience.

- Segmentation is the heart and soul of direct marketing.
- Measurement is king — or queen.

Know your audience

Direct marketing is about creating response, a response you can use to begin a relationship with a person who has a resource—time, money, or attention—that you need. To create that response, you need to know as much as possible about the person you are marketing. Denny Hatch, in the October 1998 issue of *Target Marketing,* compared it to method acting when he wrote, "Like actors, direct marketers need to get inside the heads of their audience."

Successful direct marketing, like any true integrated marketing communication effort, requires a commitment to learning as much about your potential target audiences as possible.

Segmentation—the heart and soul of direct marketing

It is your understanding of your target audiences and their needs and expectations that allows you to individualize or segment your messages to prospective students or donors.

Effective segmentation is extremely important for effective direct marketing. As you know, the world, as demonstrated by Peppers and Rogers, is moving to personal, one-to-one marketing. You'll probably never develop individual messages for every person you communicate with, but direct marketing (I'll call it DM from now on) principles will lead you to use special messages for as many different segments of your audience as you can identify. Fortunately, a single core message can be tailored to the special interests of many different segments fairly easily.

Measurement is king—or queen

Direct marketers take great pride in knowing what they got for what they spent. Other forms of advertising have impact, but it is very difficult to measure. And so you often hear people say something like "I know 50 percent of my advertising works but I don't know which 50 percent." Direct marketers know which 50 percent works and which 50 percent does not.

One final caution

The more expensive your product, the less likely that DM can actually make a sale. This is especially true for enrollment efforts. DM can generate an inquiry. DM can convince a person to enroll in a continuing education course for a week, possibly. But can DM by itself cause someone to enroll in a complete degree program? Not likely. In other words, evaluate your DM degree-enrollment efforts by the number of inquiries you receive, not by the number of students who enroll. Whether or not a prospect enrolls depends very much on other elements: the product itself, and the nature of the recruitment program that begins after the inquiry is received.

Similarly, DM can work to generate a large number of small annual fund contributions. It probably will not get you a $100,000 capital campaign gift or a substantial deferred-giving commitment. To get a major gift, you have to follow your DM efforts with comprehensive relationship-building activities that may, in the end, depend on the skill and persuasiveness of the individual fund raiser asking for the desired commitment.

Timeless principles

Direct-marketing guru, Bob Stone, once outlined 30 timeless principles of direct marketing. For our discussion, I will hone his list down to seven:

- Success depends first on the list, then the offer, and then copy and graphics
- Follow-up mailing to the same list within 30 days will pull 40 to 50 percent of the first mailing
- "Yes/no" offers consistently produce more return than offers that do not request "no" responses
- Time-limit offers out-pull offers with no time limit
- People buy benefits, not features
- The longer you can keep someone reading your copy, the better your chances of success
- Self-mailers are cheaper to produce but practically never out-pull envelope-enclosed mailers

Principle 1: Success depends primarily on the lists you use; next, on the offers you make; and last, on your copy and graphics.

Not everyone agrees with this, but I do. You can use great graphics to present a great offer but you have to present it to the right people. If the people who receive your offer aren't interested in it, they are not going to respond. So the first thing you have to do is concentrate on building lists that are right for what you want to do. We will review how to build strong prospect pools for enrollment and annual fund giving later in this chapter.

Principle 2: A follow-up mailing to the same list within 30 days will pull 40 to 50 percent of the first mailing.

Most colleges don't do this, but it works all the time. All the time. When responses to the first mailing have started to fall off (usually within about three weeks), send a slightly amended version of the first message again to increase your response rate. The better the first response, the better the second will be. In fact, there are only two times not to do this:

1. When the first response is so small that another 40 percent isn't worth the expense of doing the second mailing.
2. When you have all the qualified enrollment inquiries or gifts that you need from a first mailing.

Principle 3: "Yes/no" offers consistently produce more return than offers that do not request "no" responses.

People don't like to say "no" to something that might be a benefit to them. If your message creates even the possibility that your offer might be a good one, placing people in the position of having to say "no" puts them in a decision situation. Not giving them this choice allows them to more easily ignore the consequence of taking no action at all. So given this choice, people who think that what you are offering might be good for them are more likely to answer "yes" and give you the inquiry you are after.

Principle 4: Time-limit offers out-pull offers with no time limit.

Don't worry about turning off response from people who aren't ready to do it. You'll always have some response for months after a direct-mail program. But you will have a faster and larger response in the first two weeks after your mailing if you give people a deadline to respond. You don't have to explain the reason if you don't want to, just giving them a date is enough. You might want to include an incentive to respond by a certain date if it is appropriate to your audience. Incentives might include waiving an application fee, a financial aid planning guide, or a career-planning guide for prospective students. For an annual fund campaign, an alumni directory, tickets to an upcoming athletic event, or some form of special recognition for early givers should boost response by a specific date.

Principle 5: People, even students, buy benefits, not features.

This is one of the hardest things for colleges to grasp since most people in higher education love to list things like the number of books in their libraries, the number of faculty with the "highest degrees common in their field," and the number of students from different states. These features don't create messages that help people differentiate one college from another. People want to know how many of your graduates get what kinds of jobs for what kind of salaries, or are accepted at graduate and professional schools. Students pay us to help them do that— it's the primary benefit they expect of us.

Principle 6: The longer you can keep someone reading your copy, the better your chances of success.

David Ogilvy said it best in *Confessions of an Advertising Man*: "There is a universal belief in lay circles that people won't read long copy. Nothing could be further from the truth." What is important is not whether your message is short or long, but whether it is of interest to the person you send it to. If it is interesting to the reader, a well-written, four-page letter can be more effective than a single-page letter. People often tell me they don't think high school students will read a letter. Of course they will, if it is on a subject that interests them, like the academic subject they plan to study. But not if it is about your core curriculum or mission statement.

Principle 7: Self-mailers are cheaper to produce but practically never out-pull envelope-enclosed mailers.

When you spend the money to use an envelope, you are saying that your offer is more serious than when you use a self-mailer. More people will pay more attention to it. And your image as a serious institution of higher education will benefit. Too many people use self-mailers just because it's an easier and less expensive way to get the mail out the door. Don't be one of those people. If you are trying to get people to give serious money for a serious purpose when you solicit for your annual fund, for instance, your investment in direct marketing should reflect that.

Three keys to a successful direct marketing campaign

After you've absorbed the timeless principles listed above, you're ready for the next step: three key points that require research and planning before your campaign begins. The first two keys prompt you always to think like the person receiving your message. After you've done that, the third key guarantees that more people will respond to your message.

Key 1: Seek an emotional connection with your prospect.

For each target audience, the most important thing to search for is an area of interest that will connect you with the person you are contacting. The purpose of this first touch is to begin a relationship-building process that results in the person's enrollment, graduation, and continued support as an active alumnus.

In most cases, the one thing you will know about your prospect is an area of academic interest. For high school students taking the ACT or SAT, for graduate students competing the GMAT or GRE, or for law school students taking the LSAT, you will already know what they plan to study. Use that interest as the center of your first contact and you are more likely to create qualified inquiries from people who otherwise might not consider your college. Consider the connection made with this heading from a pre-med section at a SUNY-Buffalo Web site page: "How do you make Harvard Medical beg for you?"

The same is true for alumni. For most, their strongest connection with their alma mater is through their academic program and the professors and students they remember. Nearly every college prefers unrestricted gifts that can be used anywhere, but alumni participation rates and total giving will increase if an appeal focuses on an area of special alumni interest and most often that is the academic area from which they graduated.

Key 2: Research prospect motivation.

In addition to academic interest or reason for giving, you should know as much as possible about other characteristics of your target audiences.

First-generation college-bound students and their parents are very interested in how well an institution will prepare the student for his or her first job after graduation. Children whose parents are college graduates, on the other hand, are more interested in how the institution will prepare them for graduate or professional school. In their own way, each is concerned with the reputation of an institution, but for different reasons. Each is searching for different information; each needs a different communication plan.

And consider adult students in their mid-20s or older who are already working but never earned a bachelor's degree. Research by the College Board's Office of Adult Learning Services shows that a college's reputation is less important than the location and scheduling convenience of its programs. Again, your communication plan for these students must differ from what you do for students just out of high school.

The same is true for annual fund drives. Advancement officers would not ask a major gift prospect for a substantial donation without knowing what that person wanted to have happen with the gift. Similarly, research among your alumni as a whole should alert you to what types of projects are most likely to generate support. For both enrollment and gift giving, research leads to effective segmentation, which increases your desired response.

Key 3: Always call for an action response and be clear on how to act.

The DM research here is quite clear. Ask people to do what you want them to do and more people will do it. Do you want them to call you with an inquiry or return a reply card? Tell them to do that at the end of your letter, possibly again in a P.S. to the letter, and certainly on the reply card itself. And later in the recruitment cycle, continue using this principle when asking for a campus visit appointment, an application for admission, or an enrollment deposit. The same principle applies to annual fund solicitations. Including not only a date but also a desired amount of money will make you more likely to get what you want, when you want it.

> " For each target audience, the most important thing to search for is an area of interest that will connect you with the person you are contacting. "

Building effective lists—the high school student marketplace

This is the area where many colleges spend too many marketing dollars buying too many names. The points I am making in this section are designed to decrease the numbers of names you purchase and to increase your response rate at the same time. First, let's review the three primary sources of names of college-bound high school students: ACT from American College Testing, PSAT and SAT from The College Board, and NRCCUA from the National Resource Center for College and University Admissions.

Should you use ACT or SAT/PSAT? Both offer very similar selection criteria, but perhaps the most important difference is this: The PSAT is taken by most college-bound students in most states in December of their junior year, probably because it is the qualifying exam for the National Merit Scholarship competition. PSAT has some limitations noted below for people who wish to use it outside their primary recruitment territories, but it does offer the earliest and largest selection of names available from these sources. Because names are available by February, this is the most popular of the list sources.

If you don't use PSAT, your choice of ACT or SAT will be determined largely by which exam is most popular in the states you are recruiting in. In New England, for instance, almost nobody takes the ACT. In Illinois, Ohio, and Michigan, the ACT is the preferred exam. In a few states like Texas and Florida, substantial numbers of both ACT and SAT names are available. Most students take the ACT in the second semester of their junior year in high school and names are available to colleges in late spring and midsummer. Many students take the SAT in August and these names are not available until the senior year has started. For many institutions, this is too late to begin an effective recruitment program.

NRCCUA names are also available in winter of the junior year. These lists are compiled from surveys completed for career planning purposes in many, but not all, high schools throughout the United States. In many states, this is the best source if you plan early high school recruitment programs beginning in the sophomore year or even earlier. In Michigan, for instance, Washington University in St. Louis conducts a direct marketing program among high school freshmen. One drawback: if you have a minimum test score for admission, you will have to rely on a correlation between self-reported GPA and the test score when these students take an ACT or SAT.

Understanding the detailed discussion that follows will be easier if you have ACT and PSAT/SAT brochures available: the "ACT Assessment EOS Educational Opportunity Service" booklet and the SAT/PSAT "Student Search Service User Guide." These are the publications that list in great detail the range of selections available in compiling your lists. How you use them will have a great impact on your cost and the quality and quantity of your response. NRCCUA provides a similar but less detailed guide for list selection.

> 66 **For most academic institutions, the primary enrollment area is usually no more than a 100-mile radius from the campus.** 99

An illustration: Tip Top College

To set up a benchmark to illustrate how you might improve your results by using the techniques recommended here, I have created a hypothetical college, Tip Top College (TTC). TTC is a four-year liberal arts college with a strong regional reputation that takes a very traditional approach to direct mail. The admissions director buys the names of 50,000 high school juniors each year, mails a single publication to the entire group, and receives a response rate of 8 percent, or 4,000 names. (Your own response rate will be higher or lower depending on several variables: quality and clarity of your offer, the geographic proximity of your institution to your prospect pool, your reputation and quality perception, your cost, and the accuracy of targeting to prospects like those you already enroll.)

TTC does not segment its initial message to these 50,000 people. Each receives the same search mailing (once most likely a four-color brochure; today very possibly a personal letter with a reply card), telling them something about TTC and the students who enroll there. Those who already know something about TTC are most likely to respond; those who do not know anything about TTC will probably just throw it away.

A DM approach is different. It requires a great deal of segmentation of the prospect pool and the creation of a different message for each segment. It may sound complicated, but it is not. And more important, it will almost always increase your response rate.

There are four important steps to effective segmentation:
- ■ Clarify the reasons for your segmentation/selection criterion.
- ■ Vary your initial message to each segment.
- ■ Track and evaluate your response by each segment you use.

■ Evaluate your success by your response rate.

Have reasons for each selection criterion.

Since so many criteria are available when using high school names, you first need to define in detail the students you are looking for. The best research you can do is among the new freshmen you enroll each year. Your best results will come from building your list from among the same type of students. If you are a conservative Catholic college in the South, you are not likely to draw a strong response from Presbyterian students in Michigan. Direct marketing cannot perform miracles. The key is to deliver your message to people you know in advance might be interested. If you don't, expect your return to be low.

For nearly every institution, the first criterion should be the academic program your prospect plans to study in college.

Research shows that this is the most important reason a student selects an academic institution, and therefore it is usually the best way to begin your segmentation. And if you are contacting someone who is not already likely to be considering your institution, the best way to get your message read is to make it clear from the beginning that it is about the specific academic program of interest to the person receiving your message. Use a teaser on the envelope about the academic program mentioned inside.

Your next criterion should usually be academic ability, a combination of test score and GPA that best fits what your institution is looking for.

Avoid the temptation to select only from the top tier unless you are in fact a top tier institution as measured by the test scores and GPAs of those you enroll each year. It is OK to "stretch" yourself a little, but never at the expense of excluding those who are most likely to enroll. And since you've segmented your pool by academic program, you can set different ability levels for different areas. Let's say, for instance, that you'd like to search among the top 50 percent of test takers in each academic area. That will give you different test scores for premed and engineering students than for education or business students since the mean score is higher for the first two groups than for the second two.

Your third criterion should be geographic. Buying too many names in too wide a geographic area accounts for the greatest waste of money when buying student names. Concentrate on the primary recruiting area you actually enroll students from, not the areas where you are able to draw inquiries with a low application rate or applicants with a low enrollment rate.

For most academic institutions, the primary enrollment area is usually no more than a 100-mile radius from the campus. Purchase the names of every prospect in this area who plans to major in a program you offer and who meets your academic criteria. Not only will you generate a high response, it will be the people you are most likely to persuade to visit your campus. For prospects not giving you strong consideration at the beginning of a recruitment cycle but who are interested enough to inquire, your best chance to move higher on their choice list rests with a successful campus visit. And your best chance for a visit is with prospects who can get to you in a single day's drive. So before you spend direct-mail money anywhere else, buy everything in your primary market that fits your primary criteria.

If you still have money left in your budget, how should you spend it? Consider two recommended research steps first:

■ Identify the academic programs that have the highest conversion rates from inquiry to enrolled students. These are your strongest programs as measured by prospective students and are therefore the ones that you should consider when you reach out beyond your primary recruiting area. Even if you have no capacity for expanded enrollment in these programs, you may want to generate more applications to build your selectivity ratio or to be less generous with your institutional financial aid.

■ Identify geographic areas currently experiencing some enrollment success and those where you currently have clusters of alumni who contribute to the annual fund. If you are lucky, these will turn out to be the same areas, but, if not, either one can serve as a guide for your prospecting efforts. If you don't turn up either, then you have even more reason to limit your search to your strongest programs.

(Note: Chapter 4 of this book outlines a number of research methods and strategies for your consideration.)

The next step is simple. Purchase the names of students interested in your strongest programs who live in secondary enrollment areas where you already have some students or where you have alumni living who might be willing to volunteer time to contact your best prospects. At this point, you can use other geographic selection criteria to reduce names you do not need. Both ACT and SAT allow you to select according to how far from home a prospect says he or she is willing to go to college. In both instances, you should delete students who say they plan to live at home and are not willing to travel out of state. You'll find these under the "Location" and "Living Plans" sections on the SAT (but not the PSAT) form and under "Distance Willing to Travel" and "Residence Plans" on the ACT form.

These are the three major DM criteria that almost every academic institution should use: academic program, academic ability, and geography. Employ these to build a strong prospect list of the students most likely to respond to your offer. We'll consider additional criteria later, but now it's time to turn to the second step for effective segmentation and review what you will say to the people on your list.

Vary your initial message to each segment.

In this section, I assume that you have created from five to 20 segments in your prospect pool. Your next task is to create five to 20 different contact messages to maximize your response rate. And the best way to do that is with a letter.

But if you already have a four-color search piece, what are you going to do with it? I know you are not going to create 5 to 20 of these this year. But note the sidebar on digital printing capabilities. The time may not be far off when you can easily create a different search piece for each segment. Here are the choices for your four-color search piece:

■ Do not use the piece at all and save even more money by reducing the printing budget.

■ Use the piece, but put it inside an envelope with a personalized letter. You designed it as a self-mailer for quick and easy mailing? Redesign it, put it in an envelope with a letter anyway, or do not use it. Actually, with the number of letter-only searches proliferating, sending it as a self-mailer might be the best way for you to be different in the mailbox.

Whatever you do, you should be writing a letter. The fact is, you don't have to use a four-color search piece to get the response you want. A good letter will also do well. Better to invest your search piece money in really nice, distinctive envelopes that will help distinguish you from the standard white envelopes your competitors use.

I only name names for something really good—the best envelopes I've ever seen were used by C.W. Post College of Long Island University in 1995. They were a rich green color completely unlike those used by any other Long Island college or university and well worth the investment. I've also seen a very strong envelope from Ball State University in Indiana in 1998.

Now back to the letter.

You only have to write one basic letter with a key paragraph that will change for each academic area segment that you have selected. That's it. By just doing that, you've told your prospects you know something about them that most other colleges contacting them do not. And their reward if they return your reply card or call you is more information about the academic program that interests them. It's not one-to-one marketing, but it is certainly different from most of the initial, generic messages that come to college-bound students. You can pay to have that first letter written by a professional. Or you can write one yourself after you've read Lewis's *Sales Letters that Sizzle* or Lewis and Nelson's *World's Greatest Direct Mail Sales Letters*.

You might want to consider a different letter for those far from your campus. In that case, a simple P.S. that speaks to the fact that you know they are far away will give you another set of letters without having to create an entirely new one.

And here is another very strong recommendation. Personalize your letter. Remember when we said that DM was best used to begin a relationship-building process that might continue well after graduation? To accomplish that, start things right. You've paid for the name of a live person. Use it. "Dear College-Bound Person" just doesn't have the same impact as "Dear Bob," and you are striving for maximum impact. Almost all the search letters I received in spring 1998 were personalized. But some were not.

Track and evaluate your response by each segment you use.

This is essential so that you can make intelligent decisions about which segments to continue and which to discard. You'll need computer software that lets you do this. Your recruitment system may already track inquiries from such sources as self-reported ACT and SAT scores, college fairs, high school visits, different college guidebooks, telephone calls, letters, alumni references, and more. Now you'll want to add individual tracking ability for each direct-mail segment you create, from five to 20.

Since you ordered your search names by different segments, you'll receive them already divided into segments you can download into your database. Your computer software should let you tag a name when a response is received, make any data updates necessary, and move that person along to an active inquiry. What you have left are the people who didn't respond, ready for a second mailing a few weeks after the first. This is also very helpful when your response from some segments is so strong that you just do not want any more inquiries for one or two program areas but you do need more for everything else. Just select the names left in the segment from which you'd like more inquiries and contact them again.

The easy part is creating the different codes in your computer system to track the segments. Most systems will let you use terms that relate closely to the actual source so you don't have to match number codes with real names like ACT and SAT. The more difficult task (at least the first time you do it) is making sure the reply cards you use are marked in advance with the computer tracking code for rapid, easy entry. This will complicate your print order and make it more expensive, but if you overlook this step there is really no practical way to evaluate anything later on. If you've been using a single code for your ACT or SAT search mailings, you know how to do this. Now you just have to apply the same principle to each segment you use and turn in five print orders for five different batches of cards. Or 20 print orders for 20 different batches.

Evaluate your success by your response rate.

Isn't the number of people who eventually enroll more important than the initial response rate? It is, in the long run. But two other variables can intervene to limit that ultimate effect:

- Most of your DM inquiry prospects will need to be persuaded to apply and enroll, and the quality of that recruitment effort will increase or decrease the final enrollment rate from your direct-mail program.
- A number of prospective students may investigate your academic program in depth and decide for a variety of reasons that it is not right for them.

As a result, your evaluation of a direct-mail program should start with the initial response.

ACTS, PSAT, and SAT

If you are using ACT lists, here are some additional tips to minimize your expenses:

- When selecting your academic majors, you may notice you can also select "by occupation desired after college." ACT tells you which selection will get you the most names. Usually it is the academic major, and I recommend picking that to get the maximum number of names. In some cases, however, (nursing is one) you'll find more students by checking "occupation" and so you should select that criterion. The percentages are printed clearly in the booklet. But do not pick both academic major and occupation unless you want to send the same message to the same people twice in the first mailing. (Many students make a selection in both categories and ACT does not remove duplicates of this type when you order).

■ For your geographic segments, consider using the EIS (Enrollment Information Service) areas instead of an entire state or lists of zip codes and counties. ACT has these for every state in which a reasonably large number of students take the ACT. It's an easy way to pick an entire urban area, or to avoid one.

■ To increase or decrease the size of your prospect pool without changing the three most important criteria, consider using the information on "certainty of educational plans." Students report if they are "very sure," "fairly sure," or "not sure" of their intent to major in a particular area. You won't know how these differ for each major, but, overall, 36 percent are very sure and 43 percent are fairly sure of their academic selection. You might select all three for maximum impact in critical majors close to home, while limiting distant choice to those who are very, or at least fairly, sure of their academic plans.

■ Special lists can be built from a variety of other criteria: religion, ethnicity, honors program interest, and students with advanced placement courses.

If you are using PSAT or SAT, these steps will help build more responsive lists:

■ The number of academic majors available from SAT tests is larger than for PSAT but since many of the categories are small, the difference should not present a real problem. All the major categories are available on both tests: engineering, premed, prelaw, education, business, psychology, communications, science, and more.

■ You can use the EPS (Enrollment Planning Service) territories within states as an alternative to zip codes and counties, which are also available, and you can easily use them to focus on major metropolitan areas throughout the United States.

■ SAT (but not PSAT) allows selection by class rank, something not available from ACT.

■ With SAT you can also build other pools using these criteria and more: religion, ethnicity, high school activities, individual high school courses, and advanced placement.

Tip Top College's new costs and new results

Back at Tip Top College, the director of admissions is smiling. Inquiries have increased and costs have dropped from using the new DM techniques. I've used examples from both PSAT and ACT in Table 14-1 to show what TTC's high school direct-mail program looked like before the changes, but as you can see, the results are similar in both cases:

■ In its first attempt at segmentation, TTC broke its prospect pool of 50,000 names into 10 segments, and overall response increased from 8 percent to 12 percent, or from 4,000 to 6,000 inquiries. Cost per inquiry also fell substantially.

■ In the second phase (Table 14-2), TTC's response rate has increased but it is still buying the same number of names. Total cost has increased, but the cost

```
50,000 PSAT names @ $.22=$11,000
1 participation form @ $200=$200
Total cost = $11,200
8 percent response or 4,000 = $2.79 per
```

```
50,000 ACT names @ $.20=$10,000
1 participation form @ $200=$3,000
Total cost = $10,200
8 percent response or 4,000 = $2.55 per
```

Table 14-1
DM Program, Phase I

```
50,000 PSAT names @ $.22= $11,000
15 participation forms @ $175 = $2,625
Total cost = $13,625
12 percent response or 6,000= $2.27 per
```

```
50,000 ACT names @ $.20= $10,000
15 participation forms @ $200 = $3,000
Total cost = $13,000
12 percent response or 6,000 = $2.16 per
```

Table 14-2
DM Program, Phase 2

```
40,000 PSAT names @ $.22 = $8,800
15 participation forms @ $175 = $2,625
Total cost = $11,425
15 percent response or 6,000 = $1.90 per
```

```
40,000 ACT names @ $.20 = $8,000
15 participation forms @ $200 = $3,000
Total cost = $11,000
15 percent response or 6,000 = $1.83 per
```

Table 14-3
DM Program, Phase 3

Note: Prices in these 3 tables are based on 1998 figures.

per response has decreased about 19 percent for PSAT and just over 15 percent for ACT.

■ In the third phase (Table 14-3), the admissions director reviewed the results from each of the 15 segments and decided to reduce the size of the prospect list to 40,000 names. The response rate increased to 15 percent since the least productive segments were dropped and total inquiries stayed at 6,000. Total cost decreased from phase two but is still a bit higher than in the beginning approach. But now, cost per inquiry since the first approach has decreased over 31 percent for PSAT and about 28 percent for ACT. At the same time, the number of responses has increased 50 percent for both PSAT and ACT.

How will your experience compare to Tip Top College's? No two colleges are exactly alike, but if you are now doing your high school direct-mail programs the way TTC was at the beginning of this section, you will experience similar results. At first, you'll achieve a higher response rate because you are sending better marketing communication messages to different segments of your prospect pool. Next, you will be able to reduce your total purchase of names because you will have better evidence of what works and what does not.

The part-time adult student marketplace

For many academic institutions, part-time adult students have become an important part of the enrollment mix. By adult students, I mean people about 23 years of age or able to enroll as part-time students. The majority are women. They can be either graduate or undergraduate students.

The quest for part-time adult students is fiercely competitive, especially in urban areas. The University of Phoenix, born in the West and increasingly interested in the East, now enrolls about 50,000 students. UP practices the most sophisticated and well-financed blend of print, radio, and mail marketing in the United States. The principles of direct marketing are employed in each area.

Most colleges market themselves to adult students with ads on radio and in print media, a bit of TV, and some billboard and other outdoor efforts. This is a recommendation to try something different. You won't be surprised when I say that direct mail can give you a new ability to target your audience, qualify your inquiries, and lower your costs. It's not as easy to identify the right target groups to build prospect pools as it is with high school students. But it can be done.

DM and adult students

There are a number of important DM realities that make it an ideal option for reaching adult students.

First, direct mail is cost-effective when compared to media ads. But isn't it more expensive than radio and print advertising? It depends on how you measure expense. It is true that direct mail costs more to contact each individual person than most media do, but if you do it right, direct mail will often produce a lower cost per inquiry than radio and TV.

Media reps are very fond of quoting reach figures on a sales call. A popular radio station might reach hundreds of thousands of people and the cost per contact will be low. Radio has to give you frequency as well. So when your media rep tries to sell you several spots per day, that's exactly what you need, together with reach, to make an impression and get a response. If you're advertising on a popular station at a high listening time, the cost will add up pretty quickly. Network TV is even more expensive.

My advice is simple. Beware of reach preachers unless you want to reach everybody they can deliver. If you're selling toothpaste, cars, or long-distance phone service, you probably want lots of reach. And you can probably afford it. For most educational programs, you don't need it. (TV and radio can play important roles in image and visibility campaigns, but that's a different subject.)

Second, with direct mail, you only need to mail to as few as possible—but the right few. Building a strong direct-mail list for adult students is more difficult than it is for high school students, however. Adults don't sit down several times a year and take ACT and SAT tests. GMAT and LSAT takers are exceptions to this, but this is a small part of your entire pool.

In addition, in the list of adults that you do build, most will not be in the market for a college degree when you contact them. Your response rates are going to be lower (from 2 percent to 6 percent is good with this group), and your cost per inquiry is going to be higher—much higher than the $2 per inquiry that Tip Top College was spending on high school students.

How do you begin? By getting to know your current adult students as completely as possible so that you learn what marketing segments they comprise. This can start with a geodemographic analysis of the students you already enroll.

Geodemographic research will:

■ Identify the demographic populations in each of your major academic programs. You'll likely find differences among those who enroll in different academic areas. This will be your first indication that you should be developing different messages for each group if you want to speak to them about the things that most interest them. A 40-year-old returning to college for teacher certification and a 28-year-old striving for an MBA are very different people. One radio ad isn't nearly as likely as two different letters (or two different radio ads) to hit their respective "hot buttons."

■ Identify the magazines (and other media) used by your target populations. When you commission your research, ask for a list of the specific print and broadcast media the students in your segments are reading and listening to. This is essential for everything that comes next. You'll end up with a very long list, but it won't be hard to pick out the ones that are most likely to put you in touch with your target audiences.

Your geodemographic report will describe lifestyle characteristics of your audiences to guide not only your first contact communication, but also your post-inquiry enrollment conversion messages.

Third, employ the power of magazine subscriber lists. When you have completed your research, you are ready to begin building your list. What are you going to use? Magazine subscriber lists. You are not going to advertise in the magazines, although you could. You're going to buy the names of magazine subscribers who match the profile of your current students and who live in zip codes in your primary recruiting area.

Most magazines offer the ability to build your list using some combination of these qualifiers:

■ *Education.* You'll know if the magazine is primarily useful for undergraduate or graduate recruitment or in some cases about equally useful for both. And, in a few cases, you might decide to ignore a particular magazine subscriber list because nearly all the readers already have master's degrees. (None of these few cases are recommended for recruiting Ph.D. students either).

■ *Income.* You will know the average income of either the subscriber, the family of the subscriber, or both.

■ *Ethnicity.* You'll know if subscribers are predominantly African American, White, Hispanic, or Asian. Of more interest, you'll know when magazines you might not have considered for an entire ethnic group are in fact very good sources for a portion of it, say an upper-income portion. *Architectural Digest,* for instance, is a source for wealthy African Americans, or those aspiring to be wealthy and capable of investing in an education that might help fulfill those aspirations.

■ *Sex.* If you only want the female readers of *Time* and *Newsweek,* you will be able to buy just those.

- *Age.* You will know the average age of the subscribers, but you cannot actually buy specific age groups.
- *Academic interest.* Match the magazines with the reading preferences of students in your various academic programs. Or infer it from the subscriber profiles of magazines like *Byte.*
- *Area of residence.* Select the zip codes right for you. It would be great if magazines would sell lists by census tract; so far they do not.

To give you a more direct sense of what you'll know about the subscribers to a particular magazine, ask a list broker to obtain typical profiles from the companies authorized to sell the magazine lists. Some typical profiles are:

- *Essence.* A magazine for black women: median age 32; average household income $38,500; 30 percent married; 29 percent hold professional/managerial positions; 31 percent attended or graduated from college. Active subscriber cost: $70/M. Minimum order 5,000
- *Shape.* A health lifestyle magazine that connects with today's woman: median age 30.9; 80.5 percent employed; 58.3 percent attended/graduated from college; 68.7 percent household income $30,000+; 51.9 percent at $40,000; 41.6 percent married; 42.3 percent mothers. Active subscriber: cost $80/M. Minimum order 10,000
- *Byte.* Average age 40; 78 percent college grads; 52 percent have studied beyond the college level; average personal income is $55,500; average family income is $70,300; 49 percent in management positions; 58 percent work in their company's MIS departments. Mostly men. Active subscriber cost: $125/M. Minimum order 5,000

From these magazines and more, you can build a list (or lists) for adult students that will serve the same purpose as your ACT and SAT/PSAT pools. With this preliminary work complete, you are ready to begin prospecting for new inquiries.

> " Your geodemographic report will describe lifestyle characteristics of your audiences to guide not only your first contact communication, but also your post-inquiry enrollment conversion messages. "

The traditional graduate and professional school marketplace

Many graduate students planning to study for a doctorate of some sort will take their lead from favorite professors. But if you have a special program that you think might capture the interest of a select few, the time and expense of experimenting with a direct-mail contact is not great and it might be worth it. So let's look briefly at how you might apply the principles we've been presenting to the search for more traditional graduate students, people planning to enroll directly from their undergraduate studies as full-time students for either a doctorate or a master's degree. Our examples will concentrate on the Graduate Record Exam, but you shouldn't have any difficulty designing a program around prospects purchased from GMAT or LSAT tests.

At the start, note that we have returned to that happy land where everyone is in the market for the product. Why else would anyone be taking one of these exams? Expect a response rate somewhere between your high school program rate and your adult student program rate.

Using the Graduate Record Exam names

The GRE offers three options when you want to buy names, but only one allows you to really use the new DM knowledge you've been gaining in this chapter—the "Single Discipline Extract" selection. And these names can be a bargain compared to what we've been paying above: a set-up fee of $100 for each discipline the first time you use it, then $25 a cycle for three additional test dates during a year. There is no charge for each name included, although if your criteria are strict and interest in a program is small, you may not end up with very many names. But that's OK, we are striving for prospect pools of people most likely to enroll at our institutions, not just big pools of people.

Here are the most important GRE selections available when you select the Single Discipline Extract method:

- Undergraduate major
- Graduate degree objective, primarily master's or Ph.D.
- Undergraduate grade point average
- GPA in the major
- Geographic preference for grad study
- Permanent state of residence
- Citizenship
- Ethnicity
- Sex
- Intent to study full-time or part-time

You won't be able to get estimates of how many names are in your specific target group, but GRE will provide this information between an actual test date and the time you receive your order so that you can order materials. This will make budgeting a bit imprecise until you have gone through at least one full cycle.

There are four significant points to consider when building your GRE pool:

- Begin by selecting appropriate academic majors.
- Select an appropriate level of academic ability.
- Select a suitable geographic area.
- Select full-time or part-time students.

Select appropriate academic majors.

Building a pool first requires a review of the "Major Field Code List" to determine which academic areas listed match programs available at your institution. In most cases, the areas listed are very discrete but they do not include every program imaginable. Separate searches for minority students are possible if your enrollment goal is to build ethnic diversity within a particular academic area.

Select an appropriate level of academic ability.

Unlike the ACT and SAT/PSAT pools, you cannot sort by the GRE score received by a test taker. The GRE pool academic ability criteria are two self-reported GPAs, one for overall GPA and one for your prospect's major in college. As with high school searches, I strongly recommend you limit your search to students with GPAs similar to those who now enroll in your programs. This will help you achieve both maximum initial inquiry response and maximum eventual enrollment. If you are a midlevel university not now competing with Yale and the University of Michigan for graduate students, direct mail isn't going to put you in their level of competition. Be realistic. And save your precious dollars.

Select a suitable geographic area.

You might use a suitable geographic area, for instance, to identify students throughout the United States who plan to attend graduate school in your home state. More typically, you would use this criterion to eliminate anyone in your home state who was planning to study elsewhere for a graduate degree.

Select full-time or part-time students.

If you know that the absence of graduate assistantships to support full-time study makes it very unlikely that you would enroll a full-time student in a particular major, then limit your selection to part-time students. Similarly, if most of the students you now have in a program are part-time, then select only the names of people planning that type of study. These are likely to be prospects who are going to work full-time after graduation, so you can already see how you might shape your initial contact letter; let people know that your program caters to people like them.

A word on the GMAT

If you require the GMAT for MBA students, you can build a similar prospecting program. The selection criteria include cluster ranges of test results, undergraduate GPA, years of work experience, expected date of graduation, intent to study full-time or part-time, and ethnicity.

Unlike the GRE, you can receive GMAT estimates in advance. Names are available four times a year, approximately six to eight weeks after test dates in October (the largest testing date), January, March (the smallest testing date), and June. Cost of a single set-up is $75 per test date; if you select set-ups for two profile groups, a third is available at no extra charge. Using three set-ups, you might select full-time and part-time students in your primary recruiting area and then out-of-state students planning to work in your home state. And the GMAT wins our prize for the most expensive list we have ever priced. You will pay $.23 per name, or $230 per thousand.

Annual fund campaigns benefit from direct mail

As you move from enrollment to advancement, you enter a somewhat different direct-marketing world. Building effective lists for annual fund campaigns changes the challenge. You are not going to be buying lists from vendors. Instead, you will most likely be compiling "in-house" lists from a roster of living alumni with known addresses. But the communication principles that power direct marketing remain the same. Segmentation is essential. Understanding the motivation of your potential donor remains important. Beating the competition for dollars is vital.

Let's return to Tip Top College. It has 25,000 alumni in its database. The president is concerned that the annual alumni giving rate of 27 percent is more typical of a public university than a private college. Not only can Tip Top use more money from increased givers, this participation rate hurts its rankings in the *U.S. News and World Report* annual college guide. And in the last year, two major corporations have declined to fund capital improvement projects, citing the limited support from Tip Top graduates. The president wants the annual alumni giving rate raised to 37 percent in three years. That requires 2,500 new donors if none of the current 6,750 end their giving. That is a formidable task.

The new annual fund director starts with a careful review of current giving patterns and past solicitation efforts. She is looking for new ways to segment the database according to the interests and giving propensities of the alumni. She knows that the limitations of past annual fund campaigns are not the sole reason Tip Top alumni are not giving at a greater rate, but she also suspects that changes in tactics can produce better results.

The first two segments are obvious: 18,250 nondonors and 6,750 donors. But what distinguishes those who give from those who do not? The director and her assistant soon discover that annual fund donors are at least 10 years out of college. Other than that, there does not seem to be much of a pattern. Giving increases a bit as notable graduation anniversaries come and go. She does note that almost all annual fund efforts focus on unrestricted contributions to the general fund but giving spikes occur whenever alumni are approached to support something in their major academic area or in an area of major extracurricular interest. And there are a significant number of lapsed donors among those not currently giving. They are a third segment, reducing the group of 18,260 nondonors to 6,022 lapsed donors and 12,228 who have never given at all.

To begin her efforts, the director starts with the basics. All three primary segments are subdivided according to their major academic interest area. Those segments are further divided into those who graduated more than 10 years ago (and who have therefore probably finished paying educational loans) and more recent graduates. From there, a simple strategy emerges. The basic effort will focus on developing annual fund support for individual academic areas. Alumni will be allowed to select the specific area of relief they wish to support from three possibilities: student scholarships, new computers and computer software, or faculty-student research projects. Tip Top College can use extra money for all of these in each academic area.

Since TTC offers majors in 31 subjects, it has a large number of segments, 186. But that does not mean that we will have 186 completely different messages and packages to prepare. One or two paragraphs in each letter will focus on the three types of giving history. One or two paragraphs will focus on the key part of the solicitation plan, the academic major. The section on possible giving areas will be the same for each segment. And everyone will be reminded that a gift of any sort will boost the giving rate and improve Tip Top's rating prospects in *U.S. News and World Report*.

The annual fund director then codes the segments of her database and ships the names and addresses to a fulfillment house that will match the letters, reply cards, and envelopes so that everyone receives the right mailing. TTC has never done anything this complicated or ambitious before. But it has never tried to boost its annual fund participation by 37 percent in three years, either.

TTC's alumni magazine editor is also featuring the new campaign in the alumni magazine, including the fact that donors for the major with the highest percentage of participants will receive special recognition in a future issue. Other awards will recognize the academic major(s) with the highest donor renewal percentage each year and with the highest percentage of new donors each year.

Can direct marketing really help our new annual fund director achieve these results? Yes. Consider these examples from the real world of not-for-profit fund raising. The similarities to annual fund campaigns are many.

Example 1: *The power of an emotional connection*
Citymeals-on-Wheels in New York City had a significant problem acquiring new donors and was concerned about a declining continuation rate for current donors. By employing a new direct-marketing approach, Citymeals increased its donations by 20 percent, raising $3.3 million from 35,000 active donors between fiscal year 1997 and fiscal year 1998.

Citymeals was satisfied with the list being used for new donors but not with the response rate. A new strategy focused on increasing the response by placing a new more personal message on the envelope to evoke a more emotional response from the recipient: "I am 100 years old and I can't cook." This was not the creation of a talented copywriter. The phrase was taken from an actual letter received from a beneficiary of Citymeals. (The envelope message actually reproduced the handwriting of the writer.) Inside, the letter requesting a donation quoted two more thankful people.

The impact of this approach was powerful. The new donor rate from the mailing rose from under 1 percent to nearly 2 percent. An article in the *DM News* of September 17, 1998, reported that the campaign was "extremely cost-effective" compared to a print ad placed in the *New York Times*. Citymeals raised $1 for every 66 cents spent to acquire a new donor. The print ad at best broke even.

Example 2: *Linking mail with the Web for increased response*
The Polycystic Kidney Research Foundation started its first direct-marketing fund-raising effort in 1998 to raise its annual support from $2 million to $5 million. Donations sought were a modest $5 to $25 from a mailing campaign that sent out 10 million to 20 million letters in six mailings over a year. The package is a basic letter and reply card sent to a list of people who have contributed to similar organizations. This effort expands traditional telemarketing, major donor solicitation, and sponsorship programs according to a June 5, 1998, *DM News* report.

An unusual feature in this mailing was a prompt to visit the organization's Web site and make a donation directly from the site using a credit card number. Academic institutions might consider adding the same response option. Use of the Web for financial transactions is growing at a steady pace. Donations over the Web will save return postage costs. But if you do this, be sure to use a Web site URL that takes the potential donor directly to the appropriate place to give. Do not make them start at the front page and navigate their way to the giving location.

Example 3: Segment, track, and never stop prospecting your list for new donors

The Chesapeake Bay Foundation, according to a May 13, 1998, *DM News* article, increased its new donor acquisition response from 1.5 percent to nearly 4 percent in "just under" two years as it expanded a donor base of 83,000 people.

The prospecting list did not change, but the single direct-mail package was changed to three different pieces sent to three different list segments. The Foundation made this change at the recommendation of a direct-marketing consultant who warned them that the worst action to take was to abandon direct-mail solicitation from fear that the list being used was "tired."

> **If you're writing to alumni for the annual fund, it is even more imperative to use actual names.**

In this case, what was really needed was a new campaign that recognized that different approaches, from premium to basic, would appeal to different segments. The consultant added two points. In the first year, most acquisition programs lose money. So constant tracking of the response from different segments is essential to know what works and what does not. Donor acquisition is an expensive, continuous, and necessary process. The "average" nonprofit loses 50 percent to 60 percent of its first-time donors each year. And that makes it a great incentive to know what works best with each segment to replenish the supply.

Example 4: Research does pay dividends to the bottom line

Not everyone has the time and money to conduct marketing research before a direct-mail campaign. But sometimes circumstances make it imperative. That was the situation faced by the Bowery Mission in New York City as its active donor file decreased. The Mission switched to new direct-mail efforts after telemarketing and other efforts were unsuccessful. Donations had dropped by 60 to 70 percent in a few years. Times were desperate.

Since nothing seemed to be working and everything was collapsing, the Mission invested in donor focus groups and demographic and psychographic profiles of the remaining donor pool. Since research is expensive, none had ever been done before. But this research proved vital in guiding a complete repositioning campaign that involved using general advertising to correct image problems and, for the same reason, relocating the mailing address for donations from a New York suburb to Manhattan's Lower East Side where the Mission is located.

This work has been in progress since 1992 and was reported in the February 19, 1998, *DM News*. The donor base has increased by 100 percent to about 50,000 people, and annual donation revenue has increased by 20 percent in the last two years. According to the Mission's director of development, none of this would have happened without the investment in marketing research to guide the effort.

A detailed look at a letter package

Your lists have been purchased or compiled. Now it is time to do a mailing to your prospects. There are three elements in a DM letter package:

- The letter
- The reply card
- The envelope

The letter

The first element of your direct-mail package is the letter. There are seven components of a powerful letter:

- Make it personal.
- Open strong.
- Go for length.
- Remember that longer letters allow for better qualification.
- Highlight your main copy points in the letter.
- Sign the letter in blue.
- Use the P.S.

Make it personal

If you are recruiting students, you have paid good money for the names of real people. Use them. Take the time and pay the money to make sure that every letter you send addresses the recipient by name. Do this even if a list broker doubts whether or not it will increase the response rate sufficiently to justify the cost. You are initiating a relationship, not just getting an inquiry. Think of it as part of your image building. Sometime later you are going to send those who respond a publication that tells them about the high level of personal attention they will receive at your college. Build credibility for that statement right from the beginning by personalizing your first contact.

If you're writing to alumni for the annual fund, it is even more imperative to use actual names. The people on this list have already paid you thousands of dollars and invested a great deal of time to become a member of your alumni family. Don't insult them now with a "Dear University Graduate" salutation or anything similar. If you do, you'll pay for it with lower donations.

Open strong

Create a strong, visible first sentence. The first sentence is often the second thing a person reads in a letter after the subheads. Make it as strong as possible, introducing an important benefit of your offer and using one or two "can't miss" words. Strive for something that will make an emotional connection with the reader. And more often than not, it should probably be its own paragraph right after the greeting. In DM, one-sentence paragraphs are OK. Consider these openings:

- "How do you make Harvard Medical beg for you?"

- "Are you finally ready to finish your college degree?"
- "Now is the time to start the rest of your life."
- "Is your head lost in the clouds?"
- "Are you ready to make more money doing what you love?"

Go for length

Use a two-page to four-page letter. A major reason you are putting your money into direct mail is the opportunity it gives you to say more to the people who receive it than you can say in a 60-second media spot. Don't throw away that opportunity. How long should your letter be? It depends on your audience and what they want to know. You shouldn't feel compelled to use only a one-page letter because you think people won't read any more than that. Remember Bob Stone? And David Ogilvy? Trust them. Take the time to deliver the right message. People will read it.

Longer letters are better

When you are recruiting students, you don't necessarily want the largest possible response. You want the largest possible response from people who are likely actually to enroll at your college. Anything else will just cost you extra money and time. Find out what questions telephone inquiries typically ask about your programs and identify the "negatives" that cause people to turn elsewhere. Cost? Location? Scheduling? Length of degree program?

If you can identify your negatives, use that information in a positive way in your prospecting letter. You want to receive inquiries from people who already know your negatives, but either discount them completely or weigh them against the positives and still respond. This may take a bit of courage, since you are deliberately discouraging response. Do it anyway. Your subsequent recruitment efforts with the inquiries you do receive will be far more rewarding as a result.

Highlight your main copy points in the letter

Don't present people with long lines of unbroken copy. Do not force them to start at the beginning and read everything to get your main points. Most people won't do it. (Maybe that's how the "long letters don't get read" myth started.) Your goal here is to communicate all your main points without forcing anyone to actually read your letter. How are you going to do that? You have several options to discuss with your copywriter.

You might start with a Johnson Box (not named after the co-editor of this book) at the top of your letter before the salutation. It would contain the single most important thing you want to say to capture attention and prompt people to read more. Continue with either subheads or indented paragraphs (perhaps printed in bold) throughout the letter. People will scan these before reading the letter and then decide to read the letter if they are interested, so these subheads should convey several very important points. And a restrained use of underlining can add other important highlights. Just be sure not to overdo it. You do not want such a jumble of Johnson boxes, subheads, indents, bullets, and underlining that nothing stands out.

Sign the letter in blue

Blue is a nice touch that says you cared enough at least to make your letter look as if it were signed individually. Not many people will believe this, but it reduces the immediate impression of a mass-produced letter. Do we have to mention that the signature should be a person's name? I didn't think so until I recently received a well-written, personalized letter signed by "The Admissions Staff." A nice try that missed on an important point.

Use a P.S.

This is one of the most read parts of any letter, sometimes the first part in a one-page letter. Use it to repeat a very important benefit or actually to introduce it when the P.S. is read before the rest of the letter .

The reply card

The second element of a successful direct-mail package is your reply card. In higher education mailings, the importance of the business reply card (or BRC) is too often overlooked as an important communication device. This is unfortunate because the reply card is often the first thing your reader will look at after opening the envelope. So the first thing seen should be the primary benefit contained in your letter, right at the top of your BRC in letters too big to miss. "Yes! I want to make Tip Top College tops in computer science!" Do this and your donations will increase.

Print the name and address of the person receiving your letter on your reply card. This will cost more money, both for the printing and to match the right BRC with the right envelope and letter. Do it anyway. Not only have you made responding easier, you have made it much easier for your data entry people to enter the response with maximum accuracy and minimum delay.

What about enclosing a prepaid envelope to hold the response card? Again, this will cost more money but you might want to consider it, especially if your information system is dependent on social security numbers to identify records. I don't have proof, but I believe that more and more people are reluctant to put their social security number on a card and send it through the mail, in plain view of everyone. And a prepaid envelope fosters a more upscale image.

What about not including postage? If you have qualified your prospect pool well, you don't need to further qualify the inquirer's level of interest (which is what forcing someone to find—and use—his or her own stamp will do) by not including postage. This would make sense (as one high school guidebook boasts) if you have no control over who is receiving your message and you want to prevent a host of nonproductive inquiries. On the other hand, why use a high school guidebook like that in the first place? You should not have to worry about this for your annual fund campaign solicitations. Almost by definition, you are not mailing to unqualified prospects.

Once you have written your letter and reply card, there are some other points to consider about the package you deliver it in. I'm not going to prescribe definite right or wrong approaches, but I do want to introduce you to some of the questions that will arise.

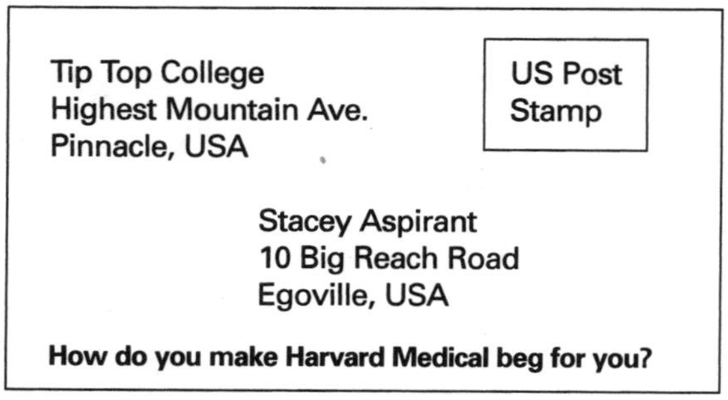

```
Tip Top College                      US Post
Highest Mountain Ave.                Stamp
Pinnacle, USA

          Stacey Aspirant
          10 Big Reach Road
          Egoville, USA

     How do you make Harvard Medical beg for you?
```

Figure 14-1
**Standard Business
Envelope With Teaser**

Plan your envelope with first impressions in mind

Should you use a standard college business envelope? This should work just fine. Should you include a teaser on the envelope? Perhaps it might increase the number of people who open the envelope if it directly addresses something of interest to them. This is another way of saying that the more accurately you can segment your population, the more likely you are to be able to include a good teaser. But a plain business envelope with no teaser can also produce a fine response rate. The only way to know the difference is to test with and without the teaser.

Should you use a label or print the address directly on the envelope? Avoid labels. For some programs and audiences (the MBA, for instance, or upper-level annual fund donors), I recommend high-quality printing directly on the envelope to achieve an appearance worthy of the value of the product you are offering. Most people know that labels are another quick and easy feature to get the mail out the door as quickly as possible. Again, the question here is not just the impact on response, but the impact on image.

But what about window envelopes with the address printed on the letter? DM folks say that window envelopes are an accepted business practice (and therefore will not hurt your image) and do not reduce response. I agree, but I still prefer a regular envelope for special audiences, including, in nearly every case, your alumni who are by definition more special to you than an enrollment prospect. You can make your decision here based on cost. It costs more to match personal letters to the right envelope with a laser-printed address on it. So if you want to save some money with a window envelope, go ahead. But no labels.

Should you use a stamp on the envelope? I like the special nonprofit bulk-rate stamps you can add to your envelope. Few people pay extra to use a stamp (perhaps because the standard bulk-rate mailing permit does not cover their use) but a stamp says that you care a little bit more about what you are doing. It just looks better. Very experienced direct marketers say that stamps do not increase response over metered envelopes although nearly everyone recommends not using a preprinted envelope. The bottom line is use stamps unless money is very tight. If you cannot use a stamp, at least use metered postage.

Creating the best DM format

Let us revisit five ways to contact prospective students and donors that will make your efforts more successful.

First, expensive four-color publications are not mandatory. A properly crafted letter and reply card package can generate just as many inquiries or more as an expensive publication, at less cost. Sometimes, depending on your audience, your goal, and your competition, a four-color publication is worth the investment. But do not assume it is mandatory at the beginning .

Second, difference counts in the mailbox. Everyone from high school students to alumni are swamped by mailings from people they do not know. Most routinely discard much of what they receive without a serious look. If your mailing is different from the others, it stands a better chance of at least getting noticed. Again, that may mean just a letter in an envelope with a teaser relevant to something you know about the prospect, usually their academic interest area or their probable giving preferences. (But pay attention to your competition. If nearly all their mailings use only a letter and reply card, consider something different to stand out in the mailbox.)

Third, pay attention to your real competition. Student recruiters should know what the institutions they compete with are doing. Get on their mailing lists and then pay attention to what you receive—the level of personalization, the quality of the materials, the attention to special requests, the skill of the letters. Always be looking for ways to gain a competitive edge. If you look, you'll find them.

Annual fund operations also need to take into account their competition. Your local orchestra, the zoological society, the nature preservation group, and many more organizations are competing with you throughout the year for a limited supply of donation dollars. Pay careful attention to what is being mailed. How does your message stand up to these others? Is it as emotional? Is fulfillment as easily described? Earlier we described the investment in direct mail made by several organizations competing for scarce donor dollars. You have one edge over them: your letter to your alumni will probably be opened. But you also know that money will not automatically flow back. So do not let your competition in the philanthropic arena appear better organized and smarter than you.

Fourth, use professional, direct response copywriting. Read the books recommended at the end of this chapter. Either discover a special talent on your staff or hire someone to write your letters. Avoid sending typical "academic" letters from anyone, including deans and faculty. Take the initiative yourself and always prepare a recommended letter for someone you want included in your communication system.

Fifth, tell people what you want them to do and make it easy for them to do it. If you build your prospect list with care, you will expect maximum response. Direct-marketing research shows that more people will do what you want them to do when you tell them to do it. The simple "return this card today" will capture enough of the uncertain to make a difference in your response rate. And of course, you want to make it as simple as possible for your qualified prospects to respond. Make instructions very clear. Preprint your prospect's name and address and give him or her the postage.

A final word or two

Direct marketing is a state of mind. Think about segments, think about one-to-one communication, think about relationship building, think about connecting with your prospects' reasons for investing time and money in education. Talk to them in language they can understand. Do these things, and your marketing communications will become far more effective than those used by competitors who are just getting the word out about how good they are. You will make an important contribution to the prosperity of your institution. And both your clients and your prospects will thank you for it.

Recommended Readings

Lewis, Herschell Gordon. *Sales Letters that Sizzle: All the Hooks, Lines, and Sinkers You'll Ever Need to Close Sales, 2nd ed.* Lincolnwood, IL: NTC/Contemporary Publishing Group, 1999.

Lewis, Herschell Gordon and Carol Nelson. *World's Greatest Direct Mail Sales Letters.* Lincolnwood, IL: NTC/Contemporary Publishing Company, 1995.

Ogilvy, David. *Confessions of an Advertising Man.* Lincolnwood, IL: NTC/Contemporary Publishing Company, 1994.

Peppers, Don and Martha Rogers. *The One-to-One Future: Building Relationships One Customer at a Time.* New York: Doubleday, 1993.

Peppers, Don and Martha Rogers. *Enterprise One-to-One: Tools for Competing in the Interactive Age.* New York: Doubleday, 1997.

Schultz, Don E.; Tannenbaum, Stanley I.; and Robert F. Lauterborn. *Integrated Marketing Communications: Putting It Together and Making It Work.* Lincolnwood, IL: NTC/Contemporary Publishing Group, 1993.

Schultz, Don E.; Tannenbaum, Stanley I.; and Lauterborn, Robert F. *Integrated Marketing Communications: The New Marketing Paradigm.* Lincolnwood, IL: NTC/Contemporary Publishing Group, 1997.

Stone, Bob. *Successful Direct Marketing Methods, 6th ed.* Lincolnwood, IL: NTC/Contemporary Publishing Group, 1997.

15

Marketing on the Web: Blending the New and the Newer

Robert Johnson

- Do you want to reach the most technologically advanced members of your audience?
- Are you interested in a high degree of message customization?
- Can you afford—or not afford—a cutting-edge interactive Web site?
- Can you quickly respond to e-mail communications you receive from the Web?
- Are you prepared to encourage intense, one-to-one relationships with faculty, students, and staff?

What is this thing called the Web?

This chapter focuses on ideas and predictions about how the Web is going to work out for you in your work in the future. I developed it by combining my own background in direct marketing with the best thoughts of many other marketing people. Nobody can tell you "how to do" marketing on the Web. You have to look at the information sources (Appendix C), follow what's happening in the field, and think about the results being achieved. Above all, you can't be afraid to experiment. Web marketing is not for the faint of heart. But if you like to explore new frontiers, you will love the challenges of this new arena.

And note that you won't always find examples of academic institutions actually doing everything that you read about in this chapter. Most of us haven't advanced far enough yet. But each activity noted here is feasible. All you need is the institutional vision and commitment to start doing them before your competitors.

The Web is the home of millions of impatient people of all ages who are looking for information and interactive communication with people who share their interests. The best Web sites weave copy with animation, use visuals without long download times, and provide access to chat rooms where like-minded people can gather and exchange information and opinions.

The Web is introducing the greatest change in the way people communicate since the telephone. In fact, today's teenagers with Web access would rather talk to friends through fast e-mail services than use a telephone. And that introduces an important message in this chapter. As fascinated as we can all become with a "full-featured" Web site, we should never forget that the simplicity of e-mail communications is still the most attractive feature of the Internet. Web sites must be designed to take advantage of this attractiveness and not act as a barrier to it.

> **"The Web is introducing the greatest change in the way people communicate since the telephone."**

Prospective students increasingly use the Web to explore possible academic institutions. When they arrive at your Web site, you can better capture and hold their attention if you offer such features as:

- Financial aid estimators and updates
- Contact with students and faculty in academic areas
- Graduate school and career information

New alumni will expect to use your Web site services to keep in touch with friends and to donate to their alma mater's annual fund. Maintain their connection with you by offering them:

- Personal Web sites that continue after graduation
- On-line employment searches
- Athletic updates

For both alumni and students, your Web site can be an ideal vehicle to cultivate long-term relationships that bring mutual benefits to both parties. That, after all, is the essence of successful marketing.

Give thanks for the annual survey of Web use conducted by the Graphic, Visualization, & Usability Center at the Georgia Institute of Technology in Atlanta. (*www.gvu.gatech.edu/user_surveys*). This is the most authoritative source of information about Web users today. The survey is biased in favor of frequent Web users, a useful bias if you are planning for an increase in the number of frequent users. The bias occurs because survey respondents are solicited with banner ads placed on Web sites. The more you use the Web, the more likely you are to be solicited and the more likely you will be to respond.

Here are some of the most significant findings from the ninth survey in 1998:

- Web users are becoming more typical of the population as a whole: Female users continue to increase, (now 38.7 percent but are increasing at a much slower rate than in the period between the seventh and eighth surveys), and average annual income continues to drop (now $52,000). Note especially that 43.8 percent of Web users between 11 and 20 years of age are female.

■ New Web users (active for less than a year) are slightly more likely to be women than men (51.7 percent) and more likely to be under age 20 and over age 50. Web growth, therefore, is ideal for those contemplating communicating with high school student prospects and soliciting deferred gifts from alumni.

■ For the first time since the surveys began, the most indispensable technology cited by survey respondents was e-mail, which rose 9 percent in use from the previous year. The indispensability of Java/Java Script also rose rapidly, an increase of 8.1 percent.

■ Web speed (measured by the time required to download a Web page) is slow and continues to frustrate 64.8 percent of respondents, and this response level is consistent over the previous two surveys. Note especially that 53 percent of respondents reported leaving a commercial Web site rather than wait for a page to download. The dissatisfaction continues despite relatively constant upgrading of modems.

■ Web pages contain more "images, animations, scripts, programs . . . ," which decrease modem speed.

Here are some important things for Web marketers in higher education to consider:

■ Colleges with a primary dependency on traditional-age students need to pay close attention to the changing communication habits not only of teenagers but also of preteens. By the time preteens are ready for college, Web use will most likely reflect the general population of college-bound students. That's less than 10 years from now.

■ Be cautious of the creative impulse to do everything that is technologically possible on a Web site. Technology is advancing far faster than access speed. Web designers should test the result of their creativity on a home PC connected to a medium-speed modem and a phone line. If your Web site is slow to download, most people will leave it before it is loaded.

■ Pay special attention to the power and speed of e-mail. People of every age love e-mail, and the affair appears to be growing. Include it as a distinct part of your Web marketing plans.

■ Do plan to adopt the innovations possible with Java Script. Visit the University of Dayton site *(www.udayton.edu)* to see what this can do for your Web site.

People over the age of 50 are becoming more involved with the Web each year. This is a tremendous opportunity for alumni relations offices that relatively few have taken advantage of.

Planning your Web site for maximum use

In the first days of shiny new Web pages, all we cared about was how many people were visiting. And so Web designers copied automobile speedometers and an old McDonald's technique and told everyone how many "hits" had been received since the minute the Web site opened. Today, you should be able to do far more to justify the resources you need. Every Web site is capable of tracking great quantities of information about what people do when they visit your site. Here, courtesy of the November 24, 1998, e-mail newsletter of Interactive Communications International *(www.icisolutions.com),* are some examples of the good things you can do with all that data.

1. Set goals you can measure. You can track not only how many people visit, but how long they stay, how they move around your site, and how many do what you want them to do—for example, sign up for information, make a donation, or register for a campus visit.

2. Compare the popularity of different parts of your site. What's different about the popular pages? Content? Navigation? Do you think you can increase traffic to less popular pages? Or should you just eliminate the less popular?

3. When you change a site, what happens? Do people stay longer? Do more of them take the action you want? Be sure to compare what happens to sections of your site after changes to what was happening before.

4. Don't make too many changes on your site at once. If you make several changes at the same time, you won't know which ones are responsible for the changes in traffic patterns.

5. Do links to portions of your site change traffic? When a section of your site is linked somewhere else (for instance, to a newsletter you send or in an advertisement you placed) does the traffic increase?

6. Read between the lines. If most of your site visits are at night, they are probably being made from home on relatively slow 28.8 or 33.3 modems. If the visits are not as long as you would like, are your graphics too heavy for speedy downloading?

7. If you want to get inquiries, give visitors more than one place to sign up. Know what part of your site generates the most inquiries. How does that part compare to the parts that attract the most visitors? Are you perhaps losing inquiries because highly visited site locations have no place where people can sign up for your offer?

8. Profile your visitors. Why do people visit your site? Find out by paying attention to where they go. Note what interests them most by learning what they download or what information they request.

9. How do your visitors find you? You can ask them on a form. But you can also use your log files to track them back to the site they came from. Learn which Web search site is working for you, and where you might want to consider an advertisement. Where most of your traffic comes from now is probably the place you can draw more from in the future.

10. Know your conversion rates. How many prospective student Web site visitors

> **Every Web site is capable of tracking great quantities of information about what people do when they visit your site.**

sign up as an enrollment inquiry? If you know the source that produces a stream of visitors, you can calculate the value of the ads you place there. How many of your alumni visit and make a donation? If you use an e-mail newsletter to drive people to a Web location that offers a giving opportunity for each academic unit, you can compare the results.

Technology-driven change

Two technology-related developments will influence the pace of the coming communications change.

First, and most important, is the speed with which people in their homes can access information on Web sites, especially videos. At present this is infuriatingly slow over any telephone modem, and this lack of speed severely restricts what you and I can effectively do on Web sites. Web users of any age are an impatient group, and effective marketing activities today must heed this impatience and therefore be limited in scope.

But this is changing. As I write, my cable TV company has already sent the first notice of the tremendous increase in download speed that is soon coming to my neighborhood. At a probable cost of twice what I am now paying for my monthly Internet connection (not counting the extra phone line charge), my Web access speed will increase more than 50 times over its present rate. There is no mention of the exact availability date of this speed increase, but it is already operating in some nearby areas.

Despite this upgrade, don't expect speedy access for everyone to happen overnight. A November 1998 edition of the *NUA Internet Survey* reported a finding by the Gartner Group that in 2003, 63 percent of 46 million Internet access lines in the United States will still be using an analog modem, or telephones. Only 14 percent will use a cable modem and 3 percent will use a satellite connection. The message is clear. In planning your Web and Internet communications, you can't overlook the great variation in access speed that will continue for some time.

Second, the price of computers capable of effectively accessing the Web has to fall to around $500. Two years ago, even one year ago, this would have seemed a silly statement. In 1999, powerful computers (by yesterday's standard) with 200MHz+ operating speeds, 32MB of RAM, and large hard drives are available for less than $1,000. As prices continue to fall, penetration in the marketplace will spread rapidly. Within 10 years, if I can be so bold, virtually every home in the United States will have Web access as a basic utility. The change will take place even more quickly among middle- to upper-income families.

How might these changes influence student recruitment? Consider these probabilities:

■ Viewbooks as we know them will likely cease to exist. Two alternatives are possible. Prospective students will create their own "viewbooks" from a college Web site and print them on their printers at home. Or visitors will order their own individualized books at a Web site, and digital printing technology will produce a personal viewbook in 24 hours and send it to the prospect

Campus fairs will disappear. Why travel miles to a stark exhibit hall and wander among college tables competing with too many others for attention at a six-foot table? Why not sit at home and take a virtual tour of the colleges that interest you, participate in a virtual open house and chat with many students and faculty, and then decide which institutions are attractive enough to deserve your personal visit?

How might these changes influence alumni relations programs? Here are some possibilities:

■ College magazines will change from their present format. Instead of the "one set of contents fits everyone" limitation of present publications, articles will be mixed to best fit the interests of different alumni groups or segments. Alumni Web visits will be monitored to collect information on the topics of greatest interest, and information will be designed to meet those interests. Eventually, printed magazines will have an electronic version on the Web.

Alumni giving rates will increase. Web technology will allow the building of very sophisticated databases, and digital printing technology will allow fund-raising campaigns to use publications that focus much more directly on the interests of individual alumni prospects.

■ The percentage of donations received directly from Web site solicitations will increase steadily over the next 10 years.

If you are a marketing person working in higher education today, you can't afford to overlook the potential of Web-based or Internet marketing. In just a few more years, it will transform the way you do business. The problem is, we don't exactly know how. And that is also the challenge and the caveat of writing this chapter. Whatever I include here now may be superseded by new experiments with new technology. There is no way to make this chapter completely up-to-date. So why write it? Two reasons. First, Internet marketing, particularly the use of e-mail in conjunction with Web sites, is here, and some people are using it effectively. Second, it will alert you to the awesome change that is about to happen.

Don Schultz of Northwestern University may have said it best in a January 15, 1997, column in *DM News*, "Integration and the Internet." He wrote, "It is clear that the Internet is going to be a major factor in the communications system of the future. When that future will occur is anybody's guess. Best estimates put it at least 10 to 15 years from now."

Note that this Shultz column appeared in a publication on direct marketing. Direct marketers have been leading the exploration of the Internet marketing potential. Most important principles of direct marketing have an application on Web sites and in e-mail communications. The "integrated marketing" and "one-to-one marketing" concepts of both have strong roots in direct marketing, where the emphasis is on direct contact and interaction with potential customers on an individual basis, whether they are students or donors. The long-term goal is the creation of an ongoing relationship between the individual and a group or community of like-minded people. This concept of "community" is an excellent fit for what academic institutions attempt to do when they enroll students and cultivate relationships with them from the time they graduate until the time they die.

So let us explore this exciting new marketing area with a broad concept that will frame the remainder of our discussion—collaboration marketing.

Marketing models

To understand the nature of collaboration marketing, consider it as the third of three marketing models:
- Mass marketing
- Traditional direct marketing
- Collaboration marketing

Mass marketing

Mass marketing is based on the premise that if you communicate with enough people frequently enough over time, you will sell more products. Since you do not need to sell to everyone who hears your message to achieve success, you do not need to be especially concerned about the specific individuals you reach. Newspapers and magazines, network TV, and highway billboards all have important roles to play in mass marketing. Although it may never disappear completely, the importance of mass marketing has been diminished by traditional direct marketing.

Traditional direct marketing

Direct marketing recognizes that marketers can identify specific target audience segments interested in particular products and design different communication programs to create a transaction with individuals in the segments. According to an article in the November issue of *Response,* the newsletter of the Direct Marketing Association of Detroit, the "total reported value of direct marketing strategic transactions" increased from $14.4 billion in the first half of 1997 to $23 billion in the first half of 1998. Direct marketing works, aided by the ability to create and use increasingly sophisticated databases. Direct marketing is successfully used in mail, specialized magazines, radio, and telephone campaigns. It is used somewhat less in network TV, mass market magazines, and print media. (See also Chapter 14).

Collaboration marketing

John Hagel III emphasizes the importance of collaboration marketing in his important book, *Net Gain.* The advent of the Web and e-mail communications allows a new marketing goal to emerge: the creation of virtual communities of real people with similar interests who share a continuing involvement with one another and with the organization that offers a product or service. Collaboration marketing is designed to help people as well as sell to people.

The premise of collaboration marketing is : an organization that helps people to know more about a product or service that interests them will sell more of those products or services to them. It is an ideal concept for academic institutions in the business of recruiting and retaining students, and then building strong alumni communities that provide their alma maters with continuing financial support .

Like direct marketing, collaboration marketing can only succeed if the desired customers share a common interest. For both alumni and prospective students, this is most likely the academic program from which they graduated or in which they plan to study. An institution's Web site then becomes the source for learning and sharing information about a common interest. Chat rooms, discussion threads, and e-mail newsletters with links back to a Web site are all examples of interactive communications that build continuing involvement and therefore a sense of community.

The best example I've yet found of a Web site that practices collaboration marketing is the Car Talk site *(www.cartalk.com)* supporting the popular National Public Radio talk show. When you visit, pay special attention to the variety of ways you can communicate not only with the talk show hosts but also with fellow visitors. Also pay special attention to the variety of features on the constantly changing front page: new columns, contests, free offers of interest to visitors, and much more. Keeping the intended community in mind, it is one of the premier sites operating today.

The most unique feature of collaboration marketing is the notion that the participants themselves create and update the content of the Web site to which they return. This is a difficult premise for any organization, and especially for academic institutions, to accept. By definition, community members themselves decide what they want to know and discuss rather than what the organization thinks they should know and discuss. Your control of the communication message is lost. But in return, you gain more continuous involvement with your prospects, and that makes them ultimately more likely to enroll or give dollars.

Collaboration marketing for alumni. An important element of collaboration marketing is your opportunity to influence your community members. For example, at the same time a prospective alumni donor is returning to your Web site to talk with a fellow premed alumni, you can advertise giving opportunities for your annual fund. A small pop-up "ad" can let visitors know that the biology department is looking to upgrade its microscopes and that each new piece of equipment will have the name of the donor engraved in a place visible to every student using it. "Click here" will bring more information, including the ability to make a donation immediately using a credit card. Making the donation will instantly add the name of the giver to the "most current" supporters list that everyone visiting the biology site has an opportunity to see. Your donor will also receive an immediate e-mail "thank you," followed later by a more personal letter. None of this is difficult to do with the current state of technology.

Collaboration marketing for student recruiting. Student recruitment will benefit from collaboration marketing as well. Prospective students visiting a site can see pop-up invitations to the next campus visit program, with information on the content and how to register just a click away. Visitors to a departmental site can be offered the opportunity to visit student Web sites maintained by students majoring in the same subject area.

> " On the Web, visitors want to go where their interests take them, not where you want them to go. "

And so it goes. The opportunities for both prospective students and their parents are almost endless. Although it can be overdone, as long as those opportunities are related to the visitors' interests and they can elect to ignore your exhortations, you should not shrink from offering opportunities to the user.

To repeat an earlier observation, collaboration marketing is scary to traditional communicators who believe they must remain in control of the message sent. On the Web, visitors want to go where their interests take them, not where you want them to go. As a result, there is less opportunity for censorship or "message control." This new marketing communications model forces emphasis on what customers want to know, not what you want them to know. Technology permits you to begin this new venture the first time people visit your Web site. Just as Dell Computer does for special customers, you can allow visitors to customize the front page of your Web site to feature the areas that are of most interest to them. For an example of how one college is doing this, visit the University of Dayton *(www.udayton.edu)* site and customize the site for yourself. It's easy to do, and it's a great way to introduce the other-community-building, collaboration-marketing features at your site.

Searchable Web sites

From a marketing perspective, a Web site is not simply a place to post as much information about your institution as you possibly can. People need to be able to find what interests them quickly and easily. At the same time, they want to avoid information that is not of interest.

An effective "search" feature at the beginning of your site is critical—even more important than the indexes that someone labors over so intensively before the academic catalog is published. A good search engine should be able to do these things:

- Allow someone to type in the name of anyone who works or studies at your institution and send them an e-mail.
- Allow someone to type in the name of any academic program you offer to take him or her directly to the relevant Web page. Let that person simply type the word "premed" or "medicine" and get where he or she wants to go. Don't make visitors scroll through a list of "academic programs" to find the one they want. (Actually, a fall 1998 test to "search" for premed information at institution sites was in most cases a failure. Despite the great interest in this preprofessional program, it is lost on many academic institution Web sites since it is not an academic "major." Type "premed" or "medicine" on your institution site and see what turns up.)
- Allow someone to type in the name of any generic "key" word and obtain a list of Web sites that address the topic the key word represents.

Your Web site must compel visitors to "bookmark" the site. It must be so interesting and important to your visitors that after the first visit they tell themselves, "I've got to come back here again or I'll miss something I don't want to miss." Exactly what that is will depend on the different interests of different visitors. Your goal is to build relationships with your regular visitors, relationships that develop into a sense of belonging to a community of like-minded people. When you have done that, you are poised for effective collaboration marketing.

What features are likely to inspire bookmarking for return visits? Consider these five examples, to which you can no doubt add. Each feature presented here also addresses the fact that there is simply not enough time for you to create new content on a regular basis for your Web site. Each kind of item listed below is already being created by someone.

Student newspapers

Alumni and prospective students and their parents regularly review student newspapers. You shouldn't worry about articles that treat some aspects of your institution unfavorably. People expect this of student newspapers. They also know that nearly every institution has one. If you don't provide access to yours, people are going to wonder why you don't.

Alumni notes

Alumni notes make up another good feature for alumni and prospective students and their parents. Allow alumni to provide new information on a regular basis, including automatic e-mail links if they wish. Then make sure these notes are included in what your search engine searches. The appeal to alumni is obvious. And each time they visit your site, you can update them with information on their current class contribution to an annual fund or to a capital campaign.

Encourage alumni to post links to their favorite Web sites with mini-reviews. Group these by topic so that everyone interested can easily find them. Make sure that prospective students searching your site by topic also locate them.

The appeal for prospective students is also strong. Link a "premed" search to information provided by alumni about their medical careers and you have an obvious appeal. Do this for every major and visitors will be easily able to follow the career success of your graduates in any area that interests them.

Press releases

Virtually every institution turns out press releases on a continuous basis throughout the year, and you should post each and every one to your Web site. Neither alumni nor prospective students will visit a press release site very often and scan the topics. But if you link this site to your search engine so that a "premed" scan turns up biology professors with new grants, alumni with new medical appointments, and students with new scholarships, you are transforming the value of your releases. Whether or not your releases are ever printed in the media, visitors interested in the topics covered will see them.

Note: Additional insight on using the Web for media relations may be found in Chapter 9.

Student contact by academic area

This idea is a winner for prospective students and also for alumni who want to know more about your current students in their old academic area. Kenneth Hartman, formerly at the College Board, notes that the primary reason a prospective student visits your Web site is to find the Web pages of your students. Very few colleges make that easy to do, usually from a fear of what visitors will find. Again, this is an area where the freedom of the Web can be scary. But the concept of collaboration marketing requires just this type of access to what your Web visitors want to see. And Hartman is correct—to the high school student visitor, your students' Web sites will be far more interesting than the official college site. You know that prospective students are very curious about who else goes to your college. Access to your student Web sites will give them the answers they want—and it is collaboration marketing at work for you.

Sports news

Not all your alumni or prospective students are interested in sports. But for those who are, access to regular news about your teams is important. Whether your institution is a strong and successful NCAA Division I university or a Division III college, people are interested in your sports programs. Your sports information director should post news of every sport to your Web site as soon as an event is over. Keep it current, and interested people will visit to find out detailed results more quickly than they can by waiting for the next morning's paper. In most cases, you'll satisfy them with more information than the local TV station will report that evening.

For the record, let's list the information regularly found on institutional Web sites that will not create return visits. They include course listings, faculty names and credentials, degree requirements, mission statements, maps, and visit instructions. These are the static elements most often found on "first-generation" Web sites. In the early days, these sections were seldom updated and contained little or no interactive features. If your Web site is still dominated by these elements, fewer and fewer Web-literate people will pay much attention to it.

This is not a recommendation to exclude first-generation information, but simply a note that these are fairly static features that are not often updated and therefore not likely to create a desire to return to your site on a regular basis. You'll have them on your site, but they don't give you what you need to foster community and collaboration.

Designing the interactive marketing Web site

In this section, I am not going to write about how a Web site looks, but about how a Web site works. To start this process, let's first look at a Web version of the five "Ws" that journalists are familiar with. These come from J.D. Mosley-Matchett, a regular Web marketing columnist for the AMA's *Marketing News,* and are her recommended five "Ws" to consider in your site design.

You're Ready for Collaboration Marketing if—

- You don't mind people adding things to your site that you don't know about in advance.
- You respond to every e-mail you receive in 24 hours or less.
- You're willing to maintain conversation threads at your site.
- You regularly search for links to new Web sites that might be of interest to your visitors.
- You understand that different people are interested in different things you will have to support collaboration among several, even many, different groups at your site.
- You produce e-mail newsletters to which your collaborators can subscribe.

---

1. Who are the people you want to visit?

This first "W" may seem basic, but it is very important and too often overlooked. For our purposes, it means defining your most important visitors. Different people on your campus will answer that question in different ways. I assume that anyone reading this book is primarily concerned with prospective students and alumni. To start, the groups should have their own "front page." The content of the page should reflect what you know about the general interests of the visitors before you allow them to tailor the page to their personal interests. A Web site built on the principles of direct marketing will develop different front pages for every important group of people visiting on a regular basis.

Consider this example from Wellesley College. The college has a standard front page *(www.wellesley.edu)* and another front page *(www.wellesley.edu/admission)* to which prospective students are directed. Visit each, and you will immediately see the point in designing different pages for different groups. You can find another front page for the alumni association *(www.wellesley.edu/Alum/alumnae.html),* which includes a developing series of sites for different graduating classes.

2. What do they want to find?

Be sure to track what visitors are looking for. If you want to keep it simple and interactive at the same time, just ask people who visit to send you an e-mail about anything they want to find and cannot.

3. When do you update your site?

No, you don't need to include the date when your site was last updated, but you do need to update it regularly, and you need to make sure people know what is new. Hope College *(www.hope.edu)* does this on a regular basis on their always-changing front page. One thing you do not want to do is to leave the date on a part of your site that was last updated months (even years!) ago. All that does is send the message that you don't care much about this particular part of your site. Check your entire Web site and try to eliminate these old dates. Ask yourself why the section is even on the site if it hasn't been updated in the last 12 months.

4. Where do you place promotions?

This is tricky. Promotions shouldn't prevent people from finding what they came to see on a Web site, but neither should you avoid them. You do want to remind people of an alumni homecoming, a student visit day, an opportunity to sign up for a newsletter. You'll get ideas on how to do this by visiting the sites that receive recognition for their marketing expertise at a Web site devoted to fine sites *(www.webbyawards.com).*

5. Why should anyone care?

If you don't give people what they want, they won't care. Don't assume that just because your institution has important faculty, a great mission, and the most wonderful core curriculum in the United States that people are going to want to visit your site. If you don't pass their relevancy test, people won't visit. Put people in interactive communication with the right people about things that interest them and you will build traffic on your site.

After reflecting how your Web site answers these five basic questions, let's review the important details that implement effective marketing communications on your Web site. We start with something as basic as how you respond to e-mail.

Robert Brueckner wrote a *DM News* column (July 15,1996, "Time to Redirect Your Thinking") in which he urged marketers to respond to e-mail inquiries with a message "that blows the recipient's doors off." He went on to note that most responses (when there are any at all) are late and don't say much. In the intervening years, responses have not improved a great deal. How should you be responding? First, the best response is a personal one from someone on your staff. I received one of these within 24 hours from a person at the University of Michigan site for graduate nursing programs. It thanked me by name, included information about an upcoming open house, and had the name of a real person (and her e-mail address) at the end. It was very impressive, especially in comparison to responses from other locations.

Most of us, however, will rely on an automated system for the first response. Any response is better than none at all since it tells the visitors that their e-mail was received. At a minimum, your automated response should address the person who sent it by name, say how long it will take to send the information requested, include a real person's name and e-mail address the recipient can get back to if more help is needed, and say thank you.

If you are responding to something more than basic requests for information, someone must monitor the mail on a regular basis. A response of some type must be sent within 24 hours. Any longer, and you are not meeting the expectations of people who use e-mail on a regular basis. If your admissions recruiters, for instance, can't respond that quickly, then an automatic response should tell the sender when to expect something more personal.

Remember that we are trying to make it as easy as possible for your prospects to find what they need. If you receive an inquiry about your premed program, your response should include the URL that will take your prospect directly to that section of your site. Many e-mail systems today allow your site visitors to click on the URL you give them and get to the desired location. This, of course, is especially helpful when your site is difficult to navigate.

Communicating effectively on the Web

At this point we offer some ideas to help make your Web site more effective:

Writing right

You will want your visitors to return to your Web site regularly in search of the new information you will be providing them. To keep them happier with that experience, you need to pay special attention to how you write for your Web site. The Web is not the vehicle for a literary masterpiece. If you regularly read *USA Today* and *Atlantic* magazine, you have an idea of how to and how not to write for the Web. If you are not yet certain of the correct choice, then consider these points from the masters of copywriting in direct marketing, Hershell Gordon Lewis and Robert E. Lewis, in their book *Selling on the Net: The Complete Guide.*

Long copy isn't bad. Just as we noted in the chapter on direct marketing, visitors to the Web will read long copy if it interests them. But you need to present the copy in short, easy-to-read steps. Long stretches of continuous copy will drive people away.

Your copy should concentrate on benefits to the reader and should seek an emotional connection. Presentation of an annual fund campaign, for instance, can stress the enhancement of Tip Top College's reputation when donations to improved equipment in biology labs not only foster better education but also attract better students who will maintain Tip Top's outstanding reputation for preparing students for medical school.

Don't be afraid to sell. You are selling "community" and membership in a collaborative environment. Be sure to ask people to join. This is another area where an important principle of direct marketing works: More people will do what you want them to do if you ask them to do it. Ask people to "click here" to register for free financial aid updates, to receive a free e-mail newsletter on Viking athletics, to sign up for a campus visit, or to send in an annual fund gift and charge it to their credit card.

Keep it interesting. As you write or review every headline and every sentence, ask yourself if it keeps your interest in the subject. This is especially important when academic institutions sometimes feel compelled to present writing that violates one basic rule of effective communications. The rule: Write for the people who will read what you write. Writing in the language of an academic discipline is appropriate for an academic meeting. It is not appropriate for presenting academic information to prospective students. Know your audience and write for it.

Allow response on the Web. Some people will want more information or to donate by phone or mail after they finish reading your Web copy. But not everyone. Many will find it strange indeed that you are forcing them to use a telephone rather than allowing them to simply click on an automatic e-mail reply form. Review your Web site carefully, especially the sections developed by individual academic departments, to make sure that every response option is included. Choice is the rule here.

Words that work

The next important point in assuring effective marketing communications on your Web site is to select key words that capture your reader's attention and motivates him or her to act. Direct marketing research shows that some words are almost impossible to ignore. Consider these recommended by Ted Nicholas in his book, *Magic Words That Bring You Riches:*

- Discover
- Amazing
- Announcing
- Do you…?

> **Words designed to motivate are not appropriate for every place on your Web site, but you should pay constant attention to the locations where they do fit.**

- You
- Free
- New
- Breakthrough
- Secrets of
- Yes
- Only
- How will . . .
- Protect
- Now
- True
- At last

Here are some brief examples of how these words can enliven your Web page:

1. This sentence in your admissions section—

> "Discover the secret to your success in college—the great faculty at Tip Top College."

is much better than this sentence—

> "The excellent faculty at Tip Top College is ready to educate you."

2. And this sentence will work much better for parents—

> "Yes, I want to discover how to lower college costs—"

than this sentence—

> "Send me information about financial aid at TipTop College."

3. More alumni will respond to this—

> "Yes, I want to protect the reputation of my Tip Top College degree."

than will respond to—

> "Send your annual fund contribution to Tip Top College."

Words designed to motivate are not appropriate for every place on your Web site, but you should pay constant attention to the locations where they do fit. These will include the pop-up or banner ads that you might use on your site that are expected to motivate people to take a desired action. They might also include the headlines that introduce text sections. Consider this headline that came up after a "premed" search at the SUNY-Buffalo site *(www.buffalo.edu)*: "How do you make Harvard Medical beg for you?" For an aspiring medical school student, that would be hard to resist.

With these notes on powerful words for the Web in mind, here are nine caveats from an article by Pat Frieson in *Target Marketing* magazine (August 1997), "From Boring to Brilliant." The examples from higher education are real; only the names of the institutions have been changed.

1. *Avoid presumptuous openings.* When you are answering an e-mail inquiry, don't overstate your case. "I know Tip Top College is right for you" can't be an accurate statement when you don't know anything about the person sending the inquiry. Similarly, telling a recent graduate that "I know you care about the

reputation of Tip Top in the next *U.S. News & World Report* ratings" refers to something that you can only know if the alumnus has actually told you that he or she cares.

2. *Write in language the reader understands.* Words and terms like "core curriculum," "modes of inquiry," "co-curricular," "liberal arts tradition," and others that represent academic jargon should never be used with prospective students and seldom with alumni.

3. *Avoid overstatements.* If you write that "Tip Top College's campus is one of the most scenic in the United States," I will be prepared for an awesome sight when I visit. Can you deliver? Many campuses are attractive and some are scenic. Few can be "one of the most scenic." Make sure your statements are believable and do not create false expectations.

4. *Use real, not rounded, numbers.* Stating your enrollment as 3,717 shows you cared enough to be accurate and sets you apart from the many others who will just say "about 3,700 students attend Tip Top." Your credibility will increase.

5. *Know your reader's possible objections and address them in your copy.* This may seem scary, but if you have good research that tells you why people often don't do what you want them to do, then you should address this directly in your communications. If, for instance, your alumni survey reveals that recent graduates don't give to the annual fund because they believe that a small contribution is not appreciated, begin your alumni association Web page or e-mail solicitation with: "You're wrong if you think that we don't value a $10 gift as much as a $100 gift. Each counts equally in the *U.S. News & World Report* ratings." Of course, if you say that in your solicitation, you have to send each donor a personal letter of thanks for his or her gift.

6. *Be appropriately personal.* Don't use "we" unless you are referring to two or more people. In most communications from one person, "I" is more appropriate and believable. Leave the imperial "we" to monarchs and politicians. Similarly, use "you" to heighten the fact that you are communicating "one to one" with an alumnus or prospective student.

7. *Repeat key features and benefits.* The direct-marketing adage that "if it's worth saying once, it's worth saying twice—or three times" is applicable to your Web and e-mail writing. Say it in the headline, say it in the introduction, and say it again before you close: "If 45 percent of our alumni give to the annual fund at Tip Top College each year, our reputation will grow and so will the value of your degree."

8. *Give your reader a reason to respond.* Explain how your institution lags in fund-raising compared to your presumed peers and—because most will not know this—explain how it has a negative impact on your *USN&WR* ratings. Surely your alumni want to help correct that situation. If you don't know how fund-raising influences the ratings, go to the *U.S. News* Web site (*www.usnews.com/usnews/edu/college*) and review the rating criteria.

9. *Use an occasional parenthetical comment.* Parenthetical statements relax the severity of your writing, adding an element of informality that will increase the personal nature of what you are saying.

Capturing e-mail newsletter subscribers

Capturing newsletter subscribers should be a primary purpose of your Web site marketing plan. When visitors subscribe to newsletters, they automatically separate themselves from the visitors who do not. Subscribers are telling you that their interest level is high. Subscribers are joining your community. Subscribers give you a continuing opportunity to build strong relationships and to deliver your messages to people who want to receive them. Here are the key points to remember as you develop your e-mail newsletter marketing plan:

■ *E-mail newsletters are simple to write.* Use standard newsletter copywriting techniques. Examples are easily available on the Web, and several e-mail marketing newsletters are noted in the resource section at the end of this chapter. Most of the copywriting guidelines already covered here will work for your e-mail newsletters.

■ *Newsletters are simple to tailor to different audiences.* You don't have to use completely different copy in every newsletter to every audience but some sections should match the specific interests of the people subscribing to them. You could, for instance, have a series of newsletters built around the professional interests of your graduates that also contain general news about your institution. Similarly, prospective students can subscribe to career interest newsletters that contain information about the accomplishments of your graduates in similar areas.

■ *Build subscribers by "opt-in" lists.* Never automatically send newsletters to groups of people you think might want to receive them. But always give visitors a clear, easy opportunity to subscribe. The best approach is to direct them to a sample copy on your Web site where you present a subscription opportunity as they finish reading the sample. A special note: direct marketers are slowly coming to an agreement that an "opt-out" option (you present visitors with a prechecked box and hope they don't delete the check mark) are not as good as an "opt-in" option where visitors have to make a choice. Remember that you are seeking interactivity and involvement on the part of your visitors. The community you are building will be stronger if members make a conscious choice to join it.

■ *Give subscribers an "opt-out" option.* At the end of each newsletter, clearly tell people how to end their subscription. And pay attention to who uses it. Consider a brief, automatic questionnaire that simply asks them why they are leaving. If it doesn't take much time to complete, you are likely to get useful information. After someone leaves, send them an automatic "thank you for being with us" note.

■ *Archive your newsletters.* You'll always be adding new subscribers. Give them an opportunity to catch up to past news by reviewing your old issues. Keeping them accessible for 12 months is long enough.

■ *Link your newsletter to your Web site.* Don't miss the opportunity to bring people directly back to your Web site. Many e-mail systems present their readers with "hot" links when the URL is typed into the newsletter, and you can take advantage of this. Your athletics newsletter, for instance, can take people directly back to pictures on your Web site of your most recent game. Your announcement that a biology professor will be featured on the Discovery channel can take people right back to pictures of her search for the Loch Ness monster.

■ *Keep it simple.* Technology exists to allow you to add pictures and video to your newsletters. But for the moment, don't do it. An important feature of e-mail is that it is quick to send and receive since it is only text. Add anything, and you destroy one of the most important email features. Direct marketing research so far shows that newsletter readership decreases sharply when anything is added that increases the time to read.

■ *Keep a database of your subscribers.* As marketers, we want to take advantage of a primary function of offering e-mail subscriptions: learning more about the people who are interested enough to subscribe. Most people will complete a brief form with basic information about who they are and what they are interested in. But always give people the option not to include personal information they might not want to send. You want the maximum number of subscribers, and people who are not interested in what you are offering will not subscribe. (Recently, for instance, I attempted to subscribe to a newsletter. I received a return e-mail asking for phone and mailing address information to "confirm" that I was who I said I was when I first attempted to subscribe. It seemed like a not so-subtle-effort to solicit further business. I didn't send the information back).

> **E-mail newsletters are an obvious vehicle for long-term cultivation of alumni.**

E-mail newsletters are an obvious vehicle for long-term cultivation of alumni. And as student recruitment moves earlier into the high school years, the cultivation concept begs to be borrowed from the advancement side and used for enrollment development. Here are sample newsletter topics of interest to enrollment professionals:

■ Especially for Parents
■ New News on Financial Aid
■ Secrets of Successful Engineers

Advancement professionals cultivating increased annual fund participation might consider these topics:

■ Moving Ahead . . . Your Classmates in the News
■ Viking Athletics . . . Coach Tom's Weekly Update
■ Inside the Leadership Club . . . Monthly Updates from President Peabody

Managing your web site

In the early days of Web development, most Web operations on campus were under the control of a techie-type living in the computer center who knew how to write in HTML and create text on Web pages—a major achievement in and of itself in the early days. As institutions everywhere worked to get their admissions publications online as quickly as possible, techies were in charge.

The next people to get involved were people from public relations and communications. They were worried about what was available on the institution's Web site. Sections of an institution's Web sites were being developed by different administrative units and academic departments, often because there were no campus resources to provide central assistance. If you believed in uniform graphic design, you had nightmares. Message control, (discussed in Chapter 1) was a special problem. The Web was populated by communication anarchists who fought any form of central control.

And today? Web sites are in a mature but still evolving state. With this observation in mind, let me hazard a suggestion from a marketing perspective, namely, that you create an oversight system to manage all campus Web operations and consider important policy issues, particularly those dealing with Web input. Keep in mind that the Web is still populated by people who believe that there should be few, if any, restrictions on free expression in this medium.

Here are the most important elements to consider in this delicate area:

1. Create a Web policy group that includes representatives from admissions, alumni relations, fund raising, public relations, athletics, information technology, and academic programs. If you simply must have one, include a person designated as the Webmaster, but under no circumstances should he or she be in charge of any single element of the institution's Web site. The Webmaster will have invaluable technical expertise but, in most instances, will not be marketing proficient and, therefore, is unable to create a marketing-oriented Web site.

2. Locate the Web policy group within the marketing unit of your institution, reporting to the chief marketing person. Policy recommendations should be made to this person, who must have the authority to make final decisions when the policy group cannot reach agreement.

3. Your institutional budget should contain a specific appropriation for ongoing Web site development, a substantial one in the context of your overall resources. The policy group should have initial responsibility for determining allocation of these funds according to already developed institutional marketing priorities. It is unlikely that you will have the resources available to develop all sections of your Web site simultaneously.

4. Divide the responsibilities of your policy group to coincide with the important elements of Web site: design, navigation, and content. It is very unlikely that your Webmaster will be talented in each of these areas, so your group should have at least one person with primary responsibility for each area. Your Webmaster should play a role similar to that of a printer in a publication

process, providing essential technical expertise on what can be done at what cost.

5. Your charge to the Web policy group should include regular review of competitive Web sites and regular monitoring of Web sites that feature the most advanced sites. Web policy group members must understand that their role is to strike the best balance between what the competitors are doing and the state of the art. You will not likely be able to keep up with the Dell Computer site or others that regularly win Webby awards *(www.webby.com)*. On the other hand, being able to keep up with advances made at competitive sites will help in your struggle for institutional resources.

6. Your Web policy group must strive to ensure a uniform graphic appearance and uniform navigation throughout the Web site. People moving from one part of the site to another should not think that they have migrated from one planet to another.

7. Your institution, not the Web policy group, must establish a policy making it clear that Web development resources are available only to institutional units that agree to adopt common graphic and navigation standards. The Web policy group must enforce this policy.

8. You must train people in each unit of the institution to update the content of their sections of the site on a regular basis. No single person or small group of people can handle this task for an entire institution. Your Web policy group must take the initiative in making this happen.

9. Your Web policy group must ensure that traffic to the Web site is monitored on a regular basis and that this traffic is taken into account in ongoing Web development. This means more than counting hits. It means paying attention to which visitors spend how much time on which sections within the overall Web site. Every Web site can be designed to capture this information.

10. For some time to come, your Web policy group should prepare an annual campus report on the state of the institutional Web site. The report should note use patterns in detail, analysis of the competition, and upgrades planned for the coming year (including the reasons why these upgrades and not others have been selected).

> **We have barely begun to explore the impact that Web technology is having on marketing communications today.**

Into the future: what Web technology will do for you

We have barely begun to explore the impact that Web technology is having on marketing communications today. Nevertheless, we need to stretch our imaginations to include the possibilities the technology holds in store for tomorrow. And in the case of e-mail, we need to consider how the simplicity of the present will continue into the future. Consider these ideas.

Combine the power of digital printing and the Web
Nothing has the potential for more revolutionary change than the combination of

digital printing or "printing on demand" and databases built on information supplied by the people visiting your Web site.

Consider this step-by-step example of how it will work as reported in an October 19, 1998, *DM News* article by Mark McLaughlin, "SmartSite Shows Marketers the Future." The examples have been changed to fit higher education.

- ■ Prospective students visit your Web site and enter information into a text file about themselves and the characteristics of a college that rank highest in their college selection process. You also capture basic information on their academic interest areas and their mailing address.
- ■ The text file is transferred automatically to a database that transforms the information into a profile of the visitor and sends this profile to a digital printing system. The digital printing system then creates a personal direct mail piece that includes the individual characteristics of each choice. The publication also focuses on the academic programs that interest this student and provides financial aid information according to the economic characteristics of the residential zip code provided. (If the visitor indicates no interest in financial aid, no information is sent).
- ■ The publication is mailed directly from the fulfillment house to the visitor within 24 to 48 hours. A personalized cover letter can be included if you wish.

The technology to do this is available now and portends a rapid expansion of the one-to-one marketing concept in higher education marketing. As a result, publications received by people will be of far higher interest and impact than anything possible in what will soon be the "old" way of printing.

Digital printing is a reality now. Whirlpool Corporation, for instance, uses this technology to prepare different responses to inquiries about its products. Before it is widely adopted, however, it faces two hurdles. The first is more significant than the other.

First, digital printing is now more expensive than traditional printing. If you plan your publications based on the "cost per piece," you will find your costs increasing for the next several years. Digital printing, however, will increase the yield from publications. Your applications and your annual fund contributions will increase as your literature becomes more valuable and interesting to your audience. If, as a good marketing person, you measure the value of your dollars by the results produced rather than the marketing tools purchased, you will find that digital printing improves your yield at every stage of the enrollment and fund-raising process.

The second hurdle is the quality of the publications printed. To the trained observer (especially when equipped with a loupe), the photographic quality in a digital publication is not equivalent to traditional printing. I do not consider this a serious objection. When given the "eyes of a normal human being" test, the digitally printed publications from Whirlpool more than serve their purpose. A small loss of printing quality does not nearly outweigh the impact of more personal information.

I make one prediction with confidence. You do not want to be the last of your competitors for students or charitable dollars to combine digital printing with the Web site capabilities. To review what's being offered in this area now, visit the Web site of a printing company featured in McLaughlin's *DM News* article *(www.webcraft.com)*. Finally, to remove any doubt that substantial sums of money are being invested to promote this approach, learn what IBM is doing by visiting the company's site for digital printing *(www.printers.ibm.com)*.

Adopting this approach to publications response is an important first impression that will help you secure membership in a virtual community based at your Web site. Your printed response will signal visitors that you care enough about their interests to tailor what you do for them. This level of attention will pay important dividends as you continue to develop long-term relationships.

The future of effective Web advertising

Have you been thinking about developing "banner" advertising? Think again.

Right now "banner" ads are popular on the home page of many Web sites. Visit the Yahoo college and university section, for instance, and you may see a banner ad from the University of Phoenix for its on-line MBA program. Banner ads are similar to "teasers" on the outside of envelopes. Just as the content of the teaser is supposed to get someone to open the envelope, so the content of the banner ad is designed to get people to "click here" and open the way to another Web site. When you are finished with your business at the site to which the banner ad takes you, you can return to your original site — sometimes easily, sometimes not.

Banner ads can also be used at your own site to take people to different places within your Web page. Colleges use them to announce sports victories, special campaign results, or upcoming special events. But are they effective?

Banner ads developed as a spin-off from conventional print advertising. In the words of Sean Carton, managing partner at Carton Donofrio Interactive, "They seemed like a good idea at the time." They appear to be an easy way to segment Web advertising according to the interests of people visiting different Web locations. Unfortunately, in 1998, Web advertisers noticed fewer and fewer people actually clicking on them. Why did that start to happen?

According to Carton in "Here's What Will Save the Web," a Web article at the Click Network site *(www.searchz.com/clickz/102898.shtml)*, fewer people are using banner ads because they don't want to leave the site they are already at to visit another. In other words, it's more complicated than opening an envelope. Clicking on a banner ad makes you leave the Web site you came to visit. Donofrio uses this analogy: "Can you imagine if advertising in magazines required you to drop the magazine you were reading and pick up another to read more about the product you were interested in?"

Faced with this growing resistance to click when told to click, Web marketers have an alternative approach that allows the visitor to remain at the original Web site while receiving new information promoted by the equivalent of a banner ad. Consider how it will work:

- ■ You see a banner ad with a message of interest and you click on it. That part is no different than the present format.

- The banner expands to about one-third the size of your normal viewing page. The larger section contains the equivalent of a full ad for the University of Phoenix on-line MBA or the special biology department giving opportunity for Tip Top College's annual fund. There is a button for more information if the ad interests you. (If not, you just click to close and go on with what you were reading or looking at).

- If you click for more information, you will receive instructions relevant to the ad itself. Tip Top College, for instance, will present additional information about how a donation will help premed students and will include a form for people to donate with their credit card. The University of Phoenix will include testimonials about its MBA program, details of how long it takes to complete the program, and a form asking that a UP person contact the visitor by phone, e-mail, or regular mail. (Note, of course, the ability to tie this back to digital printing).

- When you finish, you just click to close and you return to your original Web page. Donofrio describes the experience: "You've never left the page you were on, never had to worry about hitting the 'back' button, never got confused about where you were in cyberspace. . .".

In the fall of 1998, a company (9th Square) filed for a patent on the technology (E*Banner) to do what is described above. The principle is simple: The advertiser brings content to the Web site where you happen to be, rather than requiring you to visit a different Web site. Whether or not this exact format will take hold in Web marketing, something similar is likely to happen. The message is clear: Stay alert, visit Web marketing sites regularly, and never assume that the new approach you adopted yesterday will still be effective tomorrow. Things are changing far too quickly to make such a dangerous assumption. In the meantime, consider very seriously any plans you have for "traditional" banner advertising.

'. . . in 1998 "the hot new medium is … e-mail'

The subhead above is from an April 1998 article in *Wired* magazine by David S. Bennahum. It is presented here to remind us that despite innovative technological change, one of the most rapidly growing areas of Web use is based on the reason people found the Web in the first place—to send e-mail to one another. Today, the ability to do that is far improved over the "pioneer" days, and e-mail remains one of the most popular reasons people attach themselves to the Internet. Bennahum's perceptive comment: "During all this hype about videostreaming, people have been e-mailing each other. There's been a denial about what's going on. E-mail works and people like it." People of all ages. A November 3, 1998, article in *The New York Times,* "From Yakety-Yak to Clackety-Clack," recounted in detail how high school students are using AOL features such as Instant Messenger and Buddy Groups to "talk" with one another on a regular basis. More daily time is spent on this basic use of the Web than on "surfing" for topics of interest or visiting previous Web sites.

With regard to a higher age level, Bennahum's article recounts the rapid growth in both for-profit and "virtuous" or free e-mail lists compiled by authors of e-mail newsletters. (My own free e-mail newsletter on higher education marketing increased from 400 subscribers to more than 1,100 in five months in 1998.) Most of these grew from simple e-mail exchanges between people interested in a common topic to more formal e-mail publications prepared by a single person who reviews material in many different sources and combines the best into a newsletter. Most of these free newsletters also take contributions from subscribers. Note that these are not the traditional "listservs" that allow communication among members similar to what the teenagers in the *New York Times* article are doing. Instead, many evolved from listservs that overwhelmed the participants with too many messages. A monitor arose, screened the messages for the most useful content, and began writing a newsletter.

Compare this situation with the rapid demise of several 1995 and 1996 Web magazine publishing ventures reported on the front page of *The Wall Street Journal* of January 14, 1997: "Facing Early Losses, Some Web Publishers Begin to Pull the Plug." The often elaborate publications were simply not what most Web users were looking for when they went online. E-mail newsletters, on the other hand, are much easier to receive and read and appear to be prospering for reasons that are very similar to the "virtual community" concept introduced earlier.

A final word

Marketing on the Web is different. But not that different. Anyone familiar with the principles and practices of direct marketing will be at home in the Web marketing world. People who are not familiar with them may feel a bit lost at first. And nobody, especially not today's direct marketers, know what is really going to work in Web marketing five years from now.

We can end this chapter, however, with some general observations:

- Web marketing is very different from mass marketing, with its emphasis on frequency and reach. Don't be concerned about "reaching" the millions of people who visit the Web every day. In most cases, colleges and universities should not consider placing banner ads on Yahoo and AOL. (The exception might be institutions promoting distance education programs)
- Be very concerned with what visitors will find (or not find) when they visit your site. Know what your visitors expect to find and help them find it. Most colleges and universities are not yet doing a very good job of that. See for yourself. Take the "premed" test (see above).
- Web marketing is very much an adaptation and evolution of direct marketing. Visit the *DM News* Web site on a regular basis together with the other Web sites listed in Appendix C. In effect, you need to become a good direct marketer before you can become a good Web marketer.
- Web marketing is the perfect medium for the continued personalization of marketing. It may someday bring the concept of one-to-one marketing very close to reality. The technology is here. We have not yet learned how to use it

in effective marketing communications.

■ Collaboration marketing is a concept that should work well for colleges and universities. Many alumni are gregarious people who enjoy talking with one another. In other words, they are perfect candidates for regular participation at a site designed to promote a virtual community. But we have to give up control first and let our alumni create the content of the parts of our Web sites that they inhabit. Are we willing to do that?

College and university marketers, whether working with prospective students or alumni, are in the relationship business. In that context, Web marketing is an important part of an overall mix of marketing activities designed to create and sustain relationships that result in students enrolling and in alumni giving. Web marketing will never replace direct human contact on visiting days for new students and at alumni campus reunions. It can, however, be an influence in creating an easily accessible means of communication among like-minded people in between those relatively infrequent personal meetings. In that role, it is indeed powerful.

Recommended Readings

Bayne, Kim M. *The Internet Marketing Plan: A Practical Handbook for Creating, Implementing, and Assessing your Online Presence.* New York: John Wiley & Sons, 1997.

Bennahum, David S. "The Hot New Medium is…E-Mail: List Publishing is Not Merely Information Delivered to Your Mailbox. It's the Devolution of Mass Media Into the Hands of Everyday People and It's Growing Faster Than the Web." *Wired,* 6, no. 4 (April 1998).

Brueckner, Robert. "Time to Redirect Your Thinking." *DM News.* (July 15, 1996).

"Facing Early Losses, Some Web Publishers Begin to Pull the Plug." *The Wall Street Journal.* (January 14, 1997): 1, A8.

Frieson, Pat. "From Boring to Brilliant." *Target Marketing.* (August 1997)

"From Yakety-Yak to Clackety-Clack." *The New York Times.* (November 3, 1998).

Hagel John, III and Arthur G. Armstrong. *Net Gain: Expanding Markets Through Virtual Communities.* Boston, MA: Harvard Business Review Press, 1997.

Lewis, Hershell Gordon and Robert E. Lewis. *Selling on the Net: The Complete Guide.* Lincolnwood, IL: NTC Contemporary Publishing, 1997.

McLaughlin, Mark. "SmartSite Shows Marketers the Future." *DM News* (October 13, 1998).

Nicholas, Ted. "Magic Words That Bring You Riche$" Indian Rocks Beach, FL: Nicholas Direct Inc., 1998.

Schultz, Don. "Integration and the Internet." *DM News* (January 15, 1997).

Stern, Jim. *Advertising on the Web.* Indianapolis, IN: Que Education & Training, 1997.

Stern, Jim. *Customer Service on the Internet: Building Relationships, Increasing Loyalty, and Staying Competitive.* New York: John Wiley & Sons, 1996.

16

Getting it Together

" Creating effective marketing, whether in the form of a strategic integrated marketing plan or a more basic integrated marketing communication plan, will remain important. **"**

Creating a good marketing communication program is hard work. Money helps, but more important is the dedication and commitment of people from all areas of our institutions to do the right things in the right way. And that's what we hope this book will help you do. Different people will look to different chapters for help with the major immediate challenges facing each of our institutions. But make no mistake; effective marketing is essential. Without it, academic institutions will waste resources developing educational programs that do not meet the needs of our students, legislators will limit our funding, and government agencies will take more control of what higher education does. Projections of coming increases in college enrollments do not mean a return to the days before declining traditional enrollment provoked the initial interest in marketing in the 1970s and 1980s. The American higher education system that appeared after World War II (with its tremendous expansion in the college-bound population and government funds to support the expansion through the 1970s) has fallen off the wall, and nobody is going to put Humpty Dumpty back together again quite the way he was before.

And so, creating effective marketing, whether in the form of a strategic integrated marketing plan or a more basic integrated marketing communication plan, will remain important. At some point, many of you will move from one plan to another. And given

Robert Johnson

the differences in institutional culture, politics, and circumstances, different institutions will be moving from one to the other at different times. But here is some discussion of what we think will remain constants.

Growing commitment to a comprehensive use of marketing

You shouldn't have to sneak around your campus any longer whispering the "M" word to a handful of colleagues. Conferences and seminars that directly address marketing issues in higher education are becoming more numerous each year. Institution presidents who understand the importance of marketing will become more important and sought after in the future. But they will not become universal. Those of you who are fortunate enough to work where a president "gets it" from the start will thrive. Those of you who labor in different circumstances can still succeed, but you will have to work more diligently to demonstrate the initial need for resources (time, people, and money) and to demonstrate the results of your work. But we believe that the influence of good marketers will grow on our campuses for many years to come. And that, after all, is why you bought this book.

> " Effective database management will become essential to how you raise dollars and recruit students. "

Image enhancement

Everyone's recruitment and fund-raising efforts will be easier if his or her institution is better known and understood in the marketplace. To this end, marketing professionals will guide their colleagues to a better understanding of what is important to the special publics that are most important to achieving the goals and meeting the expectations of academic institutions. You will care less about what the general public thinks of you and more about how special publics regard you. And to do that best, you will invest more in research that allows you to understand how to identify and understand those special publics. Perhaps someday, no president on any campus will complain that his or her institution is the "best-kept secret" among people who would never have an interest in Grand Old Ivy U, no matter how many media articles or radio ads appear. But special publics, on the other hand, will receive a constant stream of desired information to keep them involved in a continued relationship with Grand Old Ivy. In the minds of those publics, a fine and strong image will blossom. And students and dollars will follow.

Personal communications

Does anyone not believe that mass marketing as we have known it is dead? Note the consternation of network TV executives when the audiences of nine of the 10 highest-rated shows in the 1998 season had fewer viewers than in 1997. In 1970, a single ad placed on each major TV network would reach over 90 percent of the homes in the United States. In 1998, the estimate is that the same ad would reach no more than 50 percent of U.S. households. The individual consumer has extraordinary choices today among cable and network TV stations, Web sites, and specialized magazines and radio stations. No one, least of all educational institutions, can hope to communicate with everyone, or even a significant fraction of everyone. So you will all have to concentrate on developing marketing communications plans focused on the individual people that mean the most to each of you. And you will have to remember that nothing you can do will force these people to pay attention to your presidents, your fund raisers, or your student recruiters, unless what you offer is perceived as a benefit. People don't owe you their attention.

Database management

Effective database management will become essential to how you raise dollars and recruit students. Without the ability to segment the people in your databases effectively, you will never be able to develop personal communications that recognize the varied interests and backgrounds of the people with whom you communicate. Database management begins with effective collection of data: what things you need to know about people and the way you will record them in your database. Once recorded, do you have the capability to segment according to whatever data elements are important to your communications plan? If your software does not give you the capability to do this within your own office (and you don't have a person on your staff who knows how to work with the software), you are working with a severe limitation.

Marketing research

Today, we know of few institutions that conduct adequate marketing research. But we expect that situation to change. Doing good research requires the right "state of mind" as much as the right level of resources. Organizations like ACT and the College Board, for instance, provide annual free reports to academic institutions who use their test score results, which are excellent measures of longitudinal changes in the marketplace. But investment in real research dollars must also grow. You must not only do more general opinion surveys, you must pay the extra cost to allow analysis of different segments within your general populations of students and donors. If you do not do this, you severely restrict your ability to plan effective marketing communications strategies and measure the impact they are having on your audiences. This is especially true in the areas of "image" and "reputation," which are not completely measurable by the number of students who inquire or the number of alumni who donate. You'll still want to know about the students who inquire but do not apply and the alumni who do not donate.

Integrated internal communications

All of you who communicate with the outside world do have to talk to one another on a regular basis inside your own institutions. You all know that athletics, advancement, and student recruitment have been separate worlds on too many campuses and each world knows little if anything about what the other is saying or doing. Marketing-oriented presidents must stop that. The marketing communications organization outlined early in this book may not come to pass in quite the way we present it here, but it does represent the future in some form. Pay attention. Presidents and trustees are beginning to wonder why advancement and admissions and enrollment efforts don't work in harmony with one another. Change is coming. If you are a young professional in these areas now, you should be preparing to live your life differently than your mentors have lived theirs.

Web communications

No doubt about it, early Web advocates were overzealous in their predictions about how quickly the Web would revolutionize our lives. But the Web is going to revolutionize the way we communicate in the next 10 years. Clearly, many of us view the Web as a serious impediment to the way we would like to do business——namely, the same way we have always done business. People complain about the volume of e-mail received, about the inability to control message content, about the reluctance of Web users to read what we want them to read, about the resources that must be diverted from somewhere to create and maintain an effective Web communications system. Stop complaining. Start solving.

Unless you plan to retire in the next five years, you have no choice but to learn a new way of doing things. In this new world, you will divert resources from printed publications and Yellow Pages ads and radio advertising because your institutions cannot afford not to do so. You will answer e-mails within 24 hours because you cannot afford not to do so. And you will stop worrying about how you can present only positive messages to your publics. You can't control that any more. You will have to tell your publics what they want to know, not what you want them to know. If they visit your Web site and don't quickly find what they want to know, you have lost them. And you may never know they stopped to see you. Scary? Sure. Reality? Yes.

And so we leave you on the edge of new opportunities to take a leadership role in the future of your academic institutions. Plan to become a campus champion of your marketing efforts. Develop new areas of marketing expertise. Use them to help solve campus problems. Help shape the enrollment your president and faculty desire (that is, help make their desires realistic), and help raise the dollars everyone needs. It will be difficult work. It will also be exciting. It will even be fun.

A solid research methodology will help preserve the integrity of the data.

Section IV
Appendixes

Designing a Research Study

It is helpful when undertaking a research project to follow a basic methodology. This is especially important when the data to be gathered will be used to support decisions that have strategic, economic, or political consequences. A solid research methodology will help preserve the integrity of the data.

Robert Sevier

I suggest a protocol to guide you through the completion of a research study that embraces the following eight sequential steps:

1. Develop the research agenda.
2. Identify your target audience.
3. Develop your initial research methodology.
4. Write your research instrument.
5. Draw the sample you will use.
6. Execute the survey.
7. Input and analyze your data.
8. Present your results.

Step 1: Develop the research agenda

In many cases, your research agenda is a reiteration of the president's original communication mandate. As such, it provides direction, clarifies options, and keeps things on track. For the most part, this involves answering such questions as the following:
1. Why are you doing the research?

2. What do you hope to learn?
3. What audiences have the answers?
4. How will you use the research?

It is important to know why you are undertaking research. You might, for example, be interested in knowing who influences your major donors. Perhaps you want to know to which media prospective students are most likely to respond. Or maybe you want to test a fund-raising case statement. All of these are good reasons to conduct research, especially since they are consistent with the original communication mandate established by your president.

At the beginning of your research project, it is important to clarify exactly what it is you wish to learn. I call this the "big question." Some big questions for different studies might be:

■ How do parents perceive our institution?

■ Why don't more alumni give?

■ Why do some students who visit not enroll?

■ Why do community residents not send their sons and daughters to our institution?

The big question serves as a sort of research thesis statement and helps keep you on track as you develop individual survey questions. Later, when reviewing the first draft of the completed research instrument, keep the big question in mind. Survey questions that do not support the big question should be eliminated.

A final question that helps shape your research agenda is one of the most important: How are you going to use the data? Because of our emphasis on communications, it is highly likely the data will be used to test perceptions and misperceptions, shape vivid descriptors, create individual messages, or outline larger communication campaigns. The very best research keeps these communication-related outcomes firmly in mind. Knowing how you will use the data helps you not only shape the questionnaire but also decide how to analyze the data and present the results.

Step 2: Identify the target audience

Identification and careful definition of your target audience is an important step in developing your research protocol. Who has the answers you seek? Often the nature of your target audience will provide insight into how they might best be queried. Some time ago I wished to determine how a client college was perceived by regional chief executive officers. We knew that CEOs were reluctant to participate in focus groups and would not respond to a mail survey. Our best option was to conduct telephone surveys arranged in advance through their secretaries.

Note: As you think about your potential target audiences, you might want to take a few minutes to review the information on target audiences presented in Chapters 1, 2, and 3.

The Big Question	Audience	Methodology	Population Size	Validity Sought	Sample Size
How do major donors perceive the institution?	Major donors	Mail survey	2,000	95 percent	322
How do traditional-aged prospective students compare you with other colleges and universities?	College-bound high school students	Telephone survey	4,800	95 percent	355
How do alumni feel about the institution?	Alumni	Mail survey	12,000	95 percent	375

Table A-1
Research Strategy Grid

Step 3: Develop the initial research methodology

Now that your research agenda is beginning to take shape, you must decide which research is most practical for the study you envision. Keeping in mind the information on different methodologies presented in Chapter 4, you may well find that a comprehensive study involving more than one population will, in fact, include a number of different methodologies.

To help guide your overall research project, you might want to create a Research Strategy Grid that links the important components of each study. As you can see from Table A-1, such a grid is a useful way to keep things organized.

In this grid, the first column contains the big question, the second column defines the target audience, and the third indicates the chosen methodology. At this point, your judgment comes into play. In choosing your methodology, you will want to weigh such factors as:

■ Audience size
■ Audience importance or status
■ Amount of money available for research
■ Level of validity sought
■ Time frame for completion of the survey
■ Geographic distribution of the audience
■ Survey length
■ Survey complexity
■ Sensitivity of survey questions

For some surveys, I have chosen a telephone survey for prospective students because of their geographic distribution, because I knew the survey would be relatively short, and because I wanted a high response rate. However I chose mail surveys for major donors because of their previous ties to the institution and because of the degree of anonymity that I sought. Finally, I chose a mail survey for alumni because of the size of the sample, because of its geographic distribution, and because the intended alumni survey would be long, complex, and cover several sensitive issues. I also knew that alumni—because of their emotional attachment to the institution—were often more responsive to mail surveys than other target audiences .

Suggestions for Lowering Research Costs

For some institutions, the biggest obstacle to market research is cost. To help reduce the cost of obtaining research data, here are some strategies and resources.

• Check secondary sources.
Before you begin a primary research project, see if secondary research is available from an association or consortium to which you belong such as CASE, NAICU, NACAC, AACRAO, AGB, NASFRE, NAIS, and others. The Web can also be a good source of secondary data.

• Develop a central research registry.
It is not unusual for more than one office at an academic institution to initiate research projects, resulting in duplicate studies or portions of studies, missed opportunities to piggyback, and wasted dollars and time. To avoid this problem, consider developing a central research registry at your institution that keeps track of who is doing what study.

• Involve faculty experts.
For a sophisticated study, seek guidance from faculty experts in statistics or research design. Their input and direction may save you time and money. Take care, however, that the topic of study will have no impact on any faculty involved. For example, you would not want a psychology professor to participate in the evaluation of publications produced by his or her spouse working in campus public relations.

• Scale down the study's size.
Some insist on trying to survey an entire population when a representative sample would be satisfactory. There are options for scaling down a research project that will not affect its quality. For example, instead of trying to see how all 18 of your constituent publics perceive you, rank these publics and seek information from the most important five or six.

• Choose a less expensive type of research.
There is an enormous difference between the costs of doing 370 mail surveys and 370 phone surveys. With minor modifications, less expensive strategies may gain the same information. However, if response rates are important, sometimes the more expensive research will be more economical over the long run.

• When possible, use closed-ended questions.
Questions that ask respondents to choose from an established series of answers (yes or no; very good, good, or not very good; and the like) are much easier and cheaper to tabulate.

• Pretest your instruments.
A solid pretest can uncover questions that need rewording or are confusing. Revising your survey based on the pretest results will increase its validity.

• Develop a research cycle.
As discussed in the book, a research cycle involves doing smaller studies each year rather than one massive study every three years. Not only will you have more control over the research, you will also be able to focus on current problems and opportunities. In addition, you will be able to monitor your market continually, probably pay less for the research, and assimilate data more easily.

• Balance what you need to know with what would be interesting to know.
One quick way to cut your costs is to reduce the size of the survey. Three-page surveys can burgeon to eight or more pages after everyone in the administration has had a chance to add a few favorite questions. When looking over the questions, ask yourself, How can I realistically use these data to improve my marketing and communication efforts? If the questions don't immediately support the overall study mandate, don't use them.

• Use sound methodology.
A solid, balanced research methodology will increase the integrity and vitality of your research data. Don't cut corners and be forced to redo the study.

• Standardize your instruments.
Writing the survey instrument is one of the most expensive components of a research project. If possible, standardize your instruments and get all possible life out of them. This is extremely important if you are trying to create longitudinal data and plan to test, at a later date, the effectiveness of your integrated marketing communication strategies.

• Consider three rules as you choose your research strategy.

1. Understand that there is an important relationship between the decisions you make on research and the amount of time and money you spend to support the research. Decisions with far-reaching implications, such as those for an expensive and long-lived communication campaign, warrant more research.

2. As the complexity of your strategic research project increases, you will need to balance quantitative research methods (surveys) with qualitative research methods (interviews and focus groups). This balance will improve the overall quality and validity of your final data.

3. When designing your research strategy, make sure you hold off discussing the type of research you want until you've isolated the questions you want to ask and the audience you want to research. It can be disastrous to begin a market research study by saying "let's do a focus group" before deciding what and whom you want to examine.

Finally, remember that a good research methodology protects not only the subject and the data but the credibility of the researcher.

The fourth column gives the population size. You must know the size of your target population before you can establish the sample size shown in the sixth column. Next, to establish the level of reliability that you want in relation to the other target audiences you are studying, you must ask yourself three key questions:

- How important is this particular audience?
- How important are these data?
- What major decisions will you make as a result?

Because there is a direct relationship between cost and reliability, you will want to use these questions to guide your thinking about the level of validity you should seek.

The final column, sample size, comes from computing the reliability level sought (column 5) and the size of the population (column 4) on a standard sociometric chart such as that found in Table 4-2 in Chapter 4, or in any good statistics book.

Step 4: Write the research instrument

For many people, writing the survey instrument is the hardest part of the research process. Although experience is always helpful, these guidelines will help you get off to a quick start.

First, don't forget the research agenda. What is the big question? Why are you doing this? What do you hope to learn? What decisions will you make as a result? Your survey must focus on answering these four questions. Often the most important survey questions are asked in different ways in more than one place in the research instrument. If a question on the survey isn't supported by the big question, don't include it.

Second, keep the methodology in mind. Telephone surveys are generally shorter and less complex. Mail surveys, because the recipients will read and answer them, can be longer and cover more complex, even sensitive issues. Mail surveys can also include publications, ads, video, or interactive media samples for review and evaluation. Focus groups and personal interviews are usually more conversational in nature, and need plenty of time for responses. Focus groups and personal interviews tend to cover fewer groups than the first two methods of research but cover

Focus Groups

Believe it or not, there is a great deal of debate about the value of focus groups. Research purists, at least those with a strong quantitative bent, feel that focus groups are usually more misleading than they are insightful. Others laud focus groups and use them with great conviction.

The fact is, when used properly, focus groups can gather valuable information. For example, they can be used to gather initial information and insights early in the study, particularly at the instrument-development stage. Focus groups are also an ideal way to test concepts, tag lines, vivid descriptors, publications, and even advertising.

As you think about focus groups, it is important to keep in mind one very important fact: Focus group data are not statistically significant no matter how many groups you do. They should never be used as the sole source of data when major, expensive, and often very public decisions are to be made.

Enhancing the effectiveness of focus groups
Here are some suggestions for making your focus groups as successful as possible:

Meeting length: About 60 minutes per session. Such a session can usually be adjusted to fit during a dinner or a class period.

Number of participants: From 10 to 12 per session. It is extremely difficult to control the discussion with more than 12, and the quality of the data will suffer.

Participant profile: Screen participants so that they are as homogeneous as possible. The participants should closely match the profile of the target audience.

Location: Almost any room will do as long as it is comfortable. Because sessions are usually recorded, the room should be fairly quiet. Ideally, chairs and tables should be movable.

Note: Remember, it takes time to scrutinize a publication, so you will usually have time for only one or two during the session. If participants will be examining one publication in depth, they should receive a copy ahead of time so they can examine it before the session begins.

Mounting publication samples: If you are interested in comparing the covers of different publications (for example, you want to compare your viewbook cover with those of your competition), mount each one securely on identical, numbered mat boards.

Displaying publications: If you want to compare covers, have enough tables or easels so all are easily seen at the same time.

Refreshments: When available, it is appropriate to serve soda or coffee. However, avoid messy finger foods such as pizza at sessions where people will handle publications.

each group more thoroughly.

Third, remember to move from general questions to specific questions, from safe questions to sensitive ones. As in any good interview, save the most difficult questions for later; open with those that are easy to answer and that gain the respondent's trust.

And finally, keep the research instrument as short as possible. Nobody likes wading through endless questions. As you write the instrument, focus on what's important and not what's merely interesting.

Open-ended and closed-ended questions

Most surveys use two different kinds of questions. Open-ended questions allow respondents to answer in their own words; closed-ended questions ask respondents to choose from a list of possible answers.

A sample open-ended question might be:

What section of the newspaper do you read most often?

There are several kinds of closed-ended questions:

■ Dichotomous (no measure of intensity)

Did you attend the open house for community residents?

❑ Yes   ❑ No

■ Multiple choice (no measure of intensity or direction)

Do you prefer to listen to radio in _____?

❑ Early morning   ❑ Afternoon
❑ Mid-morning   ❑ Early evening
❑ Late morning   ❑ Late evening

■ Scaled (used to measure intensity or direction)

How important was the cost of the alumni retreat in your decision to attend?

Very important ___ ___ ___ ___ ___ Not important at all

As you might guess, there is debate about which types of questions are best. Generally, the best surveys use both kinds of questions. The majority of survey questions are closed-ended; open-ended questions are used to gather data for which you have developed no succinct sets of responses.

With closed-ended questions, the respondents must choose from the answers offered, so you must be careful that the answers cover the full range of possibilities. There is also some loss of detail. However, closed-ended questions take less space on the instrument, are easier for respondents to complete, are less likely to be misinterpreted, and are less expensive to tabulate and analyze.

Although open-ended questions allow a much greater variety of answers, they are less likely to be completed by the respondent, to be interpreted properly by the researcher, and are much more expensive to analyze. Open-ended questions, however, are especially useful in gathering anecdotal data that might be used to expand on other data or even to serve as illustrations or testimonials in messages.

Questionnaire Guidelines

As you develop your questionnaires, remember:

Seek only information that is not available elsewhere.

Make sure test directions, such as skip patterns, are clear and simple to understand.

Use examples to illustrate any questions that may be confusing.

Place personal or sensitive questions later in the survey.

Ask important questions more than once and in more than one way.

Do not put the most important questions only at the end of the survey.

All items must mean the same thing to all respondents. Clarity is essential. Terms like "several," "most," and "usually" have no precise meaning, so avoid them.

Vary the types of questions (see previous page).

Do not talk down to respondents.

Do not assume too much knowledge on their part.

Avoid hypothetical questions; you will get hypothetical answers.

Avoid negative questions; respondents often misread them. For instance, people may overlook the negative word, then give an answer opposite to their real opinion.

Avoid technical terms, abbreviations, jargon, and "big words" that some respondents may not understand.

Avoid questions that require people to respond to two separate ideas with a single answer.

Avoid biased or leading questions. If you hint at the type of answer you prefer, respondents may tell you what you want to hear.

Avoid questions that may embarrass respondents or place them on the defensive.

Use as few questions as possible; people are less likely to complete long surveys than short ones.

Note: There is as much art as science to writing good research questions. Two helpful sources are Ken Metzler's *Creative Interviewing* and Stanley Payne's *The Art of Asking Questions.*

Software	Formats Instrument	Basic Analysis	Advanced Analysis	Graphics	Telephone
StatPac	No	Yes	Yes	No	(612) 925-0159
SPSS	No	Yes	Yes	Yes	(800) 543-5815
Minitab	No	Yes	Yes	Yes	(800) 448-3555
Survey Pro	Yes	Yes	Yes	Yes	(800) 237-4505
P-Stat	No	Yes	Yes	No	(609) 466-9200

Table A-2
Statistical Software Available for Analyzing Research Instrument

Software considerations

Because there is nothing more frustrating than having a box of 375 surveys that your software cannot analyze, it is very important for you to understand the statistical software you will be using to analyze your data even as develop your research instrument. If you are not familiar with statistical software, it is even more important to review an early draft of your instrument with the people who will be doing the analysis so they can evaluate the suitability of your question formats.

The odds are high that someone in your department of psychology, sociology, or education already has statistical software that you can borrow. However, if you need to buy software, check out the ones listed in Table A-2.

When looking for statistical software packages, consider the following questions:

■ Will it help you develop the research instrument?
■ How easily can you input and verify data?
■ Does it provide the analyses you need?

- ■ Does it include a graphics package?
- ■ Will it easily export data to Excel, Access, or Lotus?
- ■ Is there a one-time cost or must you obtain annual license fees?
- ■ How often has the package been updated?

Conduct a pretest

Every research instrument can be improved with a pretest, and it is a mystery why so few researchers don't avail themselves of this opportunity to improve both the instrument and the eventual outcomes of the study. To conduct one, ask a subset of your target sample, perhaps in a focus group setting, to complete the survey. Afterward, have the respondents evaluate and comment on the survey's apparent purpose, its content and length, the order and construction of the questions, the jumps, overall instructions, and the cover letter. This will greatly improve the quality of your research instrument.

Step 5: Draw the sample

To be a statistically valid and projectionable research instrument, it is important that you draw your sample correctly. This means that everyone in the target population has an equal chance to be chosen for your study. This is important to help assure reliability.

Assume, for example, that you are developing a survey to determine how 610,000 community residents perceived your institution and that your goal is a reliability level of 95 percent. To achieve this validity level, using a sampling chart like the one shown in chapter 4 (p.56), you will need a sample of about 384.

If the population is homogeneous, you can use a basic random sample. This is sometimes called "nth name sampling" because you choose every nth name from the larger population. To obtain a basic random sample, you need to divide your population of 610,000 by 384 and then draw every 1,588th name from a randomly generated list.

Don't forget that you should never choose the first 384 people on the list. Most lists are organized alphabetically, geographically, or chronologically, and taking the sample from the first part of the list would mean that the names are not randomly selected. Fortunately, more sophisticated database software packages often include provisions for randomly generating lists, so it should not be difficult to develop a truly random sample.

If the population is heterogeneous, use a stratified random sample. This means you actually break the larger population into subpopulations and then sample each subpopulation separately. For example, you might break the larger group of 2,000 potential donors into three segments according to the size of the gift they are able to give, their age, or some other variable.

Alumni Pool	Age Range	Size of Subpopulation*	Sample Size for 95 Percent Reliability Level
Number 1	One year out	12,000	370
Number 2	Two to five years out	36,000	377
Number 3	Six to 10 years out	33,000	377
Number 4	11 to 20 years out	84,000	381
Number 5	21 to 40 years out	75,000	381
Number 6	More than 40 years out	120,000	383

Table A-3
Sample Sizes of a Hypothetical Target Population

*This is fictitious data.

I often use a stratified random sample as part of alumni research. For example, as in Table A-3, let's suppose that you are a large university located in Columbus, Ohio, with 360,000 living alumni. If you treat this has a homogeneous sample, you will need approximately 383 in your sample to achieve a validity level of 95 percent. However, you also know that the average age of the alumni population is 43 and that the range is from 20 years of
age to 97. After some thought, you decide to break the larger population into six subpopulations:

- Alumni who graduated one year ago
- Alumni who graduated more than one but less than five years ago
- Alumni who graduated more than 5 but less than 10 years ago
- Alumni who graduated more than 10 but less than 20 years ago
- Alumni who graduated more than 20 but less than 40 years ago
- Alumni who graduated more than 40 years ago

Although the exact breakdown of these age groups is somewhat arbitrary, samples drawn from these six subpopulations will, overall, be much more representative of the larger population of alumni. The next step, of course, is to ascertain the size of each subpopulation and then draw the required sampled. The resulting sample sizes are represented in Table A-3.

A stratified random sample would require you to treat each subpopulation as a separate study. In other words, you would have to draw a specific number of names randomly from each of the six pools. The level of validity you seek, of course, would determine the number of names.

If, for example, you are completing a survey of prospective students, you might want to divide your larger sample into several smaller ones that categorize students by ethnicity, household income, distance from the institution, or some other characteristic or quality you feel is important.

Of course, it is possible to stratify every large population into smaller subsets. However, you must always balance the need to stratify with expediency and economy. Stratified studies are more complicated, take longer, and cost more.

What's so special about a 95 percent reliability level?

We have referred to reliability levels of 95 percent a number of times. It is important to keep in mind that reliability levels can vary dramatically up or down from 95 percent. The goal is to balance cost and reliability. You will note, for example, that sample sizes and costs increase significantly as you move toward higher reliability. Consider a population of 4,000. A reliability level of 95 percent requires a sample of 350. At the same time, reliability levels of 97 percent and 98 percent require samples of 842 and 1,500, respectively. These marginal increases in reliability require great increases in sample size and overall project cost. So what's so special about 95 percent? Well, it represents a good balance between high validity and moderate cost. You can spend more for more validity, but the reality is that the additional cost is generally not worth it. Often, it is more important to heighten response rates than to simply use a larger sample.

At this stage in the project, you must also think about probable response rates. This is especially true for mail surveys because responses have consistently slipped over the past decade. Response rate is less of an issue for telephone surveys, however, because the researcher generally keeps calling until he or she completes an adequate number.

When you assign levels of reliability to a study, you assume a response rate of at least 50 percent for each sample. If the response rate is less, you have what is called nonresponse bias; more people didn't respond than did. There are three basic strategies for dealing with nonresponse bias.

1. Oversample your population. For example, if your study calls for a sample of 370, you should consider surveying two or even three times that many. This oversampling will help boost response rates.

2. Include incentives with your survey. Mail surveys often include incentives such as cash, the opportunity to win a larger sum of cash or a prize through a drawing, or a small gift such as a calendar, booklet, or coupon.

3. A third strategy to reduce nonresponse bias is to use ART, an acronym that reminds you to:

■ Announce the study with a postcard;
■ Remind participants to complete the survey (use another postcard or perhaps a second survey); and
■ Thank respondents for their help.

ART is especially suited for mail surveys, though the basic strategy, with a little tweaking, works for all kinds of research.

All of these strategies must be implemented up front. There is nothing you can do to salvage a study after it suffers from nonresponse bias.

Keeping records

After you have drawn the sample, it is very important to record the specifics of the sample. This will be invaluable when you write the final report and should you decide to replicate the study in the future. At the very least, this should include the following elements:

■ Size of the population
■ Size of the sample
■ Degree of validity sought

Increasing Response Rates

Nonresponse is a growing problem in mail surveys. To help increase your response rate, consider the following strategies:

- Use the two times rule (mail twice as many surveys as you need to achieve your sample size).
- Place a short announcement in an appropriate newsletter about the study's importance.
- Use monetary, emotional, or tangible incentives.
- Send participants a presurvey announcement postcard.
- Time the survey to avoid holidays and calendar conflicts.
- Use a personalized cover letter from a prestigious person.
- Use quality reproduction of all written surveys and cover letters.
- Mail it first class (hand-stamped).
- Include return postage on addressed envelopes.
- Send a thank-you/reminder postcard a few days after mailing the survey.
- Send a second survey and cover letter to people who have not returned the first survey.

- Source of the names
- How the names were chosen
- How the sample was drawn (random, stratified random, etc.)
- Subpopulations oversampled
- Later(especially for mail surveys), the response rate.

Step 6: Execute the survey

After you have chosen the research methodology and drawn the sample, it is time to execute the survey. Because each methodology has slightly different protocols, we suggest using the guidelines in Table A-4.

Step 7: Input and analyze data

As surveys are returned or interviews finished, check them for validity and completeness. It is also helpful to number each survey before you enter it into the computer so that you can later verify randomly selected surveys against the data to ensure the accuracy of the data entry.

Analysis of quantitative data

Inputting the data from closed-ended questions is usually just a matter of correctly putting in the responses correctly. Handling data from open-ended questions is more problematic. All responses must first be read, categorized, and then coded. Finally, they must be entered. In many respects, this process converts open-ended data to closed-ended data and you can analyze it with the other closed-ended responses.

In most cases, analysis is relatively straightforward and includes descriptive statistics such as percentages (frequency counts) and statistics that highlight central tenden-

Table A-4
Guidelines for Survey Protocol

Methodology	Standard Protocol	Options
Mail Survey	• Create survey package: - Cover letter - Survey - Outgoing envelope - Prepaid return envelope to respondents	• Presurvey announcement postcard • Ads in media read by respondents to announce survey • Thank you/reminder cards to respondents • Additional surveys to nonrespondents
Telephone Survey	• Review questionnaire with survey givers	• Create template for computer screen to "input-on-the-fly"
Personal Interview	• Schedule interview • Follow-up thank you letter	
Focus Group Interview	• Write moderator guide • Screen potential members • Send reminders • Audiotape meeting	• If print materials are to be evaluated by the group, send materials to members prior to focus group meeting • Precede focus group discussion with written survey that covers main points to lessen group/moderator bias

	Residences	
Class	On Campus	Off Campus
Freshmen	85.0%	15.0%
Sophomores	70.8%	29.2%
Juniors	30.0%	70.0%
Seniors	18.8%	81.3%

Table A-5
Cross-Tabbing Findings: Who Lives Where

cies and the shape of distributions such as mean, median, mode, and standard deviation. In a few cases, you might want to use more sophisticated techniques such as analysis of variance (ANOVA) or regression analysis. Generally, as you move into this kind of analysis, you are also moving from being a serious amateur to a statistics professional.

One extremely useful method of analysis is the cross-tab. The cross-tab allows you to look at the relationship between two sets of data derived from your research. For example, suppose that you now know that of 100 students on your campus, 40 are freshmen, 24 are sophomores, 20 are juniors, and 16 are seniors—and that of these, 60 percent live on campus and 40 percent live off campus.

A cross-tab (Table A-5) would allow you to examine the relationship between where students live and their year in college.

Cross-tabs allow you to pinpoint relationships between different questions and responses. Remember, however, that cross-tabs effectively reduce the sample size. If you want to compare Hispanic female alumni to Asian male alumni, you may find that the original sample of 377 alumni has been reduced to just eight or 10 people who fit all the variables of the cross-tab.

Analysis of qualitative data

Analysis of qualitative research is usually not very sophisticated. It typically involves preserving and categorizing comments drawn from in-depth interviews and focus groups and, within context, using these comments to support or illustrate quantitative data. The merging of qualitative and quantitative data is often highly insightful.

Handling qualitative data warrants at least one word of caution. It is very important that you preserve the anonymity of the respondent when presenting qualitative data if anonymity was promised as part of the data collection. In some instances, it is easy to determine who said something based on the particular words and phrases used, and even if you don't use interviewee names, people may be able to figure who said what. It is very important to sanitize some comments to protect the anonymity of the source. Of course, you must take care not to change the meaning of the response.

Table A-6
Research Report Outline

Sections	Subsections
Table of contents	
Introduction	Statement of the problem or goals of the study
Methodology	Instrument design Instrument pretesting protocol Sampling methodology Data input and verification Analysis
Data analysis	Demographic profile of respondents Review of each question Cross-tabulations Conclusion and recommendations
Executive summary	Major findings Major recommendations Recommendations for immediate action
Appendix	Sample instrument

Step 8: Present the results

Presenting the research findings actually involves two steps: writing a detailed final report and deciding which parts of it you want to present.

The written report

The written report is the document of record. If your research and its conclusions are to be accepted, they must be well organized and clearly written. At the very least, the report should include the elements listed in Table A-6.

The tone of the report must be authoritative and serious, but nontechnical. It should include a clear table of contents so readers can focus on the parts most important to them. The methodology section should explain the survey design and pretesting, the timeline for the study's execution, response rates, and describe the statistical software and analyses used.

The best reports often open with a demographic profile of the people who completed the surveys. This helps provide perspective on the findings. It is also important to keep the tone as upbeat and positive as possible. There is a strong human tendency to focus only on the negative. This makes it important to stress positive findings early to increase support for some findings that might not be so positive, and for the body of research as a whole.

The report itself should be expertly prepared, well illustrated, carefully proofed, reproduced on high-quality paper, and bound well.

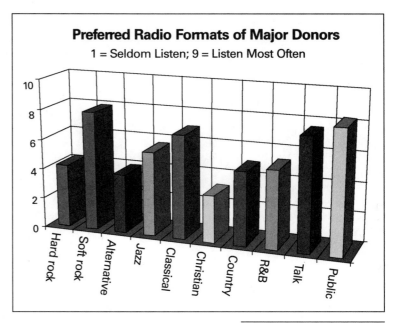

Figure A-1
Sample Presentation Graph

Oral presentation

In addition to your written report, you will probably also be asked to present the data to one or two groups. This is an opportunity to enhance not only the credibility of the research but of yourself as well. When developing the presentation, remember three cardinal rules.

1. Be judicious in deciding how much of your data to present. By emphasizing everything, you actually emphasize nothing.
2. Take the time to present the most salient bits of data in high-quality graphs such as the one shown in Figure A-1. People can absorb only so much information, and most have trouble dealing with endless columns of numbers.
3. Remember you exercise enormous power when you decide which elements of the research to present and how to present them. The simple act of graphing can make those data elements appear more important than data you did not graph.

B

Elements of a Graphics Standards Manual

Robert Sevier

Depending on the size and complexity of your organization, your graphics standards manual might include the following elements:

- New logotype and symbols
- Logotype and/or symbol on grid
- Logo sheet
- Authorized configurations
- Typography
- Color swatches
- Color samples
- Letterhead
- Layout
- Samples
- Environmental graphics and signage
- Forms

New logotype and/or symbols

A full page should be dedicated to your new image in its preferred configuration. A brief narrative can accompany the graphic, explaining the design's particular characteristics and symbolic message.

A superimposed grid pattern is printed over the image to demonstrate proper proportional relationships and spacing. This serves as a guide in instances when large-scale increases do not permit photomechanical enlargement, but you want the proper spatial relationships to be maintained.

A page that includes a variety of sizes and configurations of your logotype and symbol should be included for use in putting camera-ready copy together. You will want to prevent any re-creation of the image through handmade art or typesetting.

Authorized configurations

Several versions of the logotype and wordmark may be needed for horizontal, vertical, and other special arrangements.

Typography

In addition to the logotype, you will also need to demonstrate official institutional display and text typography. Rationale for selection, including a brief historical background of the typefaces, can contribute to interest and pride in your institution.

Color swatches

Pantone Matching Systems, Inc. (PMS), the color standard system widely used by printers, has recently undertaken an intensive effort to prevent its system from being reproduced without authorization from the company. In consideration of this, you may either print your authorized color swatches merely to show what colors a printer should match, or you may contact PMS to obtain their guidelines and swatches to include in your manual. The second option would be more suitable for loose-leaf manuals.

Color samples

Examples of acceptable black-and-white and color applications for the logotype or symbol should be shown. Also, demonstrate acceptable use of color backgrounds, screens, and reverse-outs. Give screen combinations to be used when the image is being reproduced by four-color process.

Letterhead

If the letterhead and other stationery items will be generated at noncentralized locations, include detailed layouts for each item. Give specifications and measurements for aligning the image on the page.

Layout

Basic guidelines and grid systems and some applications should be demonstrated. This function of the graphics standards manual varies greatly depending on the complexity of your applications. Concentrate on how the logotype and symbol relate to text type. Show sample layouts of simple publications with specifications for formats. It is best to keep layout specifications as simple as you can in the manual.

A graphics standards manual is not intended to be used for every publication. Your communications planning should include making decisions about which publications need such special design attention.

It is best to keep layout specifications as simple as you can.

Sample materials

If actual publications and other materials have been produced prior to designing the graphics standards manual, include a variety of them. It will demonstrate how the materials work together to create a family look. Include sample novelty and gift items, advertisements, and miscellaneous small and large objects.

Environmental graphics and signage

Even if you have not incorporated the new image into campus signs at the time the manual is being prepared, include layouts showing how it will be executed in future implementation.

Forms

Show at least one sample form with type and layout specifications. Some institutions include an order form for centrally produced items such as letterheads. The order form serves as the sample for design.

Contact information

Make it easy for users to receive guidance for applications of the new image that may not be addressed in the manual. The location of your office, hours, and telephone number can help people get the answers they need quickly. Media may call from the V station or press room, so try to make someone from your staff available to them.

Note: When developing a graphics standards manual for campus-wide use, include samples of standard institutional copy and fact sheets for use in departmental brochures and other materials. Provide guidelines for radio copy as well, including the requirement to name the institution in full (not abbreviated to initials such as UIC or WSU) at least twice on any radio advertisement, and also to provide specific locations and telephone numbers.

Appendix C

Useful Web Sites

The following Web sites are divided into seven general categories:

- U.S. agencies
- Education associations and organizations (general)
- Admissions, student recruiting, financial aid, and student services
- Fund raising, alumni relations, and foundations
- Media and public relations
- Marketing, advertising, and direct mail
- Data and research resources

Some Web sites have been listed in multiple areas.

U.S. Agencies

Smithsonian Institution
www.si.edu

U.S. Bureau of the Census
www.census.gov

U.S. Bureau of Labor Statistics
www.bls.gov

U.S. Department of Education
www.ed.gov

U.S. Department of Education Office of
Postsecondary Education
www.ed.gov/offices/ope

U.S. Department of Health and Human
Services
www.os.hhs.gov

U.S. House of Representatives
www.house.gov

U.S. Postal Service
www.usps.gov/

U.S. Senate
www.senate.gov

The White House
www.whitehouse.gov

Education Associations and Organizations (General)

American Association for Higher Education (AAHE)
www.aahe.org

American Association of Community Colleges (AACC)
www.aacc.nche.edu

American Association of University Professors (AAUP)
www.igc.apc.org/aaup/

American Association of University Women (AAUW)
www.aauw.org

American Council on Education (ACE)
www.acenet.edu

American Federation of Teachers (AFT)
www.aft.org

Association of Governing Boards (AGB)
www.agb.org

Association on Higher Education and Disability (AHEAD)
www.ahead.org

Association of Jesuit Colleges and Universities (AJCU)
www.ajcunet.edu

Coalition of Christian Colleges and Universities (CCCU)
www.gospelcom.net/cccu

Council for Advancement and Support of Education
www.case.org

Council of Independent Colleges and Universities (CIC)
www.cic.edu

European Council of International Schools
www.ecis.org

Historically Black Colleges and Universities
eric-web.tc.columbia.edu/hbcu

Internet College Exchange (ICX)
www.usmall.com/college/index.html

Multicultural Alliance
branson.org/mca

National Association of College and University Business Officers (NACUBO)
www.nacubo.org

National Association of Independent Schools (NAIS)
www.nais.org

National Association of State Boards of Education (NASBE)
www.nasbe.org

National Association of Student Personnel Administrators (NASPA)
www.naspa.org

National Community Education Association
www.idsonline.com/ncea

Council for Opportunity in Education
www.trioprograms.org/home.html

National Education Association (NEA)
www.nea.org

National Information Center for Children and Youth With Disabilities
www.nichcy.org

National Institute for Educational Planning
www.niep.com

National Institute on the Education of At-Risk Students
www.ed.gov/offices/OERI/At-Risk/ar_page1.html

Telis (TeleLearning InfoSource)
www.telis.org

Universities (All)
www.mit.edu:8001/people/cdemello/univ-full.html

University Continuing Education Association (UCEA)
www.nucea.edu/main/html

United States Student Association
www.essential.org/ussa/usaa.html

Western Interstate Commission for Higher Education
www.wiche.edu

World-Wide Graduate School Directory
www.gradschools.com

Admissions, Student Recruiting, Financial Aid, and Student Services

American Association of Collegiate Registrars and Admissions Officers (AACRAO)
www.aacrao.com

Association of Black Admission and Financial Aid Officers of the Ivy League and Sister Schools
web.mit.edu/afs/athena.mit.edu/org

Athletic Scholarship Information Search Techniques (ASIST)
www.athletes.com/assist.html

College Board Online
www.collegeboard.org

College Express
www.collegexpress.com

College NET
www.collegenet.com

College Scholarship Service
www.collegeboard.org/finaid/fastud/html/proform.htm

Educational Testing Service
www.ets.org/

Electronic Financial Aid Library
nt.scbbs.com/finaid/

Entrance Exams
www.cs.cmu.edu/afs/cs.cmu.edu/user/mkant

Financial Aid Information
www.finaid.org

National Association for College Admission Counseling (NACAC)
www.nacac.com

National Association of Student Financial Aid Administrators (NASFAA)
www.nasfaa.org

National Association of Student Personnel
Administrators (NASPA)
www.naspa.org/

National College Fairs
www.nacac.com/fairs.html

Nellie Mae Loan Link
www.nelliemae.com

Performing & Visual Arts College Fairs
www.nacac.com/exhibit/fair2.cfm

Peterson's Education
www.petersons.com

Princeton Review
www.review.com

Scholarship Scams
*www.ftc.gov/bcp/conline/edcams/scholar-
ship/index.html*

Student Services
*www.fastweb.com/fastweb/index.cgi/index.h
tml?refer=studentservices*

University Financial Aid Offices
www.finaid.org/finaid/fao-web.html

**Fund Raising,
Alumni Relations, and Foundations**

American Society of Association
Executives
www.asanet.org

Aspen Institute
www.aspeninst.org

Canadian Centre for Philanthropy
www.ccp.ca

Chronicle of Philanthropy
www.philanthropy.com

Council for Advancement and Support of
Education (CASE)
www.case.org

Council on Foundations
www.cof.org

Foundation Center
fdncenter.org/

Foundation for Independent Higher
Education
www.fihe.org/

GrantsWeb
www.web.fie.com

National Society of Fund-raising
Executives (NSFRE)
www.nsfre.org

NonProfit Times
www.nptimes.com

Philanthropy Journal OnLine
www.philanthropy-journal-org/

Philanthropy News Digest
fdncente.org/phil/philmain.html

Media and Public Relations

ABC Television
www.abc.go.com

All-Links
www.all-links.com

American Journalism Review
ajr.newslink.org/

Associated Press
www.ap.org

Black Collegian
www.black-collegian.com/

Black Issues in Higher Education
www.blackissues.com

Broadcasting and Cable Yearbook (R.R. Bowker)
www.bowker.com

Business Directory
www.businessdirectory.dowjones.com

Business Wire
www.businesswire.com

CBS Television
www.cbs.com/

CNN
www.cnn.com

C-SPAN
www.c-span.org

Chicago Tribune
chicagotribune.com

Christian Science Monitor
www.csmonitor.com

Chronicle of Higher Education
www.thisweek.chronicle.com/

Columbia Journalism Review
www.cjr.org

Dallas Morning News
www.dallasnews.com

Drudge Report
www.drudgereport.com

Ecola Newstand
www.ecola.com

Editor and Publisher
www.editorandpublisher.com

Education News
dir.yahoo.com/education/

Feature Photo Service
www.featurephoto.com

Gales Encyclopedia of Associations
www.gales.com

Gebbie Press
www.gebbie.com

InfoSeek
infoseek.com

Inkspot
www.inkspot.com

Inquisit
www.inquisit.com

Lexis Nexis
www.lexisnexis.com

Los Angeles Times
www.latimes.com

MTV
www.mtv.com

NBC Television
www.nbc.com

National Public Radio
www.npr.org

New York Times
www.nytimes.com

Newsmakers
www.newsmakers.com

O'Dwyer's Directory
www.odwyer.com

PBS Television
www.pbs.org/

PR Infofinder
www.prsa.org/ppc

PR News
www.phillips.com/prnews

PR Newswire
www.prnewswire.com

Profnet
www.profnet.com

Public Relations Society of America
www.prsa.org

Publicist
www.publicist.com

Ragan Report
www.ragan.com

Reuters
www.reuters.com

Rolling Stone
www.rollingstone.com

Standard Rate and Data Service
www.srds.com

USA Today
usatoday.com

US News Online
www.usnews.com/usnews/home.html

US Newswire
www.usnewswire.com

Voice of America
www.voa.gov

Wall Street Journal Interactive
www.wsj.com

The Washington Post
www.washingtonpost.com

WhoWhere
www.whowhere.com

Marketing, Advertising, and Direct Mail

Advertising Age
www.adage.com

American List Counsel
www.amlist.com

American Marketing Association
www.ama.org

Beyond the Wall—Advertising
www.beyondthewall.com

Database America
www.databaseamerica.com

Dependable Lists
www.dependablelists.com

Direct Mail Underground
www.rdri.com

Direct Marketing News
www.dmnews.com

Direct Marketing University
www.communicomp.com

Direct Marketing World
www.dmworld.com

Direct Media
www.directmedia.com

Fishnet Electronic Magazine for Teens
www.jayi.com

Georgia Tech University
www.cc.gatech.edu/gvu/user_surveys

Guerrilla Marketing
www.gmarketing.com

Horah Group—Direct Mail Resource
www.horah.com

Lycos—Personal Guide to the Web
point.lycos.com

Marketplace 1 to 1 (Peppers and Rodgers)
www.m1to1.com

MaxiMarketing
www.maximarketing.com

National Research Center for College and
University Admissions (mailing lists)
www.nrccua.com

Softmail Direct
www.softmail.com

Target On Line
www.targetonline.com

Wilson Internet Services
www.wilsonweb.com

WondermanCatoJohnson
www.propheus.com

Data and Research Resources

Academe Today (Chronicle of Higher
Education)
www.chronicle.com

Amazon Bookstore
www.amazon.com

American Council on Education (ACE)
www.acenet.edu

American Demographics
www.demographics.com

AskERIC
ericir.sunsite.syr.edu/

Business Directory
businessdirectory.dowjones.com

Education Commission of the States
www.ecs.org

Educational Resources Information
Center Clearinghouse (ERIC)
aspensys3.aspensys.com/eric/
barak.html#1

Educational Resources Information
Center Clearinghouse on Teaching and
Teacher Education (ERIC/SP)
www.accesseric.org/index.html

Electric Library
www.elibrary.com

Federal Web Locator
www.law.vill.edu/Fed-Agency/
Fedwebloc.html

Gale Encyclopedia of Associations
www.gale.com

Georgia Tech University Graphic,
Viualization, and Visability Center (GVU)
www.cc.gatech.edu/gvu/user_surveys

Internet Resources for Institutional
Research
apollo.gmu.edu/~jmilam/air95.html

National Council of University Research
Administrators (NCURA)
www.ncura.edu

Tattered Cover Bookstore
www.tatteredcover.com

Western Interstate Commission for
Higher Education
www.wiche.edu

Yahoo: Education: Organizations: Student
Organizations
*www.yahoo/Education/Organizations/Stud
ent_Organizations*

Yahoo: News/Newspapers: Universities
*dir.yahoo.com/news_and_media/college_an
d_university/newspapers*

Organizations and Associations

American Association of Advertising Agencies
405 Lexington Avenue
New York, NY 10174-1801
(212) 682-2500
www.commercepark.com/AAAA

American Association of Collegiate Registrars and Admissions Officers (AACRAO)
One Dupont Circle, Suite 330
Washington, DC 20036
(202) 293-9161
fax: (202) 872-8857
www.aacrao.com

American College Personnel Association (ACPA)
One Dupont Circle, Suite 300
Washington, DC 20036
(202) 835-2272
fax: (202) 296-3286
www.acpa.nche.edu

American College Testing (ACT)
PO Box 4005
Iowa City, IA 52243
(319) 337-1000
www.act.org

American Council on Education (ACE)
One Dupont Circle, Suite 801
Washington, DC 20036
(202) 939-9300
fax: (202) 833-4760
www.acenet.edu

American Marketing Association (AMA)
250 S. Wacker Dr., Suite 200
Chicago, IL 60606
(312) 648-0536
fax: (312) 993-7542
www.ama.org

American Society of Association
Executives
1575 I Street, NW
Washington, DC 20005-1168
(202) 626-2723
www.asaenet.org

American Telemarketing Association
4605 Lankershim Blvd., Suite 824
North Hollywood, CA 91602
(818) 766-5324
fax: (818) 766-8168

Association of Governing Boards of
Universities and Colleges (AGB)
One Dupont Circle, Suite 400
Washington, DC 20036
(202) 296-8400
fax: (202) 223-7053

Coalition for Christian Colleges and
Universities
329 Eighth St., NE
Washington, DC 20002-6158
(202) 546-8713
fax: (202) 546-8913
www.cccu.org

The College Board
45 Columbus Avenue
New York, NY 10023-6992
(212) 713-8000
fax: (212) 713-8282

Council for Advancement and Support of
Education (CASE)
1307 New York Avenue, Suite 1000
Washington, DC 20005-4701
(202) 328-5900
fax: (202) 387-4973
www.case.org

Council for Independent Colleges
One Dupont Circle, Suite 320
Washington, DC 20036
(202) 466-7230
www.cic.edu

Direct Marketing Educational Foundation
1120 Avenue of the Americas
New York, NY 10036
(212) 768-7277
fax: (212) 790-1561

ERIC Clearinghouse for Higher Education
One Dupont Circle, Suite 630
Washington, DC 20036-1183
(202) 296-2597
fax: (202) 452-1844
www.ericsp.org

National Association for College
Admission Counseling (NACAC)
1631 Prince St.
Alexandria, VA 22314
(703) 836-2222
fax: (703) 836-8015
www.nacac.com

National Association of Student Financial
Aid Administrators (NASFAA)
1920 L St., NW, Suite 200
Washington, DC 20036
(202) 785-0453
fax: (202) 785-1487

National Association of Student Financial
Management Systems (NCHEMS)
PO Box 9752
Boulder, CO 80301
(303) 497-0392
fax: (303) 497-0338

National Association of College and
University Business Officers (NACUBO)
2501 M St., Suite 400
Washington, DC 20037
(202) 861-2500
fax: (202) 861-2583
www.nacubo.org

National Association of Independent
Colleges and Universities (NAICU)
1025 Connecticut Ave., Suite 700
Washington, DC 20036
(202) 785-8866
fax: (202) 835-0003

National Association of Independent
Schools (NAIS)
1620 L St., NW
Washington, DC 20036-5605
(202) 973-9700
fax: (202) 973-9790
www.nais.org

National Society of Fund Raising
Executives (NSFRE)
1101 King St., Suite 700
Alexandria, VA 22314
(703) 684-0410
fax: (703) 684-0540
www.nsfre.org

University and College Designer's
Association (UCDA)
122 South Michigan Avenue, Suite 1776
Chicago, IL 60603
(312) 431-9395
www.ucda.com

University Microfilms International
300 N. Zeeb Rd.
Ann Arbor, MI 48106
(313) 761-4700

U.S. Department of Commerce Bureau of
the Census
Washington, DC 20233
(301) 457-3761

U.S. Government Printing Office
710 North Capitol St., NW
Washington, DC 20401
(202) 512-0132

About the Editors And Contributors

Editors

Robert Johnson is vice president for enrollment at Albion College, a national liberal arts college in Albion, Michigan. An executive member of the American Marketing Association (AMA), Bob is a specialist in direct-response marketing and competitive-marketing research and is expanding his interests into the continuing integration of direct marketing and Web and Internet communications. Since 1994, he has served as chair of the AMA's annual Symposium for the Marketing of Higher Education. During more than 15 years of higher education marketing, he has been a workshop presenter and consultant for several firms and associations, including the AMA, American College Testing, CASE, the College Board, Stamats Communications, and the USA Group Noel-Levitz Center for Enrollment Management. Bob sends his "no-name" e-mail newsletter on higher education marketing many times a year to more than 1,600 people. He received his bachelor's degree from Alfred University and his Ph.D. in government from the University of Massachusetts, Amherst. You can expect a quick response when you contact him by e-mail at *rjohnson@albion.edu.*

Robert Sevier is the general manager and vice president for research and marketing at Stamats Communications, Inc., an integrated marketing company serving higher education. He has written more than 40 articles for CURRENTS, *Journal of College Admissions,*

Trusteeship, Communication World, Admission Strategist, and the *College and University Journal* on such issues as integrated marketing; the social, demographic, economic, and governance trends affecting higher education image enhancement; and strategic planning. In 1998, Sevier wrote *Integrated Marketing for Colleges, Universities, and Schools: A Step-by-Step Planning Guide* published by CASE Books. He also serves on the advisory board of the American Marketing Association and has conducted more than 600 seminars and retreats for CASE, NAICU, NACAC, ACT, AACRAO, NACCAP, AMA, NCMPR, the College Board, and other organizations.

Prior to joining Stamats, Sevier worked as director of media relations for the Oregon Health Sciences University in Portland, OR; served as director of marketing communications for Denison University, Granville, OH; and taught journalism and public relations at the college level for 10 years. He earned a Ph.D. from Ohio State University, Columbus, in 1986 in policy analysis and higher education administration with an emphasis on marketing. He also holds an MS degree in journalism/public relations from the University of Oregon (1979). He can be reached at *bob-sevier@stamats.com.*

Contributors

Harry Battson, associate vice president for public affairs at the University of South Florida, Tampa, since 1995, has spent nearly 20 years in university public relations. As the media relations manager at Wright State University, he received the CASE Gold Medal for Exceptional Achievement in News Writing in 1984. While director of public relations at Wright State, he received the President's Award for Best Communication Program from the Dayton chapter of the Public Relations Society of America for his handling of a crisis involving animal research. At the University of South Florida, he has initiated a comprehensive marketing communications program incorporating research, visual identity, and integrated team efforts. The program applies media relations, marketing, and publications in sending communications messages to targeted audiences.

A. R. (Andy) Kesling is associate director of public affairs at Southern Methodist University in Dallas, Texas. Kesling has a decade of strategic and tactical experience in higher education marketing communications. He serves on a senior-level team to integrate university-wide advertising planning, placement, and creative development at SMU. Previously, he filled editorial and marketing positions with an electronic publishing service of the *Fort Worth Star-Telegram.*

Larry D. Lauer is associate vice chancellor for communications and public affairs at Texas Christian University in Fort Worth, Texas. He is a member of the Chancellor's Cabinet and chairman of both TCU's Marketing Advisory Board and its management committee. He is also assistant professor of corporate communication and teaches international communication at the university's London Center in England, and has published more than 20 articles about integrated marketing and communications. He is the author of *Communication Power: Energizing Your Nonprofit Organization,* published in 1998 by Aspen Publishers. Lauer's special interest is in adapting the latest thinking about integrated and relationship marketing to advance institutions, and he has recently been conducting seminars on that subject in this country and abroad.

Jeannie S. Morelock has 20 years of professional marketing and communications experience. She is the director of marketing and communications for Meredith College, Raleigh, NC, the largest private women's college in the southeastern United States. She earned her undergraduate degree from North Carolina State University and an MBA from Meredith. She has served as an account executive for an international cruiseline at McKinney and Silver Advertising, an educational documentary producer for NCSU, and a photographer, reporter, and editor for several television stations. She and her staff have won numerous awards for Meredith's marketing programs, advertising, publications, and public relations.

Michael Norris, director of communications at Centre College of Kentucky in Danville, has more than 20 years' experience in publications, public relations, and marketing. During his 19 years at Centre, the college has received more than 100 regional and national awards for publications and public relations projects, including national grand awards for viewbook and for student recruitment series. A songwriter and musician, Norris has recorded a CD of original songs as a member of the blues trio Halfway Home. He is also the author of a popular children's book, *Bright Blue Rooster.*

Pat Sellergren is creative group manager and editorial director at Stamats Communications, Inc., an integrated marketing company serving higher education, and is part of the creative process daily. An award-winning writer with a diverse background, she is involved in publications and interactive media projects from the conception stage through completion of the finished product. She also has more than 15 years of experience teaching college-level courses in writing and literature and has given numerous workshops and seminars on creativity and effective marketing communications. Sellergren holds a B.A. and an M.A. in English from the University of Oklahoma, where she has also completed course work toward a Ph.D. She has completed additional graduate work at the University of Iowa and the University of Iowa's Writers Workshop.